Exploring Intelligence Ar

This edited volume brings together many of the world's leading scholars of intelligence with a number of former senior practitioners to facilitate a wide-ranging dialogue on the central challenges confronting students of intelligence.

Exploring Intelligence Archives presents a series of documents, nearly all of which are published here for the first time, accompanied by both overview and commentary sections. The central objectives of this collection are twofold. First, it seeks to build on existing scholarship on intelligence in deepening our understanding of its impact on a series of key events in the international history of the past century. Further, it aims to explore the different ways in which intelligence can be studied by bringing together both scholarly and practical expertise to examine a range of primary material relevant to the history of intelligence since the early twentieth century.

This book will be of great interest to students of intelligence, strategic and security studies, foreign policy and international history.

R. Gerald Hughes is Lecturer in Military History in the Department of International Politics at the University of Wales, Aberystwyth.

Peter Jackson is Senior Lecturer in International Politics in the Department of International Politics at the University of Wales, Aberystwyth.

Len Scott is Professor of International Politics in the Department of International Politics at the University of Wales, Aberystwyth.

Studies in Intelligence Series
General Editors: Richard J. Aldrich and Christopher Andrew
ISSN: 1368–9916

Exploring Intelligence Archives

Enquiries into the secret state

Edited by R. Gerald Hughes, Peter Jackson and Len Scott

Routledge
Taylor & Francis Group

LONDON AND NEW YORK

First published 2008
by Routledge
2 Park Square, Milton Park, Abingdon, Oxon, OX14 4RN

Simultaneously published in the USA and Canada
by Routledge
270 Madison Avenue, New York, NY 10016

Transferred to digital printing 2009

Routledge is an imprint of the Taylor & Francis Group, an informa business

Typeset in Times New Roman and Helvetica by
Swales & Willis Ltd, Exeter, Devon
Printed and bound in Great Britain by
CPI Antony Rowe, Chippenham, Wiltshire

British Library Cataloguing in Publication Data
A catalogue record for this book is available from the British Library

Library of Congress Cataloging in Publication Data
Exploring intelligence archives : enquiries into the secret state / edited by
R. Gerald Hughes, Peter Jackson, and Len Scott.
p. cm. – (Studies in intelligence)
1. Intelligence service. 2. Intelligence service–Study and teaching.
3. Military intelligence. 4. Military intelligence–Study and teaching.
I. Hughes, R. Gerald. II. Jackson, Peter. III. Scott, L. V. (Leonard Victor),
1957–
JF1525.I6E97 2008
327.12–dc22
2007033700

ISBN13 978–0–415–34998–7 (hbk)
ISBN13 978–0–415–34972–7 (pbk)
ISBN13 978–0–203–02312–9 (ebk)

ISBN10 0–415–34998–2 (hbk)
ISBN10 0–415–34972–9 (pbk)
ISBN10 0–203–02312–9 (ebk)

Contents

List of documents

List of contributors

Martin S. Alexander is Professor of International Politics and Director of the Centre for Intelligence and International Security Studies at the University of Wales, Aberystwyth. A specialist on French defence planning and civil-military relations, he has written, edited or co-edited numerous books including (with Kenneth Mouré) *Crisis and Renewal: France 1918–1962* (Berghahn, 2002) and (with John F.V. Keiger) *France and the Algerian War, 1954–1962: Strategy, Operations and Diplomacy* (Frank Cass, 2002). He is currently preparing a book on the performance of the French armies in 1940.

Charles Cogan is a Senior Research Associate at the Kennedy School of Government, Harvard University. Earlier, he spent 37 years in the CIA, including as Chief Near East South Asia in the Directorate of Operations (1979–1984) and as CIA Chief in Paris (1984–1989). His recent books include *Diplomatie à la française* (Editions Jacob-Duvernet, 2005).

John Ferris is Professor of History at the University of Calgary, Canada. He has written widely on intelligence, strategy and military history. His most recent work is *Intelligence and Strategy: Selected Essays* (Taylor and Francis, 2005).

Michael Goodman is Lecturer in the Department of War Studies specialising in the study of intelligence. His recent publications include *Spying on the Nuclear Bear: Anglo-American Intelligence and the Soviet Bomb* (Stanford University Press, 2008). Since September 2007, he has been on secondment to the Cabinet Office, as the Official Historian of the Joint Intelligence Committee.

Christopher E. Goscha is Associate Professor in International Relations at the Université du Quebéc à Montréal. He specialises in Asian international history and the colonial and postcolonial history of South-East Asia, and has published in both fields. His published works include (with Thomas Engelbert), *Falling out of Touch: A Study on Vietnamese Communist Policy towards an Emerging Cambodian Communist Movement, 1930–1975* (Monash University, 1995).

David Holloway is Raymond A. Spruance Professor of International History at Stanford University, CA. His research has focused on the politics of science and technology in the Soviet Union, the Soviet atomic project, nuclear weapons and international relations. His *Stalin and the Bomb: The Soviet Union and Atomic Energy, 1939–1956* (Yale University Press, 1994) was selected by the *New York Times* as one of the 11 best books of 1994. His current research deals with the international history of nuclear weapons and the role of nuclear weapons in a changing international system.

R. Gerald Hughes is Lecturer in Military History in the Department of International Politics at the University of Wales, Aberystwyth, an associate fellow of the Centre for Intelligence and International Security Studies, reviews editor for *Intelligence and National Security* and the editor of the *Study Group on Intelligence* newsletter. His recent publications include *Britain, Germany and the Cold War: The Search for a European Détente 1949–1967* (Routledge, 2007) and, co-edited with Len Scott, *Intelligence, Crises and Security: Prospects and Retrospects* (Routledge, 2008).

Peter Jackson is Senior Lecturer in International Politics in the Department of International Politics at the University of Wales, Aberystwyth, and British editor of *Intelligence and National Security*. His books include *France and the Nazi Menace: Intelligence and Policy-making, 1933–1939* (Oxford University Press, 2000) and (edited with Jennifer Siegel) *Intelligence and Statecraft: The Use and Limits of Intelligence in International Society* (Praeger, 2005).

Rhodri Jeffreys-Jones is Professor of American History at the University of Edinburgh, and the author of a number of books on intelligence. These include *The CIA and American Democracy* (Yale University Press, 1989/1998/2003); *Cloak and Dollar: A History of American Secret Intelligence* (Yale University Press, 2002/2003); and *The FBI: A History* (Yale University Press, 2007).

Robert Jervis is Adlai E. Stevenson Professor of International Politics at Columbia University and was President of the American Political Science Association in 2000–2001. His books include *Perception and Misperception in International Politics* (Princeton University Press, 1976); *System Effects: Complexity in Political and Social Life* (Princeton University Press, 1997); and *American Foreign Policy in a New Era* (Routledge, 2005).

Loch K. Johnson is Regents Professor of Public and International Affairs at the University of Georgia. He is the author of numerous books dealing with intelligence and is the US editor of *Intelligence and National Security*. Recent books include *Bombs, Bugs, Drugs, and Thugs: Intelligence and America's Quest for Security* (New York University Press, 2002) and *Seven Sins of American Foreign Policy* (Longman, 2006).

Paul Maddrell is Lecturer in International Politics at the University of Wales, Aberystwyth. He is the author of *Spying on Science: Western Intelligence in Divided Germany, 1945–1961* (Oxford University Press, 2006), as well as many journal articles and book chapters on intelligence and German history.

David Marr has devoted 45 years to the study of modern Vietnam, with his principal monographs being *Vietnamese Anticolonialism 1885–1925* (University of California, 1971); *Vietnamese Tradition on Trial, 1920–1945* (University of California Press, 1981) and *Vietnam 1945: The Quest for Power* (University of California Press, 1995). He is currently Visiting Professor at the Research School of Pacific and Asian Studies, Australian National University, Canberra.

Peter Mauch is Lecturer in International History at Ritsumeikan University, Kyoto, Japan. He is co-author (with John Van Sant and Yoneyuki Sugita) of the *Historical Dictionary of United States-Japan Relations* (Scarecrow Press, 2007) and has published articles in *Diplomatic History* (28/5, 2004) and *Diplomacy and Statecraft* (17/2, 2006).

Merle Pribbenow is a retired CIA operations officer and Vietnamese language specialist who has published numerous articles on the history of the Vietnam War and translated the Military History Institute of Vietnam's *Victory in Vietnam: The Official History of the People's Army of Vietnam, 1954–1975* (University Press of Kansas, 2002).

Andrew Priest is Lecturer in International Politics at the University of Wales, Aberystwyth. He specialises in the history of US foreign policy and recently published *Kennedy, Johnson and NATO: Britain, America and the Dynamics of Alliance, 1962–68* (Routledge, 2006).

Len Scott is Professor of International Politics and a member of the Centre for Intelligence and International Security Studies at the University of Wales, Aberystwyth. His recent publications include *The Cuban Missile Crisis and the Threat of Nuclear War: Lessons from History* (Continuum, 2007) and *Intelligence, Crises and Security: Prospects and Retrospects* (Routledge, 2008), edited with R. Gerald Hughes.

Yigal Sheffy is Associate Professor at the Security Studies Program, Tel Aviv University, and former intelligence officer, IDF. He is the author of *British Military Intelligence in the Palestine Campaign, 1914–1918* (Frank Cass, 1998), teaches military history of the Middle East and intelligence studies and recently completed a monograph on early warning and the Israel defence perception in the 1950s and 1960s.

Matthias Uhl is a Research Fellow at the German Historical Institute in Moscow. He has published widely on Soviet defence and security policy, arms development, and intelligence operations in the Cold War era. His recent publications include *Stalin's V-2: Transfer of German Ballistic Missile Technology to the Soviet Union and the Creation of the Soviet Missile Industry, 1945–1959* (Bernard & Graefe, 2001) and *The Hitler Book* (John Murray, 2005), edited with H. Eberle.

James R. Vaughan is Lecturer in International History in the Department of International Politics at the University of Wales, Aberystwyth. He is the author of *The Failure of American and British Propaganda in the Arab Middle East, 1945–1957* (Palgrave, 2005) and is currently working on a history of Anglo-Israeli relations.

Andrew Webster is Lecturer in Modern History at Murdoch University, Perth, Western Australia. He has published several articles on the problem of international disarmament in the inter-war period, including recent articles in *Diplomacy and Statecraft* (16/3, 2005) and the *Journal of Strategic Studies* (29/2, 2006). He is presently writing a history of the international disarmament process prior to the nuclear age, to be entitled *Of Men and Arms: A History of International Disarmament from 1899 to 1945*.

Acknowledgements

This book developed from a research project, *Journeys in Shadows*, at the University of Wales Aberystwyth funded by the British Academy and the University of Wales, Aberystwyth and as part of the work of the Centre for Intelligence and International Security Studies (CIISS) at the Department of International Politics. In preparing this volume, the editors have incurred many debts and should like to acknowledge some of them here. We should like to thank our colleagues at the University of Wales, Aberystwyth for their unfailing support. Thanks are also due to all our students – past and present – for their diligence and inquisitive minds.

This book has also benefited from the proceedings of three conferences on intelligence and international relations and hosted by the University of Wales Conference Centre at Gregynog in 2002, 2005 and 2007. The purpose of this ongoing conference series, which is organised and sponsored by the Centre for Intelligence and International Security Studies at Aberystwyth, is to develop and extend the active community of scholars and former practitioners working in this field both in the UK and internationally. Thanks to all those who gave papers and/or were delegates in what were very congenial three-day sojourns in 2002, 2005 and 2007.

Thanks to the National Archives, Kew for their permission to reproduce the facsimiles of British intelligence documents which are published as part of chapters four, six, eight and nine. We should especially like to express our thanks to Hugh Alexander at the Image Library of the National Archives for his assistance with these materials. The facsimile CIA documents in chapter seven are taken from the CIA web page: 'Lt. Col. Oleg Penkovsky: Western Spy in Soviet GRU', located at: http://www.foia.cia.gov/penkovsky.asp. In chapter eight, document seventeen – SNIE 53–2–63, 'The Situation in South Vietnam', 10 July 1963 – is taken from *The Pentagon Papers: The Defense Department History of United States Decision-making on Vietnam*, Senator Gravel Edition, Volume 2 (Boston, MA: Beacon Press, 1971), pp. 729–33. Our thanks to Dan Hucker for his assistance in the preparation of the index for this volume. We would also like to thank Andrew Humphrys of Routledge for his support and (considerable) patience in the Odyssey that this volume came to represent. And finally, we should all like to acknowledge our debt to our families for their forbearance and support on so many occasions over so many years.

Introduction

Enquiries into the 'secret state'

Peter Jackson

This book brings together many of the world's leading scholars of intelligence with a number of former senior practitioners to facilitate a wide-ranging dialogue on the central challenges confronting students of intelligence. There is a clear need for greater understanding of the role intelligence has played in shaping the course of domestic and international politics over the past century. Intelligence has never played a more prominent role in international politics than it does now at the opening of the twenty-first century. National intelligence services are larger than ever and play a more public role than ever in the policy-making process of most states. Public discussion of intelligence, even the most secret intelligence, has become common in political discourse on international issues. The central objectives of this book are twofold. Like most scholarship on the subject, it seeks to deepen our understanding of the impact of intelligence on a series of key events in the international history of the past century; but it also aims to explore the different ways in which intelligence can be studied by bringing together a diverse array of both scholarly and practical expertise to examine a range of primary material relevant to the history of intelligence since the early twentieth century.

The strategy we have adopted is to present a series of documents, nearly all of which are published here for the first time, pertaining to the role of intelligence in events ranging from the London Naval Conference of 1930 through to the invasion of Iraq in 2003. Other subjects covered include French assessments of the international situation before that war, the creation of the famous British deception programme during the Second World War, North Vietnamese conceptions of the role and function of an intelligence service, a comparison of British and American net assessments of the situation in South-East Asia in 1963 and East German Security Service assessments of the relative performance of the Soviet *Komitet Gosudarstvennoi Bezopastnosti* (KGB) and the American Central Intelligence Agency (CIA).

There is also considerable variety in the type of documents included in the collection. Four are wide-ranging assessments of the strategic situation: in Europe in 1936 (Chapter 3), two on South-East Asia in 1963 (Chapter 8) and one on the Middle East in 1965 (Chapter 9). Chapter 2 provides a good example of raw intelligence by presenting a series of British decrypts of the communications of other participants in the London Naval Conference of 1930. The internal memoranda presented in Chapters 4, 5 and 10 provide fascinating insights into the way British, Vietnamese and Soviet bloc officials understood key issues pertaining to the nature and functioning of intelligence. In Chapter 6, the Security Service record of a key interview with atomic spy Klaus Fuchs is a window into a crucial aspect of counter-intelligence work. Chapter 7 focuses on the Western agent Colonel Oleg Penkovsky, whom many see as the hero of the Cuban Missile Crisis. It provides insights into Penkovsky's career as well as the nature of intelligence tradecraft. The two final chapters present very different forms of primary evidence. The document in Chapter 11 is an interview with William E. Colby, Director of Central Intelligence under Presidents Richard M. Nixon and Gerald R. Ford between 1973 and 1976. Chapter 12 presents a key section from a public enquiry into the performance of the British intelligence services and policy-makers during the period leading up to the invasion of Iraq in March 2003. The diversity of the material assembled in this volume is testimony to the range of sources available for scholars interested in intelligence. But there are many other types of sources that are not included. A preliminary list of such material would include popular culture depictions of intelligence; documents illuminating the role of secret services in different types of covert action (from propaganda and political subversion to assassination), and material pertaining to criteria used in recruitment and training. There is ample room for further volumes devoted to exploring the intelligence archives in this way.

Each document is preceded by an 'overview' providing essential background information on the authorship of the document, the political and bureaucratic context in which it was drafted, as well as some analysis of the reasons *why* it was drafted. This is then followed by a 'commentary' section providing detailed textual analysis of the content of the document by one or two experts on the subject. Inevitably, there is often substantial overlap between the overviews and commentaries. Many of the overviews include analytical insights and many of the commentaries provide interesting and important background information. The aim throughout is to consider, first, what these documents can tell us about the nature of intelligence and the character of intelligence practices and, second, the way they illuminate challenges inherent in the study of intelligence.

Interpretation of the archival record (as indeed the non-archival record) lies at the heart of historical enquiry. On one level, the challenges inherent in interpreting intelligence and intelligence-related texts are no different from those facing historians of all persuasions. They raise many of the same methodological and epistemological issues confronting scholars using Church records from the late Middle Ages or propaganda films from the height of the Cold War. Any attempt to draw meaning from historical texts requires the scholar to deploy pre-existing matrices of understanding which are always, to some degree, products of his or her own belief systems and are therefore influenced by the wider cultural context in which interpretation takes place. Epistemological questions, which pertain to the problem of how we 'know' things and thus how we interpret meaning in the social world, are at least as relevant to intelligence research as they are to any other branch of scholarly enquiry. Methodological and epistemological issues are addressed either directly or indirectly in virtually all of the documentary analyses that follow.

On another level, however, it is possible to argue that the study of intelligence does throw up distinct challenges for scholars. Not only do intelligence documents not speak for themselves, some may also dissemble and some may even lie. Thus, one of the central concerns at or near the surface of many of the contributions in this volume is the particular difficulties inherent in the search for, and interrogation of, intelligence and intelligence-related archival material. Deception, deceit and manipulation are central elements in many of the day-to-day practices of many intelligence agencies – particularly those involved in gathering secret intelligence and in mounting covert actions in other states. Does this have implications for the historical record? In terms of methodology, therefore, it is worth reflecting upon how scholars go about finding archival material on intelligence and intelligence-related issues and how they decide what material is relevant and what is not. The reality is that even the most seasoned scholar faces formidable obstacles when conducting research into state agencies whose activities have long been subject to the most rigorous secrecy (when their existence has been acknowledged at all). For decades, the response of many historians was to ignore intelligence as a factor in national and international politics.

This attitude was unfortunate. The role and activities of intelligence services provide an especially fertile area for scholars seeking to understanding the inter-play between belief systems, cultural reflexes and wider structural factors in the making of policy. The relationships between intelligence services and their targets, between different intelligence agencies in co-operation and in competition with one another, and between intelligence officials and policy-makers, all provide excellent windows not only into the social dynamics of policy-making but also into the nature of international politics. The way intelligence analysts interpret threats and make sense of the world provides insight into the political, bureaucratic and ideological context in which they are operating. A focus on the role of intelligence can thus provide telling insight into the belief systems and institutional reflexes that condition policy-making. These are questions of interest to scholars from a wide range of disciplines trained to deploy a diverse array of conceptual approaches.

One of the benefits of gathering together such a variety of contributors in a volume like this is the different perspectives that result. The majority of contributors are historians. But there are also four political scientists, several of whom have extensive experience working both inside and outside government. Three other contributors are former intelligence practitioners, two of whom held senior posts within the CIA and one of whom is a veteran of the Israeli Defense Forces (IDF). The historians involved, moreover, bring a wide range of expertise to bear on the documents in this collection. In terms of the regional expertise, there are specialists on Western Europe, the Soviet Union, the Middle East, South-East Asia and the United States. Thematically, areas of expertise range from the history of science and technology to the international politics of disarmament, colonialism and decolonisation to strategy and diplomacy more generally.

A happy consequence of this diversity is the interesting array of strategies used to interrogate the intelligence documents under scrutiny. The approach adopted by Merle Pribbenow in his analysis of documents originating shortly after the establishment of the North Vietnamese government is very different from that deployed by Martin Alexander, for example, in his consideration of the document emanating from the intelligence section of the General Staff of the French army in 1936, or by John Ferris in his discussion of the creation of the British 'double-cross' system. Such differences in approach stem from the different backgrounds and expertise of the three scholars, the different subject matter of the texts and the different national-cultural contexts in which the documents were drafted. There is, in addition, an important difference in the character of the documents in question. Two of the texts analysed in this chapter are drawn from the French military archives and were obtained and translated by French signals intelligence in 1947 and 1950. As Christopher Goscha (who discovered and translated the documents in this section) stresses, both are translations of translations. Both of the commentators, however, judge them to be genuine. This, in turn, suggests a significant vote of confidence not only for Goscha's language skills, but also for the effectiveness of French signals intelligence in Indochina during this period.

Perhaps even more interesting are the differences in emphasis and interpretation between commentators writing about the same document. The analytical focus of CIA veteran Pribbenow, for example, differs from that of David Marr, an historian of Vietnam. The former focuses in considerable detail on what the document tells us about the structural evolution of the Vietnamese security and intelligence community. The latter is more inclined to link the texts to wider developments in the political development of North Vietnam. Together, the two commentaries provide a fascinating discussion of the role of political and institutional culture in shaping the security apparatus of the new state. The variety of perspectives on offer, and the interesting differences in their analyses of the range of documents under scrutiny, provide eloquent testimony to the potential of intelligence material to deepen our understanding of contemporary history. Exploring and exploiting this potential is the overarching aim of a cognate project devoted to exploring methodological issues in the study of intelligence. This has resulted in the development of a network of scholars, journalists, former intelligence analysts and former practitioners, many of whom are contributors to this volume.[1]

Exploring Intelligence Archives: a user's guide?

The practice of ignoring the role of intelligence in international politics – usually justified either by allusions to the difficulty in gaining access to relevant archival material or by a snobbish dismissal of intelligence history as the preserve of journalists and popular historians – is thankfully no longer tenable. While historians had long touched on aspects of espionage and secret service work in writing political and diplomatic history, systematic consideration of the role of intelligence in the history of war and international relations is a far more recent phenomenon. It can be traced to the appearance of a series of ground-breaking works on British intelligence over the space of little more than half a decade from 1979 through 1986. The first such study was the initial volume of the official history of British intelligence in the Second World War, co-written by a team of scholars led by Sir Harry Hinsley.[2] This was followed in 1984 by a collection of essays on governments and intelligence communities edited by Christopher Andrew and David Dilks and then in 1985 with the publication of Andrew's *Secret Service: The Making of the British Intelligence Community*. The latter study, in particular, made an important contribution to the history of British strategy and diplomacy during the first half of the twentieth century and demonstrated the possibilities of serious historical research into the role of intelligence.[3] In 1986, Andrew collaborated with Michael Handel in establishing *Intelligence and National Security*, the first academic journal devoted to intelligence and intelligence-related issues. Study of intelligence from an historical perspective has continued to gather momentum ever since, to the point where it is now a relatively well-established sub-discipline of historical research with a significant presence in scholarly journals and in the catalogues of academic publishers.

And yet, as Scott and Hughes emphasise in this volume, substantial access to intelligence and intelligence-related archival material is a fairly recent development. Levels of access, moreover, vary dramatically across, and sometimes even within national boundaries. The case of the two most heavily studied foreign intelligence agencies illustrates this point. While the CIA has adopted a relatively liberal declassification policy in the United States, the archives of the British Secret Intelligence Service (SIS) remain effectively closed to researchers. At the same time, however, the British Security Service (still widely referred to as MI5) has released substantial material to the British National Archives, while access to the records of the American Federal Bureau of Investigation (FBI) is more restricted.[4]

For decades, success in gaining access to primary source material on the role of intelligence required persistence and ingenuity. Christopher Andrew's experience working on the British intelligence services in the late 1970s and early 1980s illuminates the difficulties involved. At this juncture the British government refused even to acknowledge the peacetime existence of SIS. Declassification policy reflected this absurd official posture. Not only was all SIS material withheld, all documents making reference to SIS of any kind, even those where SIS merely appeared on the circulation list, were held back. Access to SIS material thus required imagination and lateral thinking. The far more relaxed attitude to secrecy that prevailed among senior government officials during the first half of the twentieth century proved a major boon in this regard. Before the Cambridge spy ring was uncovered and exposed to the public, it was not uncommon for ministers and senior civil servants to take copies of sensitive documents home and even to keep these documents among their personal papers. Although such a security breach is scarcely imaginable now, the happy consequence for historians, however, is that there are numerous allusions to the role of secret intelligence in the private papers of key political figures such as Lloyd George and Lord Curzon. The diaries of senior policy-makers proved another precious source for Andrew. References to SIS are redacted from the published version of the diaries of Sir Alexander Cadogan; but they remain in the original diary held by the Churchill Archives Centre in Cambridge.[5] The interlocking character of government in Britain also helped. SIS heads of station worked under the cover of Passport Control Officers in British embassies and ministries. With this knowledge, Andrew was able to use the records of the Treasury to identify SIS operatives abroad. Finally, he benefited from isolated breakdowns in declassification procedures. SIS material inevitably slipped through the archival weeding process and into the FO 371 series of Foreign Office 'General Correspondence'. One of the most notable of such instances is an SIS memorandum drafted during the Czechoslovak Crisis of 1938 and entitled 'What Should We Do?' that found its way into the FO 371 files for 1938. Andrew and David Dilks both made extensive reference to this document in their respective reinterpretations of British appeasement at this crucial moment in the international history of the inter-war period.[6]

The case of intelligence and French policy before the Second World War poses a very different set of challenges from the British example. For many years professional historians in France had avoided systematic investigation of the role of intelligence in shaping policy on the grounds that the necessary source material had been lost or destroyed during the Second World War.[7] This ill-founded, yet widely held, assumption was first challenged during the 1980s by non-French scholars Robert Young and Martin Alexander.[8] Both pointed out that, despite the loss of the French secret service archive to Germany in 1943, there was a wealth of unexploited material openly available for consultation in the French military archives in Vincennes. And this material included numerous secret intelligence reports of the kind that remain officially closed in the British archives.[9] Indeed, the problem confronting anyone desiring to research this topic was not a paucity of sources but rather an over-abundance of potentially relevant archival material. And this problem has only been amplified since the mid-1990s when the Russian government began returning the intelligence and security archives lost to the Germans in 1943. The Red Army captured this material in 1945 and it had been held in Moscow throughout the Cold War. The material now available for consultation comprises nearly 100,000 dossiers and constitutes a major new source for the history of twentieth-century France.[10] Research into the role of domestic and foreign intelligence in politics and policy-making during this period is therefore relatively virgin territory burgeoning with unexploited archival sources.

Hence the challenges facing the historian of intelligence can vary substantially and change constantly. The situation in Britain, for example, has been revolutionised over the past decade and a half with the release first of material from the archives of the Joint Intelligence Committee (JIC), followed by a vast *tranche* of files from Britain's twentieth-century signals intelligence organisations and, beginning in 1999, substantial material from the archives of the Security Service (MI5).[11] All of this is in addition to the records of the Defence Intelligence Staff and the service intelligence departments, many of which are open in compliance with the thirty-year rule.[12] While ingenuity, persistence and a critical perspective on the source material all remain vital requirements for the historian, the vast quantity of archival source material now available (at least in the case of the British, American and

French services) is a challenge with which the first generation of intelligence scholars did not have to cope.

There are other considerations that merit the close attention of all scholars working with official records that have been released as a result of state-controlled declassification regimes of one kind or another. Richard Aldrich has provided an interesting and important series of reflections on this issue that pertain not only to the academic study of intelligence but to all scholars interested in the history of the state. Aldrich warns that archives are ultimately 'controlled material' because 'Government files that are allowed into the public domain are placed there by authorities as a result of deliberate decisions.' He adds that those who work on this material are in danger of becoming 'something close to official historians, albeit once-removed'. In support of this argument, Aldrich cites the case of the 'Ultra Secret', where a deliberate policy of government deception succeeded in keeping secret the crucial successes of British signals intelligence during the Second World War. A special Whitehall committee was convened to deal with the problem of 'how to handle history and historians'. The decision was taken to recruit a select few historians to write the official history of the Second World War, to reveal to them the secret of Ultra and then to persuade them to excise all mention of it from what they wrote. An official body was then created to review their work and further sanitise the role of signals intelligence in the course of the war. Similar efforts aimed at keeping the success of British deception out of the public domain. Depressingly, these tactics succeeded in limiting the conceptual horizons of an entire generation of gifted scholars.[13]

Aldrich is therefore sceptical of the greater openness that both the British and American governments have displayed in implementing more liberal declassification policies for intelligence and security material. He warns that, 'Well-packaged programmes of document release have allowed governments to move beyond an old-fashioned "stonewalling" approach . . . into a new era in which the authorities set the agenda for archive based researchers.'[14] Within both the British and American programmes of declassification and destruction 'there is ample scope to massage the representation of the more secretive aspects of government'. He argues for a methodological approach 'more sceptical of archives that have been laundered by the very subject that one is attempting to study'.[15] He notes that:

> Contemporary historians who explore the state are quite unique. Nowhere else is the researcher confronted with evidence precisely managed by their subject. From astronomy to agriculture, from botany to the built environment, no investigator confronts information so deliberately pre-selected.

Aldrich laments that 'most historians are remarkably untroubled by this and some have come to think of the selected materials in the Public Records Office as an analogue of reality'.[16]

These are obviously important considerations that bear careful reflection. But Aldrich has arguably pressed the case too far. It is to be hoped that few professionally trained historians believe everything they read in the archives or assume that they are working with some form of unadulterated 'truth'. At the heart of his argument is the assumption that there is a 'secret' story to most policy decisions that never makes it into the official record. Aldrich refers to this as the 'inner stuff of secret history' and concludes that we may never know the 'full story' of the role of intelligence in the Cold War.[17]

The assumption that the 'real' story behind policy-making is usually either hidden or excised from the archival record is also open to question. This seems to attribute an unrealistic level of efficiency to government machinery engaging in the ongoing struggle to maintain secrecy and shape popular perceptions. The case of the 'Ultra Secret' is an ominous warning to scholars. The British government demonstrated both the desire and the ability to manipulate records of the past. But it is also important to remember that this secret was eventually leaked – and leaked before the effects of the thirty-year rule made it possible for historians to write histories of the Second World War based on a comprehensive survey of the archival record. Moreover, it is highly unlikely that such a secret could be kept secret in the present era of increasingly intrusive mass media. The 'inner stuff of secret history' has a way of turning up somewhere. It surfaces often in the form of leaks to the press, in private papers, in memoirs or published diaries, and, increasingly, in oral testimony. Indeed, the more controversial the event or decision, the more likely that its 'secret' dimension will eventually emerge. Thereafter, it is usually possible for the patient and dedicated researcher, using time-honoured methods of cross-checking and verification and adopting a multi-level and multi-archival approach, to find traces of the 'inner' history in the archival record. The recent discovery by Matthew Jones of plans to assassinate high-ranking Syrian officials during the 1950s, plans seen and approved by US President Dwight D. Eisenhower and British Prime Minister Harold Macmillan, are a good illustration of this point. This particular discovery was made in the papers of Duncan Sandys (Defence Secretary from 1957 until 1959) held at the Churchill Archive Centre, Cambridge.[18]

The fact that Aldrich was able to turn up documentary evidence of a systematic Whitehall programme to control the work of historians is a case in point. It seems equally plausible to assume that most of the really important 'secrets' have left traces in the documentary record. The interlocking nature of modern government is once again a valuable ally for the historian. Bureaucratic rivalry, between as well as within departments, is a particularly valuable asset to ongoing efforts to reconstruct policy processes. Internecine quarrels often motivate officials to write things down. They do this for any number of reasons: sometimes to protect themselves or their department, sometimes with an eye fixed on the future historical record. While it is essential to use such material carefully, it often provides vital insight into the dynamics of policy making. Adopting a multi-national approach to research is another crucial way to study state behaviour in general and the role of intelligence in particular. It is difficult enough for governments to control the material contained in their own national archives, but they have little or no control over declassification and destruction procedures in other countries. Comparing and contrasting intelligence and intelligence-related material in archives generated by different states can therefore provide new perspectives on both intelligence practices and decision-making. It can also highlight gaps and inconsistencies in the official record.

A good recent example of possibilities of an international approach is an important article by Mathilde von Bülow on the role of French covert action in the Federal Republic of Germany during the Cold War. Von Bülow has found fascinating material in the archives of the West German security services which she uses to make a powerful case that attacks on North African émigrés living in Germany during the Algerian War were carried out not by renegade vigilantes (the 'Red Hand') but instead by the French foreign intelligence service, the *Service de Documentation Extérieure et Contre-Espionnage* (SDECE). She also shows that this covert action was carried out with the full approval of senior figures in the French political leadership. There is predictably little or no evidence of this dimension to French policy in the available French archives.[19] A multi-national approach to research provides the opportunity to alleviate the problem of systematic distortion of the archival record by state authorities seeking to shape historical interpretation.

Nor should we necessarily assume that there is always a 'hidden history' that will transform our understanding of past events. It is, in any case, a dubious proposition to assume that we can ever know the 'full story' of any historical event. Our understanding of complex historical phenomena is too contingent on the temporal and ideological context in which we operate. Indeed, an excessive preoccupation with turning up new and hitherto secret information is a potential weakness of intelligence history. In the words of one distinguished scholar, intelligence studies is 'a field that cannot stand on its own'.[20] The special importance placed on turning up new information for its own sake can sometimes overshadow the scholar's responsibility to provide a systematic analysis of what this new material tells us about the dynamics of policy-making and politics more generally. This requires a fairly comprehensive knowledge of the machinery of policy-making and the specific place of intelligence within this machinery. The historian must develop a feel for how papers moved within and across departments, as well as a sense of the institutional cultures of these organisations in general and prevailing attitudes towards intelligence information in particular. Nor can one ignore the wider political and cultural dynamics in society as a whole – which inevitably condition the way intelligence is interpreted by analysts and received by decision-makers. These requirements, significantly, are by no means unique to the study of intelligence. They are essential prerequisites for all serious political, cultural and diplomatic historians.

To conclude, the observation made by John Ferris that progress in the field of intelligence studies 'requires not only new evidence but also new approaches' is worth reiterating here.[21] It is our hope that the documents, overviews and commentary in this collection will prove useful not only to researchers but also to teachers of intelligence and intelligence-related courses and especially to students. The continued vibrancy of this new field depends on our ability to attract and inspire a new generation of students to take the academic study of intelligence on through the twenty-first century.

Notes

Introduction: Enquiries into the 'secret state'

Peter Jackson

1   See L.V. Scott and Peter Jackson, *Understanding Intelligence in the Twenty-First Century: Journeys in Shadows* (London: Routledge, 2004), also published as a special issue of *Intelligence and National Security* 19/2 (Summer 2004).
2   F.H. Hinsley *et al.*, *British Intelligence in the Second World War: Its Influence on Strategy and Operations*, vol. I (London: HMSO, 1979).
3   C. Andrew and D. Dilks (eds), *The Missing Dimension: Governments and Intelligence Communities in the Twentieth Century* (London: Macmillan, 1984) and C. Andrew, *Secret Service: The Making of the British Intelligence Community* (London: Guild Publishing, 1985).
4   The FBI website does include a 'Freedom of Information Act' (FOIA) page with links to its inventories and various digitised files. The material on espionage available on this site is extremely limited however (eight files as of 5 July 2007): see http://foia.fbi.gov/spies.htm
5   Churchill Archives Centre, Cambridge, GBR/0014/ACAD, Section 1; volumes 5–15 (1936–1945). Andrew also found similar material in the diary of Major-General Sir Walter Kirke.
6   Great Britain, The National Archives, FO 371, 21659, C14471/42/18. See also Andrew, *Secret Service*, pp. 398–400 and David Dilks, 'Flashes of Intelligence: The Foreign Office, the SIS and Security before the Second World War', in Andrew and Dilks (eds), *The Missing Dimension*, pp. 101–25.
7   There were two notable exceptions: George Castellan's seminal, *Le réarmement clandestin du Reich, 1930–1935: vu par le 2e Bureau de l'Etat-major de l'Armée française* (Paris: Plon, 1954) and an important article by Maurice Vaïsse, 'L'évolution de la fonction d'attaché militaire en France au XXe siècle', *Relations Internationales*, 32 (1982), pp. 507–24. Of these two works, only that of Vaïsse examines the role of intelligence in policy-making. As its title suggests, however, the focus of Castellan's study was German rearmament rather than French policy.
8   Robert Young, 'French Military Intelligence and Nazi Germany 1938–1939', in E. May (ed.), *Knowing One's Enemies: Intelligence Assessment before the Two World Wars* (Cambridge, MA: Harvard University Press, 1984), pp. 271–309, and Martin Alexander, 'Did the 2e Bureau Work? The Role of Intelligence in French Policy and Strategy, 1919–1939', *INS*, 6/2 (1991), pp. 293–333.
9   The catalogues of the French military archives for this period give an idea of the scale of available material. See France, Ministère de la Défense, Service historique de l'armée de terre, *Inventaire des Archives de la Guerre, Serie N (1920–1940)*, vols I and II (compiled by Jean Nicot and Pierre Waksman) (Vincennes: Service historique de l'armée de terre, 1981). Nearly 700 of the 1,027 pages of volume II are devoted to the holdings of the intelligence department (the Deuxième Bureau) of the army general staff.
10 The return of these archives was carried out in two waves, one in 1993–94 and another at the end of the decade. The first wave (comprising more than 40,000 dossiers) is now catalogued and available for consultation at the French military archives at the Château de Vincennes (for the records of the military intelligence and counter-intelligence services) or at the Centre des Archives Contemporaines at Fontainebleau (for the *Sûreté Nationale* records). The second (nearly twice as large as the first) should be completely open to scholars by the end of 2007. See Claire Sibille, 'Les archives du 2ème Bureau SR-SCR récupérées de Russie', in G-H. Soutou, J. Frémeux and

O. Forcade (eds), *L'Exploitation du renseignement en Europe et aux Etats-Unis des années 1930 aux années 1960* (Paris: Economica, 2001), pp. 27–47.

11 These are the Government Code and Cypher School (GC and CS) through 1944 and its successor the Government Communications Headquarters (GCHQ).

12 See the National Archives information sheet entitled 'Intelligence Records in the National Archives' available at: http://www.nationalarchives.gov.uk/catalogue/Rd Leaflet.asp?sLeafletID=32. R. Gerald Hughes and Len Scott provide a far more in-depth and systematic discussion of these issues in the following essay in this volume (pp. 13–39). See also Sir Stephen Lander, 'British Intelligence in the Twentieth Century', and Gill Bennett, 'Declassification and Release Policies of the UK's Intelligence Agencies', both in *Intelligence and National Security*, 17/2 (2002): pp. 7–20, 21–32 respectively.

13 Quotations from Richard Aldrich, *The Hidden Hand: Britain, America and Cold War Secret Intelligence* (London: John Murray, 2001), pp. 5, 2–3 and 6 respectively.

14 Ibid., p. 6.

15 Richard Aldrich, *Intelligence and the War Against Japan: Britain, America and the Politics of Secret Service* (Cambridge: Cambridge University Press, 2000), p. 376.

16 Aldrich, *Hidden Hand*, pp. 5, 6. The Public Record Office was the previous name for the UK National Archives, Kew.

17 Ibid., pp. 639–40 and 6 respectively.

18 Mathew Jones, 'The "Preferred Plan": The Anglo-American Working Group Report on Covert Action in Syria, 1957', *Intelligence and National Security*, 19/3 (2004), pp. 401–15.

19 Mathilde von Bülow, 'Myth or Reality? The Red Hand and French Covert Action in Germany, 1956–1961', *Intelligence and National Security*, 22/6 (2007), pp. 787–820.

20 John Ferris, 'The Road to Bletchley Park: The British Experience with Signals Intelligence, 1892–1945', *Intelligence and National Security*, 17/1 (2002), p. 56.

21 Ferris, 'The Road to Bletchley Park', p. 56.

1 'Knowledge is never too dear'

Exploring intelligence archives[1]

R. Gerald Hughes and Len Scott

Never believe anything until it has officially been denied.

(Claud Cockburn[2])

Scholarship, archives and intelligence

Over two hundred years ago Daniel Defoe wrote, 'intelligence is the soul of all public business'.[3] And yet, as political history came to dominate the academic discipline of history from the mid-nineteenth century onwards,[4] intelligence was notable by its absence from mainstream scholarship. Today, while political history has lost its former pre-eminence in the discipline, it remains very significant and is the main domicile for those scholars engaged in the study of intelligence. The emergence of intelligence history over recent years is the catalyst for this volume's consideration of issues arising from the study of intelligence using archival material. Such issues arise chiefly from two sources. First, from the traditional limitations of archive-based scholarship faced by all historians and, second, from those problems more intimately associated with the inherent secrecy of the activity of intelligence. In the specific case of intelligence history, recent years have seen a number of developments that can only be of assistance to the scholar. The reform of archival release policies internationally, allied to innovations in information flow, means that official histories are no longer the sole source of information on the intelligence dimension of international history. While it is true that there is no right and wrong approach to working with archives, a rigorous methodology is the vital element in the art of writing history. The acquisition of archival access is by no means the end of the process. E.H. Carr noted that while 'Bricks are important . . . a pile of bricks is not a house. And should the master-builder spend his time in a brick-field?'[5] In construction, as in historical scholarship, it is the manner in which the 'bricks' are put together that determines the quality of the product. For the individual scholar, this 'construction' process is crucial and it takes time to perfect. Ferdnand Braudel was quite right when observing that the discipline of history 'cannot be understood without practising it'.[6] And, as Gary Player, the legendary South African golfer, used to say: 'The more I practice, the luckier I get.'[7]

Yet, scholars of intelligence have often found it hard to practise anything at all due to a paucity of available sources. In 1992, Wesley Wark asked in exasperation, 'Where are these records?'[8] While it is at least now possible to answer that question, Wark makes a crucial point by emphasising that intelligence is not simply concerned with the activities of the security and intelligence services themselves. This reflects broader debates about the nature and definition of intelligence, which for most commentators involves the input of secret intelligence into the analytical and policy processes. Wark proffers a helpful definition of the intelligence archive as the 'record of all those government departments who receive, incorporate, digest and report on intelligence that comes to them from both secret and overt sources'.[9] Nevertheless, questions remain about the potential distinctiveness of the intelligence archive. One expectation might be that intelligence and security services live and breathe through their records as access to information and cross-referral are the life-blood of the work of intelligence and counter-intelligence. Efficient intelligence systems require efficient information management and retrieval. Whether this expectation is borne out in reality and across time and space is, of course, another matter.

The study of intelligence by means of archival analysis should recognise certain limitations from the outset. Here, we might usefully recall Otto von Bismarck's famous dictum that 'Politics is not an exact science.'[10] Neither is intelligence history. Richard Aldrich is right to inveigh against the gullibility of historians who take official British archives to be an 'analogue of reality',[11] fearing, as he does, that British Cold War historians 'often appear feeble supplicants before the state'.[12] In support of such views, Aldrich demonstrates how a generation of British historians was manipulated to conceal crucial aspects of wartime British intelligence and provide a distorted and misleading portrayal of the Allied conduct of the Second World War. In some ways, such arguments echo those of contemporary Western critics of accounts drawn from Soviet intelligence archives and raise the question of whether intelligence history is too readily manipulated. Counter to this perspective, Sir Stephen Lander, the then Director-General of the Security Service (MI5), spoke in 2002 of a common appreciation among the security and intelligence agencies that they 'do not own the past and certainly cannot change it'.[13] That is all well and good but official records, like all other records, are written for a purpose (and declassified or withheld for a purpose), and the marked reluctance of intelligence agencies to disclose their archives has meant that they have owned substantial portions of the past as far as scholars are concerned.

Like any archival depository, the intelligence archive contains many different kinds of record. Different phases in the intelligence cycle raise different issues. Similarly different forms of intelligence gathering may present different challenges. The paucity of archival sources concerning Signals Intelligence (SIGINT) remains a significant obstacle to understanding the role of intelligence in world politics in the Cold War and beyond. Human Intelligence (HUMINT), and specifically espionage, proffer more material and more evidence of challenges and opportunities. How, for example, case officers record their dealings with their agents, and how intelligence officers report back to headquarters raise generic questions about professionalism and politicisation. Do we expect the telegrams of intelligence officers back to headquarters to compare in terms of veracity to those of their diplomatic colleagues? How far do ideological and political factors impinge on construction of reports?

This collection aims to address such questions while discussing documents, many introduced into the public domain for the first time, that illustrate themes and issues vital to understanding intelligence. Some of the contributions, based on French, German, and Vietnamese archives, illustrate the changing nature of intelligence studies and herald a greater awareness of the long-standing bias towards British, American and Soviet intelligence history.[14] In Britain, as in many other states, such reflection on the archival foundations of the study of intelligence comes at an opportune time, as new phases in declassification are reached amidst unprecedented public scrutiny of British intelligence and the war on Iraq. This can only be healthy. Excessive secrecy has, in the past, served only to cause suspicion both of intelligence and of histories of intelligence. In his classic *The Structure of Politics at the Accession of George III*, Lewis Namier outlined a once commonly held view of intelligence among historians when he wrote:

> Legends naturally surround all 'secret service'; its very name inspires fear and distrust and stimulates men's imagination – it is believed to be wise and wicked, efficient and powerful. In reality the most common characteristic of political secret service at all times is its stupidity and the unconscionable waste of money which it entails. Where its task is 'intelligence', it most frequently produces tales which could not stand five minutes cross-examination in a law court, but which, by the presumed nature of the service, are secured against effective criticism, and are made credible by being framed to suit the bias of the employers.[15]

Namier is correct in stating that the secrecy associated with intelligence means that its place in state activity is often exaggerated. This suspicion of 'intelligence' as a subject of serious historical enquiry was reinforced by the paucity of the archival record on that subject in the 1950s. Despite this, Namier felt the subject of intelligence of sufficient importance to devote a chapter of the above-named book to 'Secret Service Money'.[16] However, while Namier's charges had much substance fifty years ago, the last quarter of a century has seen the erosion of such negative views of intelligence history. This must be allied, however, to an acceptance of Namier's legitimate criticism of the manner in which intelligence has too easily been regarded as omnipotent by its adherents. Certainly, more enlightened archival release policies are at the core of the stripping away of what Namier refers to as the 'legends' surrounding intelligence. That is not the whole story however. Ironically, the nature of intelligence activity today remains the worst enemy of intelligence scholarship.

One question posed in this collection is the degree to which the nature of intelligence presents particular challenges to the historian, given that intelligence is irreducibly concerned with secrecy.[17] Deception, deceit and manipulation are often integral to intelligence gathering. Indeed, a Second World War practitioner of intelligence is on record as stating that 'Intelligence work is by definition illegal. If it is very effective intelligence work, it is very illegal.'[18] Furthermore, intelligence services do not publicly reveal sources or methods because of the necessity of protecting sources and methods. Yet protection does not end at the front door. All intelligence organisations – and the policy communities within which they operate – have codified procedural arrangements and safeguards. Information is provided on the basis of a need to know and a need to preserve the anonymity of the source or method of exploitation.[19] Declassification policies are designed to protect this principle.[20] Intelligence services believe they have a duty of care for their agents, which may extend over generations, and without which their ability to gain the trust of those who would risk all to betray their country would be weakened. Equally, one reason why the British were so reluctant to reveal the Ultra Secret was the number of states (including friendly states) who were using the Enigma-style machines to the benefit of British signals intelligence. All of this is rather daunting, for as Michael Warner recently warned, 'Intelligence . . . by definition resists scholarship.'[21]

So what are the implications of all of this for the veracity of the historical record? To start with, a cautionary note should be added here. Intelligence archives can readily acquire the same mystique as secret intelligence itself, and this brings the same risk that disproportionate significance may be given to the preserved (and released) historical record. The advisability of such caution was reflected in the 1983 Franks Report which concluded that, in the build-up to the invasion of the Falkland Islands in April 1982, Whitehall may have placed too great an emphasis on secret intelligence, and that more attention could have been paid to diplomatic and political information (and, indeed, to the Argentine press).[22] In sum, it is important to remember that intelligence records may generate unhelpful expectations about the significance of what they hold simply because they have been wrapped in such secrecy. In this vein, A.J.P. Taylor cautioned that:

> There is a danger of taking . . . new sources too seriously simply because they have previously been secret . . . A statement of fact in a secret document is regarded as necessarily truer and an argument as necessarily wiser than one made . . . in public . . . Experience of human beings does not confirm this view. Taylor's law states: 'The Foreign Office knows no secrets.' Much the same applies to other departments of state and even to the cabinet office.[23]

Taylor is, for once, no maverick in this regard. In 1923, Sir Charles Webster spoke of the perpetual 'instinctive and intense' distrust displayed by governments towards scholars.[24] In this spirit, Herbert Butterfield urged scholars 'never [to] lose sight of the separate interests of officialdom . . . and the academic historian'. Owen Chadwick was blunter: 'The needs of government and the wishes of the historian conflict.'[25] In 1963, Donald Watt argued that the rights of the citizen were inseparable from the needs of the scholar in terms of archival access.[26] Here, Watt is simply acknowledging the fact that the increasing democratisation of Western societies was – and is – a powerful ally for the historian. Rather uniquely for an academic article, Watt's article was read and digested by a leading politician, Harold Wilson, the leader of the Labour Party. In 1965, Wilson, by now Prime Minister, wrote a Cabinet memorandum alluding to Watt's piece which recommended the adoption of a thirty-year (as opposed to a fifty-year) rule for the declassification of documents.[27] Wilson's reasons for adopting this path included the following responses to Watt's points. First, given the rapid end of Empire, if Britain failed to give proper access to historians, the former colonies would do so and 'our side of the story will be liable to go by default'. Second, the same was true internationally as other nations (particularly the United States) were more generous in their archival access procedures. And third, 'an objective and dispassionate analysis of the recent past can . . . promote a more informed public understanding of contemporary issues'.[28] While Wilson's recommendations were adopted by Cabinet on 5 August 1965, such models of consensus between scholars and politicians are, historically speaking, all too rare.

Of course, even democratic states have a wide variety of traditions and practices on the subject of archival access. Differences in organisational culture and bureaucratic procedure generate different patterns of declassification. According to Gill Bennett, 'The principal reason why the CIA has released so much material is that the form and content of its records have made it possible to do so.'[29] Acknowledging international variations, this collection aims to explore how a variety of people involved in the study of intelligence view primary material with their own distinct national and personal perspectives.[30] This is linked to a cognate project exploring methodological issues in the study of intelligence, which has developed a network of scholars, journalists, former intelligence analysts and former practitioners.[31] Such networks are of great utility in reminding one of the very disparate natures of opportunities to study intelligence across the globe. Internationally, we can, however, generalise that debates are often framed in terms of the official insistence on national security against the insistence of the democratic 'right to know'. As an example here, one might usefully refer to one of the more spectacular leaks in American history – the so-called 'Pentagon Papers' (a portion of which is examined in this collection). These papers, documenting the highly sensitive history of US involvement in Vietnam, came into the public domain through the actions of State Department official Daniel Ellsberg in 1971.[32] While over 50 per cent of the 7,000 pages comprising the Pentagon Papers were published in the *New York Times* and, subsequently, in book form, the remainder were kept locked away in a vault at the Lyndon Baines Johnson Library in Austin, Texas.[33] Subsequently, the LBJ Library has released portions of the remaining classified sections of the Pentagon Papers and in June 2002, for instance, 115 more pages were released into the public domain. The press brief announcing the release noted:

> While the new material is a small fraction of the entire Pentagon Papers, its release marks a significant milestone in the history of this controversial and significant study. The events surrounding the journey of these documents from government secrets to publication and release are perhaps even more interesting

and are very topical at the moment. How are we to manage government secrecy, freedom of the press, and individual rights in the interests of both national security and democracy?[34]

Such sentiments were not shared by National Security Advisor Henry Kissinger, for whom Ellsberg had once worked,[35] who complained in 1979 that, 'The massive hemorrhage of state secrets was bound to raise doubts about our reliability in the minds of other governments, friend or foe, and indeed about the stability of our political system.'[36] For his part, President Richard Nixon was characteristically blunt:

> [O]n this national security thing, we have the rocky situation where the sonofabitch thief is made a national hero . . . And the *New York Times* gets a Pulitzer Prize for stealing documents . . . *What in the name of God have we come to?*[37]

Ellsberg responded to this by asserting that, in fact, 'What we had come back to was a democratic republic . . . a government under law, with Congress, the courts, and the press functioning to curtail executive abuses, as our constitution envisaged.'[38] The suspicion of intelligence agencies and governments, allied to a dislike of official secrecy, has thus created a community of interest between the whistle-blower and the academic historian.[39]

Freedom of information: the way forward?

The fear of damaging disclosures, such as that initiated by Ellsberg, allied to the controversial nature of certain aspects of intelligence work, can lead to a natural temptation for policy-makers and officials to simply destroy the archival record.[40] Unsurprisingly, the US Freedom of Information Act (FOIA), enacted as long ago as 1966 (and amended in 2002),[41] continues to encounter opposition from interested parties.[42] In the American context, this often takes the form of the deliberate obstruction of researcher requests by the military and intelligence establishments.[43] Nevertheless, given that historians have been, and remain, the largest single group of academics utilising the FOIA, the positive implications of greater archival access for scholars of intelligence are clear.[44] In recent years Freedom of Information legislation, allied to a number of executive initiatives, notably under the Clinton Presidency, have enabled scholars and citizens to scrutinize the record of US intelligence agencies and the policy process in general. In 1993, President Clinton issued a letter in which he urged Federal Agencies to comply fully with the Act (this was followed in 1995 by an executive decision to disclose files dating from more than twenty-five years).[45]

Despite all of this, the CIA has been criticised for being the most recalcitrant of the branches of Federal government in the declassification of its files.[46] Constraints remain on sources in the USA, and, long before September 11, the administration of George Bush Sr. (1989–93) sought to impose restrictions on archival access.[47]

In the wake of 11 September 2001, the controversial Executive Order 13233 of 1 November, drafted by White House Counsel Alberto R. Gonzales, sought to restrict access to the records of former presidents. This was denounced by Society of American Archivists President Steve Hensen 'as far from being a "further implementation," is more like a complete abnegation of the original 1978 Presidential Records Act'.[48] Critics charge that there was a 60 per cent increase in the number of documents classified between 2001 and 2003;[49] while it has been claimed that 15.6 million new documents were classified in Fiscal Year 2004 (an increase of 81 per cent over the year prior to 11 September 2001).[50] There are those who argue that even before these recent developments US declassification was far too restrictive, and encouraged conspiracy theories about the US government.[51] In an attempt to improve perceived failings in US disclosure policy the Attorney General, Alberto R. Gonzales, made a number of recommendations to President George W. Bush in October 2006.[52] But these recommendations were deemed insufficient by many critics and, in response, an unsatisfied National Security Archive called for 'congressional oversight hearings to make optimistic FOIA processing goals a reality'.[53] On 14 March 2007, the National Security Archive General Counsel, Meredith Fuchs, informed the Senate Judiciary Committee that the proposed Open Government Act of 2007[54] was essential for 'improving the functioning of FOIA'.[55] Yet, despite its shortcomings, American declassification policy remains the most liberal globally[56] (certainly by comparison with other liberal-democracies).[57] These declassification policies have facilitated an extensive and sophisticated literature that provides understanding and debate beyond that of any other country (although many countries also have freedom of information legislation).[58] Raymond M. Lee goes so far as to note that 'From the point of view of research, agencies subject to the FOIA can [now] be thought of as archival repositories.'[59] The culture of greater openness in the USA is reflected in the willingness of officials and retired officials to co-operate with journalists, as well as in the writing of memoirs. These are important sources for students of intelligence. But, even by American standards, one rather extraordinary recent development has been the publication of books by a serving CIA officer dealing with contemporary national security issues, written with the explicit aim of influencing public opinion.[60]

For students of American intelligence, these privileges and opportunities can sometimes be taken for granted. But other scholars can only envy such opportunities. Bernard Wasserstein argued forcefully in 2001 that his own experiences with the US FOIA demonstrated the huge potential advantages for historians working in Britain of similar legislation being enacted there (at the time of his writing such measures were indeed being considered by the UK Parliament).[61] Is FOI legislation really the panacea advocates of greater archival access have long imagined? Certainly, advocates of such legislation often link the traditional absence of FOI to the lack of a written British constitution.[62]

We should not, however, exaggerate the extent to which the UK is the exception in democratic states' approach to intelligence archives by virtue of its lack of a written constitution. In France, that nation of prolific constitution writers, secrets pertaining to national security are exempt from freedom of information legislation.[63]

Yet it is true that, in Britain, the relationship between secrecy and disclosure has changed significantly in recent years. Certainly, there is a long tradition of official secrecy in matters pertaining to intelligence in Britain. The Foreign and Commonwealth Office seem positively proud of this legacy and their webpage includes the following observation from the Sixteenth Century: 'There is no government on earth which divulges its affairs less than England, or is more punctually informed of those of others.'[64] Despite being a global pioneer in the provision of opportunities for scholarly archival research,[65] British attitudes towards intelligence-related material were exemplified by the Official Secrets Act of 1911.[66] In 1924, Foreign Secretary Austen Chamberlain famously declared that:

> It is of the essence of a Secret Service that it must be secret, and if you once begin disclosure it is perfectly obvious to me as to Honourable Members opposite that there is no longer any Secret Service and that you must do without it.[67]

In retrospect, it seems barely believable that it was not until 1992 that Prime Minister John Major abandoned the constitutional convention that the Secret Intelligence Service (SIS or MI6) did not exist in peacetime[68] (although former Prime Minister Callaghan wrote of his dealings with the Chief of SIS in his 1987 auto-biography).[69] One consequence of this attitude toward SIS was that any record which even mentioned MI6 was withheld,[70] even when the information was entirely banal.

The Waldegrave Initiative in 1993 began a process of change in declassification which from 1997[71] resulted in the records of the Security Service reaching the Public Record Office (PRO – now the National Archives).[72] Of note here is the development of an Operational Selection Policy, drafted by the PRO and the Security Service, governing the release of MI5 records.[73] Subsequently the files of the other foreign intelligence gathering agency, Government Communications Headquarters (GCHQ) began to be transferred to the National Archives, and the wartime records of the Government Code and Cypher School, GCHQ's wartime predecessor, are now open.[74] GCHQ also undertook joint declassification of the Venona Project, providing details of Western decryption of Soviet cipher communications.[75] SIS did facilitate the opening of the wartime Special Operation Executive (SOE) records. While SIS archives themselves are not declassified, there is co-operation with other government departments to allow greater release of SIS papers held in their departmental files.[76]

Other changes in declassification procedures have advanced the cause of openness, most importantly the practice of redacting documents rather than withholding them altogether. The potential significance of this is illustrated by the CIA's estimate that under a pass-fail approach, it was only able to release 15 per cent of documents under review. With redaction the figure was increased to between 50 and 75 per cent.[77] Looking to the future, the United Kingdom's Freedom of Information Act (2000), which came into force on 1 January 2005,[78] is bound to have significant long-term consequences for scholars.[79] Of course, legal precedent will be crucial in all of this and a potentially important development saw a recent judicial decision to require SIS to explain its policy on disclosure over the case of a Second World War agent.[80] The law, it seems, is now an ally in the historians' quest for greater archival access.

Official histories, internal histories

The complex relationship between governments and historians is a recurrent theme for scholars engaged in the study of state activity. Official histories, for so long the best available source for the intelligence historian, have thus traditionally been viewed with distrust (and even disdain) by scholars.[81] Thus, any co-operation between governments and historians has produced, at best, uneven results.[82] There have, however, been certain successes in the US and British cases especially. In the United States, the seven volumes resulting from the Church Committee's deliberations, published in 1975 and 1976, were a revelation in terms of public knowledge of American intelligence activity, and these volumes have recently been termed 'the bedrock for academic work on the Intelligence Community'.[83] Across the Atlantic, notwithstanding the British culture of secrecy, intelligence records have been accessed with official sanction in a variety of ways.[84] Thus, in contrast to the official histories of the Second World War, the official histories of British intelligence in the Second World War are seen as highly detailed and authoritative accounts.[85] These remain 'seminal accounts' and of immense utility to scholars interested in all Allied and European Axis, as well as British, intelligence activities in the Second World War.[86] Despite this, and almost inevitably, the critical views of these volumes were voiced by some insiders. Sir Maurice Oldfield, erstwhile Chief of SIS, described the first volume as 'a book written by a committee, about committees for committees'.[87] Moreover, the studies were criticised for their omission of the war against Japan and far having made no attempt to scrutinise the penetrations by Soviet intelligence before and during the war. Furthermore, the fifth volume, by Sir Michael Howard, dealing with strategic deception, was not published until 1990, a decade after completion, apparently because of the concerns of Prime Minister Thatcher.[88]

The experience of involving professional academic historians has clearly proved successful and the authorised histories of MI5 and MI6, to commemorate their centenaries in 2009, are being written by Professor Christopher Andrew of Cambridge University and Professor Keith Jeffery of Queens' University Belfast, respectively.[89] Both historians have been given access to service archives[90] although, as SIS's web-site emphasises, the 'commitment to the protection of intelligence sources remains paramount and the [official history of SIS] will not reveal operational details which remain sensitive'.[91] Not to be outdone, the Historical Records Branch of the British Foreign and Commonwealth Office has also undertaken important intelligence-related projects.[92] The material included previously unseen records of the Permanent Under-Secretary's Department and, in 1999, Gill Bennett published an evaluation of the famous Zinoviev Letter which had been used to smear the British Labour Party in 1924.[93] Bennett's assessment drew upon SIS files as well Soviet records made available by the Russian government.[94] Nevertheless on present trends it could be a decade or more before records of MI5 and GCHQ are available to post-1945 Cold War, post-colonial and other historians. Again, the US example inspires envy by virtue of the wealth of material available because the declassification of CIA records has been on a far greater scale. The CIA's staff of historians has produced a variety of operational histories and document collections relating to the Cold War. Many of the documents, together with declassified articles from the CIA's in-house journal, *Studies in Intelligence*, are accessible on the CIA web-site.[95] Such documents and sources are pre-selected, and for cynics and sceptics, irredeemably tainted. Yet, to its credit, the CIA declassification of its record of covert action at the height of the Cold War has provided considerable ammunition for scholars critical of the Agency's record.[96] Most remarkable in this vein was the release in June 2007 of the so-called 'family jewels', a comprehensive account of CIA misdemeanours compiled on the orders of James R. Schlesinger during his tenure as DCI (Director of Central Intelligence) in 1973.[97]

But scholars are not entirely dependent upon the goodwill of intelligence agencies for their sources. Other, discrete, relationships also exist. As in many societies, journalists and writers trusted by the authorities are able to gain information and access. Usually this is undertaken in order to serve political or bureaucratic agendas. Sometimes it is to assist historical inquiry. Various writers on British intelligence have been given access to pre-war SIS records. These include Gordon Brook-Shepherd – who used SIS files for his study of Western intelligence and the Bolshevik Revolution, which included SIS involvement in coup-plotting against Lenin.[98] In addition, Alan Judd (former personal assistant to the Chief of SIS)[99] received similar access for his biography of the first Chief of SIS, Sir Mansfield Cumming while, more recently, Andrew Cook used SIS records for his biography of the famous SIS officer, Sydney Reilly.[100]

A further category of disclosure concerns accounts and histories written contemporaneously, usually for in-house consumption, which have subsequently been published. This hidden historiography includes such examples as John Curry's history of the Security Service between 1908 and 1945 (completed in 1946 and published in 1999); Roger Hesketh's account of the D-Day deception campaign (completed by 1948 and published in 1999); and the account of the British Security Coordination organisation in the US between 1940 and 1945 (completed by BSC officers in 1945, and published in 1998).[101] An important aspect of these and other in-house histories is that they were written by officers intimately involved in the operations they were describing. The most notable such work was Sir John Masterman's account of British counter-intelligence and the Double-Cross Committee in the Second World War,[102] an in-house history written in 1945. In 1972, he published a copy that he had retained for himself, in order 'to give credit to those [intelligence officers] who deserved it' as well as to help rehabilitate the public reputation of British intelligence after the debacles of the moles and molehunt sagas of the post-war period.[103] One consequence of the book was that it contributed to a climate of opinion in which the decision could be taken to sanction the official histories of British intelligence in the Second World War.

A slightly different venture concerns in-house operational histories written by CIA History Staff for internal CIA consumption, but which have subsequently been published. Nick Cullather's account of CIA covert action against the Guatemalan government in the 1950s was completed in 1993 and published in 1999.[104] The book also contains a report written in 1954, entitled 'A Study of Assassination', which examines how assassination options were explored by the CIA in its Guatemalan campaign. The CIA also published a report by the CIA Inspector-General into the Bay of Pigs fiasco, which was highly critical. This had been written in 1961 for the purpose of assessing responsibility and learning lessons for the conduct of covert action and was released in 1998 onto the CIA's web-site before publication in book form.[105] Also in 1998, the CIA partially declassified an account of the operation to overthrow the government of Iran in 1953 written by its History Staff.[106] But the document was very heavily redacted and omitted any reference to the (very significant) role of British intelligence. However, in 2000, the *New York Times* received a copy of a contemporary in-house CIA history of the coup written by Dr Donald Wilber, who was involved in planning the operation,[107] and various articles based on this appeared in that newspaper.[108] When, in June 2000, the document itself was posted on the Internet, attempts to digitally black out names of individual Iranian agents failed. A revised method of redaction was then used and the resulting document appeared in both the *New York Times* and on the National Security Archive web-site.[109] Significantly, the contemporary CIA history did provide details of the identity of British secret service officers and agents, Foreign Office involvement and the draft outline plan for the operation prepared by SIS.

Notwithstanding the value of in-house histories, it should be emphasised that such accounts, usually based on still-classified sources, are not a substitute for public access to the sources themselves. Such histories are often compiled with the explicit purpose of providing lessons for the conduct of future operations, and may well reflect pre-existing assumptions and perspectives of those involved in the operations. On the other hand, Sir John Masterman contended that:

> A history of double cross commissioned a few years later would have become to a great extent a *livre de circonstance* or a piece of propaganda; written in 1945 it was a report, coupled with my own observations and comments on secret intelligence work.[110]

Of course, different kinds of covert action pose different challenges for historians. In some of the more controversial activities there may be a risk that the historical record may be weeded or pruned, if indeed it was ever planted at all. Despite intensive academic, as well as US Senate, scrutiny of the archival record, nothing has emerged to prove that President Kennedy authorised CIA-sponsored attempts to assassinate Fidel Castro.[111] Conversely, some archival evidence has revealed Presidential involvement in, and the authorisation of, the assassination of foreign heads of government. In this vein most notable is the evidence that made clear that President Eisenhower in 1960 authorised the CIA to assassinate the Prime Minister of the Republic of Congo, Patrice Lumumba.[112] The scope (and duration) of British targeted killings are equally unclear. The role of the SIS in coup-plotting and assassination planning, particularly in the Middle East, and in a variety of post-colonial contexts is apparent, though archival corroboration of Prime Minister Eden's (and elements of the SIS) desire to assassinate the Egyptian President, Gamal Abdel Nasser, has yet to emerge. Nevertheless, archival evidence has appeared of joint SIS-CIA planning to overthrow the Syrian government, including the assassination of key leaders, for which Prime Minister Macmillan gave his support in 1957.[113]

Stolen histories, third parties, fire and theft

Unsurprisingly, the paucity of archives has caused historians of intelligence to become extremely catholic in their choice of suitable sources. In this vein, unauthorised disclosure has provided valuable insights into our understanding of intelligence. One category of unauthorised disclosure[114] is that of defectors, most notably, although not exclusively, from the Soviet Union.[115] Given the closed nature of Soviet society,[116] such people have traditionally formed an important source of intelligence for the West. British intelligence authorities have facilitated publication of several books based on testimony from Soviet defectors who, moreover, have provided documentary sources from KGB records. Christopher Andrew has co-written several such books illuminating Soviet intelligence operations. The first was written with Oleg Gordievsky, who worked for SIS for eleven years, and was KGB *Resident*-designate in London before his 1985 exfiltration from Moscow after coming under suspicion.[117] In addition, Andrew and Gordievsky also co-edited a collection of KGB documents that revealed Moscow Centre's instructions to its overseas *residentura*.[118] In 1999, Vasili Mitrokhin and Christopher Andrew published an account of KGB operations in Europe based on copies of KGB documents which had been illicitly made by Mitrokhin when working as a KGB archivist (he too being exfiltrated from the USSR by SIS – in 1992).[119] There is an axiom that intelligence success remains hidden while intelligence failure is publicised. These officially sanctioned collaborations are clearly – and successfully – designed to demonstrate the effectiveness of British intelligence in the Cold War espionage.[120]

The ongoing revolution in global media means that the ability of governments to control information will continue to weaken. Part of the rationale for the US National Security Archive's extensive use of the Internet is surely derived from the recognition that this medium affords unlimited opportunities for global dissemination of documentary sources. Of course, such opportunities exist for governments and 'whistle-blowers' alike. For example, some of the claims made by David Shayler, the erstwhile MI5 officer imprisoned for breaches of the Official Secrets Act, were seemingly corroborated by a document posted on the Internet. What appears to be an SIS CX report describes SIS involvement with those attempting the overthrow and assassination of Colonel Qadahfi.[121] Of note is that the revelation of these allegations did not form part of the prosecution's case in Shayler's trial and were therefore not exposed to judicial or public scrutiny.[122] For the state this reflects the uncomfortable truth that in such matters the 'playing field' of litigation against the 'whistler-blower' is level to an extent previous generations could never have imagined.

If the jurisdiction of the state often fails to cover cyberspace, the existence of international borders similarly limits the ability of governments to control information flow. Thus, international collaboration, co-operation and interaction between states provide various opportunities for historians. As noted, the 1954 CIA report on the efforts of the CIA and SIS to overthrow the government of Iran provided insight into the role of British intelligence. Similarly, much SOE material was discovered in the American National Archives after the files of the Office of Strategic Services were deposited there in the 1980s. These may contain material that has not been retained or indeed has been destroyed by the original service. Finally, the archives of the adversary may include documents acquired by espionage. Nigel West and Oleg Tsarev, for example, assess some of the materials in the KGB archive provided by Anthony Blunt and Kim Philby, based on Tsarev's access to the files.[123] A recent example of the appearance of documents is the minute of a joint SIS/CIA planning meeting in 1953 to intercept Soviet landline communications in Berlin. The document was acquired for the KGB by their spy in SIS, George Blake. It was then copied from the Soviet archive by Sergei Kondrashev (who was Blake's case officer in 1953) and published in 1997 in a book by Kondrashev and two former CIA officers.[124]

Methodology: truth, objectivity and the archives

All too often there is a disinclination amongst historians to reflect on the limited and problematic nature of knowledge in the field of historical enquiry.[125] Yet, the question as to whether historical archives can ever be an analogue of reality is, in a fundamental sense, flawed. The idea that one can strive for objective truth is certainly a favourite target for critics of historical method who hold that historians believe just that. Patrick Karl O'Brien decries the manner by which postmodernist critics labour under the mistaken impression that historians hold 'that properly footnoted historical statements are analogous to proofs in the natural sciences'.[126] George Macaulay Trevelyan – not a scholar who would figure on the reading list of most postmodernists – asserted that 'the collection of facts, the weighing of evidence as to what events happened, are in some sense scientific; but not so the discovery of the causes and effects of these events.'[127] Historians have thus been long since aware of the perils of believing that one can create the past in exactitude. John Lewis Gaddis is right to note that, 'Historical Landscapes differ in one important respect from cartographic landscapes . . . [in that] they are physically inaccessible to us.'[128] This may seem a banal point but the historian needs to repeat it, or similar, on occasion just to remind their critics of the fact that historians are acutely aware of such matters.

Having accepted the inherent limitations in historical study, it is important to give due credit to the advances made by virtue of archival research. Georg Iggers has argued convincingly that archive-based 'micro-history' has played a significant role in the evolution of historical method over the past hundred years. This, far from entrenching statist or conservative methodologies, has led to a huge increase in the diversity of approach and of scholarly sophistication.[129] Despite this, few serious historians would advance anything other than the notion that the greater part of archival history draws upon incomplete sources.[130] Indeed, even the most complete archival records have to be treated with caution. When Minister of Housing in 1953, Harold Macmillan complained of Cabinet minutes that,

> Historians reading this fifty or a hundred years hence will get a totally false picture. They will be filled with admiration and surprise to find the Cabinet were so intellectually disciplined that they argued each issue methodically and logically through to a set of neat and precise conclusions. It isn't like that at all.[131]

Further, the interpretation of the past is constantly evolving and, as Collingwood noted, 'no historical conclusion is closed in perpetuity'.[132] Historians have long recognised that the process of creating, storing, declassifying and then consulting the archival record is an inherently problematic process. Sources themselves reflect the bias and misperception of the author, to which the historian additionally brings his or her perspectives and priorities.[133] In an attempt to address this inevitable bias, J.H. Hexter has argued that, rather than seeking evidence to bolster the thesis with which one sets out, the historian should look for that evidence which challenges (or even disproves) their case thus forcing one to either modify (and strengthen) one's case or even discard the original thesis altogether.[134] The need to address questions of bias is especially important, it has been suggested, in the case of the 'intelligence scholars . . . given the paucity of reliable source material. Therefore the obligation to adhere to objective standards and judgments is all the heavier.'[135] Such views reflect nothing so much as the long process of self-reflection that has always characterised the evolution of historiography.

Marc Trachtenberg asserts that the documentary record remains by far the best available source not least because of the extra dimension that confidentiality can add to what is gleaned from the study and interpretation of such open-source materials that are available to us.[136] The scholar should, of course, have a philosophical and conceptual framework to hand when approaching documents as source material.[137] The military historian and strategist Basil Liddell Hart always advised his students, 'When questioning the validity of a piece of information ask always who was the original source', and 'On every occasion that a particular recommendation is made, ask yourself first in what way the author's career may be affected.'[138] The historian Hugh Trevor-Roper (Lord Dacre) demanded that three questions be asked of every document. First, is it genuine? Second, was the document written by someone who was in a position to know what they were writing about? Third, *why* does this document *exist*?[139] E.H. Carr exhorted scholars to 'interrogate documents and to display a due scepticism as regards their writer's motives'.[140]

In addition to all of this, it is important to note that theoretical approaches are wholly compatible with archival-based history. Indeed, they can be of immense benefit. In 1996, Geoffrey Roberts wrote: 'Contrary to the impression given by some philosophers and social scientists, a large and sophisticated set of theoretical approaches are available to narrative historians wishing to defend their craft.' These included debates in the social sciences on individualism, rationality, choice and, finally, Collingwood's argument that 'history is the history of human thought and action' and philosophical and sociological debates on the concept of 'action'.[141] The discussion of such perspectives are of immense benefit to the intelligence historian and a valuable aid in honing one's ability to avoid simply 'parroting' the archival record in a vain attempt to understand the past.

Grounds for guarded optimism?

In 2003, the then US Secretary of Defense, Donald H. Rumsfeld, famously observed that:

> As we know, there are known knowns. There are things we know we know. We also know there are known unknowns. That is to say we know there are some things we do not know. But there are also unknown unknowns, the ones we don't know we don't know.[142]

These insights do have a peculiar resonance for those engaged in the study of intelligence, as there may, indeed, be no archival record of some operations and what is lost, misplaced or deliberately destroyed may leave no record of its existence.[143] Moreover, advances in Freedom of Information legislation in the UK and elsewhere may have deleterious if unintended consequences. One aspect of the recent enquiries into the British intelligence failure over Iraq is that internal communications (including e-mail) were brought into the public domain. There is reason to believe that officials in Whitehall may now be much more careful about what they commit to permanent record and much more eager to destroy it when they have.[144]

Despite this, scholars of intelligence in Britain have many reasons to be optimistic. The declassification of intelligence records has progressed more in the last decade than in the previous century. A recent example illuminates the scope as well as the limitations of that progress. The Joint Intelligence Committee (JIC) is at the heart of the British machinery of collating and evaluating intelligence. Declassification of its records began in the wake of the Waldegrave Initiative and has now reached 1977 with the intention of releasing future records in line with the thirty-year rule.[145] Although this has yielded considerable insight into the formulation of foreign and defence policy, the process by which JIC assessments were reached is less clear.[146] Critics of the JIC have complained that its conclusions were often anodyne and consensus-driven. The nature of the JIC system and of Whitehall styles of minute-taking contrast, for example, with the American National

Intelligence Estimate (NIE) where the dissent of bureaucratic protagonists is recorded in 'footnotes' and is readily discernible. Although the papers of JIC subcommittees and the JIC secretariat have begun to appear, until now, historians have drawn primarily on JIC minutes and papers alone.[147]

Michael Herman argues convincingly that such publicity will, in future, be the norm, and intelligence organisations must adjust themselves to the new situation to which 'historians can contribute valuable perspectives'.[148] Historians of the JIC have certainly been granted unique insights into how British intelligence machinery works. The various inquiries into the Iraq War by the House of Commons Select Committee on Foreign Affairs, the Parliamentary Intelligence and Security Committee, Lord Hutton, and Lord Butler and his colleagues have yielded unprecedented detail about the JIC process.[149] One of the more notable aspects open to public scrutiny, for example, was the claims made by the government about the ability of the Iraqis to fire chemical weapons within 45 minutes. The inquiries have now illuminated the role and status of the Defence Intelligence Staff, whose experts were not shown all the information provided by SIS sources. This scrutiny has been informed by the testimony, and indeed cross-examination of key officials by Lord Hutton as well as by written records, including internal e-mails. In this context, it is worth asking if we only had access to JIC papers in 30+ year's time, how would the accuracy of the accounts compare to those that we have now?

Conclusion

Upon his retirement in 1976, A.J.P. Taylor reflected:

> Every historian tries to be accurate, although none succeeds as fully as he would like to . . . As [Dr.] Johnson says, application is the main thing. Writing history is like W.C. Fields juggling. It looks easy until you try to do it.[150]

This has a universal relevance. What is clear is that many of the problems which beset intelligence historians are generic in the study of history. For all its advantages, archival-based history can impose limitations. This is only heightened by working in archives derived from as complex and as secretive an activity as intelligence. Reflecting on his wartime experience in MI5 at a time (1973) when the existence of SIS in peacetime was taboo and when disclosure of the MI5 canteen menu would have breached the Official Secrets Act, Malcolm Muggeridge opined: 'Diplomats and intelligence agents, in my experience, are even bigger liars than journalists, and the historians who try to construct the past out of their records are, for the most part, dealing in fantasy.'[151] The diversity and sophistication of contemporary intelligence historiography hopefully suggest that Muggeridge's cynicism is no longer apposite – if ever it was. Nevertheless, constructing the past (including the very recent past) from historical records remains a challenging, frequently frustrating, but an ultimately necessary, component of understanding the value and limitations of intelligence. As an American scholar of intelligence cautioned recently: 'Intelligence . . . assists (or hampers) national leaders in the conduct of their duties, but it cannot perform said duties for them. Beware any piece of scholarship that says it has.'[152] Scholars of intelligence should never lose sight of this fact and seek to integrate it into their views on the nature, and limitations, of history. In a striking metaphor on the relationship between theory and practice in history, E.H. Carr identified the compass as 'a valuable and indeed indispensable guide. But it is not a chart of the route.'[153] We hope that what we have provided here is a navigational tool that, in some way, aids those who would seek a better route towards an understanding of the place of 'intelligence' in the history of nations.

Notes

'Knowledge is never too dear': Exploring intelligence archives

R. Gerald Hughes and Len Scott

1 'Knowledge is never too dear' was Sir Francis Walsingham's maxim: quoted in Paul E.J. Hammer, *The Polarisation of Elizabethan Politics: The Political Career of Robert Devereux, 2nd Earl of Essex, 1585–1597* (Cambridge: Cambridge University Press, 1999), p. 173. Walsingham (c.1530–1590) was Elizabeth I's 'spymaster' and is widely regarded as the 'Father of Modern Intelligence'. On Walsingham, see Robert Hutchinson, *Elizabeth's Spy Master: Francis Walsingham and the Secret War That Saved England* (London: Weidenfeld Military, 2006).
2 Joe Nicholas and John Price, *Advanced Studies in Media* (Cheltenham: Nelson, 1998), p. 88. Cockburn (1904–81), a cousin of Evelyn Waugh, was a radical journalist with Stalinist sympathies. This quote is also often attributed to Otto von Bismarck.
3 Daniel Defoe (1659 or 1661–1731), 'Scheme for General Intelligence', memorandum of 1704 prepared for Robert Harley, Speaker of the House of Commons. Quoted in George Macaulay Trevelyan, *England under Queen Anne: Ramillies and the Union with Scotland* (London: Longmans, Green and Co., 1930), p. 330.
4 Robert Harrison, Aled Jones and Peter Lambert, 'The Primacy of Political History', in Peter Lambert and Phillipp Schofield (eds), *Making History: An Introduction to the History and Practices of a Discipline* (London: Routledge, 2004), pp. 38–54.
5 E.H. Carr, 'Lewis Namier' [1971], in E.H. Carr, *From Napoleon to Stalin and Other Essays*, 2nd edn. (Basingstoke: Palgrave Macmillan, 2003), p. 190.
6 J.H. Hexter, *On Historians: Reappraisals of the Masters of Modern History* (Cambridge, MA: Harvard University Press, 1979), p. 145.
7 Quoted in Alan Partington, *The Linguistics of Political Argument: The Spin-Doctor and the Wolf-Pack at the White House* (New York: Routledge, 2002), p. 267 (n.).
8 Wesley K. Wark, 'In Never-Never Land? The British Archives on Intelligence', *The Historical Journal*, xxxv/1 (1992), p. 195.
9 Ibid., p. 201.
10 Bismarck speech to the Prussian *Herrenhaus*, 18 December 1863. Quoted in Melvin J. Hinich and Michael C. Munger, *Analytical Politics* (Cambridge: Cambridge University Press, 1997), p. 3.
11 Richard Aldrich, *The Hidden Hand: Britain, America and Cold War Secret Intelligence* (London: John Murray, 2001), p. 6. For a lively rejoinder to this, see Peter Jackson, 'The Politics of Secret Service in War, Cold War, and Imperial Retreat', *Twentieth Century British History*, 14/4 (2003), pp. 420–1. On a related theme, see Alun Munslow, 'Authority and Reality in the Representation of the Past', *Rethinking History: The Journal of Theory and Practice*, 1/1 (Summer 1997), pp. 75–87.

12   Richard Aldrich, '"Grow Your Own": Cold War Intelligence and History Super-markets', in Oliver Hoare (ed.), *British Intelligence in the Twentieth Century: A Missing Dimension?* Special Issue of *Intelligence and National Security*, 17/1 (Spring 2002), p. 148.

13   Sir Stephen Lander, 'British Intelligence in the Twentieth Century', in Hoare, ibid., p. 7.

14   Matthew M. Aid and Cees Wiebes, 'Conclusions', in *Secrets of Signals Intelligence During the Cold War and Beyond*, special issue of *Intelligence and National Security*, 16/1 (Spring 2001), p. 313.

15   Lewis Namier, *The Structure of Politics at the Accession of George III*, 2nd edn (London: Macmillan, 1957), p. 176.

16   'Secret Service Money under the Duke of Newcastle', ibid., pp. 173–234. Funds for such activities were very large during the reign of George III (r. 1760–1820) and the British government even engaged in what one would now term 'covert action'. On this, see A. Aspinall, 'The Use of Irish Secret Service Money in Subsidizing the Irish Press', *English Historical Review*, LVI/224 (October 1941), pp. 639–46.

17   Although, as Jennifer Sims recently noted:

> [There is] a tendency to equate intelligence with secrets, which has led to a neglect of open-source intelligence . . . [and the] fixation on secret sources amounts to a debilitating cognitive bias . . . [Of] all the influences on strategic culture, the first, relating to the neglect of open sources may be the most insidious.
>
> ('Understanding Ourselves', in Jennifer E. Sims and Burton Gerber (eds), *Transforming U.S. Intelligence* (Washington, DC: Georgetown University Press, 2005), p. 37)

For a text advocating the greater use of open and private sector sources, see Bruce D. Berkowitz and Allan E. Goodman, *Best Truth: Intelligence in the Information Age* (New Haven, CT: Yale University Press, 2000).

18   David Whipple, an OSS man based in wartime Switzerland, quoted in Michael Salter, *Nazi War Crimes, US Intelligence and Selective Prosecution at Nuremberg: Controversies Regarding the Role of the Office of Strategic Services* (Oxon: Routledge-Cavendish, 2007), p. 1.

19   The compartmentalisation of information is necessary to thwart the intelligence gathering of adversaries, although as the recent example of Robert Hansen, the Soviet/Russian agent in the FBI, demonstrates, the computerisation of records and information management has provided new opportunities for breaching internal security. On this, see David Vise, *The Bureau and the Mole: Most Dangerous Double Agent in FBI History* (New York: Grove Press, 2002).

20   For British policies, see Lander, 'British Intelligence in the Twentieth Century', and Bennett, 'Declassification and Release', in Hoare (ed.), *British Intelligence in the Twentieth Century*, pp. 7–20. For CIA perspectives, see Edmund Cohen, 'The CIA and the Historical Declassification of History Programs', *International Journal of Intelligence and CounterIntelligence*, 12/3 (Fall 1999), pp. 338–45. At the tune of his writing this article, Edmund Cohen was Director of the CIA Office of Information Management – the organisation which oversees the Agency's document declassi-fication programme.

21   Warner is the Historian for the Office of the Director of National Intelligence. Michael Warner, 'Sources and Methods for the Study of Intelligence', in Loch Johnson (ed.), *Handbook of Intelligence Studies* (London: Routledge, 2007), p. 17.

22   Lord Franks, *Falkland Island Review: Report of a Committee of Privy Counsellors* (London: HMSO, 1983), paras 316–17, p. 85.

23   A.J.P. Taylor, *English History 1914–1945* (Oxford: Oxford University Press, [1965] 1976 rev. edn.), p. 603.

24 C.K. Webster, *The Study of International Politics*, inaugural lecture at the University College of Wales, Aberystwyth, 23 February 1923 (Cardiff: University of Wales Press Board, 1923), p. 10.
25 Quotes from Keith Wilson, 'Introduction: Governments, Historians and "Historical Engineering"' in Keith Wilson (ed.), *Forging the Collective Memory: Government and International Historians through Two World Wars* (Oxford: Berghahn Books, 1996), p. 1.
26 D.C. Watt, 'Foreign Affairs, the Public Interest and the Right to Know', *The Political Quarterly*, 34/2 (1963), pp. 121–36.
27 The 'Fifty-Year Rule' was introduced by the Public Records Act of 1958.
28 'The Fifty-Year Rule', Memorandum by Harold Wilson to Cabinet, 27 July 1965 (CAB 129/ 22, C. (65) 114). Reproduced in 'Appendix: Harold Wilson and the Adoption of the Thirty-Year Rule in Great Britain', in K. Wilson (ed.), *Forging the Collective Memory*, pp. 290–3. Quotes, p. 291.
29 Bennett, 'Declassification and Release', p. 28.
30 The question of author perspective is one that has long-taxed historians. Robin George Collingwood noted:

> St. Augustine looked at history from the point of view of the early Christian; Tillemont, from that of a seventeenth-century Frenchman; Gibbon, from that of an eighteenth-century Englishman; Mommsen, from that of a nineteenth-century German. There is no point in asking which the right point of view was. Each was the only one possible for the man who adopted it.
>
> (R.G. Collingwood, *The Idea of History*, Oxford: Oxford University Press, 1946, p. xii)

31 L.V. Scott and P.D. Jackson (eds), *Understanding Intelligence in the Twenty-First Century: Journeys in Shadows* (London: Routledge, 2004). This volume also appeared as a special issue of *Intelligence and National Security*, 19/2 (Summer 2004).
32 For more on this, see R. Gerald Hughes, this volume, '"In the final analysis, it is their war": Britain, the United States and South Vietnam in 1963', this volume, pp. 197, 204–5.
33 *The Pentagon Papers: The Defense Department History of United States Decision-making on Vietnam*, 5 vols (Boston: Beacon Press, 1971–72).
34 'Lyndon Baines Johnson Library opens Gulf of Tonkin recordings and declassified portion of The Pentagon Papers', LBJ Library, 6 June 2002, http://www.lbjlib.utexas.edu/johnson/Press.hom/tonkinpentagonpapers.shtm
35 Fred Emery, *Watergate: The Corruption of American Politics and the Fall of Richard Nixon* (New York: Times Books, 1994), p. 42.
36 Henry A. Kissinger, *The White House Years* (London: Weidenfeld & Nicolson and Michael Joseph, 1979), p. 730.
37 Richard Nixon, H.R. Haldeman and Alexander Haig meeting at the Oval Office, 11 May 1973. Stanley I. Kutler, *Abuse of Power* (New York: Free Press, 1997), p. 473. Italics in the original. Nixon had originally seen the 'Pentagon Papers' as a political opportunity because the bulk of the papers were focused on criticisms of his Democratic predecessors, Kennedy and Johnson. This mood, however, did not long persist. Emery, *Watergate*, pp. 39–40.
38 Daniel Ellsberg, *Secrets: A Memoir of Vietnam and the Pentagon Papers* (New York: Viking, 2002), p. 457. Ellsberg is responding directly to the Nixon quote reproduced here.
39 The British civil servant Clive Ponting seemed to personify this community of interest when, after leaking two documents concerning the 1982 sinking of the Argentine cruiser *General Belgrano* to the Labour MP Tam Dayell in 1984, he became a writer and academic himself. On Ponting's leaking of the documents, his subsequent trial

(and acquittal), see Richard Norton-Taylor, *The Ponting Affair* (London: Cecil Woolf, 1985).

40 Arthur Marwick, excerpts from 'Two Approaches to Historical Study: the Metaphysical (including "postmodernism") and the Historical', *Journal of Contemporary History*, 30 (1995), in John Tosh (ed.), *Historians on History* (London: Longman, 2000), p. 302. For example, the minutes of the meetings of the US Chiefs of Staff for practically the whole Cold War after 1947 were destroyed by military officials. Marc Trachtenberg, *The Craft of International History: A Guide to Method* (Princeton, NJ: Princeton University Press, 2006), p. 157. On this, see 'Joint Staff Letter, 25 January 1993, Regarding the "Destruction of Recorded Minutes of the Meetings of the Joint Chiefs of Staff"', National Security Archive, http://www.gwu.edu/~nsarchiv/nsa/ DOCUMENT/940228.htm. Upon the death of J. Edgar Hoover in 1972, his longtime secretary also destroyed decades' worth of official and unofficial FBI records.

41 It was modified again in 2002, for the FOIA, see http://www.usdoj.gov/oip/ foiastat.htm. In 1996, the Act was updated by means of the 'Electronic Freedom of Information Act Amendments of 1996': http://www.usdoj.gov/oip/foia_updates/ Vol_XVII_4/page2.htm

42 Raymond M. Lee, 'Research Uses of the U.S. Freedom of Information Act', *Field Methods*, 13/4 (November 2001), pp. 371, 378–9.

43 See, for instance, 'Federal Court Finds Air Force Engages in a Pattern or Practice of Violating the FOIA: Archive Lawsuit Forces the Air Force to Process FOIA Requests', 19 April 2006. National Security Archive, http://www.gwu.edu/~nsarchiv/news/ 20060419a/index.htm; 'FOIA Requests to Air Force Lost, Delayed and Ignored: Air Force Sued for a Pattern and Practice of Unresponsiveness to Freedom of Information Requests: Over 150 FOIA Requests, Some as Old as 17 Years Languishing at Air Force Without a Response', 18 March 2005. National Security Archive, http://www. gwu.edu/~nsarchiv/news/20050318/index.htm

44 H.C. Relyea, 'Public Access through the Freedom of Information and Privacy Acts', in P. Herman and C.R. McClure (eds), *Federal Information Policies in the 1980s: Conflicts and Issues* (Norwood, NJ: Ablex, 1987), p. 65. Cited in Lee, 'Research Uses of the U.S. Freedom of Information Act', p. 373.

45 Lee, 'Research Uses of the U.S. Freedom of Information Act', p. 371.

46 For example, J.X. Dempsey, 'The CIA and Secrecy', in Athan G. Theoharis (ed.), *A Culture of Secrecy: The Government Versus the People's Right to Know* (Lawrence, KS: University of Kansas, 1998), pp. 37–59. Lee points out that the CIA utilises its right to withhold information on sources and methods used by the agency and virtually any request for information can be denied if so desired. Lee, 'Research Uses of the U.S. Freedom of Information Act', pp. 377–8.

47 Craig Eisendrath (ed.), 'Introduction', in *National Insecurity: US Intelligence after the Cold War* (Washington, DC: Center for International Policy, 1999), p. 3.

48 'Call to Action on Executive Order 13233', 15 November 2001, http://www.archivists. org/news/actnow.asp

49 For instance, Arthur Schlesinger, 'Take Two: 9/11 Letters', *The Guardian*, 11 September 2004.

50 Bill Moyers, 'In the Kingdom of the Half-Blind', 20th anniversary address to the National Security Archive, 9 December 2005, http://www.gwu.edu/~nsarchiv/ anniversary/moyers.htm

51 See, for example, Robert A. Goldberg, 'Who Profited from the Crime? Intelligence Failure, Conspiracy Theories, and the Case of September 11', in Scott and Jackson, *Understanding Intelligence*, pp. 99–110; Robert A. Goldberg, *Enemies Within: The Culture of Conspiracy in Modern America* (New Haven, CT: Yale University Press, 2001).

52 'Attorney General's Report to the President Pursuant to Executive Order 13,392,

Entitled "Improving Agency Disclosure of Information",' 16 October 2006, http://www.gwu.edu/~nsarchiv/news/20061019/AG_Report_to_President_EO13392.pdf
53 'Attorney General's Report Ignores Serious Problems in Agency FOIA Programs: National Security Archive Calls for Congressional Oversight', http://www.gwu.edu/~nsarchiv/news/20061019/index.htm; 'National Security Archive Letter to Attorney General Alberto Gonzales, October 19, 2006', http://www.gwu.edu/~nsarchiv/news/20061019/Letter_to_Gonzales.pdf. On oversight and accountability in the United States, see Hans Born, Loch K. Johnson and Ian Leigh (eds), *Who's Watching the Spies? Establishing Intelligence Service Accountability* (Dulles, VA: Potomac, 2005). For a comparable study of ten European states, see Jean-Paul Brodeur, Peter Gill and Dennis Töllborg (eds), *Democracy, Law and Security: Internal Security Services in Contemporary Europe* (Aldershot: Ashgate, 2003).
54 Proposed by Senator Patrick Leahy (D-VT) and Senator John Cornyn (R-TX).
55 'Archive Testifies in Support of Senate FOIA Reform Efforts: Archive General Counsel Testifies that FOIA Executive Order Does Not Go Far Enough to Enforce Compliance with FOIA: Congress Must Mandate Solutions for Delay, Agency Obstruction on FOIA', 14 March 2007. http://www.gwu.edu/~nsarchiv/news/2007 0314/index.htm
56 On this, see James J. Wirtz, 'The American Approach to Intelligence Studies', in Johnson (ed.), *Handbook of Intelligence Studies*, pp. 29–31.
57 Wolfgang Krieger, for instance, highlights the paucity of sources for scholars of German intelligence history (especially for West Germany prior to 1990). Wolfgang Krieger, 'German Intelligence History: A Field in Search of Scholars', in Scott and Jackson, *Understanding Intelligence*, pp. 42–3. But things are changing. On 1 January 2006, the German Freedom of Information Act (*Informationsfreiheitsgesetz*) came into force. This Act creates, for the first time, a legal right of access to official information held by Federal authorities. The Act does, however, exclude the right of access if

> the information [requested] could have unfavourable effects on . . . military and other sensitive interests of the German Federal Armed Forces, . . . the interests of internal or external security . . . [Or, in specific] relation to the intelligence services . . . [If] the information can endanger public security.

For the full text of the Act, see 'Gesetz zur Regelung des Zugangs zu Informationen des Bundes (Informationsfreiheitsgesetz – IFG), 5 September 2005 (BGBl. I S. 2722), http://www.bundesbank.de/download/presse/publikationen/ifg.pdf
58 Subsequent to the US FOIA of 1966, some forty countries have drawn up legislation guaranteeing rights of access to government information. These include: Denmark, Norway, Holland and France (in the 1970s); Australia, New Zealand and Australia (1980s); Hungary, Ireland, Thailand, South Korea, Israel and Japan (1990s). Lee, 'Research Uses of the U.S. Freedom of Information Act', p. 370.
59 Lee, 'Research Uses of the U.S. Freedom of Information Act', p. 376.
60 Anonymous, *Through Our Enemies' Eyes: Osama Bin Laden, Radical Islam, and the Future of America* (Dulles, VA: Brassey's Inc, 2002) and *Imperial Hubris: Why the West is Losing the War on Terror* (Dulles, VA: Brassey's Inc, 2004). The author, Michael Scheurer, subsequently resigned from the CIA in 2004.
61 Bernard Wasserstein, 'Joys and Frustrations of FOIA', *Twentieth Century British History*, 12/1 (2001), pp. 95–105.
62 For example, the pressure group Charter 88, http://www.charter88.org.uk/
63 For a useful collection of essays on the state of archival release policy in France, see Sébastien Laurent (ed.), *Archives «secrètes», secrets d'archives? Historiens et archivists face aux archives sensibles* (Paris: CNRS Editions, 2003).
64 Sagredo, Venetian Ambassador to London, Foreign and Commonwealth Office, Historical Papers: History Notes, http://www.fco.gov.uk/servlet/Front?pagename= OpenMarket/Xcelerate/ShowPage&c=Page&cid=1007029395906

65 A Parliamentary Commission recommended the establishment of the Public Record Office (as Britain's first official archive) as long ago as 1838. This eventually led to the construction (in Chancery Lane) of the world's first purpose-built archival repository after 1858. Robert Harrison, Aled Jones and Peter Lambert, 'The Institutionalisation and Organisation of History', in Lambert and Schofield (eds), *Making History*, p. 30.

66 Subsequently amended in 1920 and 1989. For the 1989 Act, see 'Official Secrets Act 1989 (c. 6)', http://www.opsi.gov.uk/acts/acts1989/Ukpga_19890006_en_1.htm. On the implications for scholarly research raised by these Acts, see Raymond M. Lee, *Doing Research on Sensitive Topics* (London: Sage, 1993), pp. 22–3. For overviews of official British attitudes to secrecy, see K.G. Robertson, *Secrecy and Open Government: Why Governments Want You to Know* (London: Macmillan, 1999), and David Vincent: *The Culture of Secrecy: Britain, 1832–1998* (Oxford: Oxford University Press, 1998).

67 Austen Chamberlain, *Hansard*, House of Commons Debate, 5th series, vol. CLXXIV, col. 674, 15 December 1924.

68 One former Foreign Secretary has reflected that 'It could only happen in Britain that the Foreign Intelligence Service, MI6, responsible to the Foreign Secretary, officially does not exist.' See David Owen, *Time to Declare* (London: Penguin, 1992), p. 343.

69 James Callaghan, *Time and Chance* (London: Collins, 1987), p. 375.

70 Gill Bennett, 'Declassification and Release Policies of the UK's Intelligence Agencies', in Hoare (ed.), *British Intelligence in the Twentieth Century*, p. 24.

71 Of course, the British culture of secrecy pervaded both archival release policy and the status and accountability of the intelligence organs of the state. Certain authors have argued that, despite official rhetoric, British liberalisation of archival release policies in the 1990s was not necessarily accompanied by a greater measure of democratic accountability of intelligence. In 1996, for example, Peter Gill argued that British measures to increase the accountability of the intelligence services masked a cosmetic shift from a 'defensive' to an 'offensive' strategy of secrecy. Peter Gill, 'Reasserting Control: Recent Changes in the Oversight of the UK Intelligence Community', *Intelligence and National Security*, 11/2 (April 1996), pp. 313–31.

72 For archival sources available in the UK, see Royal Commission on Historical Manuscripts, *Record Repositories in Great Britain: A Geographical Directory*, 9th edn (London: HMSO, 1992); J. Foster and J. Sheppard, *British Archives: A Guide to Archive Resources in the United Kingdom*, 4th edn (London: Palgrave, 2002); Royal Commission on Historical Manuscripts, *Surveys of Historical Manuscripts in the United Kingdom: A Select Bibliography*, 3rd edn (London: HMSO, 1997).

73 'Operational Selection Policy OSP8: The Security Service', Appendix to Lander, 'British Intelligence', pp. 15–20.

74 'Release of Records of GCHQ: Signals Intelligence Relating to the Venona Project', 1 October 1996, PRO Press Pack. The most relevant class at the National Archives/ Public Record Office for researching Venona is HW15 (the Venona Project records).

75 On Venona, see Robert Louis Benson, *Venona: Soviet Espionage and the American Response 1939–1957* (Laguna Hills, CA: Aegean Park Press, 1996).

76 Bennett, 'Declassification Policies', p. 27.

77 Cohen, 'The CIA and the Historical Declassification of History Programs', p. 344.

78 Freedom of Information Act 2000, http://www.opsi.gov.uk/acts/acts2000/2000 0036.htm. Typically, information 'for the purpose of safeguarding national security . . . the defence of the British Islands or of any colony, or . . . the capability, effectiveness or security of any relevant forces . . . the promotion or protection by the United Kingdom of its interests abroad' etc. is specifically exempt by the Act.

79 On this see, Raymond M. Lee, 'The UK Freedom of Information Act as a Research Tool', *International Journal of Social Research Methodology*, 8/1 (2005), pp. 1–18. On a related theme, see Meredith Cook, *Balancing the Public Interest: Applying the*

Public Interest Test to Exemptions in the UK Freedom of Information Act 2000 (London: UCL, The Constitution Unit, 2000).
80   Michael Evans, 'MI5 Ordered to Explain Secrecy over Superspy', *The Times*, 7 May 2007.
81   On this, see Herbert Butterfield, 'Official History: Its Pitfalls and Criteria', in his *History and Human Relations* (New York: Macmillan, 1952), pp. 182–224.
82   As outlined with illustrations from a number of states by Keith Wilson, 'Introduction: Governments, Historians and "Historical Engineering"', in Wilson (ed.), *Forging the Collective Memory*, pp. 1–28.
83   Warner, 'Sources and Methods for the Study of Intelligence', p. 22.
84   For an overview, see Richard Aldrich, 'Policing the Past: Official History, Secrecy and British Intelligence since 1945', *English Historical Review*, CXIX/483 (September 2004), pp. 922–53.
85   F.H. Hinsley, E.E. Thomas, C.F.G. Ransom and R.C. Knight, *British Intelligence in the Second World War*: vol. 1, *Its Influence on Strategy and Operations* (London: HMSO, 1979); F.H. Hinsley, E.E. Thomas, C.F.G. Ransom and R.C. Knight, *British Intelligence in the Second World War*, vol. 2, *Its Influence on Strategy and Operations* (London: HMSO, 1981); F.H. Hinsley, E.E. Thomas, C.F.G. Ransom and R.C. Knight, *British Intelligence in the Second World War*, vol. 3, Part 1, *Its Influence on Strategy and Operations* (London: HMSO, 1984); F.H. Hinsley, E.E. Thomas, C.A.G. Simkins and C.F.G. Ransom, *British Intelligence in the Second World War*, vol. 3, Part II, *Its Influence on Strategy and Operations* (London: HMSO, 1988); F.H. Hinsley and C.A.G Simkins, *British Intelligence in the Second World War*, vol. 4, *Security and Counter-Intelligence* (London: HMSO, 1990); Michael Howard, *British Intelligence in the Second World War*, vol. 5, *Strategic Deception* (London: HMSO, 1990).
86   Warner, 'Sources and Methods for the Study of Intelligence', p. 22.
87   Quoted in Philip Knightley, *The Second Oldest Profession: The Spy as Patriot, Bureaucrat, Fantasist and Whore* (London: Pan, 1987), p. 111.
88   On this, see Sir Stephen Lander, 'International Intelligence Cooperation: An Inside Perspective', *Cambridge Review of International Affairs*, 17/3 (October 2004), pp. 481–93.
89   The reluctance of SIS to extend its centenary history beyond 1949 (in contrast to MI5) indicates a different approach to Cold War declassification as well as what appears a different approach to sources and methods.
90   The MI5 web-site states that 'Professor Andrew is working on the history as a member of the Service, with exceptional access to its archives from which his book is being written', http://www.mi5.gov.uk/output/Page232.html
91   'SIS History and Records', http://www.mi6.gov.uk/output/Page5.html
92   For example, documents covering the mass expulsion of Soviet intelligence officers from Britain in 1972 were published in 1997. G. Bennett and K.A. Hamilton, *Documents on British Policy Overseas, Series III vol 1. Britain and the Soviet Union, 1968–72* (London: Stationery Office, 1997).
93   The Foreign Office has an extensive on-line section on the letter (containing documents and commentary), 'The Zinoviev Letter', Foreign and Commonwealth Office, Historical Papers: History Notes, http://www.fco.gov.uk/servlet/Front/TextOnly?pagename=OpenMarket/Xcelerate/ShowPage&c=Page&cid=1007029395681&to=true
94   Gill Bennett, *'A Most Extraordinary and Mysterious Business': The Zinoviev Letter of 1924* (London: FCO, 1999).
95   CIA Center for the Study of Intelligence, https://www.cia.gov/csi/studies.html
96   See, for example, William Blum, *Killing Hope: US Military and CIA Interventions since World War Two* (London: Zed Books, 2003).
97   These disclosures detail CIA assassination plots against foreign leaders, drug testing on unwitting subjects, the illegal opening of mail of selected American citizens and

spying on Vietnam War protesters. National Security Archive, 'The CIA's Family Jewels: Agency Violated Charter for 25 Years, Wiretapped Journalists and Dissidents', 21 June 2007, http://www.gwu.edu/~nsarchiv/NSAEBB/NSAEBB222/index.htm. The entirety of the 'family jewels' were released – and posted on-line – on 26 June 2007 and are available at: http://www.gwu.edu/~nsarchiv/NSAEBB/NSAEBB222/family_jewels_full.pdf

98 Gordon Brook-Shepherd, *Iron Maze: The Western Secret Services and the Bolsheviks* (Basingstoke: Macmillan, 1998).

99 Nigel West, 'Fiction, Faction and Intelligence', in Scott and Jackson, *Understanding Intelligence*, p. 123; Alan Judd, *The Quest for Mansfield Cumming and the Founding of the Secret Service* (London: HarperCollins, 1999).

100 Andrew Cook, *On His Majesty's Secret Service: Sidney Reilly ST1* (London: Tempus Publishing, 2002).

101 John Curry, *The Security Service 1908–1945: The Official History* (London: Public Record Office, 1999); Roger Hesketh, *Fortitude: The D-day Deception Campaign* (London: St Ermin's Press, 1999); Nigel West, *British Security Coordination: The Secret History of British Intelligence in the Americas 1940–45* (London: St Ermin's Press, 1998).

102 J.C. Masterman, *The Double-Cross System in the War of 1939 to 1945* (New Haven, CT: Yale University Press, 1972).

103 Ibid., p. xviii.

104 Nick Cullather, *Secret History: The CIA's Classified Account of its Operations in Guatemala, 1952–1954* (Palo Alto, CA: Stanford University Press, 1999).

105 www.foia.cia.gov/bay_of_pigs.asp; Peter Kornbluh, *Bay of Pigs Declassified: The Secret Report on the Invasion of Cuba* (New York: The New Press, 1998).

106 Scott A. Koch, *"Zendebad, Shah!" The Central Intelligence Agency and the Fall of Iranian Prime Minister Mohammed Mossadeq, August 1953* (Washington, DC: CIA History Staff, 1998).

107 Donald Wilber, *CIA Clandestine History: Overthrow of Premier Mossadeq of Iran, November 1952–August 1953*, National Security Archive, www.gwu.edu/%7Ensarchiv/NSAEBB/NSAEBB28/index.html#documents

108 The CIA history was first disclosed in articles by James Risen of the *New York Times* (16 April and 18 June 18 2000), http://www.nytimes.com/library/world/mideast/041600iran-cia-index.html

109 *New York Times*, www.nytimes.com/library/world/mideast/iran-cia-intro.pdf; National Security Archive, www.gwu.edu/%7Ensarchiv/NSAEBB/NSAEBB28/index.html#documents

110 Masterman, *Double-Cross*, p. xvii.

111 US Congress, Senate Select Committee to study Governmental Operations with Respect to Intelligence Activities, Interim Report: Alleged Assassination Plots Involving Foreign Leaders, 94th Congress 1975.

112 'American President "Ordered African Killing"', *The Guardian*, 10 August 2000; 'Eisenhower Ordered Congo Killing', *The Independent*, 14 August 2000. For details of the role of the Belgian government in the actual assassination of Lumumba, see Ludo de Witte, *The Assassination of Lumumba* (London: Verso, 2001). De Witte's book prompted a parliamentary inquiry into Belgium's role which led to a formal apology by the Belgian government to the people of the Congo. The full 1,000-page report of the committee (*Parliamentary Committee of Inquiry in Charge of Determining the Exact Circumstances of the Assassination of Patrice Lumumba and the Possible Involvement of Belgian Politicians*) has its conclusions summarised at: http://www.africawithin.com/lumumba/summary.htm

113 Matthew Jones, 'The "Preferred Plan": The Anglo-American Working Group Report on Covert Action in Syria, 1957', *Intelligence and National Security*, 19/3 (Autumn 2004), pp. 401–15.

114 'Unauthorised' refers of course to the original allegiance and not to the service to which they have defected, whose involvement and authorisation are usually apparent.

115 For useful insights on this (including a list of major Cold War defectors), see Nigel West, 'Cold War Intelligence Defectors', in Johnson (ed.), *Handbook of Intelligence Studies*, pp. 229–36.

116 Hitler's Germany, too, had severe difficulties in assessing the Soviet Union due to the near-impossibility of obtaining open-source information or of infiltrating agents. Bernd Wenger, 'The Tottering Giant: German Perceptions of Soviet Military and Economic Strength in Preparation for "Operation Blau" (1942)', in Christopher Andrew and Jeremy Noakes (eds), *Intelligence and International Relations, 1900–1945* (Exeter: Exeter University Press, 1987), p. 294.

117 Christopher Andrew and Oleg Gordievsky, *KGB: The Inside Story of Its Foreign Operations from Lenin to Gorbachev* (London: Hodder and Stoughton, 1990).

118 Christopher Andrew and Oleg Gordievsky, *Instructions from the Centre: Top Secret Files on KGB Foreign Operations, 1975–1985* (London: Hodder and Stoughton, 1991).

119 Christopher Andrew and Vasili Mitrokhin, *The Mitrokhin Archive: The KGB in Europe and the West* (London: Allen Lane, 1999). A second volume – covering Soviet operations in the rest of the world – was published in 2005. Christopher Andrew and Vasili Mitrokhin, *The Mitrokhin Archive II: The KGB and the World* (London: Allen Lane, 2005). The material supplied by Mitrokhin was deemed of sufficient importance for the British Prime Minister and his Home Secretary to order the House of Commons Intelligence and Security Committee 'to examine the policies and procedures adopted by the Security and Intelligence Agencies for the handling of information supplied by Mr. Mitrokhin.' Intelligence and Security Committee (chaired by Tom King MP), The Mitrokhin Inquiry Report, June 2000, http://www.archive.official-documents.co.uk/document/cm47/4764/4764.htm. Quote from Tom King's letter to Tony Blair (reproduced at the beginning of the official report), 20 April 2000, http://www.archive.official-documents.co.uk/document/cm47/4764/4764-let.htm.

120 By contrast, Kim Philby's *My Secret War* (New York: Grove, 1968), produced under KGB auspices in Moscow, sought to embarrass the West by its mockery of, among others, CIA counter-intelligence chief James Jesus Angleton. Warner, 'Sources and Methods for the Study of Intelligence', p. 23.

121 'Qadahfi Assassination Plot', www.cryptome.org/qadahfi-plot.htm

122 On the Shayler affair, see Mark Hollingsworth and Nick Fielding, *Defending the Realm: MI5 and the Shayler Affair* (London: André Deutsch, 1999).

123 The documents themselves have not been released, indicative of how access to Soviet archives has been managed and controlled by Russian intelligence. Nigel West and Oleg Tsarev, *The Crown Jewels: The British Secrets Exposed by the KGB Archives* (London: HarperCollins, 1999), pp. 279–345. For an overview of access to Russian intelligence archives, see Amy Knight, 'Russian Archives: Opportunities and Obstacles', *International Journal of Intelligence and CounterIntelligence*, 12/3 (Fall 1999), pp. 325–37. On Russian archives generally (including intelligence records), see Patricia Kennedy Grimsted, *Archives of Russia Five Years After: 'Purveyors of Sensations' or 'Shadows Cast to the Past'?* International Institute of Social History, Research Paper 26 (Amsterdam: IISH, 1997).

124 David E. Murphy, Sergei A. Kondrashev and George Bailey, *Battleground Berlin: CIA vs KGB in the Cold War* (London: Yale University Press, 1997), pp. 449–53.

125 For a discussion of the epistemological questions associated with the assessment of knowledge-based claims, see Martin Bunzl, *Real History: Reflections on Historical Practice* (London: Routledge, 1997). For perspectives on intelligence, see Len Scott, 'Sources and Methods in the Study of Intelligence: A British View', in Loch K. Johnson (ed.), *Strategic Intelligence*, Vol. 1: *Understanding the Hidden Side of Government* (Westport, CT: Praeger, 2007), pp. 89–108.

126 Patrick Karl O'Brien, 'An Engagement with Postmodern Foes, Literary Theorists

and Friends on the Borders with History', *What is History?*, issue 2, http://www. history.ac.uk/ihr/Focus/Whatishistory/obrien.html. O'Brien commends Bethan McCullagh's *The Truth of History* (London: Routledge, 1998) for the manner in which it 'survey[s], reposition[s] and redefin[es] the "truth" claims of modern historians in ways that will hopefully undercut postmodern misrepresentations'. Hayden White is at least asking the right question (if not necessarily supplying the right answer) in his article, 'An Old Question Raised Again: Is Historiography Art or Science?', in *Rethinking History: The Journal of Theory and Practice*, 4/3 (2000), pp. 391–406.

127   Richard Evans, *In Defence of History* (London: Granta, 1997), p. 25.

128   John Lewis Gaddis, *The Landscape of History: How Historians Map the Past* (Oxford: Oxford University Press, 2002), p. 35.

129   George G. Iggers, *Historiography in the Twentieth Century: From Scientific Objectivity to the Postmodern Challenge* (Hanover, NH: Wesleyan University Press, 1997).

130   Trachtenberg, *The Craft of International History*, p. 157. On the impossibility of achieving a totality of information from sources, see Rüdiger Graf, 'Interpretation, Truth and Past Reality: Donald Davidson meets History', *Rethinking History*, 7/3 (2003): 387–402.

131   Quoted in Anthony Adamthwaite, 'Introduction: The Foreign Office and Policy-making', in John W. Young (ed.), *The Foreign Policy of Churchill's Peacetime Administration, 1951–55* (Leicester: Leicester University Press, 1988), pp. 2–3. On a theme related to Macmillan's concerns, see Paul Rock, 'Some Problems of Interpretative Historiography', *The British Journal of Sociology*, 27/3 (September 1976), pp. 353–369; Evans, *In Defence of History*, p. 104.

132   R.G. Collingwood, *The Principles of History and Other Writings in the Philosophy of History*, (eds) W.H. Dray and W. J. van der Dussen (Oxford: Oxford University Press, 1999), p. 156. Jonathan Haslam suggests that 'only the intellectually immature . . . choose to read those thinkers who re-inforce their pre-existing beliefs.' Jonathan Haslam, 'New Introduction for the 2nd Edition', in Carr, *From Napoleon to Stalin and Other Essays*, p. xxi.

133   Collingwood, *The Principles of History*, pp. 213, 210. On this, see Peter Novick, *That Noble Dream: The "Objectivity Question" and the American Historical Profession* (Cambridge: Cambridge University Press, 1988); Chris Lorenz, '"You got your history, I got mine": Some reflections on truth and objectivity in history', *Österreichische Zeitschrift für Geschichtswissenschaft*, 10 (1999), pp. 563–84.

134   Hexter, *On Historians*, pp. 250–1.

135   Warner, 'Sources and Methods for the Study of Intelligence', p. 26.

136   Trachtenberg, *The Craft of International History*, p. 153.

137   The classic treatment of the hermeneutical problems associated with the interpretation of documents is Hans-Georg Gadamer, *Wahrheit und Methode: Grundzüge einer philosophischen Hermeneutik* (Tübingen: JCB Mohr, 6th edn, 1990).

138   Alan Clark, diary entry for 19 December 1990. Alan Clark, *Diaries* (London: Phoenix, 1994), p. 375.

139   Ron Rosenbaum, *Explaining Hitler: The Search for the Origins of His Evil* (London: Macmillan, 1998), p. 225.

140   Alan Knight, 'Latin America', in Michael Bentley (ed.), *Companion to Historio-graphy: An Introduction* (London: Routledge, 1997), p. 747.

141   Geoffrey Roberts, 'Narrative History as a Way of Life', *Journal of Contemporary History*, 31/1 (January 1996), pp. 223–224. Quote, p. 223.

142   Department of Defense News Conference, 12 February 2003. Quoted in 'Introduction', in Hart Seely (ed.), *Pieces of Intelligence: The Existential Poetry of Donald H. Rumsfeld* (London: Simon and Schuster, 2003), p. 2.

143   For discussion, see Scott, 'Sources and Methods', p. 97.

144   Richard Aldrich, 'Whitehall and the Iraq War: the UK's Four Intelligence Enquiries', *Irish Studies in International Affairs*, 16 (2005), p. 83. Aldrich notes how the

destruction of documents on 'shredding day' (the disposing of compromising material) has become a familiar routine among civil servants.

145 On the Waldegrave Initiative, see Richard J. Aldrich, 'The Waldegrave Initiative and Secret Service Archives: New Materials and New Policies', *Intelligence and National Security* 10/1 (Spring 1995), pp. 192–7; 'Did Waldegrave Work? The Impact of Open Government upon British History', *Twentieth Century British History*, 9/1 (1998), pp. 111–26.

146 For a carefully nuanced assessment of the role of the Committee based on these records by a former chair of the JIC, see Percy Cradock, *Know Your Enemy: How the Joint Intelligence Committee Saw the World* (London: John Murray, 2002).

147 On the other hand, as Cradock notes, the bulk of the records of the JIC's outposts in Germany, the Middle East and the Far East have disappeared, ibid., p. 2.

148 Michael Herman, 'Intelligence's Future: Learning from the Past', *Journal of Intelligence History*, 3/2 (Winter 2003), http://www.intelligence-history.org/jih/Herman-3-2.html

149 House of Commons Select Committee on Foreign Affairs, 'The Decision to go to War with Iraq', ninth report of the session 2002–3, HC 813-I, vol. 1, 3 July 2003; Intelligence and Security Committee, 'Iraq Weapons of Mass Destruction: Intelligence and Assessment' , Cm 5972, 9 September 2003; Lord Hutton, *Report of the Inquiry into the Circumstances Surrounding the Death of Dr. David Kelly*, http://www.the-hutton-inquiry.org.uk. Hutton's report also provides, in full, the documentary evidence submitted to the inquiry, http://www.the-hutton-inquiry.org.uk/content/evidence.htm#full; 'Review of Intelligence on Weapons of Mass Destruction: Report of a Committee of Privy Counsellors' [The Butler Report], HC 898, 14 July 2004. For discussion, see Aldrich 'Whitehall and the Iraq War'; Alex Danchev, 'The Reckoning: Official Enquiries and the Iraq War', *Intelligence and National Security*, 19/3 (Autumn 2004), pp. 436–66; Anthony Glees and Philip H.J. Davies, *Spinning the Spies: Intelligence, Open Government and the Hutton Inquiry* (London: The Social Affairs Unit, 2004); Eunan O'Halpin, 'British Intelligence and the Case for Confronting Iraq: Evidence from the Butler and Hutton Reports', *Irish Studies in International Affairs*, 16 (2005), pp. 89–102; Mark Phythian, 'Intelligence Oversight in the UK: The Case of Iraq', in Johnson, *Handbook of Intelligence Studies*, pp. 301–14; Nigel West, 'Commentary: Making War Controversial', *International Journal of Intelligence and Counterintelligence*, 17 (2) (Summer 2004), pp. 358–63; see also Peter Jackson, 'The Butler Report as an historical document', this volume, pp. 277–91; Robert Jervis, 'The Butler Report', this volume, pp. 309–13; Loch K. Johnson, 'The Butler Report: a US perspective', this volume, pp. 313–17.

150 A.J.P. Taylor, 'Accident Prone, or What Happened Next', *Journal of Modern History*, 49/1 (March 1977), pp. 1–18. Quote, p. 18.

151 Malcolm Muggeridge, *Chronicles of Wasted Time, II: The Infernal Grove* (London: Collins, 1973) p. 149. Muggeridge had served as a wartime member of MI5.

152 Warner, 'Sources and Methods for the Study of Intelligence', p. 26.

153 E.H. Carr, *What is History? The George Macaulay Trevelyan Lectures Delivered in the University of Cambridge, January–March 1961* (London: Macmillan, 1961), p. 116.

2 British SIGINT decrypts on the London Naval Conference, 1930

Andrew Webster, John Ferris and Peter Mauch

OVERVIEW: BRITISH SIGNALS INTELLIGENCE AND THE LONDON NAVAL CONFERENCE, 1930

Andrew Webster

Despite a thick London fog which delayed the arrival of many of the attending dignitaries, the London Naval Conference opened with great glitter and ceremony in the Royal Gallery of the House of Lords, on 21 January 1930, with a speech of welcome from King George V. Attended by the world's five major naval powers – Britain, the United States, Japan, France and Italy – it would meet continuously until late April in an attempt to extend the regime of naval limitation that had been agreed to eight years earlier at a conference in Washington. But there was more to these naval disarmament negotiations than met the eye. Conferences of this sort provided manifest opportunities for the intelligence services of the host nation, as control over the telegraphic facilities into and out of the country allowed for the easy interception of communications made by the delegations of visiting powers. It was an advantage which the Americans had seized at the Washington Naval Conference of 1921–22 to read the Japanese diplomatic traffic, giving them a significant advantage in negotiations.[1] At the London conference, one of the chief weapons in the British negotiating armoury was its similar ability to read most of the messages exchanged between the various delegations and their respective home governments. The British signals intelligence body, known as the Government Code and Cypher School (GCCS), 'was one of the world's largest code-breaking agencies [and] . . . possibly the best on earth between 1919 and 1935'.[2] In the course of each month during 1929–31, for example, it developed a file averaging about 300 decrypted diplomatic intercepts, ranging over American, Japanese, Italian, French, Greek, Persian, Spanish, Scandinavian and other minor states' transmissions.[3]

The signals decrypted by the GCCS are now located in the National Archives, Kew, in series HW 12. The series comprises 338 volumes of intercepted diplomatic communications that stretch over the period 1919 to 1945; the earliest files began to be released for public inspection in 1996. The two documents presented here come from the special file opened by the GCCS to cover its work during the London Naval Conference: HW 12/126, 'International Naval Conference for Fleet

Reduction, January–April 1930' (available for public consultation since 1997). It contains a total of 397 transmissions made by the attending parties that the GCCS succeeded in intercepting and deciphering. They had only partial success with American ciphers, leaving those decrypts with numerous gaps that could make interpretation difficult, while the French and Italian use of the diplomatic bag for many of their critical transmissions meant a less decisive intelligence yield. The Japanese traffic was a sparkling success, however, as their codes were almost completely penetrated, though there was sometimes a significant time lag in cracking particular messages. It is here, therefore, that the most significant influences on the London negotiations might be looked for.

What was at stake between Britain, the United States and Japan at the London conference was the global balance of naval power. The Washington Naval Treaty of 1922 had imposed a system of ratios to limit the total tonnage of capital ships (warships over 10,000 tons) among these three powers at 5:5:3, respectively.[4] This had successfully averted the threat of an Anglo-American naval race in battleships, yet other problems remained. The Washington conference left unsettled the limitation of warships displacing less than 10,000 tons, namely cruisers, destroyers and submarines, the main weapons for attacking and defending maritime lines of communication. In addition, Japanese navalists were left deeply unhappy at being forced to accept a 60 per cent ratio in capital ships, rather than the 70 per cent they saw as essential for national security and as an element of Japanese national prestige. More moderate naval voices in Tokyo had perceived the necessity for Japan to accept the proffered 60 per cent ratio, both for political considerations in easing strained American–Japanese relations and to avoid a ruinously expensive naval race in the Pacific. The debate within Japanese naval circles over the question of relative strength compared to the United States would reverberate throughout the following decade. Following the failure of the first attempt to limit warships under 10,000 tons, at the Geneva Naval Conference of 1927, these two issues came to a head at the London conference in 1930, which again sought to tackle the problem. The Japanese were determined not to allow another denigration of their claims. All Japanese policy-makers believed that any naval agreement should assure Japan's predominance in the western Pacific. In particular, there was widespread consensus on the absolute need for a 70 per cent ratio in heavy cruisers carrying 8-inch guns, which the Japanese admirals viewed as 'semi-capital' ships that could help offset the hated 60 per cent ratio in battleships.[5] In contrast, the main goal of the British government at the London conference was a three-power agreement with the United States and Japan that would maintain the delicate Anglo-American-Japanese naval balance and preserve a naval regime that entrenched British superiority.[6] An Anglo-American compromise was successfully achieved in the conference's opening weeks; the task of finding a formula that dealt with Japan's demands for an increase in her tonnage ratio took nearly two months before the London Naval Treaty was finally signed on 22 April.[7]

The documents below come from key moments in this complex negotiation. Document One is a telegram sent from the Japanese Admiralty in Tokyo to the Japanese delegates in London during the opening weeks of the conference, demanding firmness in Japan's negotiating position. Document Two is a telegram from the delegation in London to the Japanese Foreign Minister in Tokyo near the end of the conference, indicating a willingness to accept a compromise solution. Both were intercepted and more or less completely decrypted by the GCCS. Some technical information will be helpful in reading and evaluating these two intercepts. The underlined summary title at the top was provided by GCCS. Immediately below it is the GCCS intercept number and the date of decryption, followed by the information on sender and recipient and the original despatch number and date of transmission. Items in square brackets are reprinted as they appeared in the original documents.

DOCUMENT ONE:

MOST SECRET

Naval Conference: Japanese Admiralty Views on American Proposals
No: N.C. 199
Date: 14th March, 1930.

From: Head Military Affairs Bureau, Admiralty, TOKIO.
To: Japanese Naval Delegation, LONDON.
No: 39.
Date: 8th February, 1930

Plenipotentiaries' telegram Nos. 105 and 106 [our N.C. 97 and N.C. 88]. Telegraphic instructions regarding the American draft proposals have already been sent, and whilst we believe the Plenipotentiaries will take the best action in the circumstances, the views here, which are as follows, are communicated for information:-

1. Although the principal points of our demands are already known to the other side, to give no consideration at all to them is not only unfair, but from another point of view must be considered an insult.

    Thus if we make a numerical agreement in accordance with the earnest desires of the other side our faith will more or less come to nought.

2. According to the American draft plan not only would they abandon the claim for twenty-one cruisers but in certain circumstances, it appears, they would be satisfied with fifteen.

At the same time as they make this concession, they compare us with 60 per cent, and would use this concession as a powerful argument in checking our claim for 70 per cent. This is nothing more than a 'bargain'.

Whichever way you take it, the American concession in eight-inch cruisers shows that considerable concerted action has been set up between GREAT BRITAIN and the UNITED STATES. Thus, showing a combined front they plan to defeat first JAPAN and then FRANCE and ITALY in exactly the same way as at the Washington Conference.

It goes without saying that this is the parting of the ways so far as the success or failure of our demands is concerned.

3.   According to our observations on the frequent telegrams from our Plenipotentiaries, a slight anxiety has been noticed in both ENGLAND and AMERICA. As the promoters of the Conference, that is their affair, and we may be composed and calm.

However, if they maintain their firm demands without conceding anything and proceed selfishly, ignoring us, then it will be our best plan to lead affairs into a situation where there is little hope of agreement between the three Powers.

4.   Whilst GREAT BRITAIN and the UNITED STATES on one hand admonish [us] for leakage of the private negotiations, it is extremely difficult to understand how on the other hand they take advantage of a favourable opportunity and publish things at will. A typical example of this was the recent STIMSON statement, where he took formal steps to secure an understanding beforehand.

Thus it is most disadvantageous to us, as it is impossible for us to appeal to the fair judgment of public opinion.

We consider it important that we must of a necessity, as a counter-measure, secure a rigid understanding regarding the limits within which there shall be freedom to publish.

5.   It goes without saying that whilst we adopt the above-stated attitude we must make preparations to draw up our concrete counter-proposals, and to present them at a favourable opportunity.

6. The suggestion in the American plan that we should each build one capital ship of 35,000 tons is contrary to the spirit of reduction which we and AMERICA have always advocated, and not only would it cause loss of confidence at home and abroad but as it would create a reason for making reduction in the future difficult, the Imperial Government could never agree.

Further the [?warship reduction proposals] in the American plan would cause a change in the substance of the WASHINGTON Treaty:-

(a) By the postponement of replacements our object of reducing burdens can be easily achieved. If it is not, a reduction in ordinary expenditure can be made [? depending on the type of ship].
    If you especially scrap, it can be understood that in [three groups] you would rather increase the burden; and finally you would not achieve the object. Therefore it is not agreeable to carry out the [?warship reduction] plan.
(b) As there will be large differences in the effect on fleet strengths caused by scrapping the KONGO type with fourteen-inch guns and scrapping American vessels with twelve-inch guns, it is considered that careful examination of this point and others should be made before deciding yes or no.

COMMENTARY: COMMUNICATIONS INTELLIGENCE AND CONFERENCE DIPLOMACY, LONDON, 1930

John Ferris

These documents illustrate an important but overlooked matter. Diplomatic intelligence illuminates the attitudes of states and their factions. It shows concealed levers and hidden hands and means to manipulate them: how to act or to signal. It gives good news and shows the limits to bad, increasing one's certainty that unknown and unpleasant developments are not happening. Minor comments in a good source can determine the plausibility of major statements in an uncertain one. The reports of one party can reveal the intentions of another. So, too, knowledge may be useless. The point of diplomatic intelligence is to aid action, by shaping one's policy or another's. This is not easy. More often than not, intelligence provides first-rate information on third-rate issues, or knowledge which one cannot apply to policy. Actions, usually words of influence or threat, may be hard to deliver as desired or with effect, and have unintended or counter-productive consequences.

Intelligence has greater value in cases of bargaining, when every party must act, and on the same issues. Then, the power of sources like journalists or officials rises, even more the ability to steal papers, bug offices or intercept signals. Meanwhile, information on the bargaining strategy and tactics of other players can help one take tricks, though their value depends on the stakes. Thus, at the Washington Conference of 1921–22, American code-breakers solved secret Japanese telegrams which outlined the lowest ratio it would accept in the strength of battleships and aircraft carriers compared to the American and British navies. This knowledge helped American negotiators force Japan to a 5:5:3 ratio, rather than the 5:5:3.5 ratio it wanted. Sailors on both sides thought that difference important in case of war. Yet the 5:5:3 ratio might have emerged anyway, as the United States wanted it and had a strong bargaining position, while Japan's break point was guessed by the *New York Times*.[1]

A decade later, Britain had an analogous opportunity. As the London Naval Conference occurred at its capital, it had unmatched opportunities to pump the rumour mill, and to intercept traffic to and from the American, French, Italian and Japanese delegations. The GCCS, the best code-breaking agency of that era, mastered these messages, and the aims and means of other players. Britain could monitor any diplomacy between other parties by cross-checking reports from several sources, including the codes of one, usually more, participants. Yet intelligence matters only insofar as it aids action. Here, as often, it did not affect the formulation of policy but did guide the execution. The Prime Minister, Ramsay MacDonald, dominated British policy. He called the conference primarily to spur world disarmament, rather than to further narrow interests. When bargaining over the tonnage of warships, MacDonald aimed less to strengthen Britain's position against the United States, than to change American attitudes, and gain their support for further moves toward liberal internationalism. To impress Washington, he accepted many of its demands, abandoning earlier British positions. In the long term, this crippled British sea power; immediately, it weakened Britain on disputes with the United States, and forced it into intricate negotiations over naval strength with all participants. Here, intelligence mattered. It was avidly used by the Admiralty, Foreign Office and Labour politicians. Whitehall and Washington hoped everyone would reason together, but also believed a naval treaty could be reached even if France and Italy refused to sign (as eventually happened). That was not true of Japan. Neither the United States nor Britain would accept a formal change in the 5:5:3 ratio, although American unwillingness to finance its navy really had reduced it almost to 5:4.5:3. Japan, however, demanded a ratio of 5:5:3.5 for cruisers and destroyers and large strength in submarines under any new treaty. Unless that conflict could be resolved, the conference would fail, making international relations worse than they would have been without it. Equally, compromise was possible. Britain worked for one, using the clash between Japan and the United States to play each against the other, and reduce both their demands.

Intelligence is about secrets. As the point was bargaining, everyone had to signal its position, while the Japanese, American and British civilian delegations were open with each other, in the freemasonry of liberalism. Yet each had a bottom line to hide and Britain had an edge. It had means to discover secrets, they did not. Before the conference, the GCCS provided the first, though predictable, news that Japan would demand a 70 per cent ratio. It showed policy formation in Tokyo and Washington and the abortive discussions between them; it let politicians ensure British sailors were not working with Japanese ones to thwart arms control, although Labour distorted this danger. When the conference began, the GCCS did better than American code-breakers had done at Washington. It showed, usually in real time, all reports of the Japanese delegation, including material its naval and civilian sides hid from each other.[2] Britain knew their divisions as well as did their members. Against this, Japanese civilians did not hide the fact of these splits, which improved their bargaining position against other countries – thus, code-breaking reinforced Britain's will to compromise. By 13 March 1930, after a month of secret talks, the British, American and Japanese delegations accepted a complex deal which let all claim victory. Delaying the construction of three out of 18 large American cruisers gave Japan almost a 70 per cent ratio during the tenure of the treaty in practice, but not in theory, while containing construction on both sides. Britain's chief negotiator, Robert Craigie, originated this alchemy, and secretly suggested the Japanese delegation fall back on it in case of deadlock with the Americans. This action stemmed from his knowledge of the issues, and intelligence on them. Press reports, statements by American and Japanese delegates, and especially solutions of their traffic, showed the details of their discussions, the internal politics of their policy, and that their governments wanted a deal. Above all, politicians in Tokyo told the civilian delegation that when they made the best settlement they could, the government would sell it at home, and make the admirals accept it. Craigie pressed the other sides to negotiate, fed them a solution which met their bottom lines while pushing their programmes down as Whitehall wanted, and rejected any alternatives that Britain disliked. This triumph of policy and intelligence overcame Britain's bargaining weakness and met its aims over cruisers and world disarmament.

Then came the two telegrams under review. In one (N.C. 220, Document Two), solved quickly, the delegation told Tokyo this deal was the best possible. The other message (N.C. 199, Document One), as often happened with telegrams from the Japanese Admiralty, the *Kaigunsho*, was read only a month after being dispatched. Had it been solved when sent, on 8 February, Whitehall would have been concerned and might have changed its actions. This message (like some others solved between 13–18 March, but even more so) showed the *Kaigunsho* insisted on the 70 per cent ratio. Rather than accept anything less, it was preparing the ground to wreck the entire conference by working with another party. Whitehall feared France might wish to do the same. The GCCS closely followed all French and Japanese reports of their discussions, which showed they had common ground, while the French minister to Tokyo pressed Japan toward positions on submarines which might sink the conference. British and American diplomats soon queried Japanese and French officials on these matters, aiming to destroy any intrigue by showing it was known, though these actions posed small danger.

This material illuminated a major issue and in time to act, though that would have happened in any case. The *Kaigunsho*'s position was public knowledge four days after the GCCS detected it. The Foreign Office saw 'a strong possibility of the naval element in the Japanese delegation overwhelming their political colleagues and preventing an agreement', while 'a most determined effort is being made by Japanese naval authorities to reject this compromise and nothing should be left undone to prevent such a disaster occurring'.[3] In hindsight, this assessment was alarmist; in practice, little could be done about it. As Britain opposed further concessions to Japan, it could neither appease sailors nor strengthen civilians. It could gain nothing by working on, or through, the delegation; useful action could be taken only in Tokyo. The Foreign Office thought the *Kaigunsho* had little power, while the Cabinet was strong and wise enough to accept the compromise and not subvert the conference. Still, the Foreign Office immediately reported the facts (though not the source) to American authorities, including the Secretary of State, Henry Stimson, and to its own ambassador in Tokyo, John Tilley. He should 'keep in close touch' with the Minister for Foreign Affairs, Shidehara Kijuro, and 'use all your influence with the Japanese Government in favour of a reasonable settlement of this particular question at the earliest possible moment'. Tilley should act with the American ambassador, William Castle, while avoiding anything which looked like 'joint or concerted pressure'. Notably, the men who decided how to act did not know first-hand the intelligence that inspired them, nor did one of their two governments. Tilley chose to work 'almost entirely' through Shidehara, refusing to contact the Prime Minister, Hamaguchi Osachi, as conversation with him 'would be most unlikely to elicit any statement of opinion and would attract great and probably unfavourable notice in the press'. Nor would he use the naval attaché to contact the *Kaigunsho*, as 'the real problem is a political one' while the position of Shidehara,

> who was disposed to defend the compromise even at the risk of having to resign, might be weakened if it were known, or believed, that a violent Anglo-American campaign was in progress and because alternately his own sympathy might be diminished if he learned that we were working by other means than through himself.

Tilley carefully avoided 'too much trace of concerted action' with Castle, but they compared notes and moved in parallel. Both contacted the Emperor's political advisor, Saionji Kimmochi; both pressed Shidehara and asked him to deliver messages to Hamaguchi from MacDonald and Stimson in praise of the 13 March compromise; neither told the full story to his superior.[4] According to Japanese records, once he realized Shidehara's resolve, Tilley told him to 'just pigeon-hole the message', as did Castle. They discarded what their superiors intended to be trump cards, so to show Shidehara how much they trusted him. He picked these cards up and played them in a game of his own, as he publicised that situation among leading liberals in Japan, presumably to show how he mastered problems with *gaijin* and Japanese.[5]

This intelligence affected British actions, but not events in Japan. Britain and the United States would have done much the same without it. Though it affected the form and timing of their approaches to Shidehara and Saionji, the latter would have acted as they did anyway. British actions merely reinforced Japanese decisions, nor were the results simple. In part, because the role of code-breaking at the Washington conference became public knowledge, delegitimized that agreement, and left the competence and patriotism of Japanese liberals in doubt, the London Naval Treaty set the stage for a political explosion which started Japan down the road to the Pacific War.[6]

COMMENTARY: THE JAPANESE NAVY AND THE LONDON NAVAL CONFERENCE

Peter Mauch

The London Naval Conference brought together delegates from the United States, Great Britain, Japan, France, and Italy for the purpose of extending and strengthening the era of naval limitation that had been ushered in by the earlier Washington conference. The Washington negotiators had not, however, agreed to limit the building of smaller vessels – including cruisers, destroyers, and submarines – and thereby unwittingly sparked a new race in cruiser construction. After a failed attempt to limit these vessels at Geneva in 1927, the chief naval powers concluded the London conference by signing a treaty which allowed Japan a ratio of 10 : 10 : 6.975 in auxiliary categories.

The United States and Britain entered the London conference convinced that the existing 60 per cent ratio in capital ship strength was equally applicable to cruisers and auxiliaries. The negotiating position of Japan's delegates, including Navy Minister Admiral Takarabe Takeshi, called instead for a 70 per cent ratio in both cruisers and auxiliary vessels, and 78,000 tons in submarines. The 70 per cent ratio *vis-à-vis* the United States Navy – the Japanese navy's chief hypothetical enemy – had long been a cardinal objective of Japan's sailors. Anything less, they reasoned, jettisoned Japan's chances of defeating the United States on the expanses of the Pacific. This much virtually all Japanese naval officers agreed on. What remained in hot dispute throughout the London conference was the question as to whether the 70 per cent ratio represented Japan's final position, or whether it was reducible in the course of diplomatic negotiations. At issue was the very rationale of the Japanese navy. Did it exist to fight its American counterpart, or was it a tool of deterrence against American attack?

Throughout the London conference, a small cadre of Japanese officers – often referred to as the 'treaty faction' – adhered firmly to the latter position. This group included the Navy Ministry 'trio' of Vice Navy Minister and Vice Admiral Yamanashi Katsunoshin, chief of the Naval Affairs Bureau, Rear Admiral Hori Teikichi, and Navy Ministry Adjutant Captain Koga Mineichi; Admirals Okada Keisuke, Suzuki Kantarō, and Saitō Makoto; and Vice Admirals Nomura Kichisaburō and Kobayashi Seizō. These men actively identified themselves with the legacy set by Admiral Katō Tomosaburō at the earlier Washington conference. They argued that the urban and industrial complexes which sustained America's maritime might were such that even a 70 per cent ratio for Japan would not bring victory in the Pacific. They were also convinced that an unbridled naval arms race could result in a ratio far less favourable for Japan than might be secured by international agreement. This shared *Weltanschauung* goes a long way toward explaining Admiral Suzuki's tart comment: 'Only the mediocre could clamour for 70 percent or nothing'.[1]

On the other side of the divide stood those officers – often referred to as the 'fleet faction' – who maintained that, because the navy existed to fight its American counterpart, the Washington conference's 60 per cent ratio in capital ship strength was a mistake that should not be repeated at London. According to this reasoning, Japan's insistence on a 70 per cent ratio was non-negotiable. Throughout the London conference, the chief proponents of this view were Chief of the Navy General Staff Admiral Katō Kanji and his immediate subordinate, Vice Admiral Suetsugu Nobumasa. These officers and their large band of followers maintained that should the London conference break down as a result of an Anglo-American refusal to meet Japan's demand, the Japanese navy would still attain the vital 70 per cent ratio, in the context not of international cooperation but of competition.

The arguments of these hawkish elements were compelling for a very good reason: the Navy General Staff, which was responsible for command and operations, maintained virtual independence from the Navy Ministry, which was responsible for the administration, maintenance and overall control of the service. This goes a long way toward explaining the first document under review (N.C. 199, Document One). Authored by Rear Admiral Hori, this document dates to a time when US-Japanese negotiations in London had reached an impasse. The Japanese delegates maintained an insistent demand for a 70 per cent ratio, while their American counterparts were equally insistent upon a 60 per cent ratio. Against this backdrop, Hori's telegram – his widely recognised position as an advocate of naval limitation notwithstanding – gave voice to an exceedingly hard-line stance. In what amounted to an 'insult', the American delegates had given 'no consideration' to Japan's negotiating position. The United States and Britain, moreover, were working together to 'defeat' Japan. Should this situation continue, it was best for Japan to 'lead affairs into a situation where there is little hope of agreement between the three Powers'. What might be gleaned from this document is the treaty faction's need for concessions from the United States and Great Britain if it were to successfully override the fleet faction's '70 percent or nothing' arguments.

The second document under review (N.C. 220, Document Two), authored by Japan's delegates to the London conference, came against the backdrop of a Japanese-American compromise plan produced on 13 March, the Reed-Matsudaira compromise, under which Japan in fact gained many of its claims. The Japanese navy would accept a 60 per cent ratio in heavy (8-inch gun) cruisers, but only in exchange for allowing Japan a 70 per cent ratio in light (6-inch gun) cruisers and destroyers, and parity in submarines at the level of 52,500 tons. Rather than having to return to Tokyo without a treaty and be held responsible for the failure of the conference, the Japanese envoys, including Wakatsuki Reijiro, a former prime minister, and Matsudaira Tsumeo, Japan's ambassador in London, recommended accepting this formula. As the telegram made clear, the terms of the compromise plan 'practically recognized' the 70 per cent ratio. In terms of submarine tonnage, the plan fell somewhat short of the 'quota [Japan] called for', although it did offer US-Japanese 'parity'. Implicitly asking for the government's consent to the compromise plan, the delegates warned that it 'would be difficult to induce the other side to make concessions in excess of the above'. In Tokyo, the cabinet of Prime Minister Hamaguchi Osachi – which included the foremost advocate of cooperation with the United States, Foreign Minister Shidehara Kijūroō – was receptive to this plan. They believed that the negotiators in London had accomplished as much as could be expected. Japan's limited financial capabilities ruled out a naval race and they were loathe to appear responsible for breaking up the conference. The Navy Ministry also accepted the plan; though they were not entirely happy with the formula, the diplomatic, political and financial considerations meant the imperfect bargain had to be accepted. For the hard-liners of the fleet faction, however, the compromise contained both the symbolism and substance of defeat. After lengthy debate, the government finally insisted that the compromise had to be approved for the sake of the nation's foreign policy, even though the naval authorities considered it unsatisfactory from the defence standpoint. Prime Minister Hamaguchi on 1 April cabled his government's acceptance of the plan to the delegates, and some three weeks later the London Naval Treaty was signed. The aftermath of the conference was, however, messy and complicated. The Navy General Staff registered its unalterable opposition to the treaty, and in the process charged the government with having infringed its right of command.[2]

DOCUMENT TWO:

MOST SECRET
Naval Conference: Japanese Summary of the Situation and Request for Instructions
No: N.C. 220
Date: 19th March, 1930.

From: The Japanese Delegation, LONDON.
To: The Foreign Minister, TOKIO.
No: 208.
Date: 14th March, 1930
[Cypher Class A].
[This message is referred to in LONDON to TOKIO telegram of 14th March, our N.C. 213].

Confidential:

During the past two months and more we have consistently maintained our claims with the ultimate result that the British and Americans have been driven to voice their dissatisfaction at our attitude as too unaccommodating, and as being one of obstinate adherence to our own country's position and of failure to manifest the spirit of international cooperation. Nevertheless we have in wise abated our demands, but have patiently laboured to induce the British and Americans to approximate their views to ours, even hinting at a determination on our part not to shrink from breaking off negotiations, if they attempted to force upon us an unreasonably low rate.

Latterly however, as may be perceived from the WAKATSUKI-STIMSON interview of 12th instant following upon the MATSUDAIRA-REED conversations, the Americans have already practically recognised the principle of a collective seventy per cent ratio, there being in reality a disparity of something over two-hundredths. This seems to evidence anxiety on the part of the Americans to try to meet JAPAN's wishes without laying themselves open to the criticism of an absolute surrender to Japanese demands. In regard to large cruisers they have not fallen in with our views, but actually we may take it that in the main up to the next Conference we retain the strength of seventy per cent or over. As regards submarines it is a subject for regret that the quota is less than we claimed, but we may regard it as a concession on the part of the Americans that they offered parity with us by a reduction of their own quota.

In our view, so long as a new situation does not develop, it would be difficult to induce the other side to make concessions in excess of the above. Whatever may be the case if a Five Power Agreement fails to materialise with the French question as the central factor, we should on all accounts be gravely affected if a breakdown of the present Conference should supervene as a consequences of JAPAN's attitude. Careful reflection is therefore essential. Hereafter in the light of the Franco-Italian attitude and of other developments of the situation we shall of course exert our very best efforts to secure a successful realisation of our claims; but it is our hope that at this juncture the Government will consider the course of the above-mentioned negotiations and will in reply favour us with instructions.

CONCLUSIONS

Andrew Webster

As the commentaries by John Ferris and Peter Mauch make clear, these two documents represent useful examples of how signals intelligence has been intertwined
with the events of a major international conference. Yet perhaps what is most
significant about these documents is, ironically, the lack of attention that has yet
been paid to them – and to signals intelligence in general. As Ferris notes, the
American success at cracking Japanese codes during the Washington Naval
Conference soon became public knowledge, with the publication in 1931 of a book
by the chief American code-breaker, Herbert Yardley.[1] In addition, the several post-
1945 investigations into the December 1941 catastrophe at Pearl Harbor produced
widespread awareness of the success achieved by the United States in reading
Japanese codes before and during the Second World War. Yet most histories of
the Washington conference up to the present have either omitted any reference to
the role played by signals intelligence in the conference's outcome or accorded it
only passing mention.[2] It is rather only the more specialised literature on intelligence
that has given due consideration to the success of the American cryptographers.[3]
Similarly, there has been almost no mention of the role played by the GCCS in
any of the historical studies analysing the London Naval Conference. Those studies
published before any documents pertaining to the work of the GCCS became
publicly available are perhaps more understandably bare of consideration of signals
intelligence. Nonetheless, parallels with the American experience at the Washington
conference were there for those historians who wanted to look for them. That none
did shows up the same analytical blind-spot towards signals intelligence as that
contained in all studies of the Second World War before the revelation in 1974 of
the Allied ability to read the German wartime codes, the so-called 'Ultra secret'.[4]
What is more noticeable is the lack of any analysis in recent studies of the London
conference, since evidence has become available. Initially this evidence came in
limited and indirect fashion. In 1986, for example, the very first issue of the journal
Intelligence and National Security reprinted in full a highly revealing memoir of
the work of GCCS between the wars, written in 1944 by Alastair Denniston, who
had been the operational head of GCCS.[5] In it, he noted many of the code-breaking
triumphs of the service, particularly those against Japan, and recalled in one
particularly revealing line that 'throughout the period down to 1931 no big
conference was held in Washington, London or Geneva in which [GCCS] did not
contribute all the views of the Japanese government and of their too verbose
representatives'.[6] Such a pointed reference to the cities that hosted the three great
naval conferences of the inter-war period can hardly have been accidental. Specialised studies of British intelligence have indeed noted the successes of the GCCS,
including those against Japanese codes during the 1920s and early 1930s. These
have been particularly explicit and detailed since the late 1990s, when the material
in the HW 12 series first became open for consultation.[7] Overall such revelations,
it might be thought, would have prompted historians subsequently to have at least

raised the question of the possible influence of signals intelligence on British conference diplomacy in London and elsewhere, but this has not been the case.[8]

How then should historians evaluate the role of British code-breaking in its policy-making, and in particular the successes against the Japanese? The great mass of intercepted and decrypted foreign diplomatic telegrams now available in the HW 12 series are unquestionably of great importance. Antony Best, for example, has recently demonstrated the fruitful results possible from a careful use of the GCCS intercepts, concluding that 'in the field of British policy towards Japan in the interwar period it is not an exaggeration to state that no authoritative military, diplomatic or even economic history can be written in future without extensive use of the HW 12 files'.[9] But it is not a simple matter to put these files to use. The HW12 series is in many ways so large, and so undefined, that it is difficult to make effective use of it. The data is in the rawest of forms: the intercepts alone, organised solely by date. There is no indication of how they were interpreted, for the comments made on the documents by officials in the Foreign Office have been destroyed, apparently incinerated as a matter of security procedure soon after being compiled.[10] Nor is it clear who even saw this intelligence. Some of the intercepts from the naval conference carry indications as to their distribution – to the director of GCCS (Denniston), the Foreign Office (five copies) and the Admiralty – but such a list of recipients is neither surprising nor illuminating. Scattered evidence from the private diaries of some politicians and officials, and the occasional cryptic reference to secret sources in the official files, do, however, make it clear that during the time of the London conference the GCCS intercepts were given at least a limited circulation within Whitehall.[11] Stripped of their context, the problem is how to fit these intercepts into the web of other available documents on British policy-making. Consequently, a detailed knowledge of the diplomatic context is essential to making use of them in any analysis of British policy. They are not able to provide some kind of new 'complete' picture of events, but they can suggest new ways to view events and can illuminate some obscure references in private papers. MacDonald's well-known fulminations in his diary against the French during the London Naval Conference – 'They have been conspiring against us!' – only become fully comprehensible when it is realised that GCCS intercepts had shown him the extent to which the French delegation were secretly attempting to press Japan to refuse any compromise deal that heavily restricted submarines.[12] John Ferris has also warned elsewhere against the dangers of taking the GCCS decrypts during the conference strictly at face value: for example, out of his key concern to strengthen Anglo-American relations, MacDonald warned a member of the American delegation not to report anything significant in State Department codes.[13]

At first sight, it would appear that the two documents printed here exposed to the British, first of all, the firmness of the early Japanese negotiating position (N.C. 199, Document One), and then later the point at which the negotiators believed the time had come to back down and accept the deal on offer (N.C. 220, Document Two). However, as Mauch and Ferris point out, things were not so simple. In the first place, the Japanese policy-making establishment was not monolithic, and it is important to distinguish between documents sent to or received from the Admiralty and the Foreign Ministry. Second, the gap between a telegram's transmission and its decryption was critical: until a document can be read, it cannot be put to use. Thus, N.C. 220 from the Japanese delegation in London to the Foreign Minister in Tokyo was sent using 'Cypher Class A' and took only five days for GCCS to decrypt. In contrast, it took GCCS some five weeks to decrypt N.C. 199 from the Japanese Admiralty to the delegation in London, indicating the use of a much stronger form of cipher, and meaning a quite different negotiating situation had developed by the time it arrived on the desks of British policy-makers. Third, it seems clear that the British naval negotiations, and the wider diplomacy surrounding them, in many ways proceeded independently of the input from signals intelligence. What this signals intelligence provided, in the context of the 'conference diplomacy' of the London Naval Conference, was a degree of confidence and confirmation for the British representatives in their ability to secure a deal with the Japanese. While one must avoid automatically equating 'most secret' documents with being 'most important', documents such as these should, at the least, require histories of the naval conferences to take into account the ability of some host nations to play 'dirty poker' in the complex game of diplomatic negotiation.

Notes

Overview: British signals intelligence and the London Naval Conference, 1930

Andrew Webster

1   Malcolm H. Murfett, 'Look Back in Anger: The Western Powers and the Washington Conference of 1921–1922', in B.J.C. McKercher (ed.), *Arms Limitation and Disarmament: Restraints on War, 1899–1939* (Westport, CT: Praeger, 1992), p. 90.
2   John Ferris, 'The Road to Bletchley Park: The British Experience with Signals Intelligence, 1892–1945', *Intelligence and National Security*, 17/1 (Spring 2002): 67. On the GCCS, see also, Christopher Andrew, *Secret Service: The Making of the British Intelligence Community* (London: Heinemann, 1985), pp. 375–6, 499–501; Christopher Andrew, 'Secret Intelligence and British Foreign Policy, 1900–1939', in Christopher Andrew and Jeremy Noakes (eds), *Intelligence and International Relations, 1900–1945* (Exeter: University of Exeter Press, 1987), pp. 16–22; F.H. Hinsley, *British Intelligence in the Second World War* (abridged edition, London: HMSO, 1993), pp. 5–7; John Ferris, 'Whitehall's Black Chamber: British Cryptology and the Government Code and Cypher School, 1919–1929', *Intelligence and National Security*, 2/1 (January 1987), pp. 54–91.
3   The National Archives (TNA), Kew, HW 12/114–150.
4   For the text of the Washington Naval Treaty (6 February 1922), see *Foreign Relations of the United States, 1922* (Washington, DC: Government Printing Office, 1938), vol. 1, pp. 247–66. France and Italy had each been accorded ratios of 1.75.
5   On the internal debates surrounding Japanese naval policy, see, in particular, the studies by Sadao Asada: 'The Japanese Navy and the United States', in Dorothy Borg and Shumpei Okamoto (eds), *Pearl Harbor as History: Japanese-American Relations, 1931–1941* (New York and London: Columbia University Press, 1973), pp. 225–59; 'Japanese Admirals and the Politics of Naval Limitation: Kato Tomosaburo and Kato Kanji', in Gerald Jordan (ed.), *Naval Warfare in the Twentieth Century, 1900–1945:*

Essays in Honour of Arthur Marder (London: Croom Helm, 1977), pp. 141–66; 'From Washington to London: The Imperial Japanese Navy and the Politics of Naval Limitation, 1921–1930', in Erik Goldstein and John Maurer (eds), *The Washington Conference, 1921–22: Naval Rivalry, East Asian Stability and the Road to Pearl Harbor* (Ilford: Frank Cass, 1994), pp. 147–91.

6   B.J.C. McKercher, *Transition of Power: Britain's Loss of Global Pre-eminence to the United States, 1930–1945* (Cambridge: Cambridge University Press, 1999), pp. 50–8.

7   For the text of the London Naval Treaty (22 April 1930), see *Documents on British Foreign Policy, 1919–1939*, Second Series, vol. I (London: HMSO, 1946), appendix I.

Commentary: Communications intelligence and conference diplomacy, London, 1930

John Ferris

1   An excellent account is given in David Kahn, *The Reader of Gentlemen's Mail: Herbert O. Yardley and the Birth of American Codebreaking* (New Haven, CT: Yale University Press, 2004).

2   Sadao Asada discusses in some detail the telegraphic confusion within the Japanese delegation, as its civilian and naval members attempted to keep their secrets from each other. Asada, 'From Washington to London', p. 177.

3   Minute by Thompson, 25 April 1930, and Tokyo embassy to Foreign Office, dispatch no. 145, 25 March 1930, FO 371/14263, A2796; *Documents on British Foreign Policy, 1919–1939*, Second Series, vol. I (London: HMSO, 1946), pp. 249–51.

4   *Documents on British Foreign Policy, 1919–1939*, Second Series, vol. I (London: HMSO, 1946), pp. 249–66; *Foreign Relations of the United States, 1930*, vol. I (Washington, DC: Government Printing Office, 1945), pp. 66–79.

5   Thomas Francis Mayer-Oakes (ed.), *Fragile Victory: Prince Saionji and the 1930 London Treaty Issue* (Detroit: Wayne State University Press, 1968), p. 100.

6   For these events as a whole, see also Ian Gow, *Military Intervention in Prewar Japanese Politics: Admiral Kato Kanji and the 'Washington System'* (London: Routledge, 2004); James William Morley (ed.), *Japan Erupts: The London Naval Conference and the Manchurian Incident, 1928–1932, Selected Translations from Taiheyō Sensō e no Michi* (New York: Columbia University Press, 1984); John Ferris, '"It Is Our Business in the Navy to Command the Seas': The Last Decade of British Maritime Supremacy, 1919–1929', in Greg Kennedy and Keith Neilson (eds), *Far Flung Lines: Essays on Imperial Defence in Honour of Donald Mackenzie Schurman* (London: Frank Cass, 1997). Solutions referred to in this piece are in TNA, HW 12/119–125.

Commentary: The Japanese navy and the London Naval Conference

Peter Mauch

1   Grand Chamberlain Admiral Suzuki Kantarō, quoted in diary entry for 28 March 1930, Thomas Francis Mayer-Oakes, *Fragile Victory, Prince Saionji and the 1930 London Treaty Issue* (Detroit: Wayne State University Press, 1968), p. 103.

2   On these events, see Sadao Asada, *From Mahan to Pearl Harbor: The Imperial Japanese Navy and the United States* (Annapolis, MD: Naval Institute Press, 2006);

Asada, 'From Washington to London', pp. 172–82; David C. Evans and Mark R. Peattie, *Kaigun: Strategy, Tactics, and Technology in the Imperial Japanese Navy, 1887–1941* (Annapolis, MD: Naval Institute Press, 1997); Takashi Itō, *Shōwa Shoki Seijishi Kenkyū: Rondon Kaigun Gunshuku Mondai o Meguru Shoseiji Shūdan no Taikō to Teikei* (Tokyo: Tokyo Daigaku Shuppankai, 1969); Tatsuo Kobayashi, 'The London Naval Treaty', in James William Morley, *Japan Erupts; The London Naval Conference and the Manchurian Incident, 1928–1932, Selected Translations from Taiheiyō Sensō e no Michi* (New York: Columbia University Press, 1984); Minoru Nomura, *Nihon Kaigun no Rekishi* (Tokyo: Yoshikawa Kōbunkan, 2002).

Conclusions

Andrew Webster

1   Herbert Yardley, *The American Black Chamber* (Indianapolis: Bobbs-Merrill, 1931).
2   Gerald E. Wheeler, *Prelude to Pearl Harbor: The United States Navy and the Far East, 1921–1931* (Columbia: University of Missouri Press, 1963), pp. 53–8; Stephen Roskill, *Naval Policy Between the Wars*. Vol. I: *The Period of Anglo-American Antagonism, 1919–1929* (London: Collins, 1968), pp. 300–30; Thomas H. Buckley, *The United States and the Washington Conference, 1921–1922* (Knoxville, TN: University of Tennessee Press, 1970), p. 196; William R. Braisted, *The United States Navy in the Pacific, 1909–1922* (Austin, TX: University of Texas Press, 1971), pp. 599–602; Roger Dingman, *Power in the Pacific: The Origins of Naval Arms Limitation, 1914–1922* (Chicago: University of Chicago Press, 1976), p. 203; Christopher Hall, *Britain, America and Arms Control, 1921–1937* (Basingstoke: Macmillan, 1987), pp. 24–35; Robert G. Kaufman, *Arms Control during the Pre-Nuclear Era: The United States and Naval Limitation between the Two World Wars* (New York: Columbia University Press, 1990), pp. 43–72; Emily O. Goldman, *Sunken Treaties: Naval Arms Control between the Wars* (University Park, PA: Pennsylvania State University Press, 1994), pp. 121–30; Richard W. Fanning, *Peace and Disarmament: Naval Rivalry and Arms Control, 1922–1933* (Lexington, KY: University of Kentucky Press, 1995), pp. 4–8; Phillips P. O'Brien, *British and American Naval Power: Politics and Policy, 1900–1936* (Westport, CT: Praeger, 1998), pp. 166–9.
3   In particular, the path-breaking study by David Kahn, *The Code-breakers: The Story of Secret Writing* (1967, revised edition, New York: Scribner, 1996), pp. 356–9, specifically highlighted this aspect of the Washington conference. See also David Alvarez, *Secret Messages: Codebreaking and American Diplomacy, 1930–1945* (Lawrence KS: University Press of Kansas, 2000), pp. 8–16.
4   On the historiographical revolution prompted by the revelation of Ultra, see Russell M. Anderson, 'The Public Disclosure of Anglo-American Signals Intelligence since the Second World War, with Particular Reference to Ultra and Magic', unpublished PhD dissertation, Cambridge (2004). For examples of this same blind-spot towards signals intelligence in studies of the post-1945 period, see Christopher Andrew, 'Intelligence and International Relations in the Early Cold War', *Review of International Studies*, 24/3 (July 1998), pp. 321–30.
5   A.G. Denniston, 'The Government Code and Cypher School between the Wars', *Intelligence and National Security*, 1/1 (January 1986), pp. 48–70. The original copy of this memoir, dated 2 December 1944, is in the Denniston papers, Churchill College, Cambridge, DENN 1/4.
6   Denniston, 'Government Code and Cypher School', pp. 55–6.
7   Michael Smith, *The Emperor's Codes: Bletchley Park and the Breaking of Japan's Secret Ciphers* (London: Bantam Press, 2000), pp. 4–5, 17–18, 20–41. Also see works cited in note 2 on p. 55.

8   Raymond G. O'Connor, *Perilous Equilibrium: The United States and the London Naval Conference of 1930* (Lawrence, KS: University of Kansas Press, 1962), pp. 62–108; Stephen Roskill, *Naval Policy Between the Wars*. Vol. II: *The Period of Reluctant Rearmament, 1930–1939* (London: Collins, 1976), pp. 37–70; Hall, *Britain, America and Arms Control*, pp. 88–109; Kaufman, *Arms Control in the Pre-Nuclear Era*, pp. 129–38; Goldman, *Sunken Treaties*, pp. 14, 148, 151, 190–1, 204–9; Fanning, *Peace and Disarmament*, pp. 126–8; O'Brien, *British and American Naval Power*, pp. 210–18; McKercher, *Transition of Power*, pp. 50–8.

9   Antony Best, 'Intelligence, Diplomacy and the Japanese Threat to British Interests, 1914–1941', *Intelligence and National Security*, 17/1 (Spring 2002), p. 98. See in particular his discussion of the Leith-Ross mission to the Far East in 1935 (pp. 89–92).

10   Best, 'Intelligence, Diplomacy and the Japanese Threat', p. 89.

11   MacDonald diaries, TNA, PRO 30/69/1753/1, entries for 18, 24 and 25 March 1930; Ben Pimlott (ed.), *The Political Diary of Hugh Dalton, 1918–40, 1945–60* (London: Jonathan Cape, 1986), pp. 69–72, 80–1. See also John Ferris, '"Indulged in All too Little"?: Vansittart, Intelligence and Appeasement', *Diplomacy and Statecraft*, 6/1 (March 1995), pp. 124–8.

12   MacDonald diary, 18 March 1930, TNA, PRO 30/69/1753/1; Dobler (Tokyo) to Quai, 17 March 1930, Ministère des Affaires Etrangères, series SDN, vol. 1118, fos. 41–4; intercepts in TNA, HW 12/126. A complete summary of all the French manoeuvres, based upon 'secret sources', is in Foreign Office memo, 24 March 1930, TNA, FO 371/14261, A2166.

13   Ferris, 'Road to Bletchley Park', p. 68.

3 French military intelligence responds to the German remilitarisation of the Rhineland, 1936

Peter Jackson and Martin S. Alexander

OVERVIEW: A LOOK AT FRENCH INTELLIGENCE MACHINERY IN 1936

Peter Jackson

Document Three, 'Note concerning the consequences that follow, from a military point of view, from Germany's renunciation of the Locarno Treaty' is a wide-ranging assessment, prepared by the intelligence department (the *Deuxième Bureau*) of the French army General Staff in early April 1936. The document was drafted at a key moment in the history of international relations between the two world wars. By marching troops into the Rhineland on 7 March 1936, Germany smashed the last and, from the French perspective, the strongest pillar of the post-1918 order in Europe. The demilitarised status of the Rhineland had been entrenched in Articles 42 through 44 of the Treaty of Versailles. It was also guaranteed by Germany, France, Britain and Italy in the series of inter-locking treaties of mutual guarantee that made up the Locarno Accords of 6 October 1925. Locarno had been at the centre of French security policy since the mid-1920s. Its violation by Germany was therefore a challenge to the existing political order and a grave blow to French strategy and diplomacy.[1]

Martin Alexander's perceptive analysis of the document focuses on the political, diplomatic and strategic context in which it was written. Alexander shows us that there are two levels of analysis in the text. The first level concentrates on rearmament policy and France's strategic posture. The second ranges more widely to consider France's diplomatic options and to make policy recommendations. Alexander also considers the machinery in place for the making of strategic policy in France in 1936 and sets the document within the long-term context of French attempts to resurrect the military alliance with Britain that had proved so vital between 1914 and 1918. This outline will focus more specifically on the workings of France's intelligence apparatus and the precise role of intelligence in the making of foreign and defence policy during this period. It will therefore pose three questions: Who drafted the document? For whom? And for what purpose?

Who drafted the document?

Although there is no clear indication of the authorship of this document, the fact that it bears the letterhead 'État-Major de l'Armée – 2ème Bureau' means that the final version was certainly seen and approved (and quite possibly also drafted) by *Deuxième Bureau* chief, Lt. Col Maurice Gauché.[2] During the inter-war period the only permanent foreign intelligence agencies in France were the *Deuxième Bureaux* of the army, the navy and the air force General Staffs.[3] All were charged with providing their various staffs and ministries with up-to-date assessments of the strategic situation. Of the three agencies, the army *Deuxième Bureau* was by far the largest and best funded. It also produced the most comprehensive studies of international political and military issues.

The collection of secret intelligence abroad was the responsibility of the military services. France's chief secret service, the Service de Renseignements (SR), was formally attached to the army *Deuxième Bureau*.[4] The SR was funded by the war ministry (reorganised as the Ministry of National Defence in 1936) and its commanding officer was responsible both to the army high command and to the Minister of War. Its responsibilities included the management of agent networks (human intelligence), the interception and analysis of foreign telegrams and radio traffic and aerial photography. The SR offices on the Avenue de Tourville in Paris also included a counter-intelligence section, the *Section de Centralisation des Renseignements* (SCR). This unit acted in co-operation with the *Sûreté Générale* (after 1936 the *Sûreté Nationale*) and the Paris *Préfecture de Police* to combat foreign espionage and revolutionary subversion.[5]

A final essential component in the machinery of French intelligence of this era was the extensive network of service attachés posted abroad. The role of the service attaché was threefold: (1) to serve as technical counsel to the diplomatic legation; (2) to represent the French army abroad; and, (3) most importantly from the perspective of intelligence, to gather information on the political, economic and military situation inside the state to which he was posted.[6] This last function was performed in constant liaison with the 'research section' of the *Deuxième Bureau* in Paris, which directed the activity of the attaché through daily requests for all kinds of information from precise details concerning military equipment to the price of butter. Recent scholarship has rightly attributed an important role to these 'agents of international relations'. In the case of French intelligence, service attaché reports were the single most important source of information on strategic affairs in foreign states.[7]

The military thus dominated intelligence activity in France.[8] This was in contrast to the British case, where the Secret Intelligence Service was attached to the Foreign Office. Although it had long been involved in intercepting and deciphering foreign correspondence, the Quai d'Orsay (the French Foreign Ministry) did not begin developing a covert intelligence service of its own until the very eve of war.[9] And, although French embassies often provide cover for SR operatives abroad, there were significant tensions between soldiers and diplomats over this issue. Ambassador André François-Poncet took an active role in supporting SR operations in Germany. But many SR officers expressed frustration at what they perceived to be insufficient co-operation from the Foreign Ministry and lamented, with some justification, that the Quai d'Orsay under-estimated the importance of secret intelligence to policy-making.[10]

The vast majority of clandestine intelligence gathering targeted Germany and was conducted by a network of SR stations along the Franco-German frontier and in French diplomatic missions in most European states. There were four main SR posts during the 1930s. The *Bureau d'Etude Nord-Est* at Lille, the *Bureau Regional d'Etudes Metz* at Metz and the *Service des Communications Militaires* (SCM) at Belfort, all focused almost exclusively on Germany. The *Section d'Etudes Militaires* (SEM) at Marseilles gathered intelligence on both Italy and Germany. In 1937, another post, the *Bureau d'Etudes Pyrénéenes* (BEP), was established at Bayonne to monitor the Spanish Civil War. Smaller stations in Riga, Copenhagen, The Hague, Rome, Prague, Warsaw, Bucharest, Belgrade and Budapest were run by SR officers in the guise of assistant military or air attachés.[11]

The raw intelligence gathered and collated by this system was forwarded to the *Deuxième Bureau* for analysis. The tasks of synthesis and analysis were the responsibility of geographical sections within the larger *Section des Armées Étrangères* (SAE). The focus of the foreign intelligence effort was unquestionably on Germany. During the 1930s, there were more analysts attached to the *Section allemande*, responsible for preparing assessments of German intentions and capabilities, than to all other geographic sections combined. The assessments prepared by the analytical sections of the *Deuxième Bureau* drew not only on secret information obtained from the SR but also on a vast array of sources ranging from the constant flow of reports received from the Foreign Ministry's Department of Political and Commercial Affairs to a wide range of open sources. These included everything from surveys of the international press to studies of the political and economic situation in Germany prepared by research institutes attached to French universities to German telephone manuals. The latter proved especially useful for monitoring deployment of the German army and air force. Military installations were listed under *Wehrmacht* in German telephone manuals – a surprising security failure in the Nazi police state.[12] In sum, and especially in light of the relatively meagre resources at their disposal, France's intelligence gathering organs processed an imposing mass of information each week.

One area where France lagged behind Great Britain was the collection and analysis of intelligence on foreign industrial and economic potential. The French did not develop an equivalent to the British Industrial Intelligence Centre after the First World War. There was no intelligence agency charged specifically with reporting on economic and industrial issues. This task was instead the responsibility of the Secrétariat Général of France's inter-ministerial defence policy committee, the *Conseil Supérieur de la Défense Nationale* (CSDN).[13] Within this secretariat (the SGDN), economic assessment was performed by the third section, which worked in close co-operation with the three service intelligence bureaux to construct assessments of foreign economic and military potential.

The human element in France's intelligence machine also bears some consideration. Senior *Deuxième Bureau* officers, both those serving in Paris and those posted abroad as military attachés, tended to have spent their career in intelligence. The widely held assumption that intelligence was a backwater for second-rate officers does not hold true in the case of the French military.[14] It is true that career intelligence officers did not tend to rise to the very top of the military hierarchy in France. Those marked for the very highest levels of command tended to pass through the *Troisième* (operations) *Bureau* and to spend much more of their career with field units. But senior *Deuxième Bureau* officials played a major role in military policy-making at the highest level. Not only were intelligence assessments essential components in the evolution of military planning, the *Deuxième Bureau* also functioned as a useful tool in military efforts to influence foreign and defence policy through the interface with diplomatic and political elites.

As a result, high-ranking intelligence officials were typically officers of exceptional ability with distinguished service records. Like other staff officers, they tended overwhelmingly to come from conservative social backgrounds; the majority were Catholic. A combination of official regulation and long-standing tradition meant that officers refrained from expressing political views. But the majority inclined towards the conservative nationalism on the centre-right and right of the French political spectrum and had doubts about the republican regime. Judging from the personnel dossiers of senior intelligence officers, the key criteria for a career in military intelligence were personal characteristics such as 'honour' and 'dependability', a capacity for hard work, good communications skills and, above all, intellectual ability. Leadership skills appear to have been less crucial for aspiring intelligence officials than they were for those officers singled for senior command positions. The corollary to this was that career intelligence officers only rarely rose above the rank of Lieutenant-Colonel and even more rarely were given command of their own division or a seat on the *Conseil Supérieur de Guerre* (the Superior War Council: responsible for the formulation of nearly all aspects of military policy). If leading intelligence officers were not likely to rise to the pinnacle of the military establishment, they were nonetheless highly respected professionals who exercised considerable influence within the general staff of the French army.[15]

The overall calibre of *Deuxième Bureau* officers is borne out in personnel dossiers of the three senior intelligence officers in France at this time. *Deuxième Bureau* chief, Lt Colonel Maurice Gauché, was 44 years of age in 1936 – young for a senior officer of the French General Staff. He was a career intelligence officer and, like all inter-war bureau chiefs, an expert on Germany.[16] After having served as an intelligence officer on various staffs during the First World War and with the French mission to Poland in 1920, Gauché was posted first to the French army of occupation in Germany and then to the German desk of the *Deuxième Bureau* in Paris. Contacts he developed in Poland were to prove extraordinarily useful in the attack on the German Enigma machine the following decade. During the 1930s, before taking over as *Deuxième Bureau* chief, he served first as head of the German desk and then as deputy chief. Gauché was much respected within the general staff for his analytical powers and for an extraordinary capacity for detail. Weygand described him as having an 'unusually powerful and subtle intellect', and as 'an officer of the very highest calibre'. Gamelin agreed, noting that 'this is an officer who must be pushed [promoted through the system]'.[17] British officials who had frequent dealings with France's intelligence chief found him 'an unexcitable type ... unusually taciturn', who formulated 'extraordinarily accurate assessments'.[18]

The head of French secret intelligence when this document was drafted was Colonel Henri Roux (replaced by Lt. Colonel Louis Rivet in June 1936). Roux was a veteran intelligence officer who had served with both the *Deuxième Bureau* after the armistice and with the French army of the Rhine for most of the 1920s, before being reassigned as chief of the SR in 1930. Roux spoke fluent German and was one of the foremost experts on the situation in Germany within the French army.[19] A third key intelligence officer in 1936 was the French military attaché in Berlin, General Gaston Renondeau. Berlin was the most important and prestigious of the attaché posts and was occupied by Renondeau from 1932 through to the end of 1938. A graduate of the prestigious *Ecole Polytechnique*, Renondeau was also a gifted linguist who spoke fluent English, Japanese and German. Like Gauché and Roux, he was a long-serving intelligence officer who had spent most of his career representing the French army abroad. Before the First World War, he had spent four years with the Japanese army. During the war he had been attached to the French military mission in London and had then served in Russia. In 1920, he was named military attaché to the French embassy in Tokyo, where he remained until 1929 when he rejoined the General Staff as head of the SAE. In decreeing his appointment, Defence Minister Joseph Paul-Boncour stressed his standing as an officer of the 'highest distinction'. Army Chief of Staff General Maurice Gamelin described Renondeau as a 'brilliant officer' whose 'tact, judgement and formidable intellect' made him 'beyond any doubt the best choice for our Berlin posting'.[20] Intelligence was no backwater within the French General Staff. Leading intelligence officers were some of the most intelligent and accomplished members of the French military machine between the wars.

The French system as a whole had notable strengths. Foremost among these was its systematic exploitation of open source information, which was almost certainly superior to that of any other intelligence service during this period. Another was the extensive information sharing between agencies based in different ministries. From late 1935 there was daily liaison with the Department of Political and Commercial Affairs at the Quai d'Orsay. The SAE also received information as a matter of routine from all departments with an interest in national defence ranging from the ministries of the Colonies and the Interior to Public Works, Commerce and Finance. Indeed, the overriding mantra in French intelligence doctrine was that centralisation was the key to the effective exploitation of intelligence. The weekly intelligence reports prepared by the SAE of the army *Deuxième Bureau*, for example, were drawn not only from its own open and clandestine sources but also from information and assessments obtained from the air force and naval intelligence agencies, the *Sûreté Nationale* (based in the Interior Ministry), the Quai d'Orsay and frequently from the ministries of the Colonies, Commerce and Finance.[21] There can be little doubt that the French led the way among the intelligence services of the great powers in moving towards a system of 'all-source analysis' and in devising procedures for sharing of information across the defence and foreign policy establishment.[22]

Military domination of the intelligence machine placed crucial limitations on the collection, analysis and use of intelligence. In terms of collection, the first priority of the *Deuxième Bureau*, like virtually all military intelligence agencies, was to establish the 'order of battle' of foreign armed forces. It performed this task with impressive precision. It was also effective at providing accurate and timely short-term warning. As one military intelligence veteran observed with justifiable pride, France's political leadership could never complain of having been caught at unawares during any of the various coups mounted by Nazi Germany before the Second World War. But when it came to long-term assessments of key issues such as the foreign policy orientation of other powers or the performance of their armaments industries, intelligence officials tended to rely on entrenched pre-conceptions and generalisations about national character that were not always reliable.[23]

Perhaps the most important problem with military control of the collection and assessment of intelligence was the state of civil-military relations in France during this period – which conditioned the reception that intelligence estimates received from civilian decision-makers. The first half of the twentieth century was a period of ongoing tensions between the military and civilian leaders. Army intelligence had been deeply implicated in the Dreyfus Affair. In the aftermath of the affair, the entire French counter-espionage apparatus was disbanded and the skeleton staff of officers left to carry on the work of the *Deuxième Bureau* faced both the stigma of incompetence and drastic cuts in funding.[24] The reputation of the military intelligence recovered with victory in 1918.[25] But mutual suspicion was deeply ingrained and lingered throughout the inter-war period, resurfacing in the early 1930s as the defence budget was slashed as a response to the economic crisis. In this atmosphere of latent mistrust, control of the intelligence process by the military meant that intelligence assessments could be dismissed (or simply ignored) by civilian decision-makers convinced that they reflected the vested interests of the military services rather than any external reality.[26] Political imperatives intruded into the intelligence process at every level.

For whom?

Professor Alexander's commentary rightly notes that the document in question was written for several audiences. The existing document is a duplicate copy of an original that was almost certainly given wide circulation within the defence establishment. Unfortunately, there is no circulation list on this copy of the document and it is therefore impossible to know whether it made it all the way to the desk of Minister of War, General Louis Maurin. But the bureaucratic procedures in place within the ministry at the time suggest strongly that Maurin did indeed receive a copy.

Unlike service attaché reports, which were addressed directly to (and frequently read by) the relevant minister and were always circulated to the Department of

Political and Commercial Affairs within the Foreign Ministry, *Deuxième Bureau* assessments such as this usually passed through a substantial bureaucratic chain before reaching civilian officials. A typical synthesis from the analytical sections of the *Deuxième Bureau* in 1936 would first cross the desk of deputy chief (Captain Malraison) and chief (Gauché) of the *Bureau*. If it was deemed sufficiently important, it would be forwarded to a deputy chief of staff responsible for intelligence, General Victor-Henri Schweisguth, who would then decide if it merited the attention of the other Deputy Chiefs of Staff, army Chief of Staff, General Louis Colson and the Commander-in-Chief designate, General Maurice Gamelin. If Gamelin considered the assessment of especial importance, he would sometimes forward it with commentary to the Minister of War directly. Gamelin and Maurin, significantly, were old friends who graduated from the *École Supérieure de la Guerre* together in 1899. Another route to the minister went through the War Ministry's Military Cabinet. Gauché or his deputy would forward exceptionally interesting reports directly to this office, which was also responsible for digesting the weekly and monthly bulletins and studies produced by the *Deuxième Bureaux*, the assessments prepared by the SGDN as well as information from the Foreign Ministry. It was the Military Cabinets that normally decided what information was to be passed on to the minister in question.[27]

The political impact of intelligence estimates depended largely on the attitude of individual ministers towards intelligence. In the case of military intelligence assessments, it was the minister who finally decided what information should be distributed to other members of the government sitting in the *Conseil des ministres* (the Cabinet). Here we reach the real area of weakness in French government machinery. Intelligence was never summarised and distributed regularly and systematically to the Cabinet. It was instead communicated directly – usually orally – by service ministers to their Cabinet colleagues. And because the French Cabinet kept no minutes, it is impossible to discern the effect of intelligence on decision-making at this level. There was not even a permanent secretariat responsible for providing administrative support in the tradition of the British committee system. This is unfortunate as Cabinet deliberations could be decisive in matters pertaining not only to questions of war and peace but also to rearmament and financial policy. Equally important, the Cabinet was not served by an effective inter-ministerial national defence structure. There were two key organs where the various ministries and departments responsible for national security came together to debate and formulate policy. The first was the CSDN – the French equivalent of the British Committee of Imperial Defence. The CSDN had been established in 1906 to coordinate military, diplomatic and economic policy. Although it met regularly after the war to discuss various aspects of security policy, it was widely considered too large and unwieldy. By the mid-1920s, nearly all of the substantial debates were taking place in smaller sub-committees of the CSDN. In 1932 the smaller *Haut Comité Militaire* (HCM) was created to ensure more focused debate. The new committee became the focus of national security decision-making until it was replaced in June 1936 by the *Comité Permanent de la Défense Nationale*. The CSDN proper met only once after 1932. But it continued to contribute to policy formulation though its various study sections. None of these organs proved effective, however, because of the lack of permanent Cabinet machinery to coordinate their work with that of the independent ministries.[28]

This problem of insufficient coordination across ministries and departments was a major factor in the failure of intelligence to make a decisive impact on French national security policy-making. There was no inter-ministerial committee or organ charged with coordinating the collection and especially the analysis of intelligence of all kinds. The British began developing such an institution with the creation of the Joint Intelligence Committee (JIC) in 1936. The impetus for the creation of similar organ in France should have come from the offices of either the premier or the war minister. But, despite support for the idea within army intelligence, no such committee was created or even proposed.[29] The result was that the army *Deuxième Bureau* tended to operate as a self-contained community within the General Staff – deprived of the external stimulus which would have challenged the assumptions upon which analysis was based. These shortcomings should be placed in perspective however. During the 1930s no Great Power had established an effective inter-ministerial organ to coordinate the analysis of intelligence. Even the British JIC did not begin to function effectively until it was reformed on the very eve of war.[30]

A final criticism frequently made of the French approach to intelligence is that the assessments produced by the intelligence community either did not reach key policy-makers or were ignored when they did make it to the highest echelons of political and diplomatic decision-making. In a testimonial prepared after the defeat of 1940, Colonel Louis Rivet, Roux's successor as SR chief, denounced 'the bureaucratic barriers erected by poor organisation or simply by suspicion' that separated policy-makers from the intelligence services.[31] This charge has considerable validity. France's rearmament effort, for example, was delayed in part because in the mid-1930s politicians were inclined to dismiss intelligence warnings about the nature of Nazi intentions and the scale of the rearmament programmes being devised and implemented across the Rhine. They gave priority to a programme of economic recovery through financial austerity despite increasingly dire warnings from military intelligence and the army and air force high commands.[32] But such criticisms must always be placed in context. Rivet's diary, for example, reveals that he was in more or less constant contact with the head of the Military Cabinet and with the minister's civilian chief of staff at the Ministry of Defence. It also reveals that there were frequent consultations between Foreign Ministry and SR officials on a wide range of issues from signals security to counter-espionage.[33] Finally, it is important to remember that heads of state rarely saw secret service chiefs personally anywhere during the 1930s. The concept of the daily intelligence brief evolved out of the experiences of the Second World War and the Cold War.[34]

From this survey of the bureaucratic machinery of national defence policy-making in France we can make a number of educated guesses as to the likely fate of the *tour d'horizon* prepared by either Gauché or his Deputy on 8 April 1936. The survey would have been circulated in the first instance and as a matter of routine to the SAE, the chief of the SR, to Deputy Chief of Staff General Schweisguth and to General Victor Bourret, the head of the Military Cabinet at the War Ministry. Schweisguth would almost certainly have circulated it to the other Deputy Chiefs of Staff, to Chief of Staff Colson and to Gamelin. It is likely that the document would have been forwarded by General Bourret's staff to the minister's personal staff at the War Ministry and from there in all probability to the desk of General Maurin, the War Minister. Of course, there is no way of being certain of any of this. Given the fragmentary state of the French archives, one is forced to calculate the likely dissemination of this document based on the balance of probabilities in light of the way papers moved within the army General Staff and the War Ministry.

Although this is an impressive list of likely recipients, it is also worth reflecting that other key decision-makers probably did not read this document. Foremost among these were Minister of Foreign Affairs, Pierre-Etienne Flandin and Premier Albert Sarraut. The Quai d'Orsay may well have received a copy of the document. But it is highly unlikely that it would have been circulated any higher than the Director of Political and Commercial Affairs, Paul Bargeton. This is principally owing to the nature of the document, which trespasses extensively on to the terrain of foreign policy. Officials at the Quai d'Orsay tended to be ambivalent about *Deuxième Bureau* assessments. Estimates of the size of foreign armed forces, that is of the *capabilities* of other states, were accepted almost without question by diplomats. Yet these same officials tended to view intelligence assessments of the *intentions* of other states with disdain. And they were positively hostile towards the foreign policy recommendations made by military officials. This attitude stemmed from the powerful sense of ownership with which diplomats regarded the making of foreign policy. France's diplomatic corps was a long-established elite with a strong corporate identity that regarded itself as the nation's sole repository of expertise on foreign affairs. Hence, while disputes among Foreign Ministry officials were rife, the Quai d'Orsay virtually always responded to intrusions on its preserve from other departments by closing ranks in determined opposition.[35] It is therefore highly unlikely that this document, with its expansive survey of the international situation and its open prescriptions for French foreign policy, would have been attributed first importance within the confines of the Foreign Ministry.

It is difficult to judge whether this intelligence assessment was forwarded to Premier Sarraut. The lack of any centralised machinery for the analysis and dissemination of intelligence to a range of key decision-makers meant the document would only have reached Sarraut had it been forwarded to him by Maurin. But there is no evidence that this happened. Indeed there are grounds for doubt. First, although Maurin had been appointed War Minister by Sarraut when the latter assumed the premiership the previous January, the two were not well acquainted and did not work closely together. Second, Sarraut's government was a caretaker regime which was almost certain to be removed from power by legislative elections scheduled to take place less than four weeks later.[36] This crucial point underlines the importance of contextualisation when working with primary sources of all kinds and with intelligence material in particular. The policy initiatives outlined in the document were aimed less at the existing government than at whatever government emerged in its place after the May 1936 elections.

For what purpose?

The document in question provides a good illustration of the way intelligence can be used by actors in bureaucratic politics to influence the making of high policy. It thus reminds us of need to look for evidence of politicisation when working with intelligence material. As Martin Alexander rightly observes, one detects in the text of this document 'the voice of a dominant single service – one very sure of itself'.[37] Under the cover of providing a balanced and objective survey of the strategic situation in Europe in April 1936 – the classic function of intelligence assessment – this *Deuxième Bureau* memorandum articulates the convictions and prescriptions of the Army General Staff.

The use of intelligence assessments in this way by the Army High Command was far from unprecedented. During the First World War, for example, French Commander-in-Chief General Joseph Joffre used two assessments prepared by the *Deuxième Bureau* to convey his staff's vision of the future peace settlement to diplomatic and political elites. These documents advocated an extreme solution to the 'German problem' that included the annexation by France of a significant portion of the coal-rich Saarland and the reconstitution of the Rhineland into a collection of autonomous buffer states to be brought into the French orbit through a thirty-year military occupation. These documents were circulated widely within the French policy establishment and played an important role in the formulation of the French government's war aims in early 1917.[38] From 1920 through to 1934, moreover, consistently inflated assessments of German capabilities produced by the *Deuxième Bureau* were a central element in the War Ministry's successful opposition to multilateral disarmament.[39]

The document under scrutiny was part of this strategy. The remilitarisation of the Rhineland provided the Army High Command with an opportunity to drive home the danger posed by a resurgent Germany to France's political leadership. The General Staff and Foreign Ministry had been anticipating the German move since the early 1930s. Intelligence reports of an imminent reoccupation began to multiply in late 1935 and by 2 March 1936 the *Deuxième Bureau* was able to provide French decision-makers with the precise date of the operation five days later.[40] In the days and weeks following the German *coup*, *Deuxième Bureau* estimates of both the size of the German army and the pace of German rearmament were systematically inflated by General Gamelin's staff before being forwarded to civilian authorities. The aim was twofold: to justify the army's opposition to any offensive into western Germany and, equally importantly, to apply pressure on civilian leaders in general, and the incoming government in particular, to increase defence expenditure. Significantly, the High Command was simultaneously demanding a 100 per cent increase in the military outlay on rearmament for the coming year. The priority for the French military in early 1936 was to use the consternation generated by the anticipated German reoccupation to impress on civilian leaders the need for a large-scale rearmament programme which would permit France to confront Germany from a position of strength.[41]

This is the context within which the 8 April 1936 assessment should be should be interpreted. Nearly all of the hallmarks of French military intelligence assessment of the German menace during the 1930s are discernible in this document. First is the conviction that '[t]he aims of German policy are none other than those of the Führer' and envisaged the 'Germanisation of Europe'. There follows a forecast of the course of Nazi policy through 1940 which is accurate in virtually all its essentials: the incorporation of ethnic Germans into a greater Reich to be followed by territorial expansion in the east, after which the military defeat of France would bring about the isolation of Britain (as the prerequisite to a 'world policy'). One can also discern the other key elements in the image of Germany constructed by French intelligence before 1939. These included a 'formidable industrial organisation' combined with a 'centralised government whose authority is absolute' and, equally important, a national character animated by a 'warrior spirit that is unique in Europe'. There are also passages aimed clearly at supporting the military's campaign for increased funding for rearmament. The most notable of these are the sections stressing the need to accelerate the motorisation of seven infantry divisions and the creation of a second light mechanised division.

Also highly instructive in this regard are the passages discussing the relationship between the new strategic situation and France's foreign policy options. As Martin Alexander observes, the fact that the Soviet Union is mentioned only twice illustrates the ideological antipathy with which the majority of France's conservative military elites viewed the prospect of cooperation with the homeland of Socialist Revolution.[42] The USSR is mentioned, significantly, only to underline first the limited aid it could provide to those European states threatened with future German aggression and second doubts surrounding its willingness to provide such aid in any case. Much greater importance was attached to improved relations with Fascist Italy that might resurrect the short-lived military alliance negotiated with that country the previous summer. The author of the document stresses Italy's strategic interests in south-eastern Europe and then describes Italian policy as hesitating between a pro-German and a pro-French orientation. This analysis of Fascist foreign policy is as much a reflection of the ideological sympathy which characterised the views of the vast majority of French army officers towards Italy as it is a balanced reading of the likely policy choices of Mussolini's regime. Hopes for a renewed Franco-Italian front against German revisionism would crumble altogether in the bitter experience of the civil war that was about to break out in Spain the following July.[43] The document also provides persuasive evidence that the army General Staff had not written off Eastern and Central Europe as a potential theatre of operations for French troops. On the contrary, it stresses the potentially decisive importance of this theatre and argues that France must be willing to commit substantial forces to the region. This would help ensure cooperation between Czechoslovakia and its neighbours, convince Italy of the wisdom of standing with France against German aggression in the region and act as a 'catalyst for British intervention'. The document ends with the dramatic assertion that such a strategic commitment would allow France to act as the 'indispensable instrument in a powerful coalition ranged against Germany'.

In sum, this important document provides a range of insights into the military reaction to the German remilitarisation of the Rhineland as well as the role of the *Deuxième Bureau* as a mouthpiece for the army General Staff and High Command. It tells us a great deal about the way French military elites understood the increasingly intractable strategic dilemma facing France at this time. It also illuminates in interesting ways the ideological assumptions that underpinned this understanding. It is an excellent example of the potential interest of intelligence and intelligence-related material for scholars of many stripes interested in the political, diplomatic and cultural history of Europe before the Second World War.

DOCUMENT THREE:

'Note concerning the consequences that follow, from a military point of view, from Germany's renunciation of the Locarno Treaty'. France, Ministère de la Défense, Service Historique de la Défense – Département de l'Armée de Terre [SHD-DAT], Carton 7N 2521, dr. 6, 8 April 1936.

8 April 1936
Etat-Major de l'Armée
2ème Bureau

Note concerning the consequences that follow, from a military point of view, from Germany's renunciation of the Locarno Treaty

The *coup de force* of 7 March has consequences of a military order on both the Franco-German and the European levels.

We will consider the two new problems facing French military policy successively, and then envisage a solution to these problems.

I: The Franco-German problem:

Denunciation of Locarno provides Germany with:

- The offensive base necessary for a sudden attack on France and Belgium;
- The possibility to fortify its western frontier and thus to acquire the liberty of action indispensable in order to realise its political aims in central and eastern Europe.

Given that the support it might receive from its allies in the event of German aggression will be either doubtful, or insufficient and slow to arrive, France finds itself needing to meet – on its own, at any time and in the conditions of extreme speed that go with the new situation – the following requirements:

- Assuring the inviolability of its frontier;
- Being capable of intervening rapidly in Belgium and, eventually, as far as possible, holding down an important portion of German forces if the majority of the latter were to be engaged in central or eastern Europe.

I. The inviolability of our frontier requires a certain number of measures:

a) Our fortified organisation: independently of the technical improvements to be made on existing works, the following *must be completed* in the following order of priority:

As first priority:
- ○ Organisation in depth of the Sarre gap (a project that is already underway)
- ○ Completion of the fortified sector of Montmédy and cover for its left flank, between the rivers Chiers and Meuse
- ○ In lower Alsace, the defensive organisation of the Soultz gap and of the Haguenau Forest, as well as the consolidation of the Strasbourg defences

As second priority:
- ○ Reinforcement of the fortified zone between Mézières and Sedan
- ○ Reinforcement of the north and south flanks of Maubeuge
- ○ Reinforcement of the Condé-Valenciennes 'breakwater'
- ○ Construction of a barrage in the gap between the Meuse and Hirson

All of the work for these projects will be undertaken by military labour. Moreover, the defensive organisation of our right flank, in lower Alsace, would be significantly improved if we could obtain the revision of the clause of the treaty of 1815 which forbids construction of fortifications on the left bank of the Rhine in a 15 km radius around Basle. A revision of the defence of the Jura must also in time be envisaged.

b) The implementation of the essential elements of this programme must be undertaken immediately.

In this category, we must anticipated taking the following measures:

○ Improvements in the constitution of our fortress troops including notably the creation of new fortress units and the reinforcement of the first-line echelons

○ The establishment of the necessary troops on a work-footing, entailing the construction of security barracks for troops and officers

○ The establishment, forward of the position of resistance, at the most vulnerable points, of a system of surveillance, obstacles and barriers against motorised units, including the construction of light emplacements, the installation of observation posts or security detachments and the preparation of minefields.

c) Concerning the <u>larger formations earmarked for immediate intervention</u>, which will play a key role in the event of a sudden attack, their number must be increased and also, if possible, their manpower strength, along with their ability to move into action rapidly and sustain combat operations. The following measures can be envisaged to this effect:

○ Complete the planned reorganisation of our North African divisions as quickly as possible.

○ Constitute 2 new metropolitan infantry divisions by making something of the conversion of the 2 Alpine infantry divisions (27th Division at Grenoble and 29th Division at Nice) into mobile troops for the fortified sectors.

○ Station additional divisions in peacetime in lower Alsace and in the Meuse gap.

○ Restore an extra infantry regiment to the 31st Infantry Division (Montpellier) which has had only 2 regiments since the reassignment of the 80th Infantry Regiment from Narbonne to Metz.

d) We must complete, as soon as possible, the constitution of <u>our general reserve divisions</u> (at least 7 motorised infantry divisions) capable of rapid deployment and disposing of the transport necessary to get them into action with only a very short delay

e) It also matters to start constituting, in peacetime, <u>certain special elements of the general reserve</u> (battalions of armoured cars, motorised anti-tank units) that will be indispensable to enable the divisions responsible for securing the frontier to deal with the diverse situations that may occur.

f) Rapid intervention in Belgium requires the following measures:

    a) The reorganisation of our cavalry divisions: in a manner that will allow them to be placed on a combat footing on very short notice and ensure their ability to function and sustain operations with their leading echelons. This reorganisation includes the constitution of a second light mechanised division.

    b) Strengthening of the general reserve (discussed above)

    c) Constitution of covering forces with scaled down supply and support elements which will provide the units operating in Belgium with the supply structures necessary to sustain combat operations.

The different measures outlined above, whose realisation needs to be accelerated as much as possible, must not cause us to lose sight of other desirable improvements that are not of the same urgency, notably:

    ○ the modernisation of our artillery system
    ○ measures aimed at improving the quality of our conscript contingents (pre-military instruction, military and physical education of our youth)

Finally, training both the active and reserve cadres must remain our most constant preoccupations. To this effect, measures aimed at development of the training of non-commissioned officers which, for reasons of economy, were suppressed or reduced in 1935, must be re-established in their entirety and, if possible, developed further. We must equally intensify the training of our reserve cadres (both officers and non-commissioned officers).

II – The European problem

The policy of 'faits accomplis'[1] pursued by the Führer raises not just a Franco-German problem, but a European problem. We will now consider the goals of German policy, the means by which this programme might be opposed and the attitude that must be observed in the forthcoming staff talks [with Great Britain and Belgium].

A. <u>The aims of German policy</u> are none other than those of the Führer, who for the moment represents the embodiment of Germany in unprecedented conditions of prestige and unanimity. They have been clearly defined in his famous book *Mein Kampf*, whose strictures he has not renounced.

> 1) Incorporate all German-speaking territory into the Reich (Austria and by extension Czechoslovakia, the Polish corridor, Silesia, etc.).
> ii) Extend into the east of Europe into territories where the German people will find the means to live and to develop
> iii) Defeat the hereditary enemy (Erbfeind) France, before acting to the south and east by a <u>rapid and decisive</u> war; thereby achieving the isolation of Britain, an essential condition.
> iv) Obtain the colonies Germany needs as markets and as reservoirs for raw materials.

Hitler, now Head of State, has always been guided by these goals. He has also hastened to forge the instrument of war necessary to achieve them. But the military situation has changed on the Rhine as a result of French fortifications. Advised by his military chiefs, the Führer understands that if he attacks France at this point he risks a fatal war of attrition. There remains the invasion of Belgium. But this raises the problem of Britain and would range the Anglo-Saxon world against the Reich, draining the total German [war] effort without any definite gain in return.

Initial precautions must therefore be adopted:
- lacking the means to crush France quickly, and for sure, it is necessary to neutralise France and, to this end, contain it at the frontier with fortifications
- it is also necessary at all costs to reassure Britain by guaranteeing the independence of Belgium.

Then, fortified by British indifference and French impotence, without fear of an Italy absorbed on other fronts, the Reich will be able to try to achieve Mitteleuropa. In order for this plan to succeed it was necessary, first, to remilitarise the Rhineland. Hence the proclamation of integral German sovereignty over this territory – which prompted the gesture of 7 March and will dictate the responses to come.

As a result we are marching inevitably to the following situation:

A <u>sovereign</u> Germany fortifying its western frontier, <u>free to act</u> in central and eastern Europe, supported by:
- a military force superior to that of its neighbours
- a formidable industrial organisation
- a warrior spirit that is unique in Europe
- a centralised government whose authority is absolute

B. <u>To oppose the realisation of this programme</u> and thus avert the Germanisation of Europe that it will bring, there is no other means than the complete union and co-operation, on both the political and military levels, of all peoples threatened either directly or indirectly by Germany. This includes:
- The maximum development of the military forces and means of defence of each [threatened state].
- Common and immediate action by all of these states' forces against Germany in the event of German aggression against any one [of the threatened states].

The necessary agreements for the immediate and coordinated action of the forces of all powers resolved to oppose Germany must be the ultimate goal pursued unflaggingly by French policy.

I. These accords must be particularly precise when it comes to the western theatre of operations. For Great Britain, Belgium and France the necessary cooperation requires solidarity of action among their forces.
   a. Either to assure the defence of the Franco-Belgian frontier
   b. Or to use this frontier as a jumping off point for an action aimed at the Rhine.
   c. In either case the Franco-Belgian frontier must be considered the common frontier of all three powers.
   d. Moreover, we will also require the support of Italy, a guarantor of Locarno, which would be worth considerable direct or indirect military assistance.
   e. However, these circumstances [above] are not in place at the moment.

      i. British opinion, poorly informed about the dangers of the future and dominated by immediate interests, views such a course of action with repugnance.

     ii. Belgium is hesitant, taking its instructions from London, and seeks above all to escape a future general conflict.

   iii. Italy pursues its own particular objectives which absorb its activity and its resources; before aligning itself with us it legitimately demands recognition of the sacrifices it has made and the dropping of the policy of sanctions towards it. But we could never pay too high a price for the reconstitution of the Stresa Front.

II. <u>Regarding the theatre of operations in central and eastern Europe</u>: the anti-German front must extend with continuity and cohesion from the Alps to the Baltic. But, from west to east

   a. Italy, whose intervention is indispensable to prevent an Anschluss and to contribute to saving Czechoslovakia, is, as we have seen, in a situation of diplomatic expectation that it would be dangerous to prolong.

   b. The Little Entente, whose common military action is aimed uniquely against Hungary, must be reoriented against Germany, in order to provide early aid to Czechoslovakia, which is threatened with pulverisation at the outset. Yugoslavia must be protected against the German propaganda efforts that are underway there.

   c. Poland must declare its allegiance to the French alliance much more clearly than it has done so far. It must also improve relations with Czechoslovakia by settling once and for all the dispute over Teschen; it will thus become possible at the start of a war to link the Bohemian front with that around Posen by reabsorbing the German salient of Silesia.

   d. As to the USSR, its aid could only be considered limited, slow in arriving and uncertain. Its relations with Poland will have to improve so that this power [Poland] can concentrate all its forces against the Reich, even if the USSR mobilises to its rear.

The result of this rapid examination of the situation from a political point of view is that we are far from the situation we must achieve.

Success will require tenacious effort and perseverance. But it is essential to acknowledge that <u>as long as the conditions defined above are not realised, Germany will remain master of the game</u>.

The achievement of these conditions is above all of a political character and beyond the war department. But their eventual exploitation from a military point of view must, from this moment, be considered.

III. <u>General staff conversations</u> are set to take place with Britain and Belgium. It is to be hoped that analogous conversations are decided upon as soon as possible with Italy. Given the attitudes of the interested powers, these conversations can only have limited scope in relation to the scale of the problems to be resolved. They nonetheless present a real opportunity to hammer out together certain useful measures, to bring about contacts to consider the different aspects of the question, and how they can be approached, and gradually shape attitudes towards more comprehensive solutions in the future.

They must be dominated by the principle whose necessity was developed above: that the Franco-Belgian frontier is <u>the common frontier of the western powers</u>.

Once this principle is recognised the following hypotheses can be studied:

      a. <u>Germany attacks the western powers on the French and Belgian fronts</u>. Britain and France intervene immediately to aid Belgium, British forces in the region of Antwerp and French forces according to arrangements already finalised. Problems to study include: forces to be deployed by Britain, disembarkation points, lines of communication and supply offered by France, study of the eventuality of an extension of the German attack through Holland.

      b. <u>Germany attacks France, either with its main force or as a means of holding French forces down while devoting its primary effort to operations in central Europe</u>. The French army is able to ensure the defence of its own frontiers alone. But it is indispensable to maintain the principle of British-French-Belgian co-operation:

         i. On the one hand to hold down a portion of German forces on the Belgian frontier

ii. On the other hand to permit the extension of our strategic front and the development of a counter-offensive manoeuvre directed towards the Rhine.

iii. As in the previous case, the intervention of British forces must be envisaged initially in the Antwerp region, Belgian forces assuming their normal defensive deployments.

iv. Problems to study would be the same as those in the preceding hypotheses.

v. However, in the case where Belgium is not attacked, and the British do not feel able to move into Belgium (we must leave it up to them to raise the question) we should request they land all the same, in France, but stop their movement on the Belgian frontier.

vi. It would be clearly specified that we will not have need of British military aid on the Franco-German frontier. All we require is a [British] flag – for purposes of morale – <u>as far as land operations are concerned</u>.

In both of the cases envisaged above, Britain must come to our aid at sea and Belgium and Britain must both deploy their air forces to support the western front.

c. <u>Germany attacks in central Europe and covers its western frontier, remaining strictly on the defensive and manning its fortifications in the Rhineland</u>. It will be interesting to note the reactions of the British when this question is discreetly raised.

But this hypothesis is of particular interest to future conversations <u>with the Italian general staff</u>. In this eventuality in effect, although we cannot count on Belgian and, at least initially, British co-operation, the action of Italian forces in the direction of Vienna, conversely, can be envisaged.

But to confront German aggression with an appropriate system of forces including immediate action by the Little Entente in particular, the intervention of France will be imperative. In order to decide the scale of French assistance in eastern Europe in relation to the general possibilities, it is essential to determine the <u>total</u> effort France will need to furnish.

It is conceivable that, once the essential national security conditions have been met (integrity of the frontier, concentrations aimed at holding down the maximum possible German forces on the Rhine, the constitution of a force of manoeuvre to intervene in Belgium if required), the French army will retain considerable numbers of quality troops, notably in Alpine and North African divisions, that will provide the means to:

i. Intervene in central Europe with forces corresponding to the role of France in the coalition.
ii. Influence the attitude of Austria and bring about the unqualified engagement of Romanian and Yugoslav forces.

In a theatre of operations which, at an agreed stage of the war, could play a crucial role, an effort calculated with excessive parsimony will risk failing to achieve the desired objective. We must remember the case of the eastern front [in the First World War], where the Allies, after lengthy hesitation and a policy miserly reinforcement, were eventually forced to commit the equivalent of 30 divisions to obtain a decisive result. Finally, such an effort on the part of France could, sooner or later, provide a catalyst for a British intervention.

Moreover, Italy, which hesitates at the moment between different policy options, could not remain aloof from an accord in which France invested such a commitment. Without us, it is incapable of successfully defeating the course of German expansion in central Europe. Only the weight of France's armies can ensure the co-operation of the powers of the Little Entente and Czechoslovakia [sic].

Hence, in the negotiations to come with Italy, our position is a strong one, despite the events that have regrettably distanced us from this country: we will not adopt the posture of a supplicant but, on the contrary, that of the indispensable instrument of a powerful coalition ranged against Germany.

[1] Re-establishment of compulsory military service, rearmament, occupation of the demilitarised zone, and tomorrow, construction of fortifications in this zone.

COMMENTARY: THE MILITARY CONSEQUENCES FOR FRANCE OF THE END OF LOCARNO

Martin S. Alexander

This assessment presents a lengthy and substantive analysis from within the French politico-military apparatus as it reflected on the significance of Germany's 7 March 1936 unilateral remilitarisation of the Rhineland. Comprising the river's west bank and a 50-kilometre-deep slice of the east bank, the Rhineland zone had been demilitarised by the June 1919 Treaty of Versailles. The settlement was valued by France and Belgium for its provision of a protective buffer or 'glacis' to the east of their borders, making it both easier for their armies to threaten Germany's key Ruhr industrial basin and harder, or slower, for German forces to menace France and Belgium. The Rhineland's demilitarisation had been accepted by Germany's Weimar Republic, who had joined Belgium and France in signing the October 1925 Treaty of Locarno pledging the three powers not to alter these border arrangements by force.[1]

The demilitarisation was not accepted, however, by the National Socialist regime of Adolf Hitler that attained power in Germany in January 1933. Public statements by Hitler and other Nazi leaders, backed by the utterances of German army officers in private talks with the British and French military attachés in Berlin, had left no doubt that the Nazis comprehensively rejected a long-term continuation of the Rhineland's status. The demilitarisation, along with other clauses of Versailles, was condemned as an affront to German national honour and sovereignty. French, British and Belgian intelligence sources gleaned evidence from early 1935 onwards that Hitler planned to resume unfettered control over the territory when a timely opportunity presented itself. This opportunity came on 7 March 1936.

The 8 April 1936 document emanates from the *Deuxième Bureau*, the French army's intelligence department. It examines the consequences of the German coup under two headings: first, its import for immediate Franco-German defence relations and, second, its wider significance for European security.

The document's first level of analysis, addressing the remilitarisation's direct repercussions for French defence planning and force structures – the appreciation's opening three pages – sits comfortably within the traditional and well-established remit of the *Deuxième Bureau*. It was concerned chiefly with military and often highly technical aspects of the measures that the French army should take, in the department's judgement, in order to improve French security.[2] The specific challenge was to compensate for the loss of the protective 'glacis' hitherto afforded to France and Belgium by the absence of German military forces and installations in the Rhineland.[3] However, the second level of analysis – the *Deuxième Bureau*'s opinions about the general European geo-political situation – went a long way beyond the remit of a branch of the army staff. The reasons why the *Deuxième Bureau* ventured into this more controversial territory will be examined later.

First, however, it must be stressed that, as the 8 April document makes plain, Hitler's Rhineland coup caught the French army in an uncomfortable state. It was part-way through an important series of modifications to its force structure, service time, training and deployments – and was significantly disrupted in term of combat readiness, as a result, at least in the short term.[4] The loss of the Rhineland 'glacis' therefore deepened French anxieties. Jitters about France's deteriorating position and influence among third party nations all across Europe, relative to Germany's, come across throughout the document.

In part, the fears were genuine. Among French army officers and War Ministry functionaries there was an acute awareness of how slowly measures were progressing to strengthen the military forces, measures initiated back in 1933. The steps taken at that time had included the very successful conversion of one of the army's five horsed cavalry divisions into a Light Armoured Division.[5] This development was complete by September 1935, and tested to wide acclaim in large-scale army manoeuvres that month.[6] France took other steps, too, once Hitler announced the re-introduction of military conscription and his creation of an air force, the *Luftwaffe*, in March 1935. These included the retention of French conscripts with the colours for a second year of compulsory service, initiated with the autumn 1935 incorporation of recruits – something that had not yet borne fruit by spring 1936 in terms of providing a larger pool of trained army manpower.[7]

Germany's facility to station armed forces and establish aerodromes just east of the French and Belgian borders after 7 March 1936 was a further source of alarm for the French military intelligence department. This provided, as the *Deuxième Bureau* appreciation warned, the 'offensive base for a sudden attack against France and Belgium'. The coup in the Rhineland greatly enhanced the German potential to launch a sudden and surprise attack onto French and Belgian territory, provided by the presence of German military units close to the frontiers in the previously forbidden Rhineland zone.[8] Surprise attack had long been a fear haunting French defence planners. However, the proximity of German army concentration and jump-off points to the border from spring 1936 onward meant this danger was henceforth greatly magnified.

In recommending measures be instigated to counter the increased German menace, and the reduced warning time likely before any attack, the *Deuxième Bureau* was fulfilling its role in the army chain of command. Its task was to provide qualitative and quantitative evidence, and assessment derived from the data, to inform budgetary decisions, procurement choices, and operational planning by the other branches of the Army Staff and by senior officers – the army's three Deputy Chiefs of Staff and the chief of the General Staff and Commander-in-Chief designate from 1935 to 1940, General Maurice Gamelin.[9]

In the second part of the 8 April 1936 document, however, the *Deuxième Bureau* went far further than its conventional purview. Here the intelligence staff ventured analysis and recommendations not just about steps of a military-technical kind, designed to strengthen the protection of France's eastern frontiers, but also concerning much broader European geo-political measures that it felt France should take, or support, consequent on Hitler's Rhineland coup. In thus expanding its remit, the intelligence branch revealed, explicitly and implicitly, how profoundly politics and ideology infused its supposedly technocratic and impartial analyses.

Explicitly, the 8 April survey laid bare how keen the intelligence staff was to see Fascist Italy back 'within the pale', resuming its place as a partner of France and the Little Entente (Czechoslovakia, Romania and Yugoslavia) to form a barrier against German ambitions in Balkan Europe. To achieve this, the intelligence department was eager for French diplomats as soon as possible to condone, or at least overlook, Mussolini's invasion of Ethiopia in 1935.[10] Implicitly, the document's silence about the Soviet Union spoke eloquently of the detestation by conservative-minded military intelligence officers of the Franco-Soviet pact of mutual assistance. This, though one would never know it from the 8 April document, had been ratified by the French parliament just six weeks earlier, on 27 February 1936. The pact represented a cosiness with Moscow that the intelligence bureau undoubtedly hoped would fade away if, in their tabling of planning analyses and outlining of policy options, they simply ignored it.[11]

However, it was not just in terms of the politicised prisms through which military intelligence viewed the 'European problem' that the 8 April document reveals the fundamental structural shortcomings of French capacity to meet Hitler's initiatives with effective responses. In expanding its remit so far into diplomacy and politics, the army's intelligence department revealed just as much about the flaws plaguing French foreign-policy making machinery in the last years of the Third Republic (1875–1940).

At the highest level, no minutes or stenographic record were taken during meetings of the government (the 'council of ministers'). Responsibility was notoriously easy to shirk, therefore, with no record of which way individual politicians had argued, or voted, during ministerial deliberations. At lower levels of policy formulation the French bureaucrats – civilians and military alike – did not have the British habit of minuting documents with annotations, reactions and recommendations. The British *modus operandi* gives the historian at least some sight of the reception given a position paper or report as it journeyed upward from executive level functionaries or field-rank military officers to senior officials, and ultimately onto a minister's desk. Denied similar annotations, marginalia and cover-sheet commentaries on the French side, historians face a fiendishly difficult task in tracking the genesis and evolution of policy. With only the originator of a paper's name on a document, few, if any, marginal annotations and no 'seen and read' cover sheet, it is typically impossible to ascertain who was really responsible for one option, rather than another, becoming French policy.

In the world of intelligence analysis, furthermore, France had no equivalent of the British Joint Intelligence Committee (JIC), formed in the very same year, 1936, in which the *Deuxième Bureau* produced the reflections we see here on the end of Locarno. France lacked the committee machinery that might have ensured smooth coordination and rounded assessment of major geo-strategic options. It was structurally unlikely, even incapable, of producing outcomes where all the relevant diplomatic, commercial, financial and military considerations had been maturely weighed, subject to inter-departmental critique, and distilled into an agreed set of policy decisions.

To be sure, the French army, navy and air force each had a top management board known as the *Conseil Supérieur* to oversee them. These boards, however, had a remit only for their own service.[12] Above them reigned only muddle, and fierce competition for resources and influence. Most glaringly, France lacked an equivalent to Britain's CID (Committee of Imperial Defence) and its secretariat, established as far back as 1902.

In Paris, inter-service coordination took place through ad hoc meetings, when it occurred at all. The production of tri-service policy advice to the French government depended on the weak reed of, first, the High Military Committee. The then-Prime Minister André Tardieu had set this body up in 1932, but it had met infrequently and at irregular intervals thereafter. France's politico-military consideration of the best way to react to Hitler's Rhineland coup occurred in a series of hastily convoked and improvised meetings of ministers holding the armed service portfolios, along with the Chiefs of Staff, over the days immediately following remilitarisation. Two months after the *Deuxième Bureau* examined the Locarno agreement's collapse, a fresh effort was made to remedy the deficiencies in the French defence policy apparatus by establishing a Permanent Committee of National Defence, the CPDN, in June 1936. Chaired by the Minister for National Defence and War, this body was also hamstrung by the irregularity of its meetings and by its lack of a staff to ensure its decisions were implemented. Both the HCM and the CPDN were recent creations – the former giving way to the latter and the latter feeling its way in 1936 and 1937, cautiously gauging the extent of its influence and authority. Neither entity possessed the prerogative of command, and neither had the power to bang individual service heads together. Each in turn enjoyed scant success in bringing the three armed forces to arrive at a combined and agreed estimation of European security trends and present affordable, mutually supporting French defence policies.[13]

The *Deuxième Bureau* paper also makes clear the significance attached by the army intelligence officers to the opportunity presented by the Rhineland crisis to deepen British and Belgian political solidarity and improve their military coordination with France. The allusions in the later paragraphs of the document to impending military staff talks refer to Anglo-French discussions that occurred in London on 15–16 April and in Paris, with the Belgian Chief of Army Staff, General Edouard Van den Bergen, on 15 May 1936. The *Deuxième Bureau* echoed General Gamelin in seeking only a small and symbolic British deployment of ground troops on the Franco-German frontier. Its analysis reveals the hope of using a British expeditionary corps as the glue to stick together French and Belgian defensive deployments as a makeshift replacement for the loss of the Rhineland buffer.

The talks, however, ultimately disappointed French soldiers. In London, on 15–16 April, the British General Staff made clear that their assistance would not exceed two unmotorised infantry divisions in the event of European war. They also spelt out that the conversations themselves were not to be regarded in any way as connoting a political commitment to deploy British troops. This was a decision reserved to future British governments, to be taken in the light of future circumstances. The importance for French military intelligence – and for French army planners as a whole – of a British alliance shines through as clearly as does their failure to obtain one. According to one British officer who participated in the London talks, the senior French delegate, General Victor-Henri Schweisguth, frustratedly likened them to 'a football match with the referee continually blowing for offside'.[14]

Superficially, the staff talks with the Belgians went better. They led to a tour in July 1936 by Schweisguth and other French officers of sectors inside Belgium where joint defensive operations might be staged in conjunction with advancing French units, in the event of a German invasion. But appearances were deceptive. Belgium's stance was veering away from alignment with France and towards a form of neutrality that was characterised by the monarch, King Leopold III, as 'a policy of independence' in a speech of 14 October 1936 that severely attenuated Franco-Belgian strategic cooperation in practice, and killed it off in public.[15]

Bereft, then, of the mechanism for a centralised and cross-departmental analysis, it is no surprise that French governments struggled to hammer out agreed and realistic responses to Hitler's expansionism. The latter had the geo-strategic initiative, and retained it. He was highly opportunistic and tactically astute. His diplomatic coups – whether the remilitarisation of the Rhineland in 1936, the Anschluss with Austria and seizure of the Sudetenland from Czechoslovakia in 1938, or the annexation of Bohemia-Moravia in March 1939, kept his hands firmly on the reins. He remained, in the words of the *Deuxième Bureau* document here, the 'master of the game'. By contrast, French analysis remained excessively academic, while French decision-making foundered on inadequately resourced and insufficiently respected machinery for the higher direction of national security policy.

Exacerbating these problems was the typically short life of French governments of the Third Republic – each averaging some six months in office – and the 'revolving doors' situation this created among politicians handed the key portfolios for foreign and security policy. Indeed, the document of 8 April 1936 was circulated less than three weeks before the first of the two-round French parliamentary elections. These, with polling taking place on 26 April and 3 May, resulted in victory for a centre-left coalition, the Popular Front. Indeed, after what was a highly-charged and at times unsavoury campaign, the result saw Léon Blum, the country's first prime minister from the Socialist Party, take office in early June on a platform of public spending, improved welfare provision and a reduction in the working week. Throughout the weeks of electioneering the crucial political battleground consisted of the rival social and economic plans to haul France out of the Depression.[16] Against this backdrop, with the transfer of parliamentary control from the centre-right to the Popular Front always on the cards, French politicians gave foreign and strategic affairs even less attention than usual in Spring 1936.

Instead of decisive action to pick up policy suggestions made in the 8 April *Deuxième Bureau* paper, the feeble high-level direction of government and the lack of coordination bred departmental parochialism, bureaucratic rivalries and unchecked institutional self-interest. In the world of the parliamentary and ministerial merry-go-round, the senior figures within the armed services – and especially the army – represented continuity. With that continuity came authority. And this meant that, as in this 8 April *tour d'horizon* of the condition of European international relations, the articulation of policy recommendations could be as forceful as its perspective was lop-sided.

It would be to exaggerate – though not by very much – to say that a vacuum existed in French foreign and strategic policy-making in the Spring of 1936. The political class had its plate full in a febrile atmosphere whipped up by election sloganeering – especially centre-right deputies fighting to retain their seats.[17] Unsurprisingly, then, the uniformed bureaucrats of the French armed services exercised greater influence than ever in 1936. And as the second half of the 8 April document goes on to reveal, they enjoyed extensive latitude – which they did not hesitate to use – to tender advice about foreign policy matters going well beyond the traditional remit of an army intelligence department.[18]

Therefore, one returns to the question of France's defence and security decision-making apparatus. The provenance of the document reviewed here is the army's intelligence department. Its text contains not a single mention of the existence of parallel but emphatically separate intelligence branches in the French air force and the French navy. One is forcefully struck by the absence of mechanisms to generate an integrated or consolidated overall intelligence appreciation. The presentation here is the voice of a dominant single service – one very sure of itself. It is strongly marked by that vigorous tone of omniscience, even arrogance, that imbued the utterances of successive senior army leaders after 1919, from Marshal Foch and Marshal Pétain to General Weygand and General Gamelin – and which prevailed till the smashing of the army's prestige in the defeat of 1940. Yet till discredited by that debacle, the French army remained 'first among equals' in the wider French service establishment. For confirmation one need look no further than the automaticity with which Edouard Daladier, the Minister for National Defence and War, conferred on Gamelin, head of the land forces, the role of Chief of National Defence Staff when this new post was established in January 1938.[19]

As in 1940, so here in the Spring of 1936, France possessed a military organisation that was far stronger in analysing hypotheses than it was at building bureaucratic and political coalitions to implement timely and effective responses to the threats that intelligence agencies identified. Indeed, *hypothèse* was a favourite and oft-recurring word in documents drafted in the Quai d'Orsay, the French Foreign Ministry, as well as in the contingency plans formulated by the military staffs in this era. It was a word redolent of the tendency that was so characteristic of French policy circles: to review all the options, and then review them again, but settle and act upon none. Many writers have censured Gamelin for being much stronger at analysis than action.[20] This, however, is merely to personalise what was in fact a far more pervasive problem, one that was essentially cultural in nature. For the stricture, this document very strongly suggests, is one that can be just as pertinently and damagingly levelled at France's entire inter-war defence and intelligence communities.

Notes

Overview: A look at French intelligence machinery in 1936

Peter Jackson

1   For excellent discussions of these issues see, among many others, Stephen Schuker, 'The Rhineland Question: West European Security at the Paris Peace Conference', in E. Glaser, G. Feldman and M. Boemke (eds), *Treaty of Versailles: A Reassessment after 75 Years* (Cambridge, Cambridge University Press, 1998), pp. 275–312; Gaynor Johnson (ed.), *Locarno Revisited: European Diplomacy, 1920–1929* (London, Routledge, 2004) and Zara Steiner, *The Lights that Failed: European International History, 1919–1933* (Oxford, Oxford University Press, 2005), pp. 45–79, 349–456. On the centrality of Locarno to French foreign and defence policy, see Peter Jackson, 'France', in R. Boyce and J. Maiolo (eds), *The Origins of World War Two: The Debate Continues* (London: Palgrave, 2003), especially pp. 86–98.

2   On working with intelligence and intelligence-related archival material in France, see three extremely important and useful essays by Sébastien Laurent, 'Le renseignement de 1860 à nos jours: état des sources militaires', *Revue historique des armées*, 4 (2002), pp. 97–110; Laurent, 'Faire l'histoire du renseignement', and in S. Laurent (ed.), *Archives « secrètes », secrets d'archives ? Le travail de l'historien et de l'archiviste sur les archives sensibles* (Paris: Éditions du CNRS, 2003), pp. 211–20 and Laurent, 'Les archives sensibles. Du droit et des pratiques', in F. Rouquet (ed.), *L'exploitation scientifique des archives* (Rennes: Éditions Apogée, 2005), pp. 13–31.

3   Where not otherwise stated, the following section on the organisation of French intelligence is drawn from Sébastien Laurent, 'Aux « services » des Républiques: esquisse d'une histoire politique des services de renseignements (XIXe-XXe siècles)', in *Un professeur en République. Mélanges en l'honneur de Serge Berstein* (Paris: Fayard, 2006), pp. 272–8; Robert Young, 'French Military Intelligence and Nazi Germany 1938–1939', in E. May (ed.), *Knowing One's Enemies: Intelligence Assessment before the Two World Wars* (Cambridge, MA: Harvard University Press, 1984), pp. 271–309; Andrew Barros, 'Le Deuxième Bureau dans les années 1920; l'impact de la guerre totale sur les renseignements', in Frédéric Guelton and Abdil Bicer, *Naissance et évolution du renseignment dans l'espace Européen* (Vincennes: Service Historique de la Défense, 2006), pp. 189–210; Martin Alexander, 'Did the Deuxième Bureau Work? The Role of Intelligence in French Policy and Strategy, 1919–1939', *Intelligence and National Security*, 6/2 (1991), pp. 293–333, and especially Peter Jackson, *France and the Nazi Menace: Intelligence and Policy Making, 1933–1939* (Oxford: Oxford University Press, 2000), pp. 11–44. A comprehensive discussion of the evolution of France's intelligence services between the two world wars awaits the publication of Olivier Forcade's *La République espionne: Les services spéciaux militaires, le renseignement et l'Etat en France 1919–1939* (Paris: Editions Nouveau monde, forthcoming).

4   The Air Ministry did not possess a human intelligence organisation of its own. Instead a *Section Aéronautique* within the SR staffed by two officers of the air force *Deuxième Bureau* was responsible for the synthesis of secret information on the German air force provided by the espionage network of the SR. The naval staff possessed its own secret intelligence branch (Section R), which was much smaller than the army SR.

5   The activities of the SCR were dominated by counter-espionage work against Germany and counter-espionage and counter-subversion against Soviet Russia. Counter-espionage against Germany has been neglected in the existing literature. On the challenge posed by the USSR, see, above all, Georges Vidal, *La Grande Illusion: Le Parti communiste français et la Défense national à l'époque du Front Populaire* (Lyon: Presses Universitaires de Lyon, 2006).

6 SHD-DAT, 7N 666, 'Instruction sur le service des attachés militaires à étrangère', November 1903.
7 Cf. Jean-Baptise Duroselle, *Tout empire périra* (Paris: Seuil, 1984), pp. 283–7. On the role of French service attachés, see Maurice Vaïsse, 'L'évolution de la fonction d'attaché militaire en France au XXe siècle', *Relations Internationales*, 32 (1982): 507–24; M. Alexander, 'Perspectives on intra-alliance intelligence', *Intelligence and National Security*, 13/1 (1998): 4–7, and Jackson, *France and the Nazi Menace*, pp. 15–17. On the origins of the service attaché, see Maureen O'Connor, 'Sanctioned Spying: The Development of the Military Attaché in the Nineteenth Century', in P. Jackson and J. Siegel (eds), *Intelligence and Statecraft: The Use and Limits of Intelligence in International Society* (Westport, CT: Praeger, 2005), pp. 87–108.
8 On this issue see also Sébastien Laurent, 'Le service secret de l'État (1870–1945): La part des militaires', in M-O. Baruch and V. Duclert (eds), *Serviteurs de l'État: Une histoire politique de l'administration française 1875–1945* (Paris: La Découverte, 2000), pp. 279–95.
9 Jackson, *France and the Nazi Menace*, pp. 29–30 and 367–8.
10 See Jackson, *France and the Nazi Menace*, pp. 28–31.
11 On the network of SR stations, see SHD-DAT, 7N 2485–3, 'Organisation et fonctionnement des Services Spéciaux', October 1933; SHD-DAT, 7N 2486–1, 'Liste des postes SR en temps de paix', October 1929. On SR operatives posted abroad as attachés see SHD-DAT, *Fonds Moscou*, carton 152, dossier 1428, 'Officiers de renseignements adjoints aux attachés militaires', 27 March 1933. Before 1938, the Marseilles station was referred to as the *Section d'Etudes Régionales* (SER).
12 Jackson, *France and the Nazi Menace*, pp. 26–7.
13 The CSDN was the rough equivalent of the British Committee of Imperial Defence. On its structure and functions, see Frédéric Guelton, 'Les hautes instances de la Défense nationale sous la Troisième République', in O. Forcade, P. Vial and E. Duhamel (eds), *Militaires en république, 1870–1962: Les officiers, le pouvoir et la vie publique en France* (Paris: Publications de la Sorbonne, 1999), pp. 54–7 and Talbot Imlay, 'French Industrial and Economic Preparations for War between the Two World Wars: The Role of Institutions', forthcoming, in *War in History*, 15/1 (2008). On the birth of French economic intelligence, see Michaël Bourlet, 'La Section économiques du 2e bureau de l'état-major de l'armée pendant la Premiere Guerre mondiale', in Guelton and Bicer (eds), *Naissance et évolution du renseignement*, pp. 117–35.
14 This misperception is challenged effectively by Alexander in 'Did the Deuxième Bureau Work?', pp. 295–9.
15 This paragraph is based on a systematic survey of eighteen 'Dossiers du personnel' and 'États de service' held in the archives of the French army in Vincennes [SHD-DAT, series J^x and 13Y^d] and the excellent discussions of the structure and functioning of the army staff and High Command in Henry Dutailly, *Les Problèmes de l'armée de terre française, 1935–1939* (Vincennes: Imprimerie Nationale, 1980), pp. 26–38; Jean-Baptiste Duroselle, *Politique étrangère de la France, 1932–1939: La decadence* (Paris: Seuil, 1979), pp. 254–62, and Martin Alexander, *The Republic in Danger: General Maurice Gamelin and the Politics of French Defence, 1933–1940* (Cambridge: Cambridge University Press, 1993), pp. 24–35, 100–9.
16 The following paragraph is based on information obtained from General Gauché's personal dossier: SHD-DAT, 1280^G/4, 'État de Services du Général Maurice Gauché'; access to this dossier is restricted but possible with perseverance.
17 SHD-DAT, 1280^G/4, 'État de Services du Général Maurice Gauché'.
18 PRO, FO 371, 21668, C8975/65/18. See also the view of the British ambassador to Paris, Sir Eric Phipps in the Churchill College Archives, Cambridge, Sir Eric Phipps Papers, 1/16 and Maj. Gen. Kenneth Strong, *Men of Intelligence* (London: Cassell, 1970), pp. 36–7. For the opinion of the chief of Czechoslovak intelligence, see Frantisek Moravec, *Master of Spies* (London: Sphere, 1981), p. 37.

19   SHD-DAT, J^x 237, 5ème série, 'État des Services de Henri Charles Roux'.
20   SHD-DAT, 7N 2702, Paul-Boncour and Gamelin to the Foreign Ministry, 26 June 1932.
21   These bulletins are in SHD-DAT, cartons 7N 2512–2515.
22   Jackson, *France and the Nazi Menace*, pp. 41–3.
23   For a detailed analysis of the performance of French intelligence in assessing German short-, medium- and long-term intentions, see my *France and the Nazi Menace*, passim.
24   Olivier Forcade, 'Renseignement et histoire militaire: État des lieux', in P. Lacoste (ed.), *Le Renseignement à la française* (Paris: Economica, 1998), pp. 49–78 and Laurent, 'Aux « services » des Républiques'.
25   On the performance of the intelligence services during the First World War, see Olivier Lahaie, *Renseignement et services de renseignements en France pendant la guerre de 1914–1918*, a *thèse de doctorat* supervised by G.-H. Soutou, Université de Paris-Sorbonne, June 2006, 4 volumes with annexes.
26   For a more in-depth discussion, see my, 'La politisation du renseignement en France 1933–1939', in G.-H. Soutou, J. Frémeaux, and O. Forcade (eds), *L'exploitation du renseignement* (Paris: Economica, 2001), pp. 63–81, and *France and the Nazi Menace*, esp. pp. 141–59 and 389–90.
27   Jackson, *France and the Nazi Menace*, pp. 37–9; Duroselle, *La decadence*, p. 154 and Anthony Adamthwaite, 'The French Government Machine in the Approach to the Second World War', in H. Shamir (ed.), *France and Germany in an Age of Crisis, 1900–1960* (Leiden: Brill, 1990), pp. 203–13.
28   On the role of the key inter-ministerial organs responsible for national defence in France between the wars, see the excellent summary and analysis by Guelton in 'Les hautes instances de la Défense nationale', pp. 53–63.
29   Deputy-Chief of the Deuxième Bureau, Lt. Col Marie-Louis Koeltz observed in 1929 that what France needed was an inter-ministerial assessment organ that would function as 'a sort of Deuxième Bureau of the Premier's office'. He observed that the creation of such an organ was impossible 'in the face of rivalries between ministries'. See SHD-DAT, 7N 2501, dr. 1, 'Rôle et functions du 2ème Bureau en temps de paix', 15 August 1929. SR chief Rivet also supported the idea: see Jackson, *France and the Nazi Menace*, pp. 32–43.
30   This point is also stressed by Martin Alexander in 'Did the Deuxième Bureau Work?', pp. 310–11. On the JIC during this period, see Andrew, *Secret Service*, pp. 421, 483–4. On the importance of 'all source analysis', see especially Herman, *Intelligence Power*, pp. 101–13.
31   SHD-DAT, *Fonds Paul Paillole*, 1K 545, Carton 1, dr. 3, 'Rapports du SR avec le ministre', 1941. Intelligence veterans Henri Navarre and Paul Paillole endorsed this criticism, see especially Henri Navarre, *Le temps des vérités* (Paris: Plon, 1979) p. 45, and Paillole, *Services Spéciaux, 1935–1945*, (Paris: Robert Laffont, 1975) esp. pp. 67–73. Historians who have accepted their claims include Douglas Porch, *French Secret Services: Their History from the Dreyfus Affair to the Gulf War* (New York: Farrar, Straus and Giroux, 1995), pp. 134–73, and Anthony Adamthwaite, *Grandeur and Misery: France's Bid for Power in Europe, 1914–1918* (London: Arnold, 1995), pp. 157–8.
32   Jackson, *France and the Nazi Menace*, esp. pp. 143–60.
33   There are references to twenty-four separate meetings between Rivet and the chiefs of Daladier's military cabinet and seventeen meetings with the heads of the premier's civilian cabinet in Rivet's diary from June 1936 to March 1939.
34   On this question, see also Alexander, 'Did the Deuxième Bureau work?', pp. 310–15.
35   On attitudes within the Foreign Ministry at this juncture, see especially the excellent discussion in Duroselle, *La decadence*, pp. 269–89. There are indications that this attitude persists within the Quai d'Orsay. See the reflections of the eminent former diplomat and ambassador Guy Georgy, 'La diplomatie française et le renseignement',

in P. Lacoste (ed.), *Le renseignement à la française* (Paris: Economica, 1998), pp. 509–16.

36   This important point is emphasised repeatedly the literature on French politics and policy-making at this juncture. See, among many others, Stephen Schuker, 'France and the Remilitarisation of the Rhineland, 1936', *French Historical Studies*, 14 (1986), pp. 299–338; Duroselle, *La decadence*, pp. 154–7, 172–4, and Robert Young, *In Command of France: Foreign Policy and Military Planning, 1933–1940* (Cambridge, MA: Harvard University Press, 1978), pp. 120–5.

37   Alexander, this volume, p. 85.

38   SHD-DAT, 14N 35, *Deuxième Bureau* studies 'Conditions de paix' undated but certainly mid to late-August 1916 and 'Conditions de paix – le statut de l'Allemagne', October 1916. For detailed analyses, see David Stevenson, *French War Aims against Germany, 1914–1919* (Oxford: Oxford University Press, 1982), pp. 42–4 and Georges-Henri Soutou, 'La France et les Marches de l'Est, 1914–1919), *Revue Historique*, 528 (1978): 355–7.

39   Peter Jackson, 'France and the Problems of Security and Disarmament after the First World War', *Journal of Strategic Studies*, 29/2 (2006): 247–80; Andrew Barros, 'Les dangers du sport et de l'éducation physique. Une évaluation des forces allemandes par le Deuxième Bureau français (1919–1928)', *Guerres mondiales et conflits contemporains*, 210 (2003): 113–23, and Andrew Webster, 'Anglo-French Relations and the Problems of Disarmament and Security', PhD, University of Cambridge, 2001, especially pp. 88–107 and 222–31.

40   Jackson, *France and the Nazi Menace*, pp. 169–70. The best analysis of French policy at this juncture remains Schuker, 'France and the Remilitarisation of the Rhineland'.

41   Jackson, *France and the Nazi Menace*, pp. 169–77 and Olivier Forcade and Sébastien Laurent, *Secrets d'État: pouvoirs et renseignement dans le monde contemporain* (Paris: Armand Colin, 2005), pp. 132–5.

42   Alexander, this volume, p. 82.

43   Peter Jackson, 'Stratégie et idéologie: le haut commandement français et la guerre civile espagnole', *Guerres Mondiales et Conflits Contemporains*, 199 (2001): 111–33.

Commentary: The military consequences for France of the end of Locarno

Martin S. Alexander

1   The Locarno agreement was underwritten by Great Britain and Italy, two major European powers that had no land border with Germany. It should be noted that, at the time of its negotiation, Locarno was at least as much a protection for Germany, whose armaments were then still severely restricted by other clauses of Versailles, as it was an insurance for France and Belgium. See Gaynor Johnson (ed.), *Locarno Revisited: European Diplomacy, 1920–1929* (London and New York: Routledge, 2004); also Jon Jacobsen, *Locarno Diplomacy. Germany and the West, 1925–1929* (Princeton, NJ: Princeton University Press, 1972); Douglas Johnson, 'The Locarno Treaties', in Neville Waites (ed.), *Troubled Neighbours: Franco-British Relations in the Twentieth Century* (London: Weidenfeld & Nicolson, 1971), pp. 100–24.

2   See Martin S. Alexander, 'Did the Deuxième Bureau Work? The Role of Intelligence in French Defence Policy and Strategy, 1919–1939', *Intelligence and National Security*, 6/2 (1991), pp. 293–333.

3   For a perceptive general study of the Spring 1936 coup and the responses of the Locarno signatory powers (France, Belgium, Britain, Italy and Germany), see James T. Emmerson, *The Rhineland Crisis, 7 March 1936: A Study in Multilateral Diplomacy* (London: Maurice Temple Smith, 1977). Cf. Stephen A. Schuker, 'France and the

Remilitarization of the Rhineland, 1936', *French Historical Studies*, 14/3 (Spring 1986), pp. 299–338.

4   See Martin S. Alexander, *The Republic in Danger: General Maurice Gamelin and the Politics of French Defence, 1933–1940* (Cambridge: Cambridge University Press, 1993), pp. 35–74.

5   In French parlance, a DLM (*Division Légère Mécanique*), it was equipped with an array of medium tanks, armoured cars and tracked carriers for the integral infantry or 'mechanised dragoons'. The 1st DLM, entrusted to the command of a pioneering enthusiast of mechanisation, General Jean Flavigny, was principally an experimental unit, a living laboratory for mechanised and combined-arms manoeuvres, in the first three years of its existence. It was the only division-sized armoured unit in the French army at the time of Hitler's Rhineland coup.

6   The French Superior War Council (*Conseil Supérieur de la Guerre* or CSG) – the army's top management board – decided to form a second Light Armoured Division at its meeting on 29 April 1936, resisting Gamelin's call for an expansion of this force to three, not just two, divisions. SHD (Service Historique de la Défense), Vincennes, Département de Terre (Archives): Carton 1N22, Conseil Supérieur de la Guerre, vol. XVII, p. 86; General Maurice-Gustave Gamelin, *Servir* (Paris: Plon, 3 vols, 1946–47), vol. II: *Le Prologue du Drame (1930–août 1939)*, pp. 187–8.

7   See Henry Dutailly, *Les Problèmes de l'Armée de Terre française, 1935–1939* (Paris: Imprimerie nationale, 1980), pp. 207–30.

8   For a critical analysis of earlier French concerns on this score, see Robert J. Young, 'L'Attaque brusquée and its use as myth in interwar France', *Historical Reflections/ Réflexions historiques*, 8/1 (Spring 1981), pp. 93–113.

9   The French army's high-level job specifications at this time assigned one deputy chief of staff the responsibility for oversight of intelligence and relations with foreign armies, whilst a second had charge of recruits, training and operational planning, the third being tasked with the quartermaster's role (stores, supplies and military transport).

10   See Alexander, *The Republic in Danger*, pp. 52–5, 72–6; Robert J. Young, 'French Military Intelligence and the Franco-Italian Alliance, 1933–1939', *The Historical Journal*, 28/1 (March 1985), pp. 143–68; Young, 'Soldiers and Diplomats: The French Embassy and Franco-Italian Relations, 1935–36', *Journal of Strategic Studies*, 7/1 (March 1984), pp. 74–91; and more generally Franklin D. Laurens, *France and the Italo-Ethiopian Crisis, 1935–1936* (The Hague: Mouton, 1967).

11   See Alexander, *The Republic in Danger*, pp. 290–303; and more generally, William Evans Scott, *Alliance against Hitler: The Franco-Soviet Pact* (Durham, NC: Duke University Press, 1963).

12   The Superior War Council for the French army had been established in 1872, one of several reform measures instigated after the debacle of the Franco-Prussian War. The Superior Council of the Navy followed in December 1889, but the Superior Air Council was a very recent addition, having been constituted only in 1933. Allan Mitchell, 'Thiers, MacMahon and the Conseil Supérieur de la Guerre', *French Historical Studies*, 7/2 (Fall 1969), pp. 232–52; Mitchell, '"A Situation of Inferiority": French Military Reorganisation after the Defeat of 1870', *American Historical Review*, 86/1 (Feb. 1981): 49–62; Mitchell, 'The Freycinet reforms and the French Army, 1888–1893', *Journal of Strategic Studies*, 4/1 (March 1981), pp. 19–28; and information kindly supplied by M. Jean-Baptiste Bruneau, Navy Department, SHD, Vincennes.

13   The HCM and CPDN minutes and papers are found in SHD (Département de Terre) archives: Cartons 2N19–2N21.

14   General Sir Ronald Adam, correspondence with Martin S. Alexander, 15 March 1979; Schweisguth was, from early 1935 to August 1937, the French Deputy Chief of Army Staff responsible for intelligence and liaison with foreign armies. The French record

of the Franco-British talks may be found, with a scholarly commentary, in André Reussner, *Les Conversations franco-britanniques d'Etat-major, 1935–1939* (Vincennes: Publications du Service Historique de la Marine, 1969), pp. 151–60.

15 Martin S. Alexander, 'In Lieu of Alliance: The French General Staff's Secret Cooperation with Neutral Belgium, 1936–1940', *Journal of Strategic Studies*, 14/4 (December 1991), pp. 413–27; and [no author], *Les relations militaires franco-belges. Mars 1936 au 10 Mai 1940, Travaux d'un colloque d'historiens belges et français* (Paris: Imprimerie nationale, 1968).

16 Andrew W.H. Shennan, 'The Parliamentary Opposition to the Front Populaire and the elections of 1936', *The Historical Journal*, 27/3 (1984), pp. 677–95; Julian Jackson, *The Politics of Depression in France, 1932–1936* (Cambridge: Cambridge University Press, 1985); Julian Jackson, *The Popular Front in France: Defending Democracy, 1934–1938* (Cambridge: Cambridge University Press, 1988).

17 One parliamentary defence specialist who did lose his seat in spring 1936 was Jean Fabry, a retired colonel who had been severely disabled by wounds received in 1915, but who had risen to chair the Chamber of Deputies army select committee in the parliament elected in Spring 1932, before becoming Minister of War in 1935. He regained a parliamentary platform from which to campaign for stronger defence and reconciliation with Italy when he won a seat in the Senate in the autumn of 1936.

18 For a full-scale examination of the multiple ways in which French intelligence gathering, intelligence analysis and policy recommendations became politicised in this period, see Peter Jackson, *France and the Nazi Menace: Intelligence and Policy-Making, 1933–1939* (Oxford: Oxford University Press, 2000).

19 Once again, however, the reform was half-hearted: Gamelin's new title and much expanded responsibility gave him 'coordination' authority but not command over the professional chiefs of the air force, navy and colonial forces, and nor was he given a National Defence staff to assist him in his broader mission.

20 See, for instance, the essay 'General Gamelin or How to Lose', in A.J.P. Taylor, *From Napoleon to Stalin: Comments on European History* (London: The Right Book Club, 1950), pp. 144–9; cf. A.J. Liebling, *The Road Back to Paris* (New York: Paragon, 1988), pp. 25–33.

4　The creation of XX Committee, 1940

Len Scott and John Ferris

OVERVIEW: DECEPTION AND DOUBLE CROSS

Len Scott

> Oh, what a tangled web we weave when first we practise to deceive.
> (Sir Walter Scott)

The tangled webs of deception in war and statecraft can be traced back into ancient history, mythology and scripture – from when a Greek warrior posed as a deserter to lead the Wooden Horse into the city of Troy[1] to when Gideon, sometime leader of the Tribe of Israel, used deception to defeat the Midianites.[2] Modern warfare and the establishment of permanent intelligence organisations proffered new challenges and opportunities for the conduct of what became known as strategic deception. Sir Michael Howard describes this as 'the deception of the enemy High Command as distinct from his forces in the field'.[3] Such terminology underlines the distinctive military aspect to the subject, though deception in peacetime is an often integral part of intelligence operations. Among the best examples of strategic deception are those wartime operations where historians have gained access to relevant records (and in some cases to archives of the various belligerents involved).

Learning about deception, however, often presents great challenges. One recent study of Egyptian deception in the 1973 Arab–Israeli war, for example, emphasised that very little had emerged from Egyptian records on the planning and execution of Arab deception.[4] Others have shown a greater willingness to disclose their endeavours. While it took decades to learn of British deception in the Second World War, authoritative accounts have appeared of the role of deception in the American-led war against Iraq in 1990–91.[5] The Second World War has nevertheless provided the most fertile ground for understanding the central challenges and issues in the conduct and management of deception operations. In particular, studies of British strategic deception against Germany in the Second World War have demonstrated the crucial importance of the organisation of intelligence as well as the relationship between intelligence services and decision-makers.

These studies include examples of operations run over years and which required the plausibility of the intelligence to be maintained over time. Sustaining credibility presented considerable challenges. If only false or misleading information was provided, then over time the deception would be undermined. This is a generic problem in deception operations. Some real intelligence is necessary to sustain and nurture the credibility of the source. This is sometimes called 'chicken feed'. One of the great successes of the British double cross system was the manner in which the real was interwoven with the false. At the heart of this enterprise was the Twenty Committee (which through its Roman numerals XX generated the term double cross). It was the Twenty Committee that successfully co-ordinated British efforts, while MI5 case officers were at the heart of the operation. Notwithstanding turf battles between MI5 and SIS, inter-departmental co-ordination was crucial and in contrast to the lack of co-ordination and co-operation on the German side.[6]

One of the most striking examples of how real intelligence was woven into the fabric of deceit concerns the deception operation in support of the invasion of Normandy in 1944. Michael Howard describes *Operation Fortitude* as 'perhaps the most complex and successful deception in the entire history of war'.[7] One element in this was the work of Agent Garbo, a Spanish citizen, Juan Pujol Garcia, who ostensibly ran a network of agents in Britain for the *Abwehr* (German Military Intelligence). In reality he was one of three key double agents used by British intelligence to deceive the Germans about where and when the second front would be launched, and involved his warning that the invasion of France would begin on 6 June 1944.[8] MI5 ensured that the message was sent with the invasion fleet at sea, giving the Germans no time to make use of the warning.[9] The accuracy of the information nevertheless strengthened the credibility of the source who then supplied false intelligence to indicate that the Normandy landings were a feint for the main assault in the Pas de Calais. German armoured divisions were held back from the battle to face an attack that never came (from an army that never existed). Winston Churchill famously remarked to Josef Stalin in 1943 that, 'In wartime, truth is so precious that she should always be attended by a bodyguard of lies.'[10] In fact, Churchill was surely wrong: it is the lie that is so precious that she (or he) should always be attended by a bodyguard of truth.

The issue of where the allies would land in France also illustrates a particular hazard in deception. Exposure of the deception can reveal the real intent. And the costs of exposure can outweigh the benefits of success. Another documented British example concerned Operation Mincemeat, the deception for the invasion of Sicily in 1943. This was designed to convince the Germans and Italians that the allies were planning to attack Greece and Crete and later Sardinia, rather than Sicily. There was the risk that if the deception was exposed, it could be completely counter-productive. Instead of pointing away from Sicily it would in fact point toward Sicily. When this was explained to Churchill, who was required to give final approval to the plan, his reply was that it did not matter: 'Anybody but a damn fool would know it is Sicily.'[11] Nevertheless this illustrates the double-edged nature of deception.

The conduct of deception is inextricably bound up with intelligence and counter-intelligence. To conduct successful deception operations it is necessary to understand how the enemy gathers and uses intelligence and to know whether the deception is believed. Feedback is crucial. In the Second World War this was provided for the British by *Ultra* – British signals intelligence that gave effective feedback on what the *Abwehr*, the High Command, and on occasions Hitler, believed. Even more crucial is security. If the Germans had run one effective agent within the British government who knew of double cross, the whole operation could have been blown. Equally, as the Soviets had agents from within the British government who knew of the XX system, German penetration of Soviet intelligence could also have blown the efforts of the British.[12]

Deception and double cross-style operations present major challenges to the conduct of espionage. It is now clear, for example, that senior Soviet officials gave serious consideration to whether Soviet espionage on the Manhattan Project was the victim of allied deception. Churchill and Roosevelt had taken the decision not to tell Stalin about the atomic bomb until it was ready to be used. So the only source of information for the Soviets was their 'atomic spies'. For the Soviet Union to embark on atomic weapons development meant committing huge resources (and scientific genius) at a time when there was more immediate and tangible need for these. From their agents within the British government, Soviet authorities were aware of allied strategic deception against the Germans. So what the atomic bomb spies were telling the Soviet authorities had to be evaluated with care. And we now know, from Soviet records and memoirs, that the man who was eventually placed in charge of the Soviet atom bomb project, Lavrenti Beria (the feared head of the NKVD), harboured suspicions that information on the allied atomic effort was disinformation, and he warned his officers that if it was, they would be for the 'cellars' (the torture and execution chambers deep in Lubyanka).[13] The Soviet atomic project remained on a relatively small scale until the explosion of the bomb at Hiroshima. From then on the work of the atomic spies assumed a greater significance.

Similarly, in the 1960s, senior CIA counter-intelligence officials came to believe that the KGB was mounting a major campaign of strategic deception, and the head of CIA Counterintelligence, James Angleton, embraced the idea that the Sino-Soviet split represented Soviet deception rather than a crucial development in world politics.[14] The idea that significant events and changes in global politics are the results of carefully orchestrated intelligence operations is the stuff of conspiracy theory. Yet the history of deception poses unavoidable and sometimes uncomfortable challenges to our understanding. The relevance of deception to contemporary concerns and issues remains apparent. Most recently it has been claimed that the CIA mounted a deception operation against the Iranians which involved transferring scientific knowledge about the construction of an atomic device.[15] The operation apparently involved providing the Iranians with information they already had but with flawed blueprints that would help sabotage their efforts. However, it has been suggested that the ploy may have been counter-productive and 'the chicken feed' potentially important. Why officials involved in the plan have disclosed its existence is unclear. Whether we are learning of a deception or are victims of one remains to be seen. What is clear is that tangled webs of deceit remain part of the fabric of contemporary global politics.

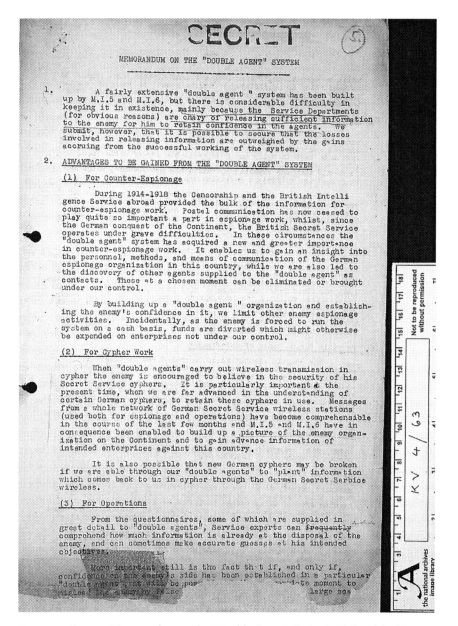

SECRET

MEMORANDUM ON THE "DOUBLE AGENT" SYSTEM

1.   A fairly extensive "double agent " system has been built
up by M.I.5 and M.I.6, but there is considerable difficulty in
keeping it in existence, mainly because the Service Departments
(for obvious reasons) are chary of releasing sufficient information
to the enemy for him to retain confidence in the agents. We
submit, however, that it is possible to secure that the losses
involved in releasing information are outweighed by the gains
accruing from the successful working of the system.

2. ADVANTAGES TO BE GAINED FROM THE "DOUBLE AGENT" SYSTEM

    (1) For Counter-Espionage

         During 1914-1918 the Censorship and the British Intelli
gence Service abroad provided the bulk of the information for
counter-espionage work. Postal communication has now ceased to
play quite so important a part in espionage work, whilst, since
the German conquest of the Continent, the British Secret Service
operates under grave difficulties. In these circumstances the
"double agent" system has acquired a new and greater importance
in counter-espionage work. It enables us to gain an insight into
the personnel, methods, and means of communication of the German
espionage organization in this country, while we are also led to
the discovery of other agents supplied to the "double agent" as
contacts.   These at a chosen moment can be eliminated or brought
under our control.

         By building up a "double agent " organization and establish-
ing the enemy's confidence in it, we limit other enemy espionage
activities. Incidentally, as the enemy is forced to run the
system on a cash basis, funds are diverted which might otherwise
be expended on enterprises not under our control.

    (2) For Cypher Work

         When "double agents" carry out wireless transmission in
cypher the enemy is encouraged to believe in the security of his
Secret Service cyphers. It is particularly important at the
present time, when we are far advanced in the understanding of
certain German cyphers, to retain these cyphers in use. Messages
from a whole network of German Secret Service wireless stations
(used both for espionage and operations) have become comprehensible
in the course of the last few months and M.I.5 and M.I.6 have in
consequence been enabled to build up a picture of the enemy organization on the Continent and to gain advance information of
intended enterprises against this country.

         It is also possible that new German cyphers may be broken
if we are able through our "double agents" to "plant" information
which comes back to us in cypher through the German Secret Serbice
wireless.

    (3) For Operations

         From the questionnaires, some of which are supplied in
great detail to "double agents", Service experts can frequently
comprehend how much information is already at the disposal of the
enemy, and can sometimes make accurate guesses at his intended
objectives.

         More important still is the fact that if, and only if,
confidence on the enemy's side has been established in a particular
"double agent", it will be possible ...   ... moment to
mislead the enemy by false ...   large sca...

Document Four: 'Memorandum on the "Double Agent" System', National Archives,
                   Kew: KV 4/63. Produced with permission of the National Archives.

Note: Certain parts of Document Four are illegible, due to poor handling.

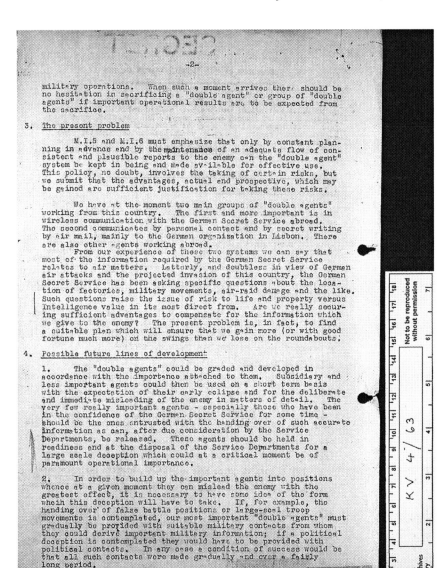

-2-

military operations. When such a moment arrives there should be no hesitation in sacrificing a "double agent" or group of "double agents" if important operational results are to be expected from the sacrifice.

3. The present problem

M.I.5 and M.I.6 must emphasize that only by constant planning in advance and by the maintenance of an adequate flow of consistent and plausible reports to the enemy can the "double agent" system be kept in being and made available for effective use. This policy, no doubt, involves the taking of certain risks, but we submit that the advantages, actual and prospective, which may be gained are sufficient justification for taking these risks.

We have at the moment two main groups of "double agents" working from this country. The first and more important is in wireless communication with the German Secret Service abroad. The second communicates by personal contact and by secret writing by air mail, mainly to the German organization in Lisbon. There are also other agents working abroad.

From our experience of these two systems we can say that most of the information required by the German Secret Service relates to air matters. Latterly, and doubtless in view of German air attacks and the projected invasion of this country, the German Secret Service has been asking specific questions about the location of factories, military movements, air-raid damage and the like. Such questions raise the issue of risk to life and property versus Intelligence value in its most direct from. Are we really securing sufficient advantages to compensate for the information which we give to the enemy? The present problem is, in fact, to find a suitable plan which will ensure that we gain more (or with good fortune much more) on the swings than we lose on the roundabouts.

4. Possible future lines of development

1. The "double agents" could be graded and developed in accordance with the importance attached to them. Subsidiary and less important agents could then be used on a short term basis with the expectation of their early eclipse and for the deliberate and immediate misleading of the enemy in matters of detail. The very few really important agents - especially those who have been in the confidence of the German Secret Service for some time - should be the ones entrusted with the handing over of such accurate information as can, after due consideration by the Service Departments, be released. These agents should be held in readiness and at the disposal of the Service Departments for a large scale deception which could at a critical moment be of paramount operational importance.

2. In order to build up the important agents into positions whence at a given moment they can mislead the enemy with the greatest effect, it is necessary to have some idea of the form which this deception will have to take. If, for example, the handing over of false battle positions or large-scal troop movements is contemplated, our most important "double agents" must gradually be provided with suitable military contacts from whom they could derive important military information; if a political deception is contemplated they would have to be provided with political contacts. In any case a condition of success would be that all such contacts were made gradually and over a fairly long period.

3. Information relating to factory sites, military defence positions and .... all kinds should mainly be ontrusted .... agents". Through these .... should be .... lies to mislead the enemy.

Document Four continued

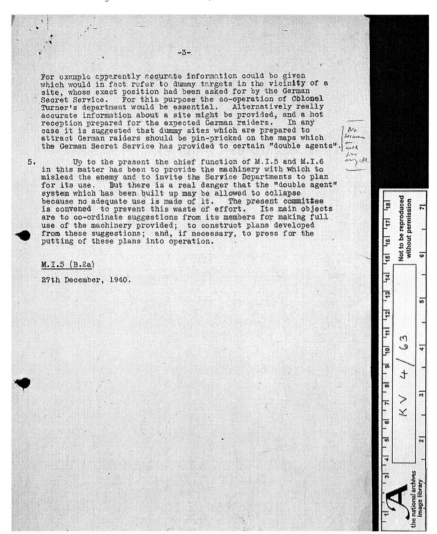

-3-

For example apparently accurate information could be given which would in fact refer to dummy targets in the vicinity of a site, whose exact position had been asked for by the German Secret Service. For this purpose the co-operation of Colonel Turner's department would be essential. Alternatively really accurate information about a site might be provided, and a hot reception prepared for the expected German raiders. In any case it is suggested that dummy sites which are prepared to attract German raiders should be pin-pricked on the maps which the German Secret Service has provided to certain "double agents".

5.   Up to the present the chief function of M.I.5 and M.I.6 in this matter has been to provide the machinery with which to mislead the enemy and to invite the Service Departments to plan for its use. But there is a real danger that the "double agent" system which has been built up may be allowed to collapse because no adequate use is made of it. The present committee is convened to prevent this waste of effort. Its main objects are to co-ordinate suggestions from its members for making full use of the machinery provided; to construct plans developed from these suggestions; and, if necessary, to press for the putting of these plans into operation.

M.I.5 (B.2a)

27th December, 1940.

Document Four continued

COMMENTARY: DECEPTION AND 'DOUBLE CROSS' IN THE SECOND WORLD WAR

John Ferris

Document Four refers to two British triumphs of intelligence during the Second World War, the 'double cross' (or XX) system, which controlled German spies, and the deception campaign, which aided the invasions of Sicily and Normandy. Controlled agents (spies ostensibly working for an enemy, but actually under your power) and deception were not unusual matters. Before the First World War, British officials knew about them, which they practised during that conflict. Britain gained from such actions; so did its enemies. Between the wars, intelligence agencies commonly used controlled agents against their foes, sometimes for deceptive purposes. What was unusual between the years 1939 and 1945 was the combination of German incompetence and British skill (and luck).

In 1939, Germany had few spies in the British Empire. Its military intelligence, the *Abwehr*, expanded these networks in an amateurish way. British security collared the lot; later, codebreakers revealed much about how German intelligence and decision-makers interpreted their reports. In 1940, MI5 created a section to manage controlled agents, ultimately named 'B1A'. Intelligence authorities then took this 'double cross' system from the normal bureaucracy and placed it under an 'XX Committee', chaired by John Masterman of B1A, with representatives from SIS and military intelligence. Masterman acknowledged that this system was odd, but wrote, 'Broadly speaking bad men make good institutions bad, and good men make bad institutions good': decades later, the official historian, Michael Howard added, 'The men who ran the Twenty Committee were good'.[1] In fact, eighteen months passed before they made this system work, and only after it changed. In the interim, deception succeeded only when a normal unit ordered that it be done by an official who could coordinate all its actions and knowledge – like Ewan Montagu, in charge of the Admiralty's internal circulation of ULTRA and member of the 'XX Committee', or John Shearer, the intelligence chief at GHQ Middle East. In order to conduct deception, many agencies had to be coordinated. This would have been difficult in ordinary times – doubly so in this one. Britain faced annihilation. The organisation of intelligence was in chaos; agencies exploded in size, their command systems imploded under the weight, and as they failed, they triumphed. 'Double cross', ULTRA and deception became self-contained silos so secret that few people knew any of them and fewer all of them – hardly anyone knew what could and should be coordinated. These developments created grounds for new demarcation disputes, especially between the central agencies involved with controlled agents. MI5 and SIS had cooperated well regarding that matter between 1914 and 1939, but during 1941, their squabbles almost wrecked the 'double cross' system. Until August 1942, whenever Whitehall confronted the chance to coordinate deception, it declined to do so, while in any case, Britain had little to hide, since it rarely could take the initiative.

This document, provided by MI5 for the first meeting of the 'XX Committee', on 2 January 1941, illustrates how hard these triumphs were to achieve. At that meeting, Masterman noted 'a real danger that the "double agent" system which has been built up may be allowed to collapse because no adequate use is made of it': 'the losses involved in releasing information are outweighed by the gains accruing from the successful working of the system'. Most of his arguments were defensive, aimed at controlling enemy intelligence. Still, deception was the great aim: if, and only if, confidence on the enemy's side has been established in a particular 'double agent', could s/he be used to deceive 'at an appropriate moment'. But, 'only by constant planning in advance and by the maintenance of an adequate flow of consistent and plausible reports to the enemy can the "double agent" system be kept in being and made available for effective use'. The 'double cross' system should be used to pass disinformation on air matters, the issue which, *Abwehr* questionnaires indicated, most interested the Germans. Again, Masterman noted, how could the 'XX Committee' achieve its aim of 'long-term operational deception – e.g. with regards to large-scale raids or invasion of enemy territory. But this needs time, & careful planning.' 'We may construct ingenious plans, but how to put them into effect?' In order to do so, the XX Committee needed a link with people who controlled planning and operations.[2] Masterman asked all the right questions; no one answered them. This silence stalled deception.

MI5 feared 'double agents' were passing material so innocuous as to wreck their plausibility, which might drive the *Abwehr* to establish new, perhaps uncontrolled, networks – that if not used for deception, the system might lose its value for security. Yet the military services would not transmit minor pieces of true information to the *Abwehr*; they were reluctant to pass even disinformation. The RN and the RAF authorised limited plans; the army felt unable to do anything. On its own initiative, but with the approval of army and air intelligence, MI5 planted false documents on the *Abwehr*, including a memorandum on 'divisional signs', an early step in the order of battle deception, which led the Germans to overestimate the number of Anglo-American divisions by about 40 per cent.[3] Such efforts had no immediate impact. Britain's record in deception during 1941 was far less good than that which backed German surprise attacks against the USSR and Japanese ones against Britain and the United States.

The tide turned in 1942, for two reasons; power – combined with the United States, the Commonwealth finally could take the initiative against Germany; and inspiration from a subordinate command. In 1940–41, the commander in Egypt, Archibald Wavell, Shearer and a specialist, Dudley Clarke, honed every old technique of deception to stimulate the enemy to bad action, and tested new ones – the false order of battle, the delivery of precise messages through controlled agents; the use of ULTRA to smoke out German preconceptions and monitor their reactions. Whitehall thought these techniques innovative and exciting; that they had worked as planned and with significance. It had faith in the British capacity to deceive, and mistakenly thought deception already had surprised several Axis forces. The western alliance was ready and able to take the initiative, through the invasion of North Africa. The time was ripe to act, thus, to deceive. An immediate operation was at hand; its success hinged on surprise, which Whitehall believed deception could provide.

Faced with the need for a practical solution to a real problem, Britain muddled through to a miracle, made on the 'old boy level', official relations emerging from personal ones. It plugged the powerful and unique edge in organisation it had forged since 1940 into normal strategic decision-making. Only after its integration within a greater system, when Britain had the initiative, did deception achieve the successes which made its reputation. A high-level synthesis emerged of all three forms of top secret knowledge – ULTRA, double cross and deception. Deception was coordinated by a few specialists. Masterman and MI5 ran the double cross system while John Bevan coordinated deception across the world, and Whitehall. Clarke handled the core work, Montagu and Charles Cholmondeley created MINCEMEAT (planting a story on Adolf Hitler, through a dead man dressed as an officer and floated off a beach in Spain, that Sicily was not the target of allied invasion), and David Strangeways oversaw FORTITUDE SOUTH, that made the Germans believe the invasion of Normandy was a feint, to cover the real attack, which would later be launched at the Pas de Calais. Germany, on the strategic defensive, still had powerful forces: deception helped to make it waste them against imaginary threats and weaken itself against real ones. The enemy could effectively prepare against seaborne assault only if it guessed allied strategy and power correctly. It did not do so. Failures with the best sources on strategic intentions and capabilities, high-level code breaking and imagery, drove Germany to rely on an inherently less useful source for such matters, spies – who, even worse, were under British control. Deception personnel, recruited through 'old boy' networks, inspired and guided by intelligence veterans of the Great War, supported by many British generals and statesmen, working with skill and creativity, defined the gold standard for deception, and shaped the Second World War.

Further reading

On the double cross system, see J.C. Masterman, *The Double Cross System in the War of 1939 to 1945* (London: Yale University Press, 1972); F.H. Hinsley and C.A.G. Simkins, *British Intelligence in the Second World War*, vol. 4, *Security and Counter-Intelligence* (London: HMSO, 1990). On deception, see Michael Handel (ed.), *Strategic and Operational Deception during the Second World War* (London: Frank Cass, 1988); Michael Howard, *British Intelligence in the Second World War*, vol. 5, *Strategic Deception* (London: HMSO, 1990); John Ferris, 'The Roots of Fortitude: The Evolution of British Deception in The Second World War', in Thomas Mahnken (ed.), *The Paradox of Intelligence: Essays in Memory of Michael Handel* (London: Frank Cass, 2003); and Thaddeus Holt, *The Deceivers: Allied Military Deception in the Second World War* (London: Weidenfeld & Nicolson, 2004).

Notes

Overview: Deception and double cross

Len Scott

1   See Richmond Lattimore (trans.), *The Odyssey of Homer* (New York: Harper and Row, 1965), Book IV, verses 266–89, Book VIII, verses 492–520, Book XI, verses 522–32.
2   *The Holy Bible: Book of Judges* (Cambridge: Cambridge University Press), Chap. 7, esp. verses 12–25.
3   Michael Howard, *British Intelligence in the Second World War*, Volume Five: *Strategic Deception* (London: HMSO, 1990), p. x.
4   Yigal Sheffy, 'Overcoming Strategic Weakness: The Egyptian Deception and the Yom Kippur War,' in L.V. Scott and R. Gerald Hughes, *Intelligence, Crises and Security: Prospects and Retrospects* (Oxon: Routledge, 2008).
5   See Anthony H. Cordesman and Abraham R. Wagner, *The Lessons of Modern War: The Gulf War* (Oxford: Westview Press, 1996), pp. 88–9, 146, 556, 585–6, 820–5.

6   For accounts of the double cross system, see J.C. Masterman, *The Double Cross System in the War of 1939 to 1945* (New Haven, CT: Yale University Press, 1972); F.H Hinsley and C.A.G. Simkins, *British Intelligence in the Second World War*, vol. 4 *Security and Counter-Intelligence* (London: HMSO, 1990) and Howard, *British Intelligence.*
7   Howard, *British Intelligence*, p. 105.
8   Roger Hesketh, *Fortitude: The D-Day Deception* (London: St Ermin's Press, 1999), pp. 135–48.
9   Communications problems meant that the Abwehr only received the message several hours after the invasion had begun. Hesketh, *Fortitude*, pp. 146–8. For discussion of Garbo's role after 6 June, see Howard, *British Intelligence*, pp. 185–200.
10   Anthony Cave Brown, *Bodyguard of Lies* (London: Star Books, 1977), p. 389.
11   Ewen Montagu, *The Man Who Never Was* (London: Corgi, 1968), p. 9.
12   For Soviet awareness of double cross and deception, see Nigel West and Oleg Tsarev, *The Crown Jewels: The British Secrets Exposed by the KGB Archives* (London: HarperCollins, 1999), pp. 159, 168–9.
13   Ibid., p. 229; David Holloway, *Stalin and the Bomb: The Soviet Union and Atomic Energy, 1939–56* (London: Yale University Press, 1994), p. 115.
14   Tom Mangold, *Cold Warrior, James Jesus Angleton: The CIA's Master Spy Hunter* (London: Simon and Schuster, 1991), pp. 89–93.
15   James Risen, *State of War: The Secret History of the CIA and the Bush Administration* (London: The Free Press, 2006), pp. 194–218.

Commentary: Deception and 'double cross' in the Second World War

John Ferris

1   J.C. Masterman, *The Double Cross System, in the War of 1939 to 1945* (London: Yale University Press, 1972), p. 65; Michael Howard, *British Intelligence in the Second World War*, vol. 5, *Strategic Deception* (London: HMSO, 1990), p 9.
2   First Twenty (XX) Committee Meeting, 2.1.41, passim, KV 4/63. MI5 described 'controlled agents' through an older term, 'double agents', which in modern parlance, means a spy one thinks is under one's control, but in fact is working for someone else.
3   Masterman, *Double Cross*, 72–3; F.H. Hinsley and C.A.G. Simkins, *British Intelligence in the Second World War*, vol. 4, *Security and Counter-Intelligence* (London: HMSO, 1990), pp. 107–9.

5　The creation of a Vietnamese intelligence service, 1945–50

Christopher E. Goscha, David Marr and Merle Pribbenow

OVERVIEW: THE EARLY DEVELOPMENT OF VIETNAMESE INTELLIGENCE SERVICES, 1945–50

Christopher E. Goscha

Few would disagree that intelligence studies could provide us with a unique insight into how newly independent nation-states born of decolonisation went about processing information on their enemies, the region, the world, as well as on their own societies, states, and religions. The problem is that precious little research has yet to be done on the role of intelligence services in the making of non-European postcolonial states, either peacefully or through the force of arms. More has been done on European nation-states emerging from the crumbling Austro-Hungarian Empire, the French 'revolutionary wars' and Ottoman domination in the late nineteenth century and in the wake of World War I. With few exceptions, the same cannot be said for the wave of new nation-states born out of the meltdown of Japanese and Western colonialism triggered by World War II and the subsequent wars of decolonization. And the process is of course still going on, as the states emerging from the former Soviet Empire confront similarly contested issues and problems.

As the documents Five, Six and Seven presented below suggests – and as I try to show in the longer piece published on this subject in *Intelligence and National Security*[1] – the Vietnamese communist case suggests that the study of intelligence in the postcolonial non-European world is perhaps not as difficult as the absence of publications on the topic would seem to suggest. In the case of Vietnam, there is in fact no shortage of sources on a wide range of security, intelligence, and espionage services for the period from 1945, when Ho Chi Minh announced the birth of the modern Vietnamese nation-state, to 1975, when the communists placed southern Vietnam under the party's leadership. Similar documentation appears to exist for communist and non-communist China.

The intelligence sources I have located on modern Vietnam can be divided into two main categories: (1) a growing collection of official Vietnamese language sources (memoirs, intelligence histories, and articles) on the role of 'public security' (*cong an*) and 'intelligence services' (*tinh bao*) during the Indochina War of 1945–54; and (2) a large body of French-captured and French-decrypted Vietnamese security and intelligence documents from the period. Many of the official intelligence histories published in Vietnam over the last two decades are 'internal' (*noi boi*) studies, destined for use within the relevant ministry or party, and not for public diffusion, much less foreign consumption. These internal publications often provide important information unavailable elsewhere. Moreover, the memoirs of high-ranking Vietnamese security and intelligence officers are also of great value if used carefully.

My aim in the following pages is simply to provide a very brief overview of the early development of the Public Security and Military Intelligence services of the Democratic Republic of Vietnam up to 1950. This provides the context for the documents translated below and, I hope, a useful point of departure for the excellent commentaries accompanying these documents. For fuller discussion and analysis, please see the longer essay from which this overview is derived.

Cong An or Public Security Forces

On coming to power in September 1945, the Democratic Republic of Vietnam (DRV) needed order and security as quickly as possible. It also needed information for policy-making and intelligence on the potential enemies of the new state, both French and Vietnamese. This is when and why the new nation-state relied most heavily on its colonial predecessor's archives, organisation, model, and staff. In the north, the DRV created the 'Bureau of Security Forces for Northern Vietnam' (*So Liem Phong Bac Bo*), modelled largely on the French Political Police (*La Sûreté indochinoise*). Le Gian directed this bureau; Tran Hieu seconded him as deputy director. The Bureau of Security Forces for Northern Vietnam consisted of a 'Scouting Intelligence Unit' (*Ban Trinh Sat*), a 'Political Bureau' (*Phong Chinh Tri*), a 'Bureau of Legal Administration' (*Phong Hanh Chinh Tu Phap*), and a 'Bureau of Identification' (*Phong Can Cuoc*). In central Vietnam, the DRV started more modestly with a simple 'Scouting Intelligence Service' (*So Trinh Sat*). In Nam Bo, the 'National Defence Guard' (*Quoc Gia Tu Ve cuoc*) came to life under the leadership of Duong Bach Mai, Nguyen Van Tran, and later Cao Dang Chiem.

From the outset, the Indochinese Communist Party (ICP) sought to control and to direct these new police and intelligence services, though this was easier said than done. In charge of this question was a discreet, behind-the-scenes man who oversaw the Party's internal security affairs, Tran Dang Ninh. In February 1946, on the orders of the Party's Central Committee, Tran Dang Ninh met with Le Gian to create a new, unified national security service. On 21 February 1946, the government promulgated Decree 23 which unified all security and police forces under one centralised entity in the Ministry of Interior. It was called the 'Vietnamese Public Security Department' (*Viet Nam Cong an vu*). It stood between the Ministry of Interior and the two lower levels of this new security administration: (1) the Public Security Services in Northern, Central, and Southern Vietnam (*So Cong An Bac Bo, Trung Bo* and *Nam Bo*) and (2) the provincial Public Security Services (*Ty Cong An*). (See Document Five).

The Public Security department was in charge of collecting information and documentation both inside and outside the country which was vital to ensuring national security. Police forces were mainly concentrated on keeping the state alive and protecting it against its internal and external enemies. This meant maintaining law and order and neutralising anti-communist opponents, such as the 'Greater Vietnam Party' (*Dai Viet*), the 'Vietnamese Nationalist Party' (*Viet Nam Quoc Dan Dang, VNQDD*) and the 'Alliance League' (*Dong Minh Hoi*). The French were of course the other major threat to Vietnamese communist power. However, given that the cities were the main sources of information on the French and the outside world, the Public Security played the leading role in intelligence gathering (*tinh bao*) in the early years of the DRV's life. To this end, three main offices were created for early espionage activities – a 'Secretariat' (*van phong*), a 'Documentary and Research Gathering Committee' (*ty tap tai lieu*), and an 'Inspection Service' (*Ty thanh tra*). The Documentary and Research centre was authorised to conduct intelligence gathering both inside and outside the country, although the cities were its main theatre of operations. Nguyen Tao ran this service and, given the nature of his work, suggested that the *Ty tap tai lieu* be renamed the 'Espionage Service' (*Ty Diep Bao*), a recommendation that was subsequently accepted.

In southern Vietnam, the situation was more precarious. For one, the southern communist leadership and its regional networks had been greatly damaged by French colonial repression following a failed communist uprising in 1940. In 1945, it would be no exaggeration to say that the communists were merely one group among several competing for the nationalist high ground. They had competition from the likes of the Hoa Hao, Cao Dai, Trotskyites and even gangsters turned patriots grouped around the Binh Xuyen. Second, the outbreak of war in September 1945 pushed the communists into the countryside and underground in the cities. Maintaining effective communications with the party centre was thus rendered extremely difficult. The Public Security existed in southern Vietnam, placed under the control of ranking communists freed from Poulo Condor prison in September 1945: Pham Hung, Le Duan, and Mai Chi Tho. However, in light of the more chaotic political, social and military situation in the south, the communist-run security forces could only begin to assert themselves effectively over the DRV state and the army in the south during 1950–51.

In upper Vietnam, the outbreak of war in December 1946 finally forced the central and northern Vietnamese Public Security services into the countryside and underground in the cities. In northern Vietnam, the Public Security Department's headquarters was moved to remote regions in the north, while the police in central Vietnam pulled back into unoccupied zones in central Vietnam. Faced with full-scale war, the security forces not only had the task of consolidating the state's power in these new and often uninviting areas, but they also had to build clandestine networks in the occupied cities in order to keep providing vital intelligence on the French and the world outside. In May 1947, an All-Country Plenum of the Public Security Department issued orders to this effect. Special investigation, scouting intelligence units, and traitor-eliminating squads were organised and dispatched to the cities. During the entire Indochina War, the Public Security ran agents in Hanoi and Saigon. Clandestine teams provided a steady stream of intelligence by monitoring the press, reporting on French troop movements, mobilising youth groups and workers' unions, and running agents between the city and the liberated zones. The city was the crucial source of intelligence on the French, their Vietnamese allies, and the world. Getting newspapers out of the city and to analysts in the mountains became an art. Faced with full-scale war, espionage became critical to political and military decision-makers. Not only were the French trying to knock the DRV out militarily, but they were also moving to create a counter-revolutionary state under Bao Dai and, to this end, sought to legitimate it at the international level. Espionage was thus essential to keeping the DRV's policy-makers abreast of changes directly affecting their state and its survival at the national and international levels. Although the Public Security forces may have sent a few agents abroad, the vital source of intelligence during this early period came from the occupied cities.

While the DRV/ICP's efforts to organise their networks, increase their surveillance, and analyse their intelligence were impressive for a nation fighting a full-scale war of decolonisation, there were serious problems. The case of the Bac Kan fiasco in October 1947 makes this clear (see Document Six). We now know that intelligence operatives in Hanoi had first learned of the date of the famous French paratrooper attack in October 1947 two days before it was to occur. Bac Kan is where much of the governmental and party leadership had been located since evacuating Hanoi since late 1946. However, because of communication problems between and the distance separating Hanoi from Bac Kan, this vital intelligence only reached the area as French paratroopers were making their raid. This intelligence failure almost cost the DRV its head.

More than anything else, Bac Kan taught the Vietnamese that intelligence gathering, analysis, and transmissions had to be improved. On 13 November 1947, a Joint Conference of the Ministry of Interior's Public Security and the Ministry of Defence's Bureau of Military Intelligence (*Hoi Nghi Lien Tich Cong An va Tinh Bao Quan*) was held in northern Vietnam on orders from the Party. The goal was to improve cooperation between the state's two main intelligence services in order to follow the enemies' moves better. Le Gian headed the Public Security's team, while Tran Hieu represented the Bureau of Military Intelligence. Given that the Public Security services were already in a position to obtain intelligence of military value in the cities, a way had to be found so that intelligence could be provided to the army's High Command quickly. The result was the creation within the police of a special 'Public Security Committee on Intelligence' (*Ban Cong an Tinh bao*). This new intelligence unit, run by the Public Security forces from the cities, was designed to share vital military and strategic intelligence with the military. This meeting also took up the question of improving the collection of intelligence, its analysis (*phan tich*) and processing (*xu ly*).

The Cuc Tinh Bao or the Ministry of Defence's Bureau of Intelligence

Military intelligence services remained weak and underdeveloped during this time. Having operated freely in upper Vietnamese cities until December 1946, the security services were in a better position to reorganise networks for channelling information and intelligence from the cities to the government zones now operating in the countryside. The guerrilla nature of the war between 1945 and 1950 also meant that military intelligence in the modern sense of the word was not yet in great demand.

However, that does not mean that the DRV did not try. Upon creating the General Staff on 7 September 1945, the Vietnamese included an intelligence section in it. Vo Nguyen Giap and his deputy Hoang Van Thai were in charge. Based on the French model, the DRV's General Staff ran organisational matters, the training of the army, and military intelligence. Hoang Dao Thuy came on board to direct communications, while Hoang Minh Dao headed up military intelligence in *Phong 2*, the rough equivalent of the French *Deuxième Bureau*. This rudimentary military intelligence service followed as best it could enemy military movements in Vietnam above the 16th parallel. Below that line, the Vietnamese army was largely on its own.

Military intelligence received a boost on 25 March 1946, when Ho Chi Minh signed into law Decree 34 which consolidated within the Ministry of Defence a separate 'Bureau of Intelligence' (*Tinh bao cuc*). In May 1947, Ho signed a second piece of legislation creating a new High Command, consisting of a revamped 'Bureau of Intelligence' (*Cuc Tinh bao*). Until June 1948, Tran Hieu headed the Bureau of Intelligence for the High Command in the Ministry of Defence. In central and especially northern Vietnam, this military intelligence service established offices at the provincial and district levels. However, until 1949, it was mainly concerned with sabotage, commando operations, assassination missions, and local espionage.

As Document Seven shows, the Ministry of Defence was apparently responsible for gathering two types of information: intelligence (*tinh bao*) and military intelligence (*quan bao*). The latter focused on gathering information on the enemy so that the high command could 'know' the enemy and respond accordingly. Its activities were limited to Vietnam and concerned with the execution of mainly military affairs. Intelligence, on the other hand, was defined in wider terms, meaning information on the enemy's social, economic, political, cultural and military situations, both inside and outside Vietnam. Intelligence would allow Vietnamese analysts to understand, in a wider purview, French politics, policy, strategy and tactics.

Judging from Vo Nguyen Giap's severe critique of military intelligence just before the Bac Kan fiasco (Document Six), the General Staff's military intelligence operations was running into serious problems. Agents were badly trained and were often French spies. Worse, since taking to the hills, the army's intelligence had little contact with the Vietnamese 'masses'. The shift from the city to the countryside meant a new geographical and social orientation in intelligence gathering. Giap stressed that the Vietnamese populations had to be used to report on French military movements. Scouting intelligence units (*doi trinh sat*) were of the utmost importance. The Bac Kan fiasco, occurring a month after this critique, only confirmed Vo Nguyen Giap's fears. Building modern intelligence services in a war of decolonisation was a chaotic and difficult business.

A chaotic and difficult business it may have been, but it was also a fascinating one, capable of providing new and exciting insights into how postcolonial, non-Western intelligence services went about processing, controlling, and interpreting information about their enemies, their own societies, the world outside and ultimately, themselves. The documents provided below and the commentaries accompanying them give us glimpses into what is a useful way of pushing Cold War era intelligence studies beyond the conventional East–West divide.

DOCUMENTS FIVE, SIX AND SEVEN:

'Three Documents on Early Vietnamese Intelligence and Security Services
Translated by Christopher E. Goscha

DOCUMENT FIVE

Source: Sac Lenh 23, in Bo Noi Vu, Vien Khoa Hoc Cong An, *Cong An Nhan Dan Viet Nam, Lich Su Bien Nien (1945–1954)*, (Hanoi: Nha Xuat Ban Cong An Nhan Dan 1994), p. 63 and in the original 2 March 1946 issue of the Democratic Republic of Vietnam's *Official Journal*: 'Sac lenh so 23 ngay 21 thang 2 nam 1946 thiet lap 'Viet Nam Cong An Vu'', in *Viet Nam Dan-Quoc Bao*, (2 March 1946), p. 118.

Democratic Republic of Viet Nam
Year Two
Independence, Freedom and Happiness

Decree no. 23-SL [Sac Lenh]

The President of the Provisional Government of the Democratic Republic of Vietnam, in accordance with the project suggested by the Ministry of the Interior, and after having been discussed by the National Assembly,

Decrees:

Clause 1: Will from this time be combined, all police and *Sûreté* (*Liêm phong*) services throughout the country, in order to create one bureau which will be called the Vietnamese Public Security Department (Viet-Nam Cong-An Vu[1]).

Clause 2: The Vietnamese Public Security Department is responsible for:

1) Gathering and centralising information and documentation, both on the inside and outside, related to national security;
2) Suggesting and implementing measures to protect against all actions which could disrupt national order and the maintenance of order, regardless of whether any of those activities are committed by Vietnamese or foreigners.
3) Investigating all actions that violate the law, as mentioned above, and tracking those who break the law in order to help the court in trying and punishing them.

Clause 3: The Vietnamese Security Department will be run by a Director, under the direct command of the Ministry of the Interior. The Director can name a Vice-Director to assist him in his work. The functions of the Vietnamese Public Security Department of the Vice Director, established by this decree of the President of the Vietnamese government, will be named in accordance with the recommendation of the Ministry of the Interior.

Clause 4: Following discussion with the Ministry of Justice, the organisational details, the security offices and the particular responsibilities of each of them will be established by ministerial order, following negotiation with the Ministry of Justice.

Clause 5: Any laws or practices in violation of this decree are hereby declared null and void.

Clause 6: The Minister of the Interior is authorised to implement this decree.

Hanoi, 21 February 1946
President of the Provisional Government of Viet Nam

Signed by the Minister of the Interior, Vo Nguyen Giap
Signed by the President, Ho Chi Minh

[Translator's note:
Documents Six and Seven are French translations of the original
Vietnamese documents. However, the original Vietnamese documents
were not attached to the French translations. What is presented below
is thus an English language translation of a French translation. Unlike
document Five, I could not refer to the Vietnamese original. This is a
problem, since such documents were sometimes translated rapidly
and carelessly. In one case below, I had to delete an entire sentence
because it was incomprehensible to me and I did not have the original
Vietnamese to resolve the problem. The translation here is thus far
from perfect and until the original comes to light cannot be considered
a completely accurate translation by any stretch of the imagination.
However, given the importance of the documents in terms of their
content, authors, and the historical contexts, I felt it important to go
ahead and provide an English translation from the French. This
seemed equally important given the lack of primary sources in English
on the early evolution of Vietnamese intelligence and public security
services.]

DOCUMENT SIX

The Democratic Republic of Vietnam, The High Command of the
Ministry of National Defence, 'Directives for the Organisation of
Intelligence Services', no. 1147/XY, Bac Bo [Northern Vietnam], 6
August 1947, signed: the Supreme Commander of the Vietnamese
National Army, Vo Nguyen Giap.

Source: Commandement des Troupes françaises d'Indochine du
Nord, Deuxième Bureau, no. 4817/2, Hanoi, 17 October 1947,
'Document Viet Minh saisi à Bac Kan', valeur : A/1, captured
document dated 6 August 1947, in file 342–343, box 10H2963,
Service historique de l'Armée de Terre, Château de Vincennes,
Vincennes, France.

The intelligence service is absolutely indispensable for the Army.
Thanks to this service, the command can know the enemy and defeat
him. There are still a number of intelligence services which are active
in our troop: the intelligence (*tinh bao*) and military intelligence (*quan
bao*) services. However, if they exist, they do so only in name. In
practical terms, they have provided few results.

The reasons for this are the following:

1) In organisational terms, we have not taken into account the necessities nor have we been realistic. [unclear sentence from French translation deleted here, translator: CEG]. The [diverse] commands persist in not taking into account the manual printed on 10 March 1947, which provided all the directives for the organisation of the intelligence services in the Army.

2) When it comes to the employment of personnel, we have been too negligent. In many places, we move into our intelligence services those who cannot fight. In other areas, we employ as intelligence agents unreliable elements. Those who meet the necessary requirements for this job – courage, risk taking and possess a sense of observation – are simple soldiers or even liaison agents [because they are brave, apparently, CEG].

3) In the development of this 'profession', we do not assist or support our personnel.

4) As for working methods, we do not assign any importance to the establishment of close relationships with [other] organisms, formations, or local populations. Nor do we use them for 'missions abroad' or solicit their cooperation in counter-espionage matters.

As a result, upon receiving these instructions, you will immediately issue orders to unit commanders at the regiment and company levels to reorganise rapidly their intelligence services according to the following guidelines:

A. Organisation: Those units which are allowed to organise their intelligence services [units] are those at the company and regiment levels. The size will be established in terms of the work needed and the material needs of each unit. However, in principle, the following table must be adopted:

  – each company must have an 'scouting squad' (*tieu doi trinh sat*)[2];
  – each battalion must have a 'scouting platoon' (*trung doi trinh sat*);
  – each regiment must have a 'scouting company' (*dai doi trinh sat*).

These intelligence units are placed under the immediate direction of the commands of the company of the battalion or of the regiment. Heretofore, the terms *tinh bao* (intelligence service) and *quan bao* (military intelligence), etc. will be abandoned and replaced by those of *trinh sat* (scouting or surveillance).

B. Personnel: The zone commands will give the order to the units under their authority to choose their personnel from their fighting units. One must avoid new recruitments, which will only increase the workforce at a time when our finances are in difficulty.

C. Distribution: One must choose men, who have gone through training courses, those who have combat experience or those who have a vocation for 'intelligence'. Intelligence agents will be chosen from among those who possess a high fighting spirit and who know the 'profession' to some extent.

D. Instructions: 'Intelligence units' will be called on not only to fight, but also to observe the enemy's situation and carry out special missions. They must also undergo a special training programme. Once these units are constituted, their instruction will begin immediately (the course curriculum and methods will be sent later).

E. Work: Whether they are garrisoned or deployed, behind the lines or at the front, the intelligence units have the task of gathering intelligence on the enemy situation, that of the populations and on the local characteristics of the terrain in order to inform the command. On arriving in an area, the intelligence unit must enter into relations with the local organisms and formations with a view to [conducting] counter-espionage and protecting the populations.

F. Armament: The intelligence unit must be armed like a combat unit and, if possible, with light arms (pistol, grenades, and sub-machine guns), which are better adapted to this type of special activity.

G. Expenses: Besides the normal subsistence expenses, the 'intelligence units' will also be accorded special allocations in accordance with the circumstances. These latter expenses will be drawn from the 'command's' purse or from the budget of the Ministry of Defence (as war expenses).

H. Liaisons: The 'intelligence units' will depend directly on the unit commands to which they belong. However, in light of their acquired experiences in special activities and in terms of their cooperation in a determined mission, they can enter into contact and help each other according to the command's directives.

In order to defeat the enemy, one must 'know' him and prevent him from 'knowing' us. This is the duty of the 'intelligence units'. The command levels will study closely these directives and report to the Ministry on the organisation of the 'intelligence units'.

Bac Bo, 6 August 1947
The Supreme Commander of the Vietnamese National Army
Signed: Vo Nguyen Giap

DOCUMENT SEVEN

Document: Ministry of National Defence, Supreme Command, No. 86/TT, 'Directives concerning the Organisation of Military Intelligence Service [*quan bao*]', dated 31 March 1950, signed for the Minister of Defence, by the Under Secretary of State Ta Quang Buu.

Source: Translation of a copy of the ministerial directives (V.M. [Viet Minh] National Defence) concerning the organisation of *Quan Bao* [Military intelligence service] (V.M. organ designed for obtaining intelligence), in file: VI, box C881, Service Historique de l'Armée de l'Air, Château de Vincennes, Vincennes, France.

Ministry of National Defence
High Command
No. 86/TT

Directives on the Organisation of Military Intelligence

The circular no. 51/TT of 14 February 1950 established the respective duties of *Tinh Bao* [intelligence] and *Quan Bao* [military intelligence].[3]

The actual directives provide precisions concerning the constitution of the new [military intelligence] organisation.

I. The Notion of *Quan Bao* in the People's War

    – The *Quan Bao* or military intelligence service (*Quan Su Tinh Bao*) is an intelligence organism located within the Army and people's troops. Its mission is to search and study all documentation on the enemy in order to help the command to 'know' him and as a result be able to establish the operational phases. Its field of action is generally limited to the inside of the country; its role is essentially military, paying particular attention to the [military] fronts.

    – The *Quan Bao* is different from the *Tinh Bao*.

The *Tinh Bao*'s character is much wider. It is active both inside the country and abroad. It combats against enemy spies or foreign ones active on Vietnamese territory. It searches out or studies all documentation concerning the enemy's social, economic, political, cultural, military and diplomatic situations in order to deduce the [enemy's] pure[4] policy, economic policy, and enemy strategy and tactics.

    – The organisation of the *Quan Bao* has obtained to this point a number of satisfactory results and has exerted itself incessantly. However, a number of weak points subsist, which must be corrected:

        The organisation is still confused and lacks unity.

        The allocation of duties between the *Quan Bao* and the *Tinh Bao* has not been defined clearly.

        There is a lack of unity in the command and reciprocal meddling [in the two service commands].

        The techniques used by the cadres of the Quan Bao are still rudimentary.

        The cadres have not understood how to 'mobilise' the possibilities of the populations for military intelligence needs.

- Our war is a 'people's war'. Military intelligence must not be the exclusive domain of the Army. The populations and above all the 'popular troops' must be a part of it. If all the possibilities of the population were mobilised in favour of the Army, we would be able to remain in charge of the situation and defeat the enemy more rapidly.

- The population is everywhere: in the occupied zones as well as in the free zones. The population does not need to camouflage itself: it lives right next to the enemy, knows the enemy and knows the country. The population provides many possibilities for military intelligence. The population can provide efficient and sensitive ears (*antennes*) for the Army, if we know how to exploit these possibilities. If every person constitutes an agent, a veritable belt would be built within the population and there is no doubt that we would win faster.

We can see then that military intelligence is of a great importance. Not only does the army have to marshal all its efforts in this direction, but the entire population and above all the people's militia must do their best to develop military intelligence. It means protecting oneself and defeating the enemy.

[*Translator's note*: Parts II-IV have not been translated. It describes in minute detail the internal organisation of the military intelligence service at the different levels of the military hierarchy.]

V. Conclusion

Military Intelligence is, in the 'people's war', a new and original organisation. Its meaning and work is extremely important, above all in the upcoming General counter-offensive, which will demand much of military intelligence services.

The success of the Military intelligence service will to a great extent assure the military victory.

It will be impossible to avoid difficulties in the start-up period. The command levels will have to study closely and carefully this current document and apply its clauses as best as possible to the material conditions in order to lead efficiently the Military intelligence and intelligence services in their missions.

31 March 1950
signed by the Under Secretary of State,
Ta Quang Buu.

1   'Vu' was added in hand and reproduced in the *Official Journal*. It replaced the original term, 'Cuc', meaning office or bureau. Vietnamese officials would soon use the term 'nha' instead of 'vu'.
2   The original Vietnamese term appears in the French translation.
3   The original Vietnamese term appears in the French translation.
4   I'm assuming that the word in Vietnamese was probably something like 'real' or 'authentic' (*chan chinh*).

COMMENTARY: ESTABLISHING A NORTH VIETNAMESE INTELLIGENCE SERVICE

David Marr

Document Five

This decree was issued at the beginning of the two most precarious weeks in the history of the Democratic Republic of Vietnam (DRV). Political parties were deadlocked over formation of a government cabinet to present to the new National Assembly, Chungking and Paris were nearing agreement for Chinese troops to withdraw from northern Indochina in favor of French forces, and the Indochinese Communist Party (ICP) was divided over whether to fight the French or compromise with them. As part of the agreement reached between Vietnamese political parties, Huynh Thuc Khang accepted the position of Interior Minister as an explicitly non-party member of Cabinet. Khang selected Nguyen Duong as Cong An (Public Security) director, and Dao Hung as head of the Cong An's vital northern bureau. Neither had any party membership, although the ICP suspected Hung of leaning towards the Vietnam Nationalist Party. In any event, ICP members remained in charge of key offices, and if called upon young Viet Minh recruits could be expected to obey them rather than the top Cong An officials.

A Sino-French agreement was signed on 28 February, a Franco-Vietnamese preliminary accord was reached on 6 March just as French ships entered Haiphong harbor, and armed Viet Minh groups obeyed President Ho Chi Minh's injunction to avoid any confrontation. Meanwhile, a quiet but intense struggle for control of the Cong An persisted, at least in Hanoi and vicinity. Not unaware of ICP tactics, Dao Hung made some appointments of his own and sacked a few ICP members. In late April, the ICP head of the Cong An's secret political investigation office arrested some Nationalist Party activists. Hung ordered the release of the detainees, without success. Nguyen Duong chose to avoid involvement, more Nationalist Party members ended up in jail, and Duong submitted his resignation to the Interior Minister. Huynh Thuc Khang may have become so irritated by this internecine conflict that he offered his resignation to Ho Chi Minh; if so, it was not accepted. However, Duong's resignation was accepted, and soon after Dao Hung went the same route.

The ICP now had outright control of the higher reaches of the Cong An. By July, armed Nationalist Party and Revolutionary Alliance groups were either imprisoned or retreating towards the Chinese frontier. It would take much longer for the Cong An hierarchy to extend across the provinces and absorb hundreds of local Viet Minh assassination squads and covert investigation teams.

Document Six

Vo Nguyen Giap drafted this directive in the wake of serious military reversals. In February 1947, the French launched attacks in Tonkin that shattered Vietnamese defenses, produced widespread panic, and sent army units fleeing in all directions. During the summer rainy season, French assaults dropped off substantially, giving regular army units time to regroup, reprovision and rethink their *modus operandi*. With government approval, Giap ordered regiments to disaggregate, with one battalion and regimental headquarters staying together while other battalions dispersed their companies, in some cases infiltrating them back to enemy-held districts. When a tactical opportunity arose, companies would recombine to battalion size, accomplish the mission, then disperse again.

Document Six can be read at two levels: organizational and conceptual. Each military echelon is being told to create reconnaissance units, train them, and make sure they learn the human and physical specifics of their operational area. In August 1947, this order was quite unrealistic. For years thereafter the principal source of tactical intelligence would not be regular army reconnaissance units, but local guerrilla groups and Viet Minh associations.

Conceptually, Giap was highlighting the importance of reliable intelligence on the enemy, the terrain, and the surrounding people. He acknowledged that military intelligence personnel had to rely on 'local organizations and formations', notably when it came to counter-intelligence and security. Rather delicately, Giap authorized different intelligence units to 'enter into contact and help each other', which must have raised eyebrows among security cadres intent on compartmentalization of information and need-to-know restrictions. Giap's directive also drew no line between those who conduct intelligence sorties and those who analyze the results.

Document Seven

Early 1950 saw momentous changes for Vietnam, with Ho Chi Minh traveling secretly to China and the Soviet Union, Beijing and Moscow extending formal recognition to the DRV (counterpoised by Washington and London recognizing the Associated State of Vietnam), a large Chinese advisory group dispatched to the border region, and the start of an ambitious re-equipping and re-training program for the army. During 1948 and 1949, Army units had been patiently rebuilt to regimental size. Now it was possible to craft infantry divisions, artillery battalions and a range of specialized units. Not least of all, the army wanted a full-fledged military intelligence service, which would integrate all the unit-level, regional and local intelligence groups that had proliferated since 1945.

This would not be easy. In practice, many army groups had been collecting political, economic and even diplomatic data as well as military information. The Cong An and the ICP were doing the same thing. As Christopher Goscha explains in his preceding Overview, there was high-level agreement in early 1950 that rationalization should occur. In February, the ICP leadership resolved to take non-military intelligence duties away from the army and lodge them with the Cong An. Document Seven, signed one month later, provided army commanders with a rationale for delineating military and non-military intelligence, and foreshadowed formation of a full-fledged military intelligence service. We know that in August a Military Intelligence Bureau was created within the General Staff, but how far down the chain of command the changes went is unclear. I doubt that the army surrendered all or even most of its non-military intelligence activities to the Cong An, and we know that the Cong An continued to collect information enabling them to conduct operations of a military character. Despite Communist Party attempts to correct the problem, army/Cong An overlap and competition continued into the 2nd Indochina War, and indeed is still evident today.

Document Seven incorporates the people and local armed groups actively into the intelligence equation in a way that is absent in Document Six. This is not a polite nod to the incoming Chinese communist advisors, since 'people's war' doctrine had been touted in Vietnam for years. It relates to the General Staff's growing appreciation of the war as an Indochina-wide endeavor, with valuable contributions coming not only from regular army divisions or regiments, but also regional and local forces. Curiously, Document Seven says nothing about physical communication of intelligence across considerable distances and hostile terrain. Transmission of intelligence in timely fashion remained the biggest practical obstacle to the end of the 1st Indochina War.

Ta Quang Buu, who signed Document Seven, is a prime example of the lively, enquiring individuals that Vo Nguyen Giap and Hoang Van Thai gathered to the army General Staff. Born to a 'feudal' family of scholars, trained as a mathematician in Paris and Oxford, Buu's only quasi-military experience was organizing Boy Scouts in the early 1940s. As Chinese political influence increased from 1951, individuals like Buu with bad class backgrounds had to be protected by Giap and Thai from party and police predators. When it came to collection, processing, evaluation and presentation of intelligence data, members of the General Staff knew how to distinguish what is and what ought to be, unlike many on the Party's Central Committee. This helps to explain DRV success in both the 1st and 2nd Indochina Wars.

COMMENTARY: THE DEVELOPMENT OF VIETNAMESE INTELLIGENCE

Merle Pribbenow

The three documents unearthed by Professor Christopher Goscha illustrate several important stages in the development of the Vietnamese communist intelligence and security services into a powerful and effective apparatus, an apparatus that was able to hold its own in the struggle against the sophisticated intelligence and security services of two modern Western powers, France and the United States.

Document Five, dated 21 February 1946, marks the birth of Vietnam's Public Security Service (initially called a department or bureau and later upgraded to become one of the most powerful ministries in the Vietnamese government). The document demonstrates that from the very first days of their ascension to power the Vietnamese communists rejected the common Western concept of separating national security (political security) functions from civil (criminal) police functions. Instead of this, whether consciously or unconsciously, the Vietnamese adopted the Soviet model, as exemplified by the KGB and its predecessor organizations (the NKVD, the MVD, etc.). Under this Soviet model, a model that the Government of the Socialist Republic of Vietnam still follows to this day, all governmental functions related to public safety, order, and national security are handled by a single umbrella organization responsible for everything from the policeman directing traffic on the street corner and the local fire department up through border defense and customs and immigration functions to national-level police, political security, espionage, and counter-espionage operations.

The reason for their decision was, and is, quite simple: any and all disruptions of internal stability, including both social and political stability, are viewed as threats to the Party's hold on the reins of power, and such threats must be dealt with in a unified, coordinated manner that is best achieved through a single, unified organizational entity. Ultimately, all crimes and all acts of social disruption, whether or not the motive is political, are considered 'crimes against the state'. Therefore, the primary duty of the umbrella organization whose birth was formalized in this document, the Public Security Department and all of its successor organizations down through the years (the Public Security Directorate, the Ministry of Interior, and today's Ministry of Public Security), has always been the protection and preservation of the Vietnamese Communist Party's hold on the reins of power. The Soviet KGB was called 'the sword and the shield' of the Soviet Union's communist regime, and it is no accident that Vietnam's Ministry of Public Security adopted the 'sword' motif from the emblem of the old KGB as part of the official emblem of the Vietnamese Public Security Service.

Professor Goscha's next document (Document Six), a 1947 document in which General Vo Nguyen Giap issues an order on regularizing the 'intelligence function' in Viet Minh military units, marks the establishment of a formalized system for carrying out tactical intelligence functions at the unit level in the Vietnamese army. The bulk of the Viet Minh's armed forces were formed in haste following the August 1945 'revolution', when Ho Chi Minh and his followers seized the reins of governmental power in Hanoi at the end of World War II. Very few of the army's unit commanders had any military experience or training, and even fewer had any understanding of 'intelligence' or 'reconnaissance' in the western sense. Initially, most of the units were locally recruited and locally based, operating only in areas where most of the unit's personnel had been born and grown up. Whatever 'intelligence' or 'reconnaissance' operations they conducted were strictly 'ad hoc' arrangements, utilizing the knowledge of the local terrain and the personal contacts (agents) and relationships that members of the units had in the local community.

In the summer of 1947, when this document was written, Ho Chi Minh and his followers had just been driven out of Hanoi and had taken refuge in the vast, remote mountain forests of the Viet Bac region, where they worked to regroup and reorganize their forces for the long struggle against the French that they knew lay ahead. In order to be able to survive and to fight successfully, all Viet Minh military units, and especially main force mobile units, would need solid, well-trained, reliable intelligence-reconnaissance units to collect the tactical information that would be required to plan and carry out combat operations.

In this document Giap spells out the weaknesses of the 'ad hoc' tactical intelligence arrangements then in effect in the Viet Minh army and sets forth guidelines for selecting, training, and organizing specialized elements in each tactical unit, from the company level upward, to ensure that Vietnamese military commanders at all levels had a standardized and reliable system for collecting the kind of tactical intelligence they required. Only a few short months after this document was written the Viet Minh leadership received a stark demonstration of the need to revamp its system for acquiring and disseminating combat intelligence in an incident that Professor Goscha mentions in his Overview. In October 1947, a raid by French paratroopers into a communist base area came very close to capturing several of Ho Chi Minh's most senior leaders, including Party Secretary Truong Chinh and Chief of Staff Hoang Van Thai. In spite of the fact that a Viet Minh intelligence agent in Hanoi had reported the build-up of French paratroopers at Gia Lam Airfield several days before the attack, the Vietnamese were taken completely by surprise because the agent's report did not reach the leadership due to 'inadequate communications arrangements'. General Vo Nguyen Giap complained in a memoir that during a headquarters staff meeting on the day of the attack the Chief of Viet Minh intelligence operations, Tran Hieu, was unable to provide no information whatsoever on the enemy operation. In his memoir, Giap commented sarcastically that, 'This type of work [intelligence] was still very new to us.'[1]

It is interesting to note that the organizational arrangement that Giap laid out in this document – one 'reconnaissance squad' [*tieu doi trinh sat* – or 'scouting squad', as the French translated the term] for each company, one reconnaissance platoon for each battalion, and one reconnaissance company for each regiment – remained the Vietnamese army's organizational standard throughout the resistance war against the French, the war against the United States and its allies, and the wars in Cambodia and along Vietnam's northern border with China during the 1980s, and is probably still in effect today.

The final document (Document Seven) provided by Professor Goscha, a 1950 document on the organization of the Ministry of Defense's military intelligence service, is illustrative of Vietnam's attempts to deal with a classic intelligence problem of priorities with which many countries, including the United States, have wrestled. The central problem here being how to strike a balance between the requirement for detailed battlefield intelligence to meet the immediate combat needs of battlefield commanders and the requirement of the nation's highest leaders for high-level strategic intelligence, intelligence that extends beyond the purely military realm into such areas as politics, diplomacy, and economics. This was the basis of the conflict between the two Ministry of Defense intelligence entities described in the document, the Ministry of Defense's Intelligence Department (*Cuc Tinh Bao*), responsible for supplying strategic intelligence to the Party and governmental leadership, and the Military Intelligence Department (*Cuc Quan Bao*), responsible for supplying tactical and campaign-level (called in the Soviet Union and the West the 'operational level') intelligence to the General Staff and to military commanders at lower levels.

In the U.S. and many other countries similar conflicts have led to the creation of two separate intelligence services – a civilian intelligence service to provide strategic intelligence to the most senior political leaders (the Central Intelligence Agency in the United States), and a military intelligence service primarily responsible for providing tactical and operational-level intelligence to military commanders (in the United States, the Defense Intelligence Agency and the intelligence arms of the individual military services). In Vietnam, however, three separate intelligence agencies were eventually formed: (1) the General Staff's Military Intelligence Department (*Cuc Quan Bao*) to satisfy tactical and operational-level intelligence requirements for military commanders; (2) the Ministry of Public Security's Intelligence Department (*Cuc Tinh Bao*); and (3) a separate strategic intelligence service located in the Ministry of Defense and responsible for conducting high-level espionage operations aimed at providing strategic level intelligence to Vietnam's most senior Party and governmental leaders.[2] This Vietnamese strategic intelligence service was originally formed in 1951 and was called (according to one source) the 'Central Intelligence Directorate' (*Nha Tinh Bao Trung Uong*).[3] Later, operating under the cover name of the Ministry of Defense's 'Research Department' (*Cuc Nghien Cuu*), the Vietnamese communist strategic intelligence service, through its operational arm in South Vietnam, COSVN'S (the Central Office for South Vietnam) Strategic Intelligence Office, recruited, trained, and directed a number of high-level agents in South Vietnam who later became famous for their espionage exploits during the war against the Americans in the 1960s and 1970s (Vu Ngoc Nha, Huynh Van Trong, Pham Xuan An, Pham Ngoc Thao, Nguyen Van Ta AKA Dang Duc Tran, etc.).

Notes

Overview: The early development of Vietnamese intelligence services, 1945–50

Christopher E. Goscha

1   Chris Goscha, 'Intelligence Studies and Decolonisation: The Case of the Democratic Republic of Vietnam at War (1945–50)', *Intelligence and National Security*, 22/1 (2007), pp. 100–38.

Commentary: The development of Vietnamese intelligence

Merle Pribbenow

1   Vo Nguyen Giap and Huu Mai, *Chien Dau Trong Vong Vay* [Fighting While Surrounded], (Hanoi: People's Army Publishing House, 2001), pp. 137, 141.
2   Hoang Hai Van and Tan Tu, *Pham Xuan An: A General of the Secret Service* (Hanoi: The Gioi Publishers, 2003), pp. 25–6; Colonel Cong Van Hieu and Lieutenant Colonel Kieu Duc Thanh, *Lich Su Tinh Bao Cong An Nhan Dan (1945–1954) – Luu Hanh Noi Bo* [History of People's Public Security Intelligence (1945–1954) – Internal Distribution Only] (Hanoi: People's Public Security Publishing House, 1996), p. 96.
3   Nguyen Thi Ngoc Hai, *Tran Quoc Huong: Nguoi Thay Cua Nhung Nha Tinh Bao Huyen Thoai* [Tran Quoc Huong: The Spy-Master of Legendary Intelligence Agents] (Hanoi: People's Public Security Publishing House, 2004), p. 94.

6 The interrogation of Klaus Fuchs, 1950

Michael Goodman and David Holloway

OVERVIEW: SIR MICHAEL PERRIN'S INTERVIEWS WITH DR KLAUS FUCHS

Michael Goodman

Background

Dr Klaus Emil Julius Fuchs is perhaps one of the most important spies the Soviet Union ever had. It has been confidently estimated that his information expedited the Soviet atomic bomb programme by 1–2 years, and more recently his hitherto unknown yet significant contribution to their hydrogen bomb programme has also begun to emerge.[1] In early 1950, Fuchs was arrested by British authorities for passing information to the Soviet Union. Sir Michael Perrin, at this time the Deputy Controller for Atomic Energy within the Ministry of Supply, was the scientist tasked with interviewing Fuchs. Perrin was chosen for two reasons: he had been involved in atomic intelligence matters since the war and so had the highest levels of clearance; and in addition he had the technical knowledge to assess Fuchs's contribution. Following his admission of guilt, Fuchs was interviewed by Perrin in January and again in March 1950.

Klaus Fuchs was no ordinary scientist. Having arrived in England in the early 1930s, he completed his doctorate at Bristol University, before moving to Edinburgh University for post-doctoral study. With the outbreak of war and with a desperate shortage of competent scientists, Fuchs – now a naturalised Briton – had his security clearance rushed through and began work on the atomic bomb. His initial involvement was concerned with intelligence information on the German programme, but before long he was dispatched to New York, first, to work at the British Diffusion Mission, and thence to Los Alamos, where he worked in the Theoretical Division. Despite the strict compartmentalisation at Los Alamos, the British group were given *carte blanche* to attend all colloquia and visit all areas. In addition, however, even had they been subjected to rigorous division, it seems this would have made little difference to Fuchs. As General Groves – the military head of the Manhattan Project – testified in the Oppenheimer hearings in 1954, 'It is important to realize [that] if we had limited [overall information] to a small group, say just the top people, Fuchs might still have been in that group.'[2] In 1946, Fuchs left Los Alamos and moved to the British Atomic Energy Research Establishment at Harwell, where he headed the Theoretical Division – a position he remained in until his arrest in 1950.

Fuchs's admission of guilt could not have come at a worse time for the British. Just a few months earlier the first Soviet atomic bomb had been detected, coming a number of years before it had been predicted. Partly as a result, there had been renewed calls on both sides of the Atlantic for the US to resurrect its technical sharing of atomic information with the UK. Talks to achieve this had progressed well, that is until the Fuchs's affair broke. It signalled an end to such discussion and left the British to go it alone.

An integral component of intelligence work is a consideration of knowing what the enemy knows about you. As such, Perrin's interview with Fuchs now provided a potential information feast to the intelligence services. It was known that Fuchs had had access to the highest levels of information both in the United States, and in the United Kingdom. He was therefore in a position to pass on not only the work he had been concerned with, but also that of everyone else. Perrin's interviews took place within this context. Perrin was to have two meetings with Fuchs. The first, in January 1950, was a general discussion of what information Fuchs had provided to the Russians. The second meeting, in March, was designed to answer questions provided by the Americans who, for various reasons, were not allowed at this stage to meet Fuchs yet who were desperate to interrogate him.[3] Intelligence on the Soviet nuclear weapons programme had been accorded the highest priority in Whitehall and Washington. With the first Soviet bomb arriving earlier than the intelligence agencies had predicted, it became paramount to know what else Fuchs had transmitted, and to adapt intelligence estimates accordingly.[4]

The espionage of Klaus Fuchs

Through his interviews with Perrin, Fuchs admitted that he had conveyed information on the origins of the British project in 1942, and of the American gaseous diffusion project once he re-located there in 1943. In February 1945, Fuchs passed a report he had written, summarising 'the whole problem of making an atomic bomb as he saw it'. He passed a subsequent report on the same topic in June, this time also using information from the relevant files at Los Alamos so that the information was correct; in addition, he provided a blueprint of the implosion bomb design to be tested at Trinity.

After returning to England, Fuchs was employed at Harwell. Harwell was concerned exclusively with the peaceful aspects of atomic energy, yet Fuchs was a frequent visitor to Dr William Penney's weapons development laboratory at Fort Halstead. According to Fuchs, he had refused to answer Soviet questions on the size of the US stockpile or about the British programme. Importantly, at this time, Fuchs provided more detailed information on the fission bomb. In regard to the hydrogen bomb, Fuchs noted that he had given 'the Russian agent the essential nuclear physics data and the general picture as far as it was then [in mid-1947] known to him of how the weapon would work'.[5]

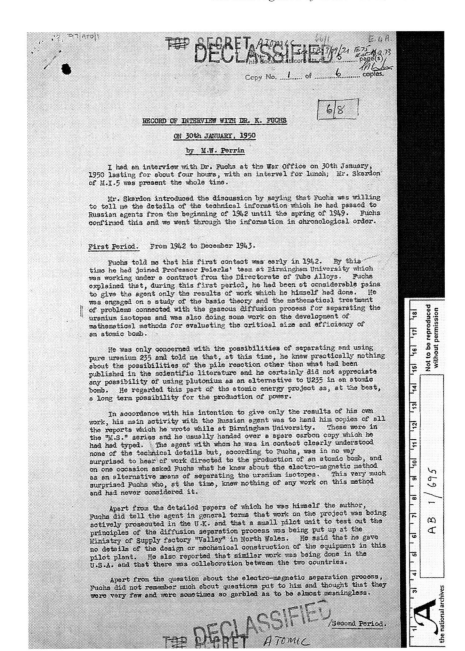

TOP SECRET ATOMIC

DECLASSIFIED

Copy No. 1 of 6 copies.

6 8

RECORD OF INTERVIEW WITH DR. K. FUCHS

ON 30th JANUARY, 1950

by M.W. Perrin

I had an interview with Dr. Fuchs at the War Office on 30th January, 1950 lasting for about four hours, with an interval for lunch; Mr. Skardon of M.I.5 was present the whole time.

Mr. Skardon introduced the discussion by saying that Fuchs was willing to tell me the details of the technical information which he had passed to Russian agents from the beginning of 1942 until the spring of 1949. Fuchs confirmed this and we went through the information in chronological order.

First Period. From 1942 to December 1943.

Fuchs told me that his first contact was early in 1942. By this time he had joined Professor Peierls' team at Birmingham University which was working under a contract from the Directorate of Tube Alloys. Fuchs explained that, during this first period, he had been at considerable pains to give the agent only the results of work which he himself had done. He was engaged on a study of the basic theory and the mathematical treatment of problems connected with the gaseous diffusion process for separating the uranium isotopes and was also doing some work on the development of mathematical methods for evaluating the critical size and efficiency of an atomic bomb.

He was only concerned with the possibilities of separating and using pure uranium 235 and told me that, at this time, he knew practically nothing about the possibilities of the pile reaction other than what had been published in the scientific literature and he certainly did not appreciate any possibility of using plutonium as an alternative to U235 in an atomic bomb. He regarded this part of the atomic energy project as, at the best, a long term possibility for the production of power.

In accordance with his intention to give only the results of his own work, his main activity with the Russian agent was to hand him copies of all the reports which he wrote while at Birmingham University. These were in the "M.S." series and he usually handed over a spare carbon copy which he had had typed. The agent with whom he was in contact clearly understood none of the technical details but, according to Fuchs, was in no way surprised to hear of work directed to the production of an atomic bomb, and on one occasion asked Fuchs what he knew about the electro-magnetic method as an alternative means of separating the uranium isotopes. This very much surprised Fuchs who, at the time, knew nothing of any work on this method and had never considered it.

Apart from the detailed papers of which he was himself the author, Fuchs did tell the agent in general terms that work on the project was being actively prosecuted in the U.K. and that a small pilot unit to test out the principles of the diffusion separation process was being put up at the Ministry of Supply factory "Valley" in North Wales. He said that he gave no details of the design or mechanical construction of the equipment in this pilot plant. He also reported that similar work was being done in the U.S.A. and that there was collaboration between the two countries.

Apart from the question about the electro-magnetic separation process, Fuchs did not remember much about questions put to him and thought that they were very few and were sometimes so garbled as to be almost meaningless.

/Second Period.

DECLASSIFIED

TOP SECRET ATOMIC

Document Eight: 'Record of Interview with Dr. K. Fuchs on 30th January 1950, National Archives, Kew: AB 1/ 695. Produced with permission of the National Archives.

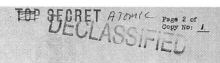

Page 2 of
Copy No: *1*

2.

Second Period.   New York.   December 1943 to August 1944.

Fuchs was a member of the British Diffusion Mission which went to
New York in December 1943 and he stayed on there when the majority came
back to the U.K.   During this period Fuchs learnt a good deal more about
the American programme and, in particular, that a large production plant
for the gaseous diffusion process was being built which would be worked
in conjunction with a second large plant using the electro-magnetic
process.   He knew that both these plants would be at "Site X" but he
told me that he did not then know where this was and could not therefore
report it to the new Russian agent with whom he was in contact in the
U.S.A.   He did, however, know of the general scale of effort of the
American programme and the approximate timing, and this information was
passed over.   By now his original intention to pass on only such
information as was the result of his own work had been dropped and he
did provide some technical information about the American gaseous diffusion
plant.   He told me that he had given the agent some general information
about the membranes and had told him that these would be made of sintered
nickel powder though he did not know any technical details.   His main
contribution was to pass over copies of all the reports prepared in the
New York office of the British Diffusion Mission.   These carried the
serial letters "M.S.N." and he handed over, usually, the manuscript of
each report after it had been typed for duplication.

During this period Fuchs said that he still had no real knowledge of
the pile process or of the significance of plutonium.   He paid one short
visit to Montreal and knew that the team there were engaged on the design
and construction of a small heavy water pile.   He took no great interest
in this work and imagined it could only be related to the long-term
possibility of the development of atomic energy as a source of power.
As far as he could remember he did not pass any of this to the Russian
agent as he regarded it as of little interest.   He told me that during
this period he got the impression from the agent that the Russians had a
great general interest in the project and that its importance was fully
appreciated, but he did not believe that anything very serious was being done
by the Russians themselves.

Third Period.   Los Alamos.   August 1944 to the summer of 1946.

When Fuchs went to Los Alamos he realised for the first time the full
nature and magnitude of the American atomic energy programme and the
importance of plutonium as an alternative to U235 became clear to him.
He also learnt then that it was intended to build large plutonium-producing
piles as an alternative to the U235 production plants at Oakridge.

The first contact with the Russian agent after he went to Los Alamos
was in February 1945, when he met him at Boston, Mass.   While there Fuchs
wrote a report, which he said would have covered several pages, summarising
the whole problem of making an atomic bomb as he then saw it.   This report
included a statement of the special difficulties that would have to be
overcome in making a plutonium bomb.   He reported the high spontaneous
fission rate of plutonium and the deduction that a plutonium bomb would
have to be detonated by using the implosion method rather than the relatively
simple gun method which could be used with U235.   He also reported that the
critical mass for plutonium was less than that for U235 and that about
5 to 15 kilos would be necessary for a bomb.   At this time the issue was
not clear as to whether uniform compression of the core could be better
obtained with a high explosive lens system or with multi-point detonation
over the surface of a uniform sphere of high explosive.   He reported the

/current

Document Eight continued

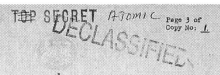

3.

current ideas as to the need for an initiator though these, at the time, were very vague and it was thought that a constant neutron source might be sufficient. Finally, when he wrote his report in February 1945 he referred only to the hollow plutonium core for the atomic bomb as he did not then know anything about the possibility of a solid core.

He met the Russian agent again in Santa Fe at the end of June 1945 and this time handed him a detailed report which he had already written in Los Alamos with access to the relevant files so that he could be sure that all figures mentioned were correct.

This second report described fully the plutonium bomb which had by this time been designed and was to be tested at "Trinity". He provided a sketch of the bomb and its components and gave all the important dimensions. He reported that the bomb would have a solid plutonium core and described the initiator which, he said, would contain about 50 curies of polonium. Full details were given of the tamper, the aluminium shell and of the high explosive lens system. He told the agent that the two explosives to be used in this system were "Baratol" and "Composition B", though he himself did not know what this really meant in terms of H.E. technology.

The Russian agent was told that the "Trinity" test was expected to produce an explosion equivalent to about 10 kilo tons of T.N.T. and was given details of the date and an approximate indication of the site.

Fuchs told me that, at this time, details of production pile design, construction and operation were still unknown to him and were therefore not passed to the Russian agent. He had several further meetings with him in Santa Fe in the autumn of 1945 and spring of 1946 but could not remember precise dates. During these meetings he gave some information on the delta phase of plutonium and "probably" made some reference to the use of gallium as an alloying constituent, but he was insistent that he gave no other information on the metallurgy of plutonium and that he did not describe the techniques needed for its preparation or fabrication.

During this latter period at Los Alamos, or perhaps soon after he returned to the U.K., Fuchs gave the Russian agent some general information about the possibilities of developing a "mixed" bomb. In particular, he emphasised the advantage of this for the U.S.A. because they already had both plutonium production piles and isotope separation plants and could make use of both materials.

The Russian agent with whom he was in contact during his whole period in the U.S.A. (while at New York and Los Alamos) was rather more capable of understanding the information which he was given than had been the case with his contact in the U.K. Fuchs described him as being perhaps an engineer or chemical engineer. He clearly had no detailed knowledge of nuclear physics or of the sort of mathematics with which Fuchs was competent to deal.

Fourth Period. Harwell. Summer of 1946 to Spring of 1949.

Fuchs explained that, during this last period, he was having increasing doubts on the wisdom of passing information to the Russians, and he assured me that he did not give them all the information that he could have given and that he did not always answer questions that were put to him. He was, for instance, several times asked for the American rate of production and stockpile of atomic bombs and about the U.K. programme.

/As to

Document Eight continued

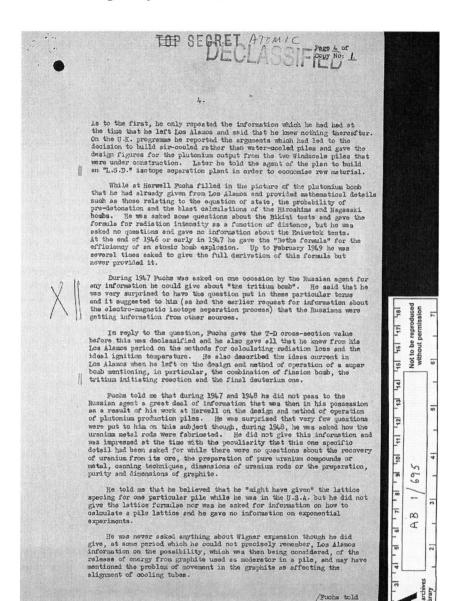

TOP SECRET ATOMIC
Page 4 of
Copy No: 1.
DECLASSIFIED

4.

As to the first, he only repeated the information which he had had at
the time that he left Los Alamos and said that he knew nothing thereafter.
On the U.K. programme he reported the arguments which had led to the
decision to build air-cooled rather than water-cooled piles and gave the
design figures for the plutonium output from the two Windscale piles that
were under construction. Later he told the agent of the plan to build
an "L.S.D." isotope separation plant in order to economise raw material.

While at Harwell Fuchs filled in the picture of the plutonium bomb
that he had already given from Los Alamos and provided mathematical details
such as those relating to the equation of state, the probability of
pre-detonation and the blast calculations of the Hiroshima and Nagasaki
bombs. He was asked some questions about the Bikini tests and gave the
formula for radiation intensity as a function of distance, but he was
asked no questions and gave no information about the Eniwetok tests.
At the end of 1946 or early in 1947 he gave the "Bethe formula" for the
efficiency of an atomic bomb explosion. Up to February 1949 he was
several times asked to give the full derivation of this formula but
never provided it.

During 1947 Fuchs was asked on one occasion by the Russian agent for
any information he could give about "the tritium bomb". He said that he
was very surprised to have the question put in these particular terms
and it suggested to him (as had the earlier request for information about
the electro-magnetic isotope separation process) that the Russians were
getting information from other sources.

In reply to the question, Fuchs gave the T-D cross-section value
before this was declassified and he also gave all that he knew from his
Los Alamos period on the methods for calculating radiation loss and the
ideal ignition temperature. He also described the ideas current in
Los Alamos when he left on the design and method of operation of a super
bomb mentioning, in particular, the combination of fission bomb, the
tritium initiating reaction and the final deuterium one.

Fuchs told me that during 1947 and 1948 he did not pass to the
Russian agent a great deal of information that was then in his possession
as a result of his work at Harwell on the design and method of operation
of plutonium production piles. He was surprised that very few questions
were put to him on this subject though, during 1948, he was asked how the
uranium metal rods were fabricated. He did not give this information and
was impressed at the time with the peculiarity that this one specific
detail had been asked for while there were no questions about the recovery
of uranium from its ore, the preparation of pure uranium compounds or
metal, canning techniques, dimensions of uranium rods or the preparation,
purity and dimensions of graphite.

He told me that he believed that he "might have given" the lattice
spacing for one particular pile while he was in the U.S.A. but he did not
give the lattice formulae nor was he asked for information on how to
calculate a pile lattice and he gave no information on exponential
experiments.

He was never asked anything about Wigner expansion though he did
give, at some period which he could not precisely remember, Los Alamos
information on the possibility, which was then being considered, of the
release of energy from graphite used as moderator in a pile, and may have
mentioned the problem of movement in the graphite as affecting the
alignment of cooling tubes.

/Fuchs told

DECLASSIFIED
TOP SECRET ATOMIC

Document Eight continued

TOP SECRET ATOMIC
Page 5 of
Copy No: 1.

5.

Fuchs told me that he was never asked for, and never gave "fundamental nuclear physics data relating to the fission reaction".

During this last period Fuchs said that he had given the agent general information on the ideas current at Harwell on new types of reactor including the "flame trap" design, the "ball" and "sandwich" reactors, fast reactors and breeders.

During the latter part of 1948 he was asked on one occasion for a specific Chalk River report, dealing with neutron distribution in the N.R.X. pile, which he had never seen. He was also told that "there is a report on mixing devices" and was asked whether he could get it. He had not, at the time, seen this report but identified it at Harwell and provided extracts from it. This information refers to a particular design detail that is relevant only to the Windscale air-cooled production piles.

He was also asked about the solvent extraction process. He knew hardly anything of this but was able to get some very limited information from Harwell reports and passed this over though he believed that this was of no great significance.

All these questions confirmed his opinion that the Russians had access to information from another source or sources.

Finally, I discussed with Fuchs the nature of the "atomic explosion" that had taken place in Russia in the autumn of 1949. He told me that he would have expected this to be due to a plutonium bomb in the light of all the information he had passed to the Russians. He, personally, believed that this conclusion was confirmed by the measurements on the airborne fission products that had been collected, though he recognised the doubt in this interpretation due to the lack of chemical evidence for the presence of plutonium in the cloud. He said that he was, however, extremely surprised that the Russian explosion had taken place so soon as he had been convinced that the information he had given could not have been applied so quickly and that the Russians would not have the engineering design and construction facilities that would be needed to build large production plants in such a short time.

I formed the impression that, throughout the interview, Fuchs was genuinely trying to remember and report all the information that he had given to the Russian agents with whom he had been in contact and that he was not withholding anything. He seemed, on the contrary, to be trying his best to help me to evaluate the present position of atomic energy work in Russia in the light of the information that he had, and had not, passed to them.

Michael Perrin

TOP SECRET ATOMIC

Document Eight continued

RECORD OF INTERVIEW WITH DR. K. FUCHS

on 22nd MARCH, 1950

by M.W. Perrin

I had an interview with Dr. Fuchs at Wormwood Scrubs on 22nd March, 1950 lasting for about an hour. As in the case of my earlier interview on 30th January, 1950, Mr. Skardon of M.I.5 was present.

This second interview was arranged with Dr. Fuchs' consent, and its object was to try to get more information from him as to what he had passed over to the Russian agents with whom he had been in contact here and in the U.S.A.

The questions which I put to Dr. Fuchs were based on discussion of the record of my earlier interview with Sir John Cockcroft and Commander Welsh, and were designed to get answers, if possible, to a list of 24 questions arising from consideration of the record of the first interview which had been forwarded to us from the Nuclear Energy Division of the C.I.A. These questions were the result of consideration by the American Joint Atomic Energy Intelligence Committee which includes representatives of the Intelligence Section of the U.S.A.E.C.

I would first emphasise two general points arising from my interview with Fuchs.

While he showed every sign of willingness to help in any way that he could, he strongly maintained his inability to remember in detail much of the information that he had passed over to the Russians. This seems surprising but may perhaps be due to his having, subconsciously, forced himself to forget his disloyalty.

The second general point is that Fuchs made it clear that, from his first contact in 1942 until his last in the early part of 1949, he only had about a dozen meetings with Russian agents here and in the U.S.A. At any one of these meetings he might have been asked two or three questions, and these were generally of a very vague nature. It is therefore extremely difficult to assess, from the nature of the questions put to Fuchs, the real interest of the Russians.

As an example of this (cf. C.I.A. question No. 10), Fuchs said that, so far as he could remember, the question about the E.M. process put to him in the U.K. in 1943 was read out from a piece of paper, and the words were something like: "What do you know of the electro-magnetic method for separating isotopes?"

Fuchs told me that he was never asked any questions on heavy water, and none about uranium production until 1948 when he was asked how the uranium metal rods for a pile were fabricated.

Fuchs confirmed his earlier statement that the information given to the Russians on the gaseous diffusion process while he was in the U.K. during 1942 and 1943, and in New York during the first part of 1944, was fairly

/complete

Document Nine: 'Record of Interview with Dr. K. Fuchs on 22nd March 1950', National Archives, Kew: AB 1/ 695. Produced with permission of the National Archives.

TOP SECRET ATOMIC Page 2 of
Copy No: 1.

DECLASSIFIED

complete as far as the theory was concerned. He did not have much
practical knowledge or engineering "know-how" and did not pass this over,
nor did he give the Russians information on construction materials in a
gaseous diffusion plant.

Fuchs was asked no supplementary questions on this subject other
than a general question about the barriers. As he told me at the first
interview, he did say, during the time when he was in New York, that these
were made of sintered nickel powder. (cf. C.I.A. questions No. 3 & 4.)

Fuchs told me, in amplification of what he had said at the first
interview, that he was fairly sure that, either at the end of the
Los Alamos period or early in the final Harwell period, he had told the
Russian agent something about the relationship between the spontaneous
fission rate of Pu 240 and the exposure time of uranium in a pile. He
believed that he had quoted 2% Pu 240 as being the permissible upper limit
due to difficulty that would be encountered from spontaneous fission
neutrons from this isotope in the detonation of a bomb. (cf. C.I.A.
question No. 5.)

Fuchs was very clear in his recollection that he had never given, or
been asked for, information about the fuzing and firing techniques in any
kind of atomic bomb. The detailed information about the Trinity Test
bomb which he had written out and passed over in June 1945 stopped short
at the H.E. lens system.

Few, if any, technical production details or "know-how" were given in
the Santa Fe meetings about weapon components, but Fuchs did describe in
detail the design of the initiator and "possibly" the nickel carbonyl
process for plating. He did not, however, give any information on the
manufacture of beryllium metal.

He did not remember giving any details about delta phase plutonium
or phase diagrams, but only referred in rather general terms to its
existence. (cf. C.I.A. questions No. 12, 13 & 22.)

The calculations of blast etc. that Fuchs passed over were based on
reports which he had written for Dr. Penney. This information was mostly
passed in the form of short summaries, but "some of the actual reports
may have been passed over". (cf. C.I.A. questions 8, 20 & 21.)

As far as the "mixed" bomb is concerned, Fuchs repeated that he had
only given the agent some general information about its possibilities.
He thought that he had "probably" referred to a 2-to-1 mixture as a
particular case, and had mentioned the critical mass that would be
involved. No sketches were given.

In my first interview with Fuchs he had told me that he believed that
he "might have given" the lattice spacing for one particular pile while he
was in the U.S.A. On think this over, however, he felt more certain
during the second interview that the lattice which he had passed over was
that designed for the Windscale piles, and that this information had been
given early in 1947. (cf. C.I.A. question No. 16.) At that time he
gave, as he had said at the first interview, the design figures for the
plutonium output from the Windscale piles.

/During

TOP SECRET ATOMIC
DECLASSIFIED

AB 1/695

Document Nine continued

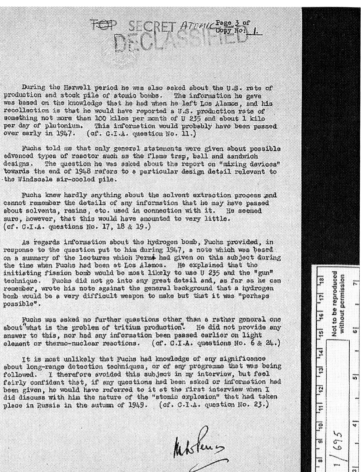

TOP SECRET ATOMIC Page 3 of
Copy No: 1

DECLASSIFIED

During the Harwell period he was also asked about the U.S. rate of
production and stock pile of atomic bombs. The information he gave
was based on the knowledge that he had when he left Los Alamos, and his
recollection is that he would have reported a U.S. production rate of
something not more than 100 kilos per month of U 235 and about 1 kilo
per day of plutonium. This information would probably have been passed
over early in 1947. (cf. C.I.A. question No. 11.)

Fuchs told me that only general statements were given about possible
advanced types of reactor such as the flame trap, bell and sandwich
designs. The question he was asked about the report on "mixing devices"
towards the end of 1948 refers to a particular design detail relevant to
the Windscale air-cooled pile.

Fuchs knew hardly anything about the solvent extraction process and
cannot remember the details of any information that he may have passed
about solvents, resins, etc. used in connection with it. He seemed
sure, however, that this would have amounted to very little.
(cf. C.I.A. questions No. 17, 18 & 19.)

As regards information about the hydrogen bomb, Fuchs provided, in
response to the question put to him during 1947, a note which was based
on a summary of the lectures which Fermi had given on this subject during
the time when Fuchs had been at Los Alamos. He explained that the
initiating fission bomb would be most likely to use U 235 and the "gun"
technique. Fuchs did not go into any great detail and, as far as he can
remember, wrote his note against the general background that a hydrogen
bomb would be a very difficult weapon to make but that it was "perhaps
possible".

Fuchs was asked no further questions other than a rather general one
about "what is the problem of tritium production". He did not provide any
answer to this, nor had any information been passed earlier on light
element or thermo-nuclear reactions. (cf. C.I.A. questions No. 6 & 24.)

It is most unlikely that Fuchs had knowledge of any significance
about long-range detection techniques, or of any programme that was being
followed. I therefore avoided this subject in my interview, but feel
fairly confident that, if any questions had been asked or information had
been given, he would have referred to it at the first interview when I
did discuss with him the nature of the "atomic explosion" that had taken
place in Russia in the autumn of 1949. (cf. C.I.A. question No. 23.)

TOP SECRET ATOMIC
DECLASSIFIED

Document Nine continued

Fuchs's post-war handler in England, KGB agent Alexander Feklisov, has commented that 'Klaus only admitted to the very minimum and was far from volunteering to confess everything to the British authorities.'[6] There is evidence that Feklisov has proof for this, as it has been claimed the KGB received British intelligence reports on Fuchs's confession, possibly courtesy of the Cambridge spy ring.[7] Despite these claims, however, there do appear great discrepancies in his testimony concerning his role, in particular, in the development of the hydrogen bomb that, it is now evident from Russian documents, Fuchs played a much greater role. At the same time though, what is crucial, in a sense, is the belief that Perrin held, that 'Fuchs was genuinely trying to remember and report all the information that he had given to the Russian agents with whom he had been in contact and that he was not withholding anything.'[8]

COMMENTARY: AN ANALYSIS OF SIR MICHAEL PERRIN'S INTERVIEWS WITH KLAUS FUCHS: COMPARATIVE SOVIET PERSPECTIVES

David Holloway

In recent years documents have been published that make it possible to look at Klaus Fuchs from the Soviet perspective. How does Fuchs's confession to Sir Michael Perrin look when matched against those documents? Did Fuchs give Perrin an accurate account of his activities? What use did the Soviet Union make of the information Fuchs provided? What value did the Soviet intelligence services and Soviet scientists place on that information?

First Period. From 1942 to December 1943

Fuchs joined Rudolf Peierls's group at the University of Birmingham in May 1941. Three months later, on August 8, Fuchs had a conversation with S.D. Kremer ('Baron'), a member of the military attaché's staff at the Soviet Embassy in London. Fuchs told Kremer about his research and reported that Werner Heisenberg was working in Leipzig on the problem of the uranium bomb. He gave a short report on the utilization of uranium and said that if only 1 per cent of the energy of a 10kg uranium bomb were realized, the yield would be equivalent to 1000 tonnes of dynamite. Two days later, the London *rezidentura* of Soviet military intelligence cabled this information to A.V. Panfilov, director of military intelligence. Panfilov recommended that a physicist be consulted, but it is not clear whether that was done or when.[1]

The cable from military intelligence arrived in Moscow some weeks earlier than the first report from the NKVD *rezident* in London, A.V. Gorskii, about atomic energy research in Britain. In late September 1941, Gorskii informed Moscow that the British had decided to make the uranium bomb and described some of the steps being taken to achieve that goal.[2] Several days later he sent further information, apparently including a copy of the report of the Maud Committee, which had made a cogent argument in the summer of 1941 that it would be possible to make an atomic bomb by the end of 1943.[3] The Maud Report, which had provided the basis for the British decision to build the bomb, played an important role in the American decision too.[4] On October 9, 1941 – at about the same time that Gorskii sent his second report to Moscow – Vannevar Bush, chairman of the U.S. National Defense Research Committee, briefed President Roosevelt on the Maud Report and received the president's approval to make a concerted effort to see if the atomic bomb could be built.[5]

Fuchs told Perrin that in this period he had provided mainly his own reports on theoretical aspects of the gaseous diffusion process for separating uranium isotopes. The Soviet documents show that the GRU (*Glavnoe razvedyvatel'noe upravlenie* – the Chief Intelligence Directorate of the General Staff) wanted information of a different kind. On September 28, 1942, the GRU wrote to the London *rezidentura*. 'The materials from "Foks" about work on the uranium bomb are of interest and are being used by us,' it stated, but it wanted Fuchs to throw light on the following questions: the work on isotope separation at Imperial Chemical Industries; work being done by Metro-Vickers in Manchester; the research of Professor Dirac in Cambridge and Professor Joliot in Paris; work on uranium in Germany and in the United States (especially in Berkeley).[6] The letter concluded by saying that Fuchs should find out what practical results had been achieved, 'since most of the materials received up to now have been basically theoretical explorations'. It is clear that the GRU was not completely satisfied with the information Fuchs was providing.

On June 27, 1943, Moscow sent another 'operational letter' with a long list of questions for Fuchs, including the question about electromagnetic isotope separation that suggested to him that the Soviet Union had sources of information other than him.[7] Other questions on the list asked how much separated U-235 there was in the world and how much uranium had been mined in different countries. It is unlikely that Fuchs provided information of this type. An assessment prepared by the GRU in 1945 suggests that Fuchs gave little information about the industrial side of the atomic project:

> During his work for the Intelligence Directorate of the Red Army Fuchs provided a series of valuable materials, containing theoretical calculations on the fissioning of the uranium atom and the creation of the atomic bomb . . . In all, in the period 1941–1943 more than 570 pages of valuable material were received from Fuchs.[8]

Fuchs did not, however, confine himself to providing copies of his own work. In the summer of 1943, he gave the GRU a list of the titles of 286 American scientific reports. Igor Kurchatov, who had been appointed scientific director of the Soviet atomic project, wrote a memorandum on this list, pointing out which reports were of particular interest.[9] On August 13, the GRU wrote to the London *rezidentura* that it would like to obtain copies of nine of these reports, but it is not clear whether Fuchs passed on any of those reports or indeed whether he was in a position to do so.[10]

The Soviet documents generally confirm Fuchs's account of his activities in this period. They help to explain Fuchs's apparent irritation at the questions he was asked. He wanted to give Soviet intelligence the results of his own research, but the GRU wanted broader and more practical information about the British atomic project. Important though Fuchs was in this period, the information Moscow received through the NKVD about the Maud Committee's work and the overall direction of the British effort appears to have been more significant than Fuchs's reports, because that information made it clear that the atomic bomb was indeed a realistic possibility.

Second Period. New York. December 1943 to August 1944

Before Fuchs left for New York in December 1943, the GRU made arrangements for him to contact a new courier, Harry Gold. Fuchs was not aware that he was now reporting to the NKVD.[11] During this period, he worked in New York as a member of the British Diffusion Mission. According to his confession, he provided the Soviet Union with information about the gaseous diffusion process of isotope separation.

I.K. Kikoin, who was in charge of the gaseous diffusion separation process in the Soviet project, wrote three analyses of intelligence material he received in the course of 1944. The material reviewed by Kikoin consisted largely of reports on various aspects of gaseous diffusion isotope separation. Kikoin's analyses of this material were written between 5 July 1944 and 28 February 1945, but the material examined in the last report had been given to Kikoin on 16 September 1944. The timing and content of Kikoin's reports suggest that in all three reports he was reviewing material provided by Fuchs. In the second of his analyses, Kikoin placed a high value on the material he had received. 'Together with the earlier material devoted to these problems,' he wrote, 'this provides a very full and valuable theoretical analysis of the productivity and stability of the plant.'[12]

Third Period. Los Alamos. August 1944 to the summer of 1946

After moving to Los Alamos, Fuchs took part in solving the most important problem Los Alamos had to deal with, i.e. designing an implosion method that would make it possible to initiate a nuclear chain reaction in plutonium, in spite of that element's high rate of spontaneous fission. Fuchs told Perrin that in February 1945 he gave Gold material on the plutonium bomb. In a memorandum written on April 7, Kurchatov analyzed what is evidently the material provided by Fuchs.[13] (Kurchatov had received the intelligence the day before, on April 6.) Kurchatov commented that the data on the spontaneous fission of heavy elements were 'exceptionally important'. He was struck by the high spontaneous fission rate of plutonium. Kurchatov was also impressed by the material on the implosion method, which he had only recently learned about and had only just begun work on. (Some weeks earlier another source at Los Alamos had provided information on implosion, but this was evidently not as detailed as the information provided by Fuchs.)[14] It is clear from Kurchatov's commentary that Fuchs gave Perrin an accurate account of what he provided to Gold.

At the end of June 1945, Fuchs gave Gold a detailed report on the plutonium bomb, which he had written at Los Alamos with access to the relevant files. He informed Gold that the plutonium bomb was to be tested in New Mexico in July and that it would produce an explosion equivalent to about 10 kilotons of TNT. On July 10, V. N. Merkulov, head of the NKGB, wrote to Beria that the NKGB had received information 'from several reliable agent sources' that the explosive test of the plutonium bomb would take place in July, probably on July 10, and that the expected yield was 5 kilotons. (The test took place on July 16 and the yield was 20 kilotons.) This information was probably given to Stalin before the Potsdam conference, which began on July 17.[15]

On October 18, as the Soviet crash program to build the bomb was getting under way, Beria received a memorandum from Merkulov containing information, presumably based on Fuchs's report, about the design of the atomic bomb.[16] Merkulov's memorandum contained a description of the plutonium bomb with all the dimensions and a description of the materials from which it had been made, including the delta phase of plutonium. Kurchatov decided to take this as the basis for the design of the first Soviet plutonium bomb, on the grounds that the quickest and most reliable way to make the first bomb was to copy a design that had already worked.

Fourth Period. Harwell. Summer of 1946 to Spring of 1949

Fuchs told Perrin that he had been asked a great many specific questions in this final period of his work as a spy. The relevant Russian documents have not been published, so it is not possible to make a judgment on the value of his answers to most of those questions. There is, however, evidence about the impact of the information he provided about the superbomb (i.e. the hydrogen bomb). Fuchs had attended a conference at Los Alamos in April 1946 at which Edward Teller presented the 'Classical Super', the design concept he had developed at Los Alamos during the war. Fuchs was well informed about the state of knowledge about the superbomb in the United States in the spring of 1946.

Fuchs did not volunteer this information. It was his new controller, A. S. Feklisov who asked Fuchs for information about the 'tritium bomb' in September 1947. Fuchs told Feklisov in general terms about the work done in the United States up to 1946. Six months later, on March 13, 1948, he gave Feklisov a package of material. Apart from the information listed in his confession, he provided a detailed description, along with a diagram, of the design of the Classical Super as it existed in the Spring of 1946. He also included information on the idea that he and John Von Neumann had come up with for compressing and igniting thermonuclear fuel.[17] The Ministry of State Security forwarded this material to Stalin, Molotov, and Beria. On June 10, the Soviet government set up a special group, under Iakov Zel'dovich, to work on the hydrogen bomb at the nuclear weapons center in Sarov, and another group, under Igor Tamm, at the Physics Institute of the Academy of Sciences in Moscow.[18]

In his confession to Perrin, Fuchs did not put much weight on the information he had provided to the Soviet Union about the superbomb. It is true that the ideas current at Los Alamos in 1945–46 turned out not to work. The path from the 1946 position to the testing of thermonuclear weapons proved to be difficult and complicated in the Soviet Union as well as the United States. Fuchs's information nevertheless provided an impetus to Soviet work on thermonuclear weapons, and the ideas he conveyed – especially the idea that he and Von Neumann developed – may have helped Soviet scientists come to an understanding of how the hydrogen might be built.[19] None of that would have been clear to Fuchs at the time of his confession to Perrin, and his dismissive attitude to the information he had given to the Soviet Union may reflect his real estimate of its value rather than an attempt to deceive Perrin.

Conclusion

Several conclusions can be drawn from this brief review. First, the Soviet documents by and large confirm the accuracy of Fuchs's confession to Perrin. Second, in 1941–43 Fuchs and the GRU appear to have been somewhat at cross-purposes, with the GRU wanting Fuchs to give it information he either could not, or would not, provide. In this period, the information Fuchs supplied was less important than that obtained by the NKVD from other sources in Britain. Fuchs's deep interest in physics, which may have frustrated the GRU in 1941–43, was, however, of great importance once Fuchs arrived in Los Alamos and had access to data on the design of the bomb. Third, Fuchs's information was treated very seriously by the Soviet intelligence services and by Soviet scientists, especially after November 1942, when Kurchatov began to receive the intelligence material for review. The material Fuchs provided may have influenced the Soviet choice of gaseous diffusion as the main process for separating uranium-235 and certainly influenced the design of the first Soviet atomic bomb, which was tested on August 29, 1949.

Notes

Overview: Sir Michael Perrin's interviews with Dr Klaus Fuchs

Michael Goodman

1 For more on this, see M.S. Goodman, 'The Grandfather of the Hydrogen Bomb?: Anglo-American Intelligence and Klaus Fuchs', *Historical Studies in the Physical and Biological Sciences*, 34/1 (2003), pp. 1–22.
2 Cited in *In the Matter of J.Robert Oppenheimer: Transcript of Hearing before Personnel Security Board* (Washington, DC: USGPO, 1954), p. 175.
3 For more, see M.S. Goodman. '"Who is Trying to Keep What Secret from Whom and Why?" MI5-FBI Relations and the Klaus Fuchs Case', *Journal of Cold War Studies*, 7/3 (Summer 2005), pp. 124–46.
4 See M.S. Goodman. *Spying on the Nuclear Bear: Anglo-American Intelligence and the Soviet Bomb* (Stanford, CA: Stanford University Press, 2007).

5   'Statement of Michael Wilcox Perrin', 31 January 1950, PRO: KV 2/1250.
6   A. Feklisov, *The Man Behind the Rosenbergs: Memoirs of the KGB Spymaster who Also Controlled Klaus Fuchs and Helped Resolve the Cuban Missile Crisis* (New York: Enigma Books, 2001), pp. 228–45.
7   S. Roberts, *The Brother: The Untold Story of Atomic Spy David Greenglass and How He Sent His Sister, Ethel Rosenberg, to the Electric Chair* (New York: Random House, 2001), pp. 216–17.
8   'Record of Interview with Dr K. Fuchs on 30th January, 1950', PRO AB 1/695, p. 5.

Commentary: An analysis of Sir Michael Perrin's interviews with Klaus Fuchs: comparative Soviet perspectives

David Holloway

1   'Rasshifrovka soobshcheniia rukovoditelia Londonskoi rezidentury v Razvedu-pravlenie Genshtaba KA o rabotakh po sozdaniiu atomnoi bomby v Anglii', [Deciphered communication from the director of the London *rezidentura* to the Intelligence Directorate of the General Staff of the Red Army about research on the development of an atomic bomb in England], Document No. 1/2, in L.D. Riabev (ed.), *Atomnyi proekt SSSR* [The Atomic Project of the USSR], vol. 1, *1938–1945, pt. 2* (Moscow: izd. MFTI), pp. 434–5.
2   'Spravka 1-go Upravleniia NKVD SSSR o soderzhanii poluchennoi iz Londona agenturnoi informatsii o "soveshchanii Komiteta po uranu"', [Information from the First Directorate of the USSR NKVD about the content of agents' information received from London about the 'meeting of the Uranium Committee'], Document No. 106, in (ed.), *Atomnyi proekt SSSR*, [The Atomic Project of the USSR], vol. 1 *1938–1945, pt. 1* (Moscow: Nauka, 1998), pp. 239–40.
3   'Spravka 1-go Upravleniia NKVD SSSR o soderzhanii doklada 'Uranovogo komiteta', podgotovlennaia po poluchennoi iz Londona agenturnoi informatsii', [Information from the First Directorate of the USSR NKVD about the content of the report of the 'Uranium Committee' prepared on the basis of agents' information received from London], Document No. 107, in ibid., pp. 241–2.
4   Margaret Gowing, *Britain and Atomic Energy* (London: Macmillan, 1964), Chapter 3.
5   McGeorge Bundy, *Danger and Survival: Choices About the Bomb in the First Fifty Years* (New York: Random House, 1988), pp. 43–4.
6   'Operativnoe pis'mo GRU Genshtaba KA rukovoditeliu Londonskoi rezidentury s zadaniem dlia K. Fuksa', [Operational letter from the GRU of the General Staff of the Red Army to the director of the London *rezidentura* with a task for K. Fuchs], Document 1/10, in Riabev *Atomnyi Proekt SSSR*, pp. 447–8.
7   'Operativnoe pis'mo GRU Genshtaba KA rukovoditeliu Londonskoi rezidentury s zadaniem dlia K. Fuksa', [Operational letter from the GRU of the General Staff of the Red Army to the director of the London *rezidentura* with a task for K. Fuchs], Document 1/11, ibid., pp. 448–50.
8   Quoted in Vladimir Lota, *GRU i atomnaia bomba* [The GRU and the Atomic Bomb] (Moscow: OLMA-PRESS, 2002), pp. 101–2.
9   'Iz otzyva I.V. Kurchatova na "Perechen" amerikanskikh rabot po probleme urana', [From I.V. Kurchatov's review of the 'List of American works on the uranium problem'], Document No. 169, in Riabev *Atomnyi proekt SSSR*, pt. 1, pp. 354–60.
10   'Operativnoe pis'mo GRU Genshtaba KA rukovoditeliu Londonskoi rezidentury s zadaniem dlia K. Fuksa', [Operational letter from the GRU of the General Staff of the Red Army to the director of the London *rezidentura* with a task for K. Fuchs], Document No. 1/15, in ibid. pt. 2, pp. 466–8.

11 Vladimir Lota, *GRU i atomnaia bomba* [The GRU and the Atomic Bomb], pp. 102–4.
12 'Zakliuchenie I.K. Kikoina o soderzhanii razvedmaterialov po diffuzionnoi ustanovke, postupivshikh iz NKGB SSSR', [I.K. Kikoin's assessment of the content of intelligence materials on the diffusion plant received from the USSR NKGB], Document No. 246; another document with the same title, Document No. 297; and 'Otzyv I.K. Kikoina o soderzhanii razvedmaterialov po diffuzionnoi ustanovke, postupivshikh iz NKGB SSSR', [I.K. Kikoin's report on the content of the intelligence materials on the diffusion plant received from the USSR NKGB], Document No. 315, all in Riabev, *Atomnyi proekt SSSR*, pt. 2, pp. 91, 196, 233–4.
13 'Zakliuchenie I.V. Kurchatova na razvedmaterialy ob effektivnosti "iadernogo vzryvchatogo veshchestva," metodakh vzryva i dr., postupivshie iz 1-go Upravleniia NKGB SSSR', [I.V. Kurchatov's assessment of the intelligence materials on the effectiveness of the 'nuclear explosive', methods of detonation etc., received from the First Directorate of the USSR NKGB], Document No. 329, in ibid. pt. 2, pp. 261–4.
14 See Kurchatov's analysis of this material in his memorandum of March 16, 1945, 'Zakliuchenie I.V. Kurchatova na razvedmaterialy (razdel "atomnaia bomba"), postupivshie iz 1-go Upravleniia NKGB SSSR', (I.V. Kurchatov's assessment about the intelligence materials (section 'atomic bomb') received from the First Directorate of the USSR NKGB], Document No. 321, in ibid., pt. 2, pp. 245–6. It appears that this information came from Ted Hall. See Joseph Albright and Marcia Kunstel, *Bombshell: The Secret Story of America's Unknown Atomic Spy Conspiracy* (New York: Times Books, 1997), pp. 122–3.
15 'Pis'mo NKGB SSSR L.P. Berii o podgotovke ispytaniia atomnoi bomby v SShA', [Letter from the USSR NKGB to L.P. Beria about preparation for the test of an atomic bomb in the USA], Document No. 371, in Riabev, *Atomnyi proekt SSSR*, pt. 2, pp. 335–6. On the likelihood that Stalin was informed about this, see the notes to the document, ibid. Kurchatov was given the same information orally on July 2; see 'Spravka 1-go Upravleniia NKGB SSSR o podgotovke k ispytaniiu atomnoi bomby v SShA', [Information from the First Directorate of the USSR NKGB about preparation for the test of an atomic bomb in the USA], Document No. 367, ibid., pp. 329–30.
16 Merkulov to Beria, October 18, 1945, in 'U istokov sovetskogo atomnogo proekta: Rol' razvedki, 1941–1946gg', [The origins of the Soviet atomic project: the role of intelligence, 1941–1946], *Voprosy istorii estestvoznaniia i tekhniki*, 1992, no. 3, pp. 126–9.
17 G.A. Goncharov, 'Osnovnye sobytiia istorii sozdaniia vodorodnoi bomby v SSSR i SShA', [The basic events in the history of the development of the hydrogen bomb in the USSR and the USA], *Uspekhi fizicheskikh nauk*, 1996, vol. 166, no. 10, 1098–9. The diagram of the Classical Super has been reprinted in Gregg Herken, *Brotherhood of the Bomb* (New York: Henry Holt, 2002), pp. 210–11.
18 Goncharov, 'Osnovnye', p. 1099.
19 G.A. Goncharov, 'Termoiadernyi proekt SSSR: Predystoriia i desiat' let puti k vodorodnoi bombe', [The thermonuclear project of the USSR: the prehistory and ten years on the path to the hydrogen bomb], in V.P. Vizgin (ed.), *Istoriia sovetskogo atomnogo proekta* [The History of the Soviet Atomic Project] (St Petersburg: The Russian Christian Humanities Institute, 2002), pp. 128–30.

7 The CIA and Oleg Penkovsky, 1961–63

Charles Cogan and Len Scott

OVERVIEW: THE ESPIONAGE OF OLEG PENKOVSKY

Charles Cogan

Overview: into the basement

Professor Christopher Andrew, the British historian and intelligence specialist, maintains there exists a serious gap in books about most world leaders, including American presidents: a lack of treatment of their role as consumers of intelligence. Andrew sought to correct this lacuna in his book, *For the President's Eyes Only: Secret Intelligence and the American Presidency from Washington to Bush.*[1]

More generally, we can say that the role of intelligence is rarely covered adequately in works on foreign policy. There seems to be a separation between the two as there is, one might say, in real life. The official diplomatic history series done by the State Department (Foreign Relations of the United States) has had to be redone in some instances (Iran, Congo) because in the original volumes there was little, if anything, on the role of the CIA and covert action in these countries, which was capital.

Where you stand is where you sit

Just as intelligence officers running an espionage operation often have an exaggerated notion of the importance of their agent's performance, so diplomats and policy officials often denigrate the importance of intelligence, especially human intelligence.

An example of the latter mindset is that of McGeorge Bundy, who was the adviser to the President for National Security Affairs under John F. Kennedy and subsequently under Lyndon Johnson. Bundy told the historian Michael Beschloss that he had managed it so that 'the spy' (meaning Oleg Penkovsky) was not mentioned once in his book, *Danger and Survival*.[2] This excellent book, subtitled, 'Choices About the Bomb in the First Fifty Years,' and which was presented as a history of nuclear weapons since their inception, contains a chapter on the Cuban Missile Crisis.

An example of the former mindset is the CIA-authorized book on Penkovsky, *The Spy Who Saved the World*,[3] by Jerrold L. Schecter and Peter Deriabin. The clear implication in the title being that Penkovsky prevented the Cuban Missile Crisis from escalating into a nuclear war.

Penkovsky and the Cuban Missile Crisis: no real-time connection

The most important question one has to ask about Penkovsky relates to his product. Regardless of how exciting, how palpable, it was to have a high-level source in Moscow, no matter how elaborate the arrangements for the clandestine meetings were, what did he produce? Was he the 'spy who saved the world', or was this the hyperbole of a title? To answer this question, and putting aside the other information he provided in 1961–62, we will focus in this article on Penkovsky's role in the Cuban Missile Crisis, the most critical confrontation between the two sides in the Cold War, when the danger of the use of nuclear weapons was greater than at any time before or since.

Penkovsky had nothing to do with the Cuban Missile Crisis in a real-time sense. According to Schecter and Deriabin, the last meeting of substance with Penkovsky took place on August 27, 1962, in Moscow.[4] Penkovsky was arrested around October 22.

The title of the Schecter/Deriabin book has nothing to do with Penkovsky having given a real-time warning that offensive missiles were being moved into Cuba. In fact, Penkovsky did not give any information that there were missiles in Cuba.[5] Other human sources reported on the existence of missiles in Cuba at the time, but not offensive missiles. A U-2 flight on August 28, 1962, revealed the existence of SA-2 surface-to-air missiles. It was followed by a warning from President Kennedy to Nikita Khrushchev on September 4. When defensive cruise surface-to-surface missiles were found shortly thereafter, the President followed on September 13 with a very stern warning to Khrushchev and emphasized that Cuba was 'under our most careful surveillance'.

It was only through the fateful U-2 flight of October 14 that the existence of offensive missiles in Cuba was discovered. An Air Force pilot flew a U-2 over the San Cristobal area where installations for Medium Range Ballistic Missiles (MRBMs) of the SS-4 variety were detected. The photo interpreters knew immediately that it was the SS-4 because of its measurements and because the SS-4 had been paraded before in Moscow.[6]

Penkovsky's contribution was minor but nevertheless important. In 1961, he had provided a manual in which there was a sketch on how the SS-4 would be field deployed. This enabled the CIA to confirm the existence of the SS-4s in Cuba and to confirm the progress of the installation as it was being photographed in successive flights of the U-2. In the words of Dino Brugioni, the author of the book *Eyeball to Eyeball*, which deals with the crisis principally from the technical point of view, 'Penkovsky provided confirmation, but the U-2 was the driving thing.'[7] In his book, Brugioni is even more emphatic on the role of the U-2: 'Without the U-2 airplane, there may have been no crisis – only an accomplished fact.'[8]

Interment

The end of the Cold War, and the arrival on scene of Robert Gates, an advocate of a policy of 'openness' for the CIA, gave the impetus for an extraordinary public authentication of Penkovsky as a leading spy of the Agency in the Soviet Union during the Cold War. Although the Schecter/Deriabin book is described above as a CIA-authorized biography, it was clearly the work of Gates himself, just as, some 40 years later, the Bob Woodward book, *Bush at War*,[9] was in part inspired by George Tenet himself, anxious to get into the public record the fact that the CIA was at the point in the swift campaign that overthrew the Taliban in Afghanistan in the wake of the September 11 attacks.

Some CIA professionals resist this marketing of the CIA while others believe it is high time that the CIA gets some credit for what it has done instead of being a constant whipping boy before the American public. Penkovsky's principal case officer, George Kisevalter, declined to participate[10] in the exercise authorized by Gates whereby Schecter would enter the basement of CIA headquarters and read documents sent down from above. According to Schecter himself, the total of documents consisted of seventeen cardboard boxes.[11] This included the complete record of the meetings. Translation of the transcripts was done by Deriabin.

Summing up

To sum up, Penkovsky was the most notable of a string of Soviet walk-in agents handled by the CIA (and in this case the British) during the Cold War. He did not 'save the world' in the Cuban Missile Crisis, as he had no real-time role. Penkovsky was an authentic high-level agent, and the best evidence is that he was not a 'double' sent by the Soviets, as some have claimed. With the end of the Cold War, the story of how this agent was run, in Moscow and in Western Europe, under most difficult operational circumstances, deserved to be told, as part of the lore of the CIA.

COMMENTARY: PENKOVSKY: A WESTERN SUCCESS STORY?

Len Scott

Introduction

Oleg Penkovsky was one of the most significant western espionage successes of the Cold War. The most extensive study of his espionage contends that: 'During the Berlin crisis of 1961 and the Cuban missiles crisis in 1962, Penkovsky was the spy who saved the world from nuclear war'.[1] Recently, a former senior SIS officer stated that Penkovsky 'averted war in Cuba'.[2] Not all those who recognise the importance of his espionage would embrace these conclusions. Yet the case of Penkovsky illuminates a range of issues concerning the study of intelligence, from understanding the challenges of collection to analysing the problems of assessment and exploitation. It also raises intriguing questions about the realm of counter-intelligence and whether, as has been claimed, Penkovsky was a triumph of Soviet counter-intelligence rather than a success for western intelligence. The case of Penkovsky further illustrates the British-American intelligence relationship. CIA documents provide details of SIS-CIA collaboration as well as insights into the roles (and identities) of SIS officers, though relevant SIS files remain classified. Nor has access been gained to the records of either the KGB who arrested Penkovsky or the GRU to whom he belonged.

The documents presented here were released to Jerrold Schecter and Peter Deriabin by the CIA and are available at their web-site.[3] They are organised into three sections. The first (Documents Ten and Eleven) illuminates tradecraft and shows details of how the CIA conducted clandestine communications. The second (Documents Twelve-Fifteen) concerns doubts about whether Penkovsky was (or became) a Soviet agent of disinformation and provides a focus on counter-intelligence issues. The third (Document Sixteen) involves information that Penkovsky provided about Soviet nuclear deployments in the DDR which might have been relevant to assessments of whether the Soviets would deploy nuclear missiles in Cuba in 1962.

Tradecraft

Document Ten[4]: *[Blank] Operational Plan*, 1 January 1961[5]
Document Eleven: *Briefing of (Blank) to Load Drop for (Blank)*, 3 May 1961[6]

It is an abiding principle that intelligence services do not disclose sources and methods. Yet in the 1990s the CIA declassified documents that provided insights into operational methods. Clandestine communication with agents is a core activity in espionage. The '[Blank] Operational Plan' provides detailed and specific instructions on reconnaissance and preparation for clandestine communication including casing and servicing 'dead drops'.[7] Procedures for signalling that dead drops have been activated are spelt out. Another document (Document Eleven) provides a record of a briefing that was prepared for a foreign diplomat from a western European ally as part of an 'elaborate backup plan' in case SIS operations in Moscow fell through.[8]

The plan is dated 1 January 1961. This was after Penkovsky made contact with the CIA but before either they or SIS had established communications with him. The plan was part of the agency's response to Penkovsky's approach and to his choice of dead drop.[9] Annex II of the plan and the May 1961 memorandum make clear that the CIA was dependent on allied intelligence services. As Schecter and Deriabin have shown, the CIA's Moscow station was not yet fully effective and the officer tasked with contacting Penkovsky failed to do so.[10] And without the active support of American diplomats, the CIA turned to SIS, who were aware of Penkovsky after he made an approach to a British businessman, Greville Wynne.

How significant are these documents? In terms of how Penkovsky was run in Moscow, they are of limited value inasmuch as it was SIS and not CIA that had operational responsibility. Although some contact became possible with the

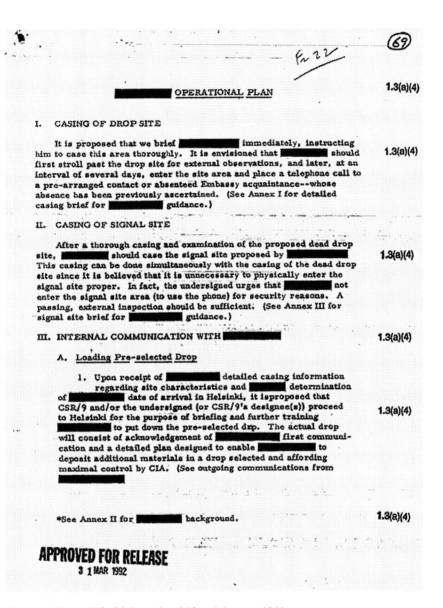

Document Ten: [Blank] Operational Plan, 1 January 1961

Reproduced from the CIA web page: 'Lt. Col. Oleg Penkovsky: Western Spy in Soviet GRU', http://www.foia.cia.gov/penkovsky.asp

2. The drop packet and contents will be prepared at
     Headquarters and should be hermetically sealed (to
deter opening by ████████ as well as to protect the contents)   **1.3(a)(4)**
and colored to match the dark green radiator drop site.
CSR/9 will hand-carry the packet to Helsinki for transmittal to
████████

3. In Helsinki, ████████ will be given intensive briefing
     on the general and specific locale, avenue(s) of approach,
loading, security factors, aborting measures, possible entrap-   **1.3(a)(4)**
ment including KGB M. O. against ████████ if apprehended,
use of telephone to call wife, exiting direction, and signalling
technique and procedure. To give realism to the briefing, a
building with foyer area, similar to the actual drop site, will
attempted to be found in the Helsinki area and actual practice(s)
will be performed.

4. ████████ will then be given the packet to secrete upon
     himself as he returns to Moscow. (Note: ████████ has
a diplomatic passport and has previously reported that he has   **1.3(a)(4)**
never been searched or asked to declare his personal items to
Customs.) Upon arrival in Moscow, ████████ will transfer the
packet to his maximum security safe to which he alone has the
key and combination. The safe is located in a secure building.
(If preferred, the packet could be retained upon his body until the
drop is effected.)

5. As soon as possible, ████████ will make a dry run up
Pushkinskaya Ulitsa for the purpose of external casing and   **1.3(a)(4)**
orientation of the building drop site. At an interval of several
days, he will make the actual drop preferably just before dusk,
late in the day. It is suggested that consideration be given to
████████ proceeding along Kuznetskiy Most, turning abruptly
right onto Pushkinskaya Ulitsa, and, at his normal (fast) pace,
proceeding directly into the drop site locale and emplacing the
drop. An alternative method might be to proceed down Kuznetskiy
Most and observe the window displays" in Meat Store No. 19,
turning onto Pushkinskaya Ulitsa, (still window shopping in the Meat
Store), pause and then proceed into the building site and place a
call to his wife inquiring as to what kind of meat or kolbasa his
wife prefers him to purchase. This would give him a convincing
cover for the use of the phone, although his surveillants might be
closer because he slowed down to window shop.

- 2 -

Document Ten continued

6. If, for any reason, ███████ is obliged to abort the actual loading of the drop, then he should make, at this time, <u>only one more</u> attempt at an interval of approximately one week. If a second attempt must be made, ███████ should use the alternate plan for approach and not the exact one as before.

       1.3(a)(4)

7. After successful loading of the drop, ███████ should allow at least one day to pass, but not more than two, before he puts down the pre-selected signal at the pre-designated site. On the basis of ███████ casing report, ███████ can proceed to this site and mark the loading signal with a red crayon or pen.

       1.3(a)(4)

IV. OUTGOING COMMUNICATION FROM ███████

       1.3(a)(4)

A. It is proposed that in our message to ███████ that we inform him of the following method in which he may communicate with us:

       1.3(a)(4)

    1. ███████ will be instructed that the American House, No. 3 KROPOTKINSKAYA NABERZHNAYA, will be the locale for the drop. He will be instructed to proceed down the right side of TURCHANIN Ulitsa (toward the Moscow River) at a specified date and time, and as he passes the wall surrounding the American House courtyard, throw the drop package over the wall. ███████ will be in place on the otherside of the wall to retrieve the package. (See attached diagram and 1955 photos of this area - Annex IV.)

       1.3(a)(4)

    2. Upon receipt of package ███████ will secrete it upon himself and return immediately to the Embassy for inclusion of package in pouch. NOTE: Dependant upon the circumstances and ███████ recommendations, it may be more propitious to use the Marine NCO (highly recommended by ███████ for actual transport of the drop packet to the Embassy. Thus, ███████ could leave empty-handed and upon safe-arrival at the Embassy could telephone ███████ at the American House. This would be the signal for ███████ to instruct the Marine NCO to leave for the Embassy. However, such action might not be amenable to ███████ without Ambassadorial knowledge and concurrence.

       1.3(a)(4)

    3. The afore-mentioned plan is contingent upon ███████ casing of the area and his recommendations for implementing the plan. (A briefing guide is attached as Annex V for ███████ guidance.)

       1.3(a)(4)

- 3 -

Document Ten continued

ANNEX I

1. As soon as possible, ███████ should take a stroll up the
right-hand side of PUSHKINSKAYA Ulitsa (going toward SADOVAYA) and
closely observe Building No. 2, situated between the Women's Shoe Store   1.3(a)(4)
and Meat Store No. 19, located near the intersection of PUSHKINSKAYA
Ulitsa and KUZNETSKIY MOST. (See Attachment No. 1 - map of area.)

2. During ███████ walk-by and visual inspection of Building No.
2 and the immediate vicinity, the following detailed information is   1.3(a)(4)
desired:

    a. What type of building does No. 2 appear to be? Apartment-
house, shop, restaurant, warehouse, etc.?

    b. Would a Westerner be able to enter the ground floor to use
the telephone without arousing undue attention?

    c. Is the telephone booth visible when walking past the building?

    d. Are there any windows flanking the entrance which would
enable passersby to look into the lobby or foyer on the
ground floor?

    e. Was the presence of any type of possible fixed security
forces noted in the immediate vicinity?

    f. Note surveillance patterns on ███████ in this area and the
closeness of ███████ surveillants, if possible (without   1.3(a)(4)
arousing their suspicions).

    g. Did ███████ note any people transiting (entering or
departing) or loitering in the lobby/foyer of Building No. 2   1.3(a)(4)
as ███████ passed?

    h. What type of building is located directly across the street
from Building No. 2 with respect to its adaptability as an
observation post?

    NOTE: To facilitate ███████ ability to observe the numerous
items enumerated above, it is suggested that ███████ pause at several   1.3(a)(4)
stores along PUSHKINSKAYA Ulitsa to "window shop." In fact,

Document Ten continued

██████████ might window shop at the ⟨⟨⟨⟨⟨⟨⟨⟨⟨⟨ ⟨⟨⟨⟨⟨⟨⟨⟨⟨⟨ ⟨⟨ on
the corner of PUSHKINSKAYA Ulitsa and KUZNETSKIY MOST (note
location on attached map) and even enter and purchase a book. Upon
exiting ██████████ could cross the street and window shop in Meat Store
No. 19. With regard to the meat store, CIA would be interested in
knowing if there is an entrance on KUZNETSKIY MOST as well as on
PUSHKINSKAYA Ulitsa. Also what are the operating hours of the meat
shop?

1.3(a)(4)

3. At an interval of several days, preferably at dusk, ██████████
should walk toward PUSHKINSKAYA Ulitsa past the PROEZD
KHUDOZHESTVENNOGO TEATRA, turn right onto PUSHKINSKAYA
Ulitsa and enter Building No. 2 and place a telephone call (telephone
No. 28) to a friend in the Embassy. (This call should be pre-arranged
to ██████████ or so arranged that ██████ will know that the
recipient of the call is not present to answer the call.) The location of
the telephone is contained in the attached map and is situated to the left
of the entrance.

1.3(a)(4)

4. The following detailed information is desired in conjunction
with this casing/observation plan:

    a. Surveillance: Number and pattern. Did any follow
    ██████████ into Building No. 2? Is it possible to enter
    Building No. 2 before the surveillance turns the corner?

1.3(a)(4)

    b. Sketch and describe interior of foyer or lobby.

        (1) Are there apt to be people loitering inside?

        (2) Where are the stairs located?

        (3) What color are the walls? Type of floor?

        (4) What type of lighting is used in the lobby? How
            bright?

        (5) Is phone booth illuminated?

        (6) Note any other entrances or exits.

- 2 -

Document Ten continued

c. Particularly note dark green radiator near wall, opposite telephone booth, and to right of the entrance.

(1) Match green color as close as possible with colors from your chart. Is finish flat or shiny? New or old? Is it smooth or cracked and peeling.

(2) If ██████ can determine a standard green available in Moscow, and visual observation confirms that this is the same shade of green as the radiator, he may possibly be able to duplicate it from Embassy stocks.   1.3(a)(4)

(3) It may be that the paint inside other Moscow building entrances is similar in color to that of the radiator site. Therefore, ██████ may be able to get a sample, away from the site, after he has observed the radiator coloring.   1.3(a)(4)

(4) How high is radiator off of floor? Length?

(5) Note peculiar or distinguishing characteristics.

(6) What is the approximate distance between wall and back of radiator?

(7) What are the lighting conditions here?

(8) Is the hook visible? What color is the hook?

(9) Would a small packet, the color of the radiator, be visible to people entering or loitering in the foyer/lobby?

(10) Are there knobs or dials for manual operation of the radiator?

(11) When will central heat be turned on in Moscow?

NOTE: In order to observe radiator area closely, ██████ might, if he deems it secure, loiter just briefly near the radiator before exiting. ██████ could be buttoning his coat, lighting a cigarette, blowing nose, etc.)   1.3(a)(4)

- 3 -   1.3(a)(4)

Document Ten continued

ANNEX II

The utilization of ████████ in the project ██████████ presupposes
that a risk assessment has been resolved in favor of using ████████
instead of an unprotected American tourist. [The involvement of
████████ also is predicated on the fact that because of the prohibition
on the use of American Embassy personnel, no active support can be
rendered by CIA staff agents attached to the American Embassy,
Moscow. The decision to use the services of ████████ was based on
the above premises plus the fact that ████████ has diplomatic immunity,
that he is trained in operational support tasks, capable, well motivated,
and has already established operational patterns. Moreover, in case of
a provocation, no American would be involved directly. On the debit
side of the ledger, it should be noted that ████████ is not CIA controlled
(joint liaison operation), that he will probably render a full report of his
operational involvement to his superiors, that ██ will become involved
in this operation, and that ████████ must be met in Helsinki in order
to rehearse all steps of the plan and to give Subject the drop instrument.

1.3(a)(4)

1.3(a)(4)

ANNEX III

SIGNAL SITE CASING

1. Approach from Ulitsa GORKOGO going toward Ulitsa
PUSHKINSKAYA via KOZITSKIY Pereulok. Walk on right side of street.
Window-shop in vegetable-fruit store which is next to site (House 2,
Korpus 8).

2. Determine type of installation where telephone is located.

3. Is telephone (and signal site) visible from sidewalk? Are there
windows on ground floor level?

4. Would a Westerner have normal access in terms of using
telephone or is telephone so hidden that passersby would never be aware
of its existence? Are there any written signs or overt indications that
there is a telephone booth in this location?

5. Observe any taxi stands or possible fixed surveillance/observa-
tion points near this building.

6. Notice if any people are loitering near entrance to building or
situated across the street.

7. If you can observe interior through window or open door as you
pass by, describe in detail interior arrangements.

8. Observe type of building(s) opposite (across the street) from
signal site.

1.3(a)(4)

Document Ten continued

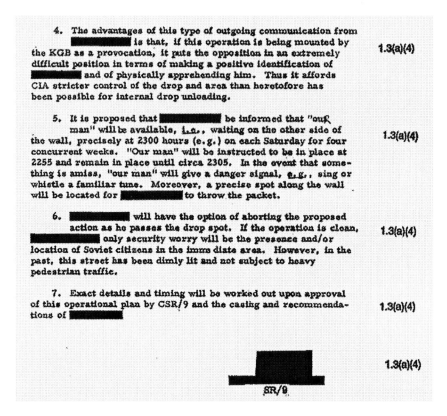

4. The advantages of this type of outgoing communication from ▮▮▮▮▮▮▮▮▮▮ is that, if this operation is being mounted by the KGB as a provocation, it puts the opposition in an extremely difficult position in terms of making a positive identification of ▮▮▮▮▮▮ and of physically apprehending him. Thus it affords CIA stricter control of the drop and area than heretofore has been possible for internal drop unloading.   1.3(a)(4)

5. It is proposed that ▮▮▮▮▮▮▮▮ be informed that "our man" will be available, i.e., waiting on the other side of the wall, precisely at 2300 hours (e.g.) on each Saturday for four concurrent weeks. "Our man" will be instructed to be in place at 2255 and remain in place until circa 2305. In the event that something is amiss, "our man" will give a danger signal, e.g., sing or whistle a familiar tune. Moreover, a precise spot along the wall will be located for ▮▮▮▮▮▮ to throw the packet.   1.3(a)(4)

6. ▮▮▮▮▮▮▮▮ will have the option of aborting the proposed action as he passes the drop spot. If the operation is clean, ▮▮▮▮▮▮▮▮ only security worry will be the presence and/or location of Soviet citizens in the immediate area. However, in the past, this street has been dimly lit and not subject to heavy pedestrian traffic.   1.3(a)(4)

7. Exact details and timing will be worked out upon approval of this operational plan by CSR/9 and the casing and recommendations of ▮▮▮▮▮▮   1.3(a)(4)

       1.3(a)(4)

SR/9

Document Ten continued

Americans at embassy receptions, Schecter and Deriabin show arrangements for communicating with Penkovsky in Moscow were conducted by SIS through its intermediaries, Greville Wynne and Janet Chisholm, the wife of the SIS Head of Station. The dead drop was a standard technique for secret communication, although Penkovsky himself strongly preferred to use clandestine human contact 'because of security considerations, as well as because he derive[d] satisfaction from personal contact'.[11] However, as discussed below, the KGB did activate a dead drop after Penkovsky was arrested when he presumably revealed its existence to them. The potential importance of this incident is discussed later.

Techniques of tradecraft are the foundation of an effective intelligence service and details are never willingly disclosed. The documents provide operational detail about the conduct of espionage in a hostile counter-intelligence environment which are intrinsically fascinating and show the considerable attention to detail in operational planning. What is also significant is that disclosure of this kind of material calls into question any blanket prohibition on the release of materials about operational matters, and provides a potential precedent.

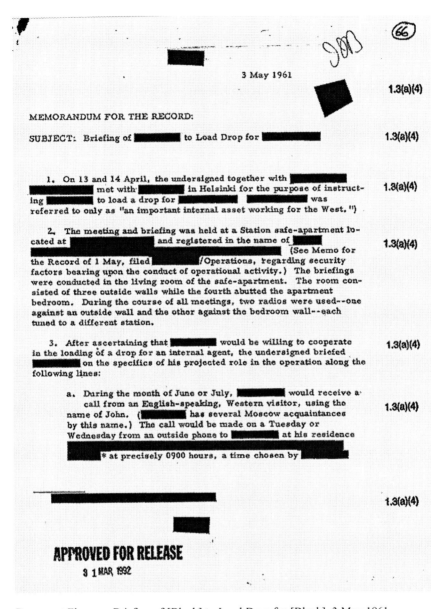

3 May 1961

1.3(a)(4)

MEMORANDUM FOR THE RECORD:

SUBJECT: Briefing of ███████ to Load Drop for ██████████   1.3(a)(4)

1. On 13 and 14 April, the undersigned together with █████████
████████████ met with ███████ in Helsinki for the purpose of instruct-   1.3(a)(4)
ing ███████ to load a drop for ██████████ ██████████ was
referred to only as "an important internal asset working for the West.")

2. The meeting and briefing was held at a Station safe-apartment located at ██████████████ and registered in the name of ████
████████████████   (See Memo for   1.3(a)(4)
the Record of 1 May, filed ████████ /Operations, regarding security
factors bearing upon the conduct of operational activity.) The briefings
were conducted in the living room of the safe-apartment. The room consisted of three outside walls while the fourth abutted the apartment
bedroom. During the course of all meetings, two radios were used--one
against an outside wall and the other against the bedroom wall--each
tuned to a different station.

3. After ascertaining that ████████ would be willing to cooperate   1.3(a)(4)
in the loading of a drop for an internal agent, the undersigned briefed
████████ on the specifics of his projected role in the operation along the
following lines:

   a. During the month of June or July, ████████ would receive a·
       call from an English-speaking, Western visitor, using the
       name of John. (████████ has several Moscow acquaintances   1.3(a)(4)
       by this name.) The call would be made on a Tuesday or
       Wednesday from an outside phone to ████████ at his residence

       ████████ * at precisely 0900 hours, a time chosen by ████████

1.3(a)(4)

APPROVED FOR RELEASE
3 1 MAR 1992

Document Eleven: Briefing of [Blank] to Load Drop for [Blank], 3 May 1961

Reproduced from the CIA web page: 'Lt. Col. Oleg Penkovsky: Western Spy in Soviet GRU',
http://www.foia.cia.gov/penkovsky.asp

as the best suited for him. Rather than tie up ███████████ `..13(a)(4)`
mobility during the months of June and July, it was agreed
that he would await the call during the week of 13-17 June
and during the weeks of 4-8 July and 25-29 July. If the
call is not forthcoming during this period, ███████ indicated that he would be amenable to fulfilling his role in the
operation at any other future date that telephonic contact can
be established with him. The conversation, setting up the
reception of the drop instrument by ███████ at American
House, will follow in this manner:

JOHN: "Hello, Gino (diminutive of Luigi). This is John.
         Could you play Bingo Thursday evening?"

███████: "Yes, I'll see you there."   `1.3(a)(4)`

JOHN: "Good, I'll see you Thursday."

                    OR

███████: "No, I'm busy on Thursday."   `1.3(a)(4)`

JOHN: "Sorry. How about next week?" (To which   `1.3(a)(4)`
         ███████ will respond affirmatively.)

b. After receiving the call on either Tuesday or Wednesday
    morning, ███████ will attend the Bingo game at   `1.3(a)(4)`
American House on Thursday evening circa 2045. (Note:
███████, in the company of his wife and other friends,
has previously attended American House. His wife is an
avid Bingo player.)

c. Between 2100-2115, either ███████ or ███████
    will load the magazine rack in the second floor toilet   `1.3(a)(4)`
with the drop instrument, previously pouched to ███████
for ███████. If the toilet is occupied during this period,
███████ or ███████ will return between 2200-2215 to load.

d. At approximately 2130 hours, ███████ will proceed to
    the men's room at 2130 (2230, if toilet is occupied) and   `1.3(a)(4)`

- 2 -

Document Eleven continued

███

retrieve the drop packet from the magazine rack. Upon
retrieving the packet, ███ will mark a red slash
on the top left side of the magazine rack. This will indicate
to ███ or ███ that the drop has been securely
serviced.*

1.3(a)(4)

e. On Friday, ███ will make a dry run past both
the drop site and signal site for ███ (Complete instructions, written in Italian, directing ███
to the precise drop and signal sites will be prepared and
wrapped around the drop packet.)

1.3(a)(4)

f. On Saturday, ███ will make the actual drop
emplacement for ███ He plans, tentatively,
to use his car, parking near the actual drop site, and will
walk immediately to the site, emplace the packet, and then
make the cover phone call. ███ pointed out that this
tactic is compatible with patterns previously demonstrated
to his surveillants. Such a maneuver forces the surveillance
car to halt some distance behind ███ By the time
the surveillance can either follow ███ into the drop
area or assume a positive surveilling posture, ███
is confident that he will be able to have the drop loaded
with time to spare.

1.3(a)(4)

g. Later the same day, if cover for action can be
smoothly devised, ███ will go to the assigned
signal site and indicate that he has loaded the drop by making
the prescribed signal for ███ If ███ is
unable to make the signal on Saturday, he will put the signal
up before 10:00 a.m., Sunday.

1.3(a)(4)

h. The same day, Saturday, after loading the drop,
███ will return (probably in the evening) to
American House, enter the second floor men's room, and
mark a red slash on the top right side of the magazine rack.
It was emphasized that this action must be performed by
2400 hours, Saturday.

1.3(a)(4)

---

*If impossible to load or service drop on this particular Thursday,
the same procedure will be invoked automatically for the preceding
Thursday.

- 3.-

███

Document Eleven continued

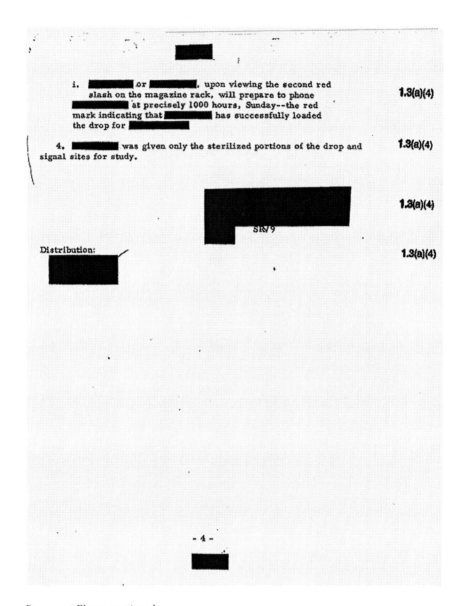

i. ████████ or ████████, upon viewing the second red
slash on the magazine rack, will prepare to phone
████████ at precisely 1000 hours, Sunday--the red
mark indicating that ████████ has successfully loaded
the drop for ████████

4. ████████ was given only the sterilized portions of the drop and
signal sites for study.

1.3(a)(4)

1.3(a)(4)

1.3(a)(4)

SR/9

Distribution:

1.3(a)(4)

- 4 -

Document Eleven continued

A wilderness of mirrors?

Document Twelve: *Translation of the letter which (Blank) passed (Blank) on 28 March 1962.*[12]

Document Thirteen: *Memorandum on Counterintelligence Activities*, 20 July 1962.[13]

Document Fourteen: *Memo for the DDP from Howard J. Osborn re Oleg V. Penkovskiy*, 23 May 1963.[14]

Document Fifteen: *Penskovskiy Case* [Minute of the President's Foreign Intelligence Board] 26 June 1963.[15]

The history of intelligence shows that those running espionage operations need to consider whether they are gathering intelligence from an agent or receiving disinformation from a double-agent. Doubts about Penkovsky first emerged from the KGB defector, Anatoly Golitsyn, who persuaded some senior officials including James Angleton, the CIA's Head of Counter-Intelligence, that this was a Soviet plot.[16] These doubts were shared by some British officials, notably Peter Wright of MI5.[17] Edward Jay Epstein made public these suspicions and stated that Penkovsky was 'a Soviet postman at the time of the missile crisis'.[18] For those who believed that the Soviets had penetrated western intelligence, the success of the Penkovsky operation was a problem. Wright, for example, claimed that the head of MI5, Sir Roger Hollis, was a Soviet mole. Yet as Gordon Brooke-Shepherd argues: 'If it is accepted that Oleg Penkovsky was not a Soviet plant, then it must follow, as night follows day, that Roger Hollis, then Head of MI5, was not a Soviet agent.'[19] Challenging Penkovsky's *bona fides* was necessary to sustain the case that MI5 had been penetrated at a high level.

Whether Penkovsky was (and remained) genuine was a concern for the American and British intelligence communities. The documents show that by the summer of 1962 there was concern within CIA that Penkovsky was under Soviet suspicion and might have been compromised to the point where he could be acting as a double agent. Sir Dick White, the Chief of SIS, believed Penkovsky might have been turned by the Spring of 1962.[20] Penkovsky's letter to his handlers nevertheless shows that Penkovsky himself alerted western intelligence to his concerns about surveillance, and his final letter continued to warn of KGB surveillance. The 'Memorandum on Counterintelligence Activities', written by the head of the CIA's Soviet Division, indicates that concerns about the security of the operation led to increased scrutiny of the material and provided delays in dissemination pending careful checks with other sources. The CIA's 1963 assessment (Documents Fourteen and Fifteen) was that Penkovsky's material was authentic. Schecter and Deriabin concur: 'He told too much, and what he provided was too damaging to Soviet interests'.[21] Everything he told the West about Khrushchev's policy on Berlin, for example, seemed designed to encourage a firm and resolute western response to Soviet demands.

Yet one reason for the inherent complexity of counter-intelligence is that to maintain the credibility of the deception some accurate information needs to be provided in some form, often termed 'chicken feed'. Moreover, the conduct of

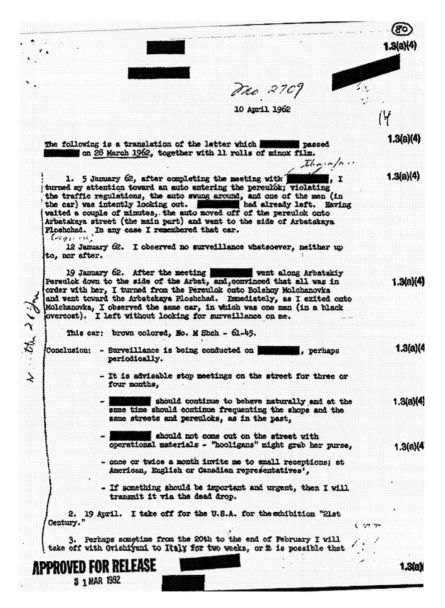

Document Twelve: Translation of the Letter Which [Blank] Passed [Blank] on 28 March 1962

Reproduced from the CIA web page: 'Lt. Col. Oleg Penkovsky: Western Spy in Soviet GRU', http://www.foia.cia.gov/penkovsky.asp

1.3(a)(4)

on 14 March I will be in Geneva at the Auto Exhibition.

4. I request that a reception be organized for between 10 and 20 February, at which I will inform ████████ more concretely of all future plans. 1.3(a)(4)

5. In the future at receptions with whom will I be able to talk and pass material, when ████████ will be absent because of pregnancy? 1.3(a)(4)

6. ████████ made a good impression, but KRO (Counterintelligence) does not like him and are watching him carefully. 1.3(a)(4)

With warm greetings

Until we meet soon my dear friends

26 January 1962

1. 27 January 1962. - ████████ was not at ████████ reception and therefore I have retained all of this until this time. 1.3(a)(4)

2. The trip to Italy was postponed until summer, and visit to Geneva in March was cancelled for M.O. *(presumably "by Ministry of Defense")*

3. If all is well then I will take off for the U.S.A. on 19 April. But at the present it's going badly as the KRO are rummaging around concerning my father (kopat'sya vokrug moego ottsa) - they are continually searching for my father's burial place, they cannot find it and therefore they are conjecturing that perhaps my father is alive, and therefore that in the future it would not be suitable to send me on overseas assignments. My command considers these fears meaningless and they are defending me from all these conjectures of the "neighbors." Everything must be decided soon.

4. In March I must meet with ████████ at a reception and I will pass detailed information about myself and plans for the future depending upon the situation which is in turmoil about me. 1.3(a)(4)

5 March 1962

1. I plan to fly to the U.S.A. on 18 April. Everything is already submitted concerning the visas. The KGB will have its say on the 15th of April. My superiors in the Committee and in the M.O. have made all

1.3(a)(4)

Document Twelve continued

1.3(a)(4)

the arrangements for my trip to the exhibition - "21st Century." If
I make the trip, then everything will be alright.

    2. If they do not give me permission to make the trip, then my
situation will change sharply and become complicated. It will be necessary
to leave the Committee, and in the fall of this year, having fulfilled
25 years of service in the army, I will be discharged. We must plan our
future work on all of these contingencies of life.

    3. If I do not come to the U.S.A., then after the 20th of April
it will be necessary to arrange a reception at which I will be able to
pass my plans for the future.

                                          28 March 1962

1.3(a)(4)

Document Twelve continued

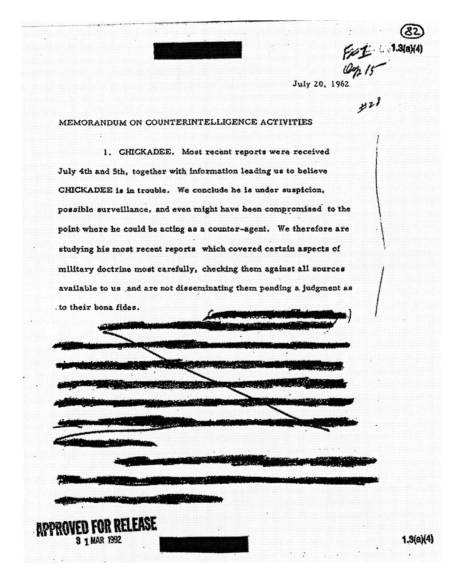

July 20, 1962

MEMORANDUM ON COUNTERINTELLIGENCE ACTIVITIES

　　1. CHICKADEE. Most recent reports were received July 4th and 5th, together with information leading us to believe CHICKADEE is in trouble. We conclude he is under suspicion, possible surveillance, and even might have been compromised to the point where he could be acting as a counter-agent. We therefore are studying his most recent reports which covered certain aspects of military doctrine most carefully, checking them against all sources available to us and are not disseminating them pending a judgment as to their bona fides.

APPROVED FOR RELEASE
3 1 MAR 1992

1.3(a)(4)

Document Thirteen: Memorandum on Counterintelligence Activities, 20 July 1962

Reproduced from the CIA web page: 'Lt. Col. Oleg Penkovsky: Western Spy in Soviet GRU', http://www.foia.cia.gov/penkovsky.asp

23 May 1963

MEMORANDUM FOR: Deputy Director (Plans)

SUBJECT: Oleg V. Penkovskiy

1. There has been a lot of speculation in foreign and U. S. press as to the fact that Penkovskiy may have been a double agent and that the documentary material might have been disinformation.

2. In the event that this comes up in your briefing of the Vinson Committee, you might find the attached helpful and I am sending it along for inclusion in your package which Elizabeth is holding for you for this purpose.

Howard J. Osborn
Chief, SR Division

Attachment

Document Fourteen: Memo for the DDP from Howard J. Osborn re. Oleg V. Penkovskiy, 23 May 1963

Reproduced from the CIA web page: 'Lt. Col. Oleg Penkovsky: Western Spy in Soviet GRU', http://www.foia.cia.gov/penkovsky.asp

Bona Fides of the Penkovskiy Operation

1. We have no reason to believe that Penkovskiy was a double agent or that any information he supplied us was wittingly provided to him as deception material by Soviet authorities.

2. Throughout this extraordinary operation, a recurrent question for us, and one also in the minds of analysts trying to cope with the resultant flood of classified Soviet documents, has been the possibility of Soviet deception. This possibility was given serious consideration each time we received new material from Penkovskiy. During the numerous long personal meetings we had with him we used subtle and varied tests of his loyalty and his information; we also checked the intelligence provided against all other information available to the intelligence community. He always passed all of the tests which could be levied on him personally and his information has stood the tests of time and comparative intelligence.

3. On the basis of these checks and counterchecks together with our familiarity with the methods and purposes of Soviet deception operations, we have concluded that there is no possibility that this case represents planned deception, build-up for deception, fabrication, or double agent activity. Rather it represents the most serious penetration of Soviet officialdom ever accomplished and one that will hurt them for years to come.

Document Fourteen continued

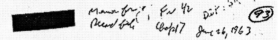

8. Mr. McCone then turned to the Board's question on implications of the Penkovskiy case as they relate to British and U.S. security. He said that Penkovskiy provided us intelligence from August 1960 through August 1962, and gave us more than 8,000 pages of translated reporting, most of which constituted highly classified Soviet defense documents. He stated that the case did not have any/implications for Britain or the U.S. as this was a controlled agent recruited by CIA and shared with MI-6, who we got into the circuit because the contact was outside the USSR and we used London on several occasions for meetings. Dr. Land asked about the motivation of Penkovskiy, and the DCI replied that it was primarily emotional—that the man resented his failure to advance higher in the regime and was motivated to work against the present leaders. He noted that the British had taken the principal rap of the case because of Wynn, who was a courier working for MI-6. We think that the case was blown because of a penetration in the British government who saw Wynn and Penkovskiy together. We also think that Penkovskiy got careless and when they searched his apartment they found all of the espionage equipment. Mr. McCone noted that they had picked up a couple of our officers and in one case implicated a clerk who had been sent to service a letter drop, but had let him go after brief questioning. These had all been png'd. He noted that Penkovskiy had no access to either FBI or CIA personnel. Mr. Coyne asked if Penkovskiy had initiated the initial contact and was there any danger that he had been planted. Mr. McCone replied that this was something that we always feared, that we had checked his bona fides extremely carefully, and held up dissemination of reports in order to insure their validity. After most careful checks with all other types of intelligence, we had come to the conclusion that this was authentic.

*added by Mr. McCone.

1.3(a)(4)

EXCERPT.

Document Fifteen: Penskovskiy Case [Minute of the President's Foreign Intelligence Board] 26 June 1963

Reproduced from the CIA web page: 'Lt. Col. Oleg Penkovsky: Western Spy in Soviet GRU', http://www.foia.cia.gov/penkovsky.asp

intelligence and counter-intelligence operations are often undertaken by different organisations with different interests. And while one organisation may be loath to disclose its own secrets, it may be more inclined to make sacrifices of others. It is now clear, for example, that the KGB learned about western communications interception in Berlin at the planning stages of the operation from their agent in SIS, George Blake. Yet for thirteen months Operation Stopwatch/Gold yielded a considerable amount of intelligence from the Soviet military in Germany because the KGB did not wish to risk Blake.[22]

Penkovsky provided a very considerable amount of material on Soviet military strategy at a time when western sources were nugatory. Is there a possibility that the KGB would have surrendered high level military secrets on such a scale? Given the scope and scale of the material, it surely stretches credulity to believe that they did. Would they have also exposed the identities of large numbers of GRU officers and, moreover, a significant number of their own?[23] What possible operation could have justified such action? There may perhaps be more scope (though no more evidence) for the supposition that Penkovsky could have been turned during the course of 1962. But by then he had conducted forty-two face-to-face meetings with his handlers and handed over much of the written material. Moreover, if Penkovsky had been an agent of disinformation, he most surely would have been used to reinforce the efforts of the Soviet leadership to project the illusion of strength rather than expose the reality of weakness. In 1961, the Soviets had only a handful of Intercontinental Ballistic Missiles (ICBMs) and the Soviet General Staff confronted the prospect of a pre-emptive first strike by the United States. Evidence has emerged that Khrushchev approved KGB deception operations, which *inter alia*, sought to persuade NATO that the Soviets had increased the capabilities of their ICBMS and their Submarine Launched Ballistic Missiles (SLBMs).[24]

One further incident relevant here (which also underlines the importance of tradecraft) was a procedure for emergency communication in Moscow. In October 1961, Penkovsky was briefed on how to provide emergency warning of a Soviet attack.[25] This involved voiceless telephone calls to the US embassy to be followed by use of a dead drop to give details (although the telephone calls were themselves sufficient to constitute emergency warning). According to the KGB, Oleg Penkovsky was arrested on 22 October. The emergency procedure agreed with Penkovsky was subsequently activated on 2 November.[26] When the coded warning was sent, news was immediately passed to the Director of the CIA, who in turn briefed the President on 3 November.[27] Although this occurred after the *denouement* of the Cuban missile crisis, Soviet-American agreement had still not been formalised, and US (and UK) nuclear forces remained at higher than normal states of alert, with the US Strategic Air Command at the unprecedented Defense Condition 2, just short of full readiness for war.

The reasons for the KGB's actions are unclear but the most plausible explanation is Raymond Garthoff's suggestion that Penkovsky deliberately tried to provoke a nuclear attack on the Soviet Union.[28] This would be consistent with his repeated suggestions to his handlers that they provide him with atomic demolition charges to plant at strategic points in Moscow to 'decapitate' the Soviet system at the necessary moment.[29] If Penkovsky was a Soviet-controlled agent, it is difficult to see what the KGB hoped to accomplish by provoking a nuclear attack on Moscow. The most plausible explanation is that the incident provides yet more support for Penkovsky's *bona fides*.

Missile intelligence

Document Sixteen: Meeting 1 (London) 20 April 1961[30]

Penkovsky travelled to Britain in April/May and July/August 1961 and to France in September/October 1961 in his work for the State Committee for the Coordination of Scientific Research Work. This role was designed to provide cover for his GRU activities. It also enabled direct contact between Penkovsky and western intelligence. The visits facilitated forty-two clandestine meetings with his two SIS and two CIA case officers. These were recorded, transcribed/translated and in 1992 declassified by the CIA.[31] Document Sixteen is an extract from the first meeting, held at the Mount Royal Hotel in London on 20 April 1961. Penkovsky stated that Soviets had deployed 150 km-range R-11 nuclear missiles (known as the SS-1 or Scud in the West) in East Germany. In subsequent meetings the Soviet deployments were further discussed and his case officers sought clarification.[32]

Penkovsky's information challenged the western belief that the Soviets had never deployed nuclear weapons outside Soviet territory.[33] Potentially this was significant for western assessments of whether the Soviets might deploy nuclear weapons in Cuba, which exercised the US intelligence community in the summer and autumn of 1962. Penkovsky did not provide intelligence on the deployment of Soviet MRBMs or IRBMs. In the meeting on 20 April, he did state that there had been talk with Castro about sending 'small caliber rockets' to Cuba and that 'possibly a few rockets are already there'.[34] The KGB stated that they arrested him on 22 October, the day the missile crisis broke publicly, and he was unable to provide any real-time intelligence during the crisis. He is nevertheless credited with providing information on which crucial decisions and assessments were made.[35]

By October 1962, the view of the British intelligence community was that 'we have no evidence that the Russians have established IRBM or MRBM sites in the satellite countries, but we have every reason to believe that shorter range tactical missiles are deployed in East Germany and possibly in Poland.'[36] It remains unclear how the CIA assessed Penkovsky's intelligence and how it was integrated into the analytical process. In September 1962, the US intelligence community carefully considered whether the Soviet Union would deploy nuclear weapons in Cuba but concluded that [it]

> would be incompatible with Soviet practice to date and with Soviet policy as we presently estimate it. It would indicate a far greater willingness to increase the level of risk in US–Soviet relations than the USSR has displayed thus far, and consequently would have important policy implications with respect to other areas and other problems in East–West relations.[37]

MEETING #1 (LONDON), 20 APRIL 1961

1. The meeting was held at the Mount Royal Hotel. Participants in the meeting were:

Harold Hazlewood
Michael Fairfield
Joseph Welk
George McAdam

2. By means of a prearranged meeting set up through Mr. Greville WYNNE as organized by Mr. ‾ (details of which are recorded elsewhere), Subject was expected at any time convenient for him to take leave of his companions under the pretext of turning in for the night. This was expected to occur at any time after 2100 hours. Subject's instructions were to report to Room 712 which was engaged by Mr. Hazlewood. Since Room 360 appeared to be far superior as a meeting place because it was much larger, with adequate meeting capacity and, more important, it was an interior court thus avoiding street noises and in addition since a clandestine recorder could be more conveniently concealed in this room, it was decided to use Room 361. Mr. HAZLEWOOD, hereafter referred to as H. and Mr. ‾ hereafter referred to as J., waited for the arrival of Subject in Room 712 for the purpose of escorting him to Room 360 where the other two members of the party waited. Subject arrived at Room 712 at about 2140 hours and after being greeted by H. and J. was told that a more adequate meeting area was set up in Room 360, to which room Subject was conducted. Subject arrived in Room 360 at 2150 hours. Upon entering Subject was introduced to G. and H. and all persons sat in a circle with a small serving table in the middle.

3. G: Would you prefer to speak Russian or English? S: I would much rather speak Russian because I can express myself much better in Russian. G: Very well, then. S: I graduated from the Military-Diplomatic Academy in 1953. In 1955 I went to Turkey. My working language there was English. I had many difficulties there and during the past four years I simply forgot much of my English by disuse. Well, Gentlemen, let's get to work. We have a great deal of important work to do. G: You have already introduced yourselves upstairs. S: Yes. G: Therefore you know now that you are in good hands. S: Yes, and I have thought about this for a long time and I have attempted to make this contact taking a very devious path about which I feel I must report to you in full. G: You must know that we are in receipt of your original letter. S: You mean the one I gave to the two teachers (the two American tourists). If you knew how many grey hairs I have acquired since that time; if you had only marked the signal just so I would have known that the message got into the proper hands. I worried so much about this. (To reassure Subject J. pulled out the original copy of Subject's first letter referred to above including the photograph he enclosed of Colonel Charles PEEKE, U.S. Military Attache, Ankara, at the time Subject served his tour there.) S: Yes, that is the photograph I sent and Colonel PEEKE was the Military Attache there. G: This was shown you to reassure you and in two words I can tell you why a response was not made to you immediately after

Document Sixteen: Meeting 1 (London), 20 April 1961

Committee and our OTHEL consists of officers who are working under cover in Moscow. We have a total of 58 officers including myself. In all ministries which have any foreign relations, there are strategic intelligence officers. As members of these ministries and committees thereof they have contact with and conduct intelligence against visiting foreign delegations, tourists, lecturers, etc..

40.   S: There is also a Fifth Directorate. The chief of this directorate is the former chief of the MDA of whom you (G.) have reminded me - Gen. Lelt. KOCHETKOV. This directorate is concerned with the placement of REZIDENTURAS in all countries including the countries of People's Democracies, and the preparation of diversionists groups. This directorate studies all critical targets such as bridges, tunnels, etc. and analyzes drop zones for large scale operations for General Staff use as well as small group operations for behind-the-lines sabotage groups.   G: Are they now engaged in sabotage activities?   S: No, they are not now engaged in sabotage activities, but they do have the personnel trained and placed in critical areas where they will act when the order is given.   G: In all countries, including the Democracies?   S: In all countries, but in the Democracies it is of a different nature, like stay-behind, because we do not conduct active intelligence against the Democracies. We have a Tenth Directorate of the General Staff which deals with all matters of a military nature with the People's Democracies through the military attaches and this Directorate controls the delivery of all rocket weapons, in the countries of People's Democracies.

41.   S: In this year all countries of People's Democracies must be furnished rocket weapons.   VARENTSOV and his people are also working on the development of bases, storage areas, launching sites, and the training of cadres for the countries of People's Democracies. The rockets which we are now delivering to these countries are those which are now being mass-produced such as the R-11 about which I gave you a report. This one, and in addition all those which are on production lines, are being given to China and all other countries of People's Democracies. (Note: Later Subject emphasized that Albania was the one exception, due to the recent "revisionistic" attitude of Gen. Enver HOXHA.)

42.   S: In the DDR we now have four brigades and of these two brigades already are equipped with atomic warheads. They also have special storage facilities and the engineers of the Artillery Academy Dzerzhinskogo are working on this. This Academy is now in the hands of MOSKALENKO, which occurred after the accidental death of Marshal NEDELIN due to a rocket disaster. That was not an aircraft accident. The report was a big lie deliberately reported to the world. But I will give you all details of this separately. I wrote a little about this but I must add to it because it is impossible to write all details.

43.   G: Let me fill out the GRU organizational chart.   S: I have given you five directorates, and there is no Sixth Directorate so designated. There is a separate Eighth OTHEL called the Coding Section and there are Rear Services units (SLUZHBY TYLA) which provide logistical support such as clothing and even diamonds and gold for agent operations.

14

Document Sixteen continued

Various accounts suggest that the assessment of CIA analysts that the Soviets would be unlikely to put nuclear weapons into Cuba was informed by the view that the Soviets had not deployed nuclear weapons outside Soviet territory. This suggests that the information Penkovsky supplied was not integrated into the assessment process. This had happened in 1961 on the much more crucial question of Soviet ICBM development. Penkovsky's information on Soviet ICBM deployments challenged US (and especially USAF) assessments, which were only revised and reduced when *Corona* satellite photography became available.[38] Until then, uncorroborated humint was insufficient to alter assumptions and assessments.

It is also now clear that Soviets had previously stationed medium-range missiles in East Germany.[39] In 1959, 1,200-km-range R-5M MRBMs were stationed in the DDR within range of London and Paris, key USAF bases in France, and the UK Thor IRBM sites being established in East Anglia. The precise reason for the deployment of these missiles remains unclear as does the cause of their hasty withdrawal later in 1959. Matthias Uhl and Vladimir Ivkin suggest that various western intelligence communities were aware of the deployment, and provide evidence of US knowledge, but there are no indications of an institutional memory of these events that could inform assessments in 1962. Whether knowledge that the Soviets had put nuclear weapons into eastern European would of itself have challenged the CIA's assumption that Khrushchev would not confront the US in Cuba is far from certain. Nevertheless, this may well illustrate a generic aspect of intelligence: however good the tradecraft and however credible the information, it is of no value unless it is effectively integrated into the assessment process and made use of.

Notes

Overview: The espionage of Oleg Penkovsky

Charles Cogan

1   Christopher Andrew, *For the President's Eyes Only: Secret Intelligence and the American Presidency from Washington to Bush* (New York: HarperCollins, 1996).
2   McGeorge Bundy, *Danger and Survival: Choices About the Bomb in the First Fifty Years* (New York: HarperPerennial, 1996). Michael R. Beschloss, *The Crisis Years: Kennedy and Khrushchev, 1960–1963* (New York: HarperCollins, 1991), p. 768.
3   Jerrold L. Schecter and Peter Deriabin, *The Spy Who Saved the World: How a Soviet Colonel Changed the Course of the Cold War* (New York: Charles Scribner's Sons, 1992).
4   Schecter and Deriabin, *The Spy Who Saved the World*, pp. 319–27.
5   Author telephone conversation with Dino Brugioni (see note 8), 25 July 2005.
6   Ibid.
7   Ibid.
8   Dino Brugioni, *Eyeball to Eyeball* (New York: Random House, 1991), p. viii.
9   Bob Woodward, *Bush at War* (New York: Simon and Schuster, 2002). See also Gary C. Schroen: *First In: An Insider's Account on How the CIA Spearheaded the War on Terror in Afghanistan* (New York: Presidio Press/ Ballantine Books, 2005).
10 Schecter and Deriabin, *The Spy Who Saved the World*, p. 441.
11 Ibid.

Commentary: Penkovsky: A Western success story?

Len Scott

1   Schecter and Deriabin, *The Spy Who Saved the World* p. 3. For a recent account based on testimony from one of Penkovsky's two CIA case officers, George Kisevalter, see Clarence Ashley, *CIA Spymaster* (Gretna, LA: Pelican Publishing Company, 2004).
2   Baroness Park of Monmouth, letter to *The Times*, 8 February 2004.
3   Schecter and Deriabin, *Spy Who Saved the World*, pp. 339–41. The documents were released in 1992 and are currently available in the National Archives, Washington. 179 are accessible at the CIA website at: http://www.foia.cia.gov/penkovsky.asp
4   Note: as part of the sequence of documents running through the volume, the CIA documents appearing on the preceding pages have been numbered Ten-Sixteen. But, for the sake of consistency, the original document identifiers (docs 1–179) allocated by the CIA on its web page at http://www.foia.cia.gov/penkovsky.asp are also used in the notes.
5   CIA: http://www.foia.cia.gov/penkovsky.asp, doc. 156. This volume, Document Ten, pp. 145–52.
6   CIA: http://www.foia.cia.gov/penkovsky.asp, doc. 140. This volume, Document Eleven, pp. 153–6.
7   A dead drop is 'a hiding place to leave materials and messages for pickup, preferably to be used only once', Schecter and Deriabin, *Spy Who Saved the World*, p. 12. Other terms used are 'dead letter drop' and 'dead letter box'.
8   Briefing of (Blank) to Load Drop for (Blank) 3 May 1961; see Schecter and Deriabin, *Spy Who Saved the World*, pp. 192–3.
9   Schecter and Deriabin, *Spy Who Saved the World*, pp. 12–14, 425–7.
10 Ibid., pp. 19–22, 33–4, 37–8.
11 CIA: 'Discussion between SR/COP, CSR/9, DCSR/9, (Blank) Re: SR/COP's European Trip', 6 February 1962, p. 1, http://www.foia.cia.gov/penkovsky.asp, docs. 71–80; Schecter and Deriabin, *Spy Who Saved the World*, p. 295.
12 CIA: http://www.foia.cia.gov/penkovksy, asp, doc. 53. This volume, Document Twelve, pp. 158–60.
13 CIA: http://www.foia.cia.gov/penkovksy, asp, doc. 35. This volume, Document Thirteen, p. 161.
14 CIA: http://www.foia.cia.gov/penkovksy, asp, doc. 15. This volume, Document Fourteen, pp. 162–3.
15 CIA: http://www.foia.cia.gov/penkovksy, asp, doc. 12. This volume, Document Fifteen, p. 164.
16 For Golitsyn on Penkovsky, see Anatoliy Golitsyn, *New Lies for Old: The Communist Strategy of Deception and Disinformation* (London: Bodley Head, 1984), p. 54; see also Schecter and Deriabin, *Spy Who Saved the World*, pp. 204–5; Tom Mangold, *Cold Warrior – James Jesus Angleton: The CIA's Master Spy Hunter* (New York: Simon and Schuster, 1991), pp. 77–8. For discussion, see Len Scott, 'Espionage and Cold War: Oleg Penkovsky and the Cuban Missile Crisis', *Intelligence and National Security*, 14/3 (Autumn 1999), pp. 37–9. For a recent exposition of the claim that Penkovsky was Soviet-controlled, see Servando Gonzalez, *The Nuclear Deception: Nikita Khrushchev and the Cuban Missile Crisis* (Oakland, CA: Spooks Books, 2002), pp. 123–35.
17 Peter Wright (with Paul Greenglass) *Spycatcher* (Richmond, Australia: Heinemann, 1987), pp. 204–12.
18 Edward Jay Epstein, *Deception: The Invisible War Between the KGB and the CIA* (London: W.H. Allen, 1989), pp. 79–80.
19 Gordon Brook-Shepherd, *The Storm Birds: Soviet Post-war Defectors* (London: Weidenfeld and Nicolson, 1988), p. 162.

20   Tom Bower, *The Perfect English Spy: Sir Dick White and the Secret War, 1935–90* (London: Heinemann, 1995), p. 282.
21   Schecter and Deriabin, *Spy Who Saved the World*, p. 194.
22   David E. Murphy, Sergei A. Kondrashev, and George Bailey, *Battleground Berlin: CIA vs KGB in the Cold War* (New Haven, CT: Yale University Press, 1997), pp. 217–18, 423–8, 449–53. For a discussion of the British side, see David Stafford, *Spies Beneath Berlin* (London: John Murray, 2002), passim.
23   Ashley states that 533 GRU and 75 KGB officers were compromised, *CIA Spymaster*, p. 225. Schecter and Deriabin state that Penkovsky identified 7–10 per cent of 7000 photographs, mostly GRU and including 200–300 KGB, *Spy Who Saved the World*, p. 173.
24   Aleksandr Fursenko and Timothy Naftali, *'One Hell of a Gamble': Khrushchev, Castro Kennedy and the Cuban Missile Crisis 1958–1964* (London: John Murray, 1997), pp. 138–9.
25   CIA: Meeting No. 37, 2 October 1961, paras 13–14, http://www.foia.cia.gov/ penkovsky.asp, docs. 101–10; Schecter and Deriabin, *Spy Who Saved the World*, pp. 262–3, 284–7, 347–8.
26   When the episode was first disclosed by Garthoff, his source had suggested that the phone call had been made on 22 October, Raymond L. Garthoff, *Reflections on the Cuban Missile Crisis* (Washington, DC: The Brookings Institution, 1987), pp. 39–41. For further details and clarification, see *Spy Who Saved the World*, pp. 337–52.
27   CIA: John A. McCone, Memorandum, 5 November 1962 (courtesy of the US Information and Privacy Coordinator); Schecter and Deriabin, *Spy Who Saved the World*, pp. 346–7.
28   Garthoff, *Reflections*, pp. 64–5.
29   Schecter and Deriabin, *Spy Who Saved the World*, p. 74, *et seq.*, Ashley, *CIA Spymaster*, pp. 194, 203, 232–4.
30   CIA: Meeting 1 (London) 20 April 1961, paras 41–2, CIA: http://www.foia.cia.gov/penkovsky.asp, doc. 149. This volume, Document Sixteen, pp. 167–8.
31   Some 140 hours of tape recording were generated, Ashley, *CIA Spymaster*, p. 194.
32   CIA: Meeting #2, 21 April 1961, para 123, http://www.foia.cia.gov/penkovsky.asp, docs. 141–50; Meeting No. 4 at Leeds, England, 23 April 1961, para 36, http://www.foia.cia.gov/penkovsky.asp, docs. 141–50; Meeting #5, 24 April 1961 in Leeds, paras 64–6, http://www.foia.cia.gov/penkovsky.asp, docs. 141–50; Meeting Number 7, Birmingham, England, 27 April 1961, para 82, 141–50.
33   See also Schecter and Deriabin, *Spy Who Saved the World*, p. 68.
34   Meeting 1, para 110. There is no evidence that R-11s were ever deployed in Cuba though in September when Khrushchev decide to send additional tactical nuclear weapons the Soviet Military recommended R-11s, Fursenko and Naftali, *'One Hell of a Gamble'*, p. 188.
35   See Schecter and Deriabin, *Spy Who Saved the World*, pp. 318–52; Christopher Andrew, *For the President's Eyes Only: Secret Intelligence and the American Presidency from Washington to Bush* (London: HarperCollins, 1995), p. 290; for a more circumspect assessment, see Scott, 'Espionage and the Cold War'.
36   National Archives: CAB 182/11, JIC Missile Threat Co-ordination Sub-Committee, JIC (MT) (62) 7th Meeting, 30 October 1962.
37   *FRUS, 1961–1963, Volume X*: Document 433, Special National Intelligence Estimate, SNIE 85–3–62, 'The Military Build-up in Cuba', 19 September 1962, pp. 1070–80.
38   Schecter and Deriabin, *Spy Who Saved the World*, pp. 271–82; Scott, 'Espionage and Cold War', pp. 29–30.
39   Matthias Uhl and Vladimir I. Ivkin, '"Operation Atom", the Soviet Union's Stationing of Nuclear Missiles in the German Democratic Republic, 1959', *Cold War International History Project Bulletin*, 12/13 (Fall/Winter 2001), pp. 299–307.

8 American and British intelligence on South Vietnam, 1963

Andrew Priest and R. Gerald Hughes

OVERVIEW: THE US AND VIETNAM IN 1963

Andrew Priest

These two documents were produced at a pivotal moment of American involvement in the Vietnam War. By this time the stability of South Vietnamese President Ngo Dinh Diem's regime was in serious doubt and, as both of these documents recognise, without immediate action, the entire political, social and economic fabric of the country was threatened. Diem had been the leader of the Republic of Vietnam since partition following the Geneva Agreement of 1954. In the opinion of both the British and American governments, the years that followed had seen some considerable successes in his country. Up until just a few months before these documents were written, Diem appeared to be dealing with the dual challenges of building up the South Vietnamese state while fighting the communist insurgency, which had been reinvigorated from 1960. His methods were often questionable and even brutal, but the US overlooked these because he seemed to be maintaining stability. Indeed, when John F. Kennedy became the US President in January 1961, the main focus of US attention in South-east Asia was the developing crisis in Laos between the communist Pathet Lao and the Royal Laotian Army.

Yet the situation in Vietnam continued to be of concern. Of crucial importance in monitoring its progress were US National Intelligence Estimates (NIE) prepared by the Central Intelligence Agency (CIA) with the co-operation of other key departments and services. These were the most important intelligence documents used by policy-makers because they were wide-ranging, explained the current situation in given areas and also made predictions of likely future developments. Documents produced by the British Joint Intelligence Committee (JIC) performed similar functions, the JIC being an interdepartmental body dealing with intelligence collection and analysis. Much of this JIC document is concerned with the military, political and economic situation. Yet it is clear that while the communist threat and lack of progress in checking it were worrying, the main concern was South Vietnam's internal situation.

The JIC note that Kennedy's decision to increase military aid to the government of South Vietnam during 1961 and 1962 undoubtedly helped bolster the government and prevent the Viet Cong from making significant advances (Document Eighteen, p. 185). Diem agreed to develop a counterinsurgency strategy and a strategic hamlet programme modelled on the one developed by the British in Malaya. This was the most controversial aspect of the American programme, involving the 'securing' of villages against communist infiltration through fortification. British influence in this programme was established and maintained through the British Advisory Mission Vietnam (BRIAM). By the time the JIC report was written, Vietnam was becoming more of a concern to the British and Peter Busch has argued that Britain 'did not counsel restraint and failed to show Kennedy more peaceful ways out of the potential quagmire in Vietnam'.[1] Busch shows that the head of BRIAM, Robert Thompson, was optimistic by late 1962 and early 1963 that the war was being won, especially because the strategic hamlet programme that he championed appeared to be yielding results.[2] The JIC document reflects some of this, suggesting that 'successful conclusion of the strategic hamlet programme would have a long-term effect' on the military situation (Document Eighteen, p. 2).

Thompson's optimism was reflected elsewhere. During late 1962 and early 1963, while still guarded, some British and American intelligence reports were becoming cautiously optimistic about the prospects for the South Vietnamese government. Roger Hilsman, Director of the State Department's Bureau of Intelligence and Research, reported in December 1962 that the government's counterinsurgency policy was being implemented effectively, although there was still considerable concern over the state of the strategic hamlet programme.[3] At the start of 1963 he was more positive, telling his superiors that he had 'the impression that things are going much much better than they were a year ago, but that they are not going nearly so well as the people here in Saigon both military and civilian think they are'.[4]

In series of developments during the first months of 1963, however, the situation deteriorated rapidly. On 2 January, South Vietnamese forces engaged the Viet Cong at the village of Ap Bac near Saigon in the Mekong Delta. The Viet Cong inflicted heavy losses before retreating into the jungle. The battle was reported in the American press as a defeat and the American government worried that this might have a negative impact on the South Vietnamese army's morale. Growing tensions between the government and members of the Buddhist majority compounded this situation. As the NIE document (Document Seventeen) notes, Diem was a Catholic and this made his position more difficult as the majority Vietnamese Buddhist population increasingly came to resent his apparent favouritism towards those of his own religion, his nepotism and his authoritarianism. At the beginning of May these tensions culminated in the shooting of nine people at Buddhist celebrations in the city of Hué. The resulting 'Buddhist crisis' referred to in the NIE document highlighted the fragility of Diem's grip on power and tensions between the South Vietnamese and US governments. Diem's brother and interior minister, Ngo Dinh Nhu, was now becomingly openly critical of the American presence and his influential wife was even more vocal.

Despite Diem and his supporters' attempts to paint the Buddhists as communist stooges, the Americans had to admit that most of the protesters were moderates demanding reasonable concessions from the regime. The initial crisis and Diem's subsequent reaction galvanised many who had previously been indifferent, and provided a rallying point for their grievances. The situation worsened in May and June and on 11 June the first in a series of public self-immolations by Buddhist monks took place on the streets of Saigon in protest at Diem's refusal to agree to a series of Buddhist demands.[5]

By now, intelligence reports were increasingly grim. The American document reflects both a pervasive pessimism in American attitudes and a realisation that the chances of a successful coup were growing. The fact that this document offers odds on the likelihood of a coup against Diem shows just how bad the situation had become. Coups attempts were a common feature of Diem's years in office, but now Diem's freedom of action appeared to be increasingly constrained. As a CIA document of 8 July 1963 had concluded, he could either relax his rule, which might lead to further demands, or tighten measures against the Buddhists, which could trigger a coup.[6] The two documents reproduced here illustrate the dilemma that policy-makers faced. While the NIE states that, 'Diem's position may have been permanently and dangerously impaired', the Americans also recognised that there were few, if any, alternative candidates to lead the country. Of greatest concern now were Nhu and his wife. They had become an embarrassment and the NIE makes it clear that the US government is increasingly aware of public opinion in the US and elsewhere 'that the US is supporting an oppressive and unrepresentative regime'. Yet they also saw that if Diem was removed from office, a successful bid for power by his brother could result in a stiffening of the regime and even an official request for the Americans to leave.

In the months that followed the writing of these documents, the situation became worse. Diem cracked down further on Buddhist dissent and the Americans increasingly entangled themselves with those plotting to oust the President and his brother. While Kennedy refused to allow the US government to become implicated in any coup attempt, from October 1963 he made it known that he was willing to 'identify and build contacts with possible alternative leadership' and that it was 'Essential that this be totally secure and fully deniable'.[7] At almost exactly the same time he produced National Security Action Memorandum 263 authorising the withdrawal of approximately 1,000 US forces.[8] There are those who argue that because the situation had become so bad and intelligence reports so negative, this NSAM can be taken as evidence that Kennedy was planning to withdraw the US military presence from Vietnam, perhaps following his successful re-election in 1964. Most notably, John Newman has argued this in *JFK and the Vietnam War* and his work has become a part of American popular culture through efforts of film director Oliver Stone in *JFK*.[9] This view has been given credence by the reminiscences of Kennedy's Secretary of Defense, Robert S. McNamara, and former CIA station chief in Saigon William E. Colby,[10] and academic Howard Jones has developed it.[11] Yet others have disagreed with this assessment.[12] Frederik Logevall, for example, argues that NSAM 263 is not the radical document some claim because it advocates no more than 'token withdrawal' when conditions are better.[13]

Both views are open to endless debate because they rely on selective evidence and supposition. By mid-1963, as the British document (Document Eighteen) suggests, the US was already 'deeply committed in South Vietnam' and although Kennedy had said he did not want to increase the United States' presence there 'it would be hard for them not to do so if faced with a choice between abandoning the country to the Viet Cong and a major intensification of their effort in South Vietnam'. What we can say with certainty is that the 'Buddhist crisis', followed by the slow withdrawal of US support for Diem and his assassination just three weeks before Kennedy's death removed the last vestiges of a stable government in Saigon. This made the job for Kennedy's successor, Lyndon B. Johnson, much more challenging[14] and ultimately brought the US closer to a large-scale military commitment in Vietnam.

DOCUMENT SEVENTEEN:

SNIE 53–2–63, 'The Situation in South Vietnam', 10 July 1963.
Source: *The Pentagon Papers: The Defense Department History of United States Decisionmaking on Vietnam*, Senator Gravel Edition, Volume 2 (Boston, MA: Beacon Press, 1971), pp. 729–33.

*SNIE 53–2–63
10 July 63

THE SITUATION IN SOUTH VIETNAM

SCOPE NOTE

NIE 53–63, 'Prospects in South Vietnam,' dated 17 April 1963 was particularly concerned with the progress of the counterinsurgency effort, and with the military and political factors most likely to affect that effort. The primary purpose of the present SNIE is to examine the implications of recent developments in South Vietnam for the stability of the country, the viability of the Diem regime, and its relationship with the US.

CONCLUSIONS

A. The Buddhist crisis in South Vietnam has highlighted and intensified a widespread and longstanding dissatisfaction with the Diem regime and its style of government. If – as is likely – Diem fails to carry out truly and promptly the commitments he has made to the Buddhists, disorders will probably flare again and the chances of a coup or assassination attempts against him will become better than even. (*Paras. 4, 14*)

B. The Diem regime's underlying uneasiness about the extent of the US involvement in South Vietnam has been sharpened by the Buddhist affair and the firm line taken by the US. This attitude will almost certainly persist and further pressure to reduce the US presence in the country is likely. (*Paras. 10–12*)

C. Thus far, the Buddhist issue has not been effectively exploited by the Communists, nor does it appear to have had any appreciable effect on the counterinsurgency effort. We do not think Diem is likely to be overthrown by a Communist coup. Nor do we think the Communists would necessarily profit if he were overthrown by some combination of his non-Communist opponents. A non-Communist successor regime might be initially less effective against the Viet Cong, but, given continued support from the US, could provide reasonably effective leadership for the government and the war effort. (*Paras. 7, 15–17*)

DISCUSSION

I. INTRODUCTION

1. The two chief problems which have faced the Government of South Vietnam (GVN) since its birth in 1954 have been: (a) to forge the institutions and loyalties necessary to Vietnam's survival as an independent nation, and (b) to counter the menace of Hanoi's subversive and aggressive designs – pursued since 1960 by a campaign of widespread guerrilla warfare. In attempting to cope with these problems, the GVN has been hampered by its lack of confidence in and its inability to engage the understanding and support of a considerable portion of the Vietnamese people – including large segments of the educated classes and the peasantry. In recent weeks these inadequacies and tensions in the South Vietnamese body politic have been further revealed and intensified.

II. THE BUDDHIST AFFAIR

2. President Diem, his family, and a large proportion of the top leaders of the regime are Roman Catholics, in a population that is

70 to 80 percent Buddhist. The regime has clearly accorded preferential treatment to Catholics in its employment practices and has favored the Catholic Church. But there have been no legal restrictions on religious freedom and, until recently, most Buddhists appeared passive in their response to the privileged institutional position occupied by the Catholic Church. There have, however, been various administrative discriminations against the Buddhists, though these may have resulted as much from thoughtlessness or misplaced zeal on the part of minor officials as from conscious GVN policy. These have obviously created an undercurrent of resentment, as is evidenced by the extent and intensity of the recent outbreaks.

3. In April 1963, the GVN ordered its provincial officials to enforce a longstanding but generally ignored edict regulating the public display of religious flags. As it happened, this order was issued just prior to Buddha's birthday (8 May), a major Buddhist festival, and just after Papal flags had been prominently flown during a series of officially encouraged celebrations commemorating the 25th anniversary of the ordination of Ngo dinh Thuc, Diem's brother, the Archbishop of Hue. A protest demonstration developed in Hue on 8 May, which was dispersed by fire from a Civil Guard unit. In the ensuing melee several persons were killed, including some children. The GVN has blamed the deaths on Viet Cong terrorists despite evidence to the contrary, and its subsequent stiff-necked handling of this incident and its aftermath has sparked a national crisis. The Buddhists, hitherto disorganized and nonprotesting, have shown considerable cohesion and force – enough to elicit a set of 'compromise' agreements from President Diem on 16 June. Moreover, the fact that the Buddhist leaders have been able to challenge the government openly without evoking serious government retaliation has presumably given them considerable confidence.

4. For the moment, the Buddhist movement remains under the effective control of moderate bonzes who have refused to accept support from or countenance cooperation with any of Diem's political opponents, Communist or non-Communist, and appear to be trying to insure that the Buddhists live up to their part of the

bargain. This leadership gave the GVN a period of grace (which expired about the end of June) in which to show that it was moving in good faith to carry out its undertakings, failing which protests would resume. So far there have been no further demonstrations, but the Buddhist leadership is clearly restive.

5. Despite Buddhist restraint in the political exploitation of the affair, it has obvious political overtones. It has apparently aroused widespread popular indignation and could well become a focal point of general disaffection with the Diem government. It provides an issue on which most of Diem's non-Communist opponents (even including some Catholics) can find common ground of agreement. There is considerable evidence that the issue itself and, even more, the Diem family's handling of it to date has occasioned restiveness at virtually all levels of the GVN's military and civil establishments, both of whose lower and middle echelons are largely staffed by Buddhists. In some cases, civil servants seem to have ignored or tempered GVN instructions, superiors have on occasion evaded their assigned task of propounding the official GVN line to their subordinates, and information on impending government actions has obviously leaked to Buddhist leaders. In any case, recent developments are causing many GVN officials to reexamine their relations with and the limits of their loyalty to the Diem regime; there is accumulating evidence of serious disaffection and coup plotting in high military and civilian circles.

6. The Buddhist affair appears to have given considerable heart to the various non-Communist political opposition splinter groups in and out of South Vietnam. There also appears to be a growing feeling among former supporters of the regime that Diem's position may have been permanently and dangerously impaired. Thus far, however, we have no evidence that the diverse opposition groups have been able to form new or effective alliances with one another.

7. The Buddhist issue would appear to be an obvious windfall for the Communists, but so far there is no evidence that they have been able to exploit it effectively. They may have penetrated the Buddhist clergy to some extent, but are not presently exerting any

discernible influence, despite the suggestions to the contrary in GVN pronouncements. To date the Buddhist crisis does not appear to have had any appreciable effect on the continuing counterinsurgency effort, though the morale and efficiency of the GVN's military and civil forces are likely to be impaired if the issue is prolonged.

8. The Buddhist crisis has also hurt the GVN internationally, with potentially important effects upon the future success of US policy towards southeast Asia. Protests are growing in other predominantly Buddhist countries, with the implication that US action could help resolve the crisis. Cambodia and Ceylon have made representations to the UN and more may be forthcoming. In other countries, including the US, the crisis has given new stimulus to criticism of US policy on the grounds that the US is supporting an oppressive and unrepresentative regime.

9. The future course of the Buddhist affair will be largely determined by the GVN's actions in the near term. It is likely that the issues recently raised can be resolved if the GVN executes its portion of the negotiated bargain. However, politically sophisticated segments of South Vietnamese society, Buddhists included, are mindful of Diem's past practice of often using negotiations as a stall for time and of making promises in order to weather an immediate crisis. The real danger in the present situation is that Diem may be tempted to employ such tactics which have served him well in the past but could prove disastrous if essayed this time. If demonstrations should be resumed, they would probably assume an increasingly political cast, and less moderate Buddhist leadership would be likely to come to the fore. Public order would be threatened. In particular, we cannot be sure how various army or police units would react if ordered to fire on demonstrations headed by Buddhist bonzes.

III. THE EFFECT OF RECENT DEVELOPMENTS ON US-GVN RELATIONS

10. The GVN has always shown some concern over the implications of US involvement in South Vietnamese affairs and from time to time has felt moved to restrict US activities and presence in South

Vietnam. This attitude springs partly from legitimate, if hypersensitive, concern for the appearance as well as the fact of Vietnam's recently acquired sovereignty. To a considerable degree, however, it springs from the Diem government's suspicion of US intentions toward it, and from its belief that the extensive US presence is setting in motion political forces which could eventually threaten Diem's political primacy.

11. The Buddhist affairs erupted at one of these periods of GVN sensitivity, and the strain has been aggravated by subsequent events. The GVN's initial handling of the issue gave the US ground for serious embarrassment and concern which, in turn, produced a succession of forceful US démarches. The Diem family has bitterly resented these US actions and may well feel that the Buddhist protests were at least indirectly due to the US presence. Under the circumstances, further pressure to reduce that presence is likely.

12. A key role in this regard will be played by Diem's brother, Ngo dinh Nhu. He has always been Diem's chief political lieutenant, but the years since 1954 have witnessed a steady accretion of Nhu's personal power and authority-an accretion due partly to circumstance and primarily to deliberate effort on Nhu's part. Nhu has political ambitions of his own and almost certainly envisages himself as his brother's successor. For a variety of reasons, Nhu has long privately viewed the US with some hostility and suspicion. American criticism of the GVN has especially irritated Nhu, for he is aware that he and his wife are often its primary targets. Above all, Nhu almost certainly doubts whether the support which the US has given to his brother would be transferred to him.

13. In the negotiations with the Buddhists, Nhu urged his brother to take a firm line and is, by his own statement, wholly out of sympathy with the concessions made. On the basis of past performance, we think it unlikely that he will help to implement the settlement; his influence on Diem will be rather in the direction of delaying and hedging on commitments, a tendency to which Diem himself is already disposed. This will be the more likely since not only the Nhus and Diem, but also his brothers Archbishop Thuc

and Ngo dinh Can, the political boss of the central provinces, obviously continue to doubt the legitimacy of Buddhist complaints and to underestimate the intensity of the crisis.

IV. THE OUTLOOK

14. If the Diem government moves effectively to fulfill its 16 June commitments, much of the resentment aroused by the Buddhist controversy could be allayed. However, even if relations between the GVN and the Buddhists are smoothed over, the general discontent with the Diem regime which the crisis has exacerbated and brought to the fore is likely to persist. Further, if-as is probable-the regime is dilatory, inept, and insincere in handling Buddhist matters, there will probably be renewed demonstrations, and South Vietnam will probably remain in a state of domestic political tension. Under these circumstances, the chances of a non-Communist assassination or coup attempt against Diem will be better than even. We cannot exclude the possibility of an attempted Communist coup, but a Communist attempt will have appreciably less likelihood of success so long as the majority of the government's opponents and critics remain-as they are now-alert to the Communist peril.

15. The chances of a non-Communist coup – and of its success – would become greater in the event renewed GVN/Buddhist confrontation should lead to large-scale demonstrations in Saigon. More or less prolonged riot and general disorder would probably result – with the security forces confused over which side to support. Under such circumstances, a small group, particularly one with prior contingency plans for such an eventuality, might prove able to topple the government. Conversely, a continued or resumed truce between the GVN and the Buddhists would serve to reduce the likelihood of such an overthrow.

16. Any attempt to remove Diem will almost certainly be directed against Nhu as well, but should Nhu survive Diem, we are virtually certain that he would attempt to gain power – in the first instance probably by manipulating the constitutional machinery. We do not believe that Nhu's bid would succeed, despite the personal

political base he has sought to build through the Republican Youth (of which he is the overt, uniformed head), the strategic hamlet program (whose directing Interministerial Committee he chairs), and in the army. He and his wife have become too much the living symbols of all that is disliked in the present regime for Nhu's personal political power to long outlive his brother. There might be a struggle with no little violence, but enough of the army would almost certainly move to take charge of the situation, either rallying behind the constitutional successor to install Vice President Tho or backing another non-Communist civil leader or a military junta.

17. A non-Communist successor regime might prove no more effective than Diem in fighting the Viet Cong; indeed at least initially it might well prove considerably less effective, and the counterinsurgency effort would probably be temporarily disrupted. However, there is a reasonably large pool of underutilized but experienced and trained manpower not only within the military and civilian sectors of the present government but also, to some extent, outside. These elements, given continued support from the US, could provide reasonably effective leadership for the government and the war effort.

COMMENTARY: 'IN THE FINAL ANALYSIS, IT IS THEIR WAR': BRITAIN, THE UNITED STATES AND SOUTH VIETNAM IN 1963

R. Gerald Hughes

> From my earliest associations with Vietnam (1951) I have been concerned about US handling of information from that area. . . . This included deliberate and reflexive manipulation of information, restrictions on collection and censorship of reporting. The net result was that decisionmakers were denied the opportunity to get a complete form of information, determine its validity for themselves, and make decisions.
> (Lt. Col. Henry A. Shockley, Former Chief, Collection and Liaison, Defense Attaché Office, Saigon, 1975)[1]

> In the final analysis, it is their war.
> (John F. Kennedy, 2 September 1963)[2]

In analysing these two documents on the early stages of US involvement in the Vietnam War (SNIE 53–2–63 and JIC 63(20)), one should recall two important facts. First, Britain was not directly involved in the war. Thus, what we have here is a British perspective on a largely American problem – South Vietnam – and a contemporary American assessment on the same issue.[3] Consequently, the British document – JIC 63(20) (Document Eighteen) – can be seen as a piece of intelligence on an ally and a commentary on an area of vital interest to the United States.[4] Second, since intelligence-gathering is traditionally directed at 'friends' *and* opponents alike, the British would have targeted South Vietnam and the United States as well as North Vietnam, the Soviet Union and the People's Republic of China, in seeking intelligence on South-East Asia at this time.[5] The function of intelligence is to provide policy-makers with as full a picture of the whole situation as possible, and not to simply assess the strengths, weaknesses and intentions of potential adversaries. While the latter functions are vital, they should not overshadow everything else.

Some of the conclusions reached in JIC 63(20) will certainly have been a result of intelligence-sharing with the Americans.[6] But the British also had a multitude of sources independent of, and sometimes superior to, those possessed by the Americans. The British had secret and open-source information from throughout the region and the possession of Hong Kong, and the British recognition of the People's Republic of China in 1950 gave London a number of sources unavailable to Washington. In addition, the British had any number of sources as a result of intelligence networks established during the long-standing British presence in East Asia. Much of this intelligence was undoubtedly passed onto the United States (including invaluable SIGINT on North Vietnam from the GCHQ monitoring station at Little Sai Wan in British Hong Kong).[7] And, as Richard Aldrich has noted, it was in the sphere of intelligence, where British decline was relatively less marked, that Britain was able to achieve the greatest measure of equality in the 'Special Relationship' with the United States.[8] But, of course, not even the closest of allies share everything.

At first sight, the British document under consideration here contains nothing that would preclude its release in line with the established Thirty-Year Rule (i.e. in 1994). However, the fact that it is an estimate produced by the Joint Intelligence Committee (JIC) meant that it was not subject to normal procedure and as a result it was not released until 2000. Despite this, a substantial proportion of the information contained within JIC 63(20) was available in other British documents – mainly emanating from the Foreign Office – from 1994 onwards. Indeed, the development of much of the thinking evident in JIC 63(20) can be traced in British (non-intelligence) documents stretching back to early 1961, when John F. Kennedy was inaugurated as US president. In January 1961, for example, Harry Hohler (British ambassador in Saigon, 1960–63) gave Lord Home (Foreign Secretary, 1960–63) a detailed report outlining increasing Viet Cong attacks, the unpopularity of the regime of Ngo Dinh Diem (President of South Vietnam, 1955–63) and the policy divisions amongst US political and military personnel in South Vietnam.[9] This file was available to the public from 1992. Given the presence of intelligence material in the files of other government departments, it is clear that unreleased (intelligence) files might not always contain new information. Thus, a broad-front approach to British archives on South-East Asia will more likely provide the

SECRET

c/L

(THIS DOCUMENT IS THE PROPERTY OF HER BRITANNIC MAJESTY'S GOVERNMENT)

J.I.C.(63) 20 (Final)   COPY-NO. 82

18th July, 1963   GUARD

CABINET

JOINT INTELLIGENCE COMMITTEE
─────────────────────────────

THE SITUATION IN SOUTH VIETNAM

Report by the Joint Intelligence Committee

SUMMARY OF REPORT AND CONCLUSIONS

In our report at Annex we review the development of
military activity by the Viet Cong in the past twelve months,
and of political activity connected with it.   The report also
covers the degree of success of United States/South Vietnamese
counter-measures, the consequences internally and abroad,
and the prospect for the next year or two.

2.   The tide flowing in the Viet Cong's favour at the end of
1961 was stemmed by massive United States military aid,
including specialised military units, in 1962.   The communist
"Front for the Liberation of South Vietnam" was given much
publicity but no official recognition by communist governments,
and has no territorial base in the country.   But it has
considerable propaganda value.   With United States help the
South Vietnamese Government is increasing its security forces
and pressing on with plans for pacification and resettlement,
including the establishment of "strategic villages and hamlets",
but much remains to be done and the South Vietnamese army has
important weaknesses, which the Viet Cong continue to exploit.

3.   We conclude that:-

(a) the greatest weaknesses of the Government forces are
indifferent leadership at many levels, too heavy reliance
on sophisticated support and a lack of Intelligence
techniques.   In particular, qualities of leadership vary
considerably and although some senior officers in command
are competent enough, overall proficiency varies and in
many cases has impeded the satisfactory execution of
operations;

(b) there is, however, evidence that the Viet Cong's
programme has been delayed, and to some extent disrupted
by the United States and South Vietnamese counter-measures;

-1-

SECRET

CAB 158/48

Document Eighteen: JIC (63)20, 'The Situation in South Vietnam', 18 July 1963
National Archives, Kew: CAB 158/ 48. Produced with permission of the National
Archives.

SECRET – GUARD

(c) the Diem Government's counter-measures have involved
a degree of regimentation and austerity which have
aroused some discontent among the general population,
but there is little or no evidence to suggest that the
general population is becoming restive or that there
is any threat to the regime from popular revolt.   The
Government must, however, show its ability to secure,
hold and administer those parts of the country in which
the Viet Cong operate and this will largely depend on
the success of their strategic hamlets and political
indoctrination programmes;

(d) the United States is deeply committed in South
Vietnam and, although President Kennedy has indicated
that the United States is unlikely to feel able to get
itself further committed, it would be hard for them not
to do so if faced with a choice between abandoning the
country to the Viet Cong and a major intensification
of their effort in South Vietnam;

(e) the military situation is unlikely to show much
improvement during the next twelve months although the
successful conclusion of the strategic hamlet programme
would have a long-term effect.   The struggle is therefore likely to continue on much the same lines as in the
past few months.

(Signed) BERNARD BURROWS

Chairman,
on behalf of the
Joint Intelligence Committee

Cabinet Office, S.W.1.

18th July, 1963

–2–

SECRET – GUARD

Document Eighteen continued

C|L

SECRET - GUARD

COPY NO. 82

ANNEX to J.I.C.(63) 20 (Final)

THE SITUATION IN SOUTH VIETNAM

GENERAL

By the end of 1961, the Viet Cong movement had gained a
clear political and military edge over the legal Government
of Vietnam. Terrorism and the Communist indoctrination of
large sections of the population had become more widespread
than ever before. The rebels not only strengthened their
hold on areas in which they were already dominant, but also
made inroads into parts of the country hitherto controlled by
neither side and even extended offensive activities generally
in traditionally Government held areas. As a result of this
expansion of Viet Cong activities, whole areas began to slip
away from Government control; morale both in the civil
administration and in the armed forces declined and national
confusion resulted from the seeming inability of the Diem
regime to seize the initiative from the Viet Cong.

2. During 1962 the United States alarmed by the situation
made a determined effort to counter the growth of the Viet
Cong movement. This consisted of overt and effective aid to
the South Vietnamese Government in the form of military and
economic advice and of material support. It included the
despatch of specialised United States military units and civil
administrative teams.

POLITICAL

3. In the early part of 1962 the North Vietnamese Government
(D.R.V.) were making considerable play with demands for an
international conference "to find effective steps designed to
preserve the 1954 Geneva agreements and to safeguard peace in
Vietnam and South East Asia". This included exerting pressure
on Prince Sihanouk to take up the cause of the neutralisation
of South Vietnam and the holding of an international conference
no doubt with the ultimate aim of achieving the reunification
of North and South Vietnam. The D.R.V. received overt support
from China, but the Russians did not commit themselves equally
to these demands, which fell away completely during the final
round of the Geneva Conference on Laos in July 1962.

4. For the time being the D.R.V. are apparently leaving
propaganda pressures for immediate reconsideration of the
position in South Vietnam to other Communist organs in
particular the "Front for the Liberation of South Vietnam".
Heavy publicity is given to the pronouncements of the Front
but neither the DRV nor other Communist Governments seem to
have gone so far as to give the Front even de facto recognition
as an alternative government, and the relations it has established appear to be with other "Front" organisations rather than
with governments. The D.R.V. probably prefer to have a
campaign mounted which weakens and aims to overthrow the Diem
regime, while themselves avoiding any commitment to accept
South Vietnamese neutrality - which has been consistently
plugged by the Front - as a final solution. Nor has there
apparently been any attempt to give the Front a territorial
base in South Vietnam to support a possible future claim
to be an alternative government. Meanwhile the

-3-

SECRET - GUARD

Document Eighteen continued

SECRET - GUARD

Front has failed to get any outstanding figure among the opponents of President Diem onto their Central Committee and those in exile have, in general, rejected the Front's neutralisation programme.   They nevertheless tend to pursue policies directed towards neutralisation and even re-unification, thus rendering their organisations particularly susceptible to Front influences.

5.   It would, nevertheless, in our view, be a mistake to underrate the value of the Front to the Communists.   The opportunity it purports to offer to the war-weary and discontented in South Vietnam for an end to the struggle without direct surrender to the North is bound to put a strain on the will to persevere.   For the Viet Cong, meanwhile, to have a possible instrument for a negotiated settlement in reserve is a useful insurance against an indefinite military stalemate, quite apart from the Front's presentational value to the DRV in giving credibility to their claim not themselves to be the mainspring of the insurgence in South Vietnam.

ECONOMIC SITUATION

6.   Despite massive United States aid - which since 1955 has amounted to two thousand million dollars - the war imposes a great burden on the economy and consumes half the budget. Communications have been disrupted, economic development retarded, taxes raised, imports controlled and credit restricted. The effects of all this have been particularly felt in the towns, notably Saigon where standards are relatively high and loyalties sensitive, and among the business community.   The insecurity of large areas also results in periodic shortages of food, fuel and other things, and upward price fluctuations which make for widespread hardship and add to the peasant's difficulties in selling his produce and buying the manufactures he needs.   Discontents arising from these economic stringencies are in themselves unlikely to have a decisive influence on the course of political events in the foreseeable future, but they must add to existing strains on the will to persevere with the war.

MILITARY

The Viet Cong Forces

7.   Viet Cong losses in 1962 were considerable.   Figures claimed by the South Vietnamese Government, however, have been inflated and even United States records include possible Viet Cong sympathisers, chance onlookers and unidentified villagers who have also come under Government fire.   The strength of the Viet Cong regular forces, has now risen, despite casualties, from a 1961 peak of about 21,000 to a present figure of between 22,000 and 25,000.   It seems probable that to the 3,500 infiltrators who arrived in South Vietnam during 1962, some 9,000 local recruits have been added.   The majority of these recruits come from the large reservoir of partly armed and trained supporters in South Vietnam;   the number of these is a matter for conjecture but it may be as high as 200,000. Arms for the new recruits seem mainly to have been obtained from losses inflicted on the Government forces, although some infiltrators are known to have brought down personal weapons. There is some evidence that Chinese communication equipment is also carried down by the infiltrating parties.

-4-

SECRET - GUARD

Document Eighteen continued

SECRET – GUARD

8. Information obtained from combat intelligence and from interrogation indicates that the following overall changes in the military organisation of the Viet Cong movement took place in 1962:-

(a) The division of Central Vietnam into two military regions: Military Region V in the north and Military Region VI in the south.

(b) The establishment of three regimental headquarters in the Military Region V. These, although capable of planning co-ordinated brigade type operations, seem to be principally administrative in character and are not designed at present to command units directly in battle.

(c) The allocation of specialists, mostly of DRV army origin, to the support elements, immediately subordinate to Military Headquarters Nam-Bo and Headquarters Military Region V.

(d) The build-up of such operational support elements which now include signal companies, artillery battalions (at present only armed with light mortars and 57 mm recoilless rifles) and engineer units.

9. Viet Cong units in the Nam-Bo region have remained much the same in character as previously, although some additional battalions are now operational. As in Central Vietnam, a separate military command structure has been established in Nam-Bo in parallel with the existing hierarchy of Party committees. Military Headquarters subordinate to the Nam-Bo Regional Headquarters now exist in each of the three inter-provincial sectors and in the Saigon/Cholon zone. (A map showing the Viet Cong military organisation is at Appendix "A".)

<u>United States/South Vietnamese Forces</u>

10. Following the United States decision to increase military aid to South Vietnam, a United States Military Assistance Command MAC(V) was set up in Saigon in January 1962 and was completely formed by May 1962. This Command replaced the United States MAAG which had operated in South Vietnam for some years, and which remains in the country, subordinate to MAC(V).

11. Simultaneously with the introduction of MAC(V), two separate projects were sponsored by the Americans. These were:-

(a) Politico-military planning of a co-ordinated design for the pacification and resettlement of the country.

(b) The immediate provision of increased military assistance in the form of arms and of support units. The latter consisted of helicopter companies and squadrons of fixed wing aircraft, all manned by United States personnel.

12. The clear determination on the part of the Americans to give massive aid overtly to the South Vietnamese had an immediate result. At practically all levels of the official South Vietnamese civil and military hierachy, morale began to rise and the defeatist sentiment, which had been widespread in 1961, began to dissipate.

-5-

SECRET – GUARD

Document Eighteen continued

SECRET - GUARD

13. The United States build-up was impressive. In late 1961, barely a thousand United States Servicemen were stationed in South Vietnam. By May 1962, five thousand United States personnel, and by the end of the year a total of between twelve and thirteen thousand, were in the country. Very large consignments of arms and equipment began to arrive in early spring 1962 and by the end of the year ample supplies were available, not only for the existing armed forces, but also for the new contingents which were being raised.

14. The increase in the South Vietnamese security forces in 1962 included:-

(a) An extra 30,000 men in the Army. This produced two new divisions, (both now operational), a new parachute battalion, additional ranger companies and certain specialist intelligence units.

(b) A small increment to the South Vietnamese Navy and Air Force.

(c) A large build-up in the para-military forces of:-

(i) from 75,000 to 95,000 in the Civil Guard;

(ii) from 50,000 to 90,000 in the Self Defence Corps;

(iii) an unknown number of armed personnel, both male and female, in the Republican Youth Movement.

This build-up continues and will reach its peak in mid-1963.

15. In addition to the basic weapons and material available to these increased forces, new equipment was introduced to give added flexibility to the field army. Amphibious armoured personnel carriers (APC), amphibious tanks and landing ships and craft were among these important items, but the support of over a hundred United States operated helicopters and a smaller number of fighter bomber and light bomber aircraft were generally of greater value as these all are of considerable tactical use over the whole country. The amphibians are most useful in the Delta area of Cochin China and certain coastal parts of central South Vietnam. (A map showing South Vietnam military regions is at Appendix "B".)

Operations in 1962/63

16. Campaigning in South Vietnam follows a seasonal trend with a low offensive ebb at the time of the monsoons. In Cochin China, the optimum period runs from late November to the beginning of June. In central South Vietnam the limits are less well defined, but the months of August to December cover the most difficult campaigning conditions.

17. Viet Cong offensive activity tends to start vigorously in late November, but from May onwards the slower moving Government forces are in a better position to develop greater offensive capacity. Heartened by their successes in 1961, the Viet Cong planned to break through into a further stage of insurgency by mid-1962 - the setting up of liberated areas protected by their armed forces and governed by a Communist hierachy.

-6-

SECRET - GUARD

Document Eighteen continued

SECRET - GUARD

18. Accelerated United States assistance had no direct effect
on the very intense Viet Cong activity during the months of
February, March and April, 1962, which hit the South Vietnamese
Government when morale was at its lowest. It was not until
May, when militarily conducted resettlement operations began
to get under way, that Government initiative increased to match
that of the Viet Cong. By June 1962, with the rains under way
in Cochin China, Viet Cong activity against the South
Vietnamese Government's forces flagged, although guerilla
operations of a local nature continued. This decrease in Viet
Cong initiative continued throughout July 1962.

19. Government operations during June, July and August
included action against the insurgents in the very difficult
flooded Delta terrain with the new amphibious APC's and a
number of damaging attacks against regular Viet Cong
battalions in the same area. Elsewhere, large-scale
operations were at a low ebb, and although the Viet Cong has
never lost the capacity to strike and inflict heavy casualties
in almost every part of the country, any attempt that the
insurgents had planned to "liberate" large areas of the country
in 1962 had failed. In addition, heavy casualties had been
inflicted on them. During the rains, which continued until
October, some pressure was maintained but when the flooding
subsided initiative once again passed to the Viet Cong.
During the respite given by the bad weather, recruiting and
training had taken place, but there is evidence that the Viet
Cong started their campaigning season with a large proportion
of raw recruits in their ranks.

20. Late November and December 1962 saw the traditional
return of the Viet Cong to the offensive. As in the same
period of 1961 they showed their ability to launch battalion
size operations and in two cases, a co-ordinated two/three
battalion attack was mounted. In January and February 1963,
their activity against the regular South Vietnamese forces
decreased once again and their efforts seemed to be directed
mainly against resettlement areas and Civil Guard detachments.
Their intelligence remains good and ambushes against small
units continue. In March there was a sharp rise in the number
of incidents though most of them were small.

Special Counter-measures

21. United States/South Vietnamese joint planning led to an
overall anti-insurgency plan being finalised and approved by
the South Vietnamese Government. When the plan was issued
in August, 1962, it was apparent that the establishment of
large resettlement areas, made up of strategic villages and
hamlets, was to be the keystone to the whole operation. This
idea, based on the advice given by the British Advisory
Mission to Vietnam (BRIAM) in late 1961, when adopted as the
essential basis for military operations accelerated the
important civil/military activities already undertaken in
this sphere. The strategic hamlets and villages are guarded
by their own Self Defence Corps and Republican Youth contingents. Thus the Civil Guard, instead of being tied to certain
fixed centres, is now able to protect vital points and
constitute small local reserves for counter-guerilla operations.

-7-

SECRET - GUARD

Document Eighteen continued

SECRET - GUARD

The Regular forces still have many static duties to perform, but most of the divisional units and the entire parachute brigade are available for mobile counter-insurgency operations. The specialised Army Ranger companies are still restricted to a provincial reserve role.

22.   The resettlement measures have helped to prevent the establishment of "liberated" areas by the Viet Cong and reduced the opportunities for intimidating the peasants and local officials. The switching of the Viet Cong attacks on to the strategic hamlets and villages may be evidence that they fear their possible effects on the insurgency. This trend may become more evident as resettlement continues. At present, approximately 60 per cent of the hamlets have been completed, although many of these require further improvement.

23.   A significant change in military tactics during 1962 has been the introduction of helicopters for troop transport. The immediate effect was to deprive the guerillas of many of the advantages that they derived from the terrain, i.e. the ability to come and go unobserved and operate in areas largely inaccessible to the South Vietnamese. Towards the end of the year however the Viet Cong had developed a counter-measure of waiting under cover for the helicopters and at the critical point of touch down subjecting the helicopters to heavy small arms and automatic weapons fire. Nevertheless a good deal of the inherent advantage of the helicopter still remains. A too heavy reliance on the "luxuries" of modern equipment has also been noted. The United States military advisors are well aware of both the existence and the dangers of this trend, which in the past, has prevented the successful conclusion of a number of anti-insurgency operations.

CONSEQUENCES OF UNITED STATES SOUTH VIETNAMESE COUNTER-MEASURES

Internal

24.   The Government's counter-measures, for example the enforced removal of some of the population to strategic hamlets and villages, have involved a degree of regimentation and austerity which has aroused some discontent among the general population. To this the Government have added both a programme of occasionally somewhat grotesque puritanism in cities and considerable ruthlessness in the use of napalm and air strafing of peasants who might (or might not) be Viet Cong, which could equally provide grounds for widespread resentment. The communists have also endeavoured to arouse resentment to the defoliation programme but they have probably had more success abroad than in South Vietnam itself. There is however little or no evidence to suggest that the general population is becoming restive or that there is any threat to the regime from popular revolt. Among the politically conscious minority there is certainly fairly widespread criticism of the Ngo family and, to a lesser extent, of the President himself. This feeling also extends to the Armed Forces where Presidential suspicion of many of the ablest officers has tended to affect morale. In May and early June

-8-

SECRET - GUARD

Document Eighteen continued

SECRET - GUARD

of this year, inept handling of Buddhist demonstrations
provoked by discontent over discrimination in favour of
Vietnamese Catholics led to a crisis between the Government
and the Vietnamese Buddhist community. An agreement on
outstanding issues was reached in mid-June, but only after
the Government, or rather the Ngo family, had gone
dangerously far towards alienating unnecessarily a large and
normally loyal part of the population. There is now likely
to be further trouble.

External

25. It is abroad that the image of the Saigon regime has
principally suffered, not least as a result of its consistent
mishandling of the American press. The Mansfield Report
expressed well-considered misgivings about the success of
American aid to South Vietnam over the last seven years, and
emphasized that, although so much effort and money had been
spent, the Diem regime has failed to harness the best
energies of the nation. Even if the report has not discouraged
the United States Administration, it will have had an effect
on Congress. The D.R.V. have made full propaganda use of
accusations of authoritarianism made against the President
and his entourage and it is disturbing for the regime that
representatives of the Front for the Liberation of South
Vietnam were recieved at the Afro-Asian Solidarity Conference
meeting at Moshi early this year, and that in April a South
Vietnamese delegation to the Afro-Asian journalists conference
in Djakarta was rejected in favour of one from the Front.
Indonesia is the only non-communist country which has received
the travelling delegation of the Front and even there it was
explained that they were not received on a governmental basis,
but there are now permanent representatives of the Front in
Algiers and Havana.

THE OUTLOOK

26. The military situation is unlikely to show much
improvement during the next twelve months although the
suffessful conclusion of the hamlet programme would have a
long term effect. The struggle is therefore likely to
continue on much the same lines as in the past few months.
The United States is now deeply committed in South Vietnam.
President Kennedy has indicated that the United States is
unlikely to feel able to get itself further committed. The
most influential thinker in the South Vietnamese Government,
Nhu, seems to be playing for less open American involvement,
and perhaps a considerable reduction in the number of
Americans in the country, but with continued material and
financial support. A token reduction in United States
servicemen, at least, would be welcome to the South Vietnamese
and to the United States Government. Nevertheless we find
it hard to believe that in the last resort, if faced with a
choice between abandoning the country to the Viet Cong and
a major intensification of its effort in South Vietnam, the
United States would decide to abandon the struggle. We have
examined in J.I.C.(62) 12 of the 5th April, 1962, the likely
implications of direct United States military intervention
in South Vietnam. We consider the conclusions of this report
remain valid.

27. The economic outlook for the next twelve months offers
little hope of improvement. The Government faces the dilemma
of finding enough money to continue the war without imposing
unacceptable levels of taxation and austerity while at the
same time providing that stimulus to commerce and investment
necessary if the economy is to keep pace with the growing
population and to be lifted eventually above its present
predominantly agricultural level.

-9-

SECRET - GUARD

Document Eighteen continued

SECRET - GUARD

28. Of South Vietnamese military weaknesses, the most important are indifferent leadership at many levels and a heavy reliance on sophisticated support, which has tended to slow down infantry operations in difficult terrain. Together these two factors endanger the satisfactory conduct of a basically anti-guerilla war.   On the other hand, there is evidence that the Viet Cong's programme has been delayed and to some extent disrupted.   If Government intelligence and operational technique improved, the strong mobile forces at their disposal would be in a position to keep the Viet Cong largely on the defensive by a succession of heavy blows against their regular units;   it would also have the effect of increasing their difficulties of food gathering. The Viet Cong would still retain the ability to operate in small groups and be in a position to terrorise those areas where the population had little or no evidence of governmental control.   Thus such military operations cannot achieve complete success in themselves.

29. The Viet Cong are fighting a guerilla war with the active or passive support of a significant proportion of the population.   They are a most highly organised and disciplined political force.   Their determination and willingness to endure hardship is well-known and their military skill and courage in the face of enormous material superiority has emerged most clearly from recent engagements. To a large extent they still appear to rely on capturing weapons and other military equipment which indicates that these are not readily available from bloc sources.   We would not expect them to use, or indeed wish to use, more sophisticated equipment, such as aircraft or A.P.C.'s, in the type of operations they carry out, but the time may come when they will need greater supplies of arms, ammunition and equipment from external sources, both because of the developing and expanding organisation of the Viet Cong and because United States aid to Government forces is beginning to take effect.

30. The population at large requires to be supplied with, and won over to, a positive national ideology and their confidence in the Government's ability to secure, hold and administer those parts of the country in which the Viet Cong have operated must be restored.   The growth of resettled areas can help here.   In this context the current political indoctrination of the population of strategic villages and hamlets through para-military organisations like the Republican Youth and Mouvement Solidaire des Femmes is a step forward from the counter insurgency standpoint.   Over 59 per cent of the population are already grouped in some 5,000 hamlets, but these must be made more secure against subversion and by rapid rescue operations when they are attacked.   Extensions must also take place in areas where the Viet Cong are more active.   On 17th April, 1963 the Government announced an "Open Arms" surrender campaign.   Here again they may have been influenced by BRIAM advice.   With surrenders claimed at 100 a week by the Government before the campaign, this could seriously weaken the Viet Cong if properly and humanely applied, as the Government seem to be trying to do.

-10-

SECRET - GUARD

Document Eighteen continued

SECRET - GUARD

31. We conclude that:-

(a) the greatest weaknesses of the Government forces are indifferent leadership at many levels, too heavy reliance on sophisticated support and a lack of Intelligence techniques. In particular, qualities of leadership vary considerably and although some senior officers in command are competent enough, overall proficiency varies and in many cases has impeded the satisfactory execution of operations;

(b) there is, however, evidence that the Viet Cong's programme has been delayed, and to some extent disrupted by the United States and South Vietnamese counter-measures;

(c) the Diem Government's counter-measures have involved a degree of regimentation and austerity which have aroused some discontent among the general population, but there is little or no evidence to suggest that the general population is becoming restive or that there is any threat to the regime from popular revolt. The Government must, however, show its ability to secure, hold and administer those parts of the country in which the Viet Cong operate and thus will largely depend on the success of their strategic hamlets and political indoctrination programmes;

(d) the United States is deeply committed in South Vietnam and, although President Kennedy has indicated that the United States is unlikely to feel able to get itself further committed, it would be hard for them not to do so if faced with a choice between abandoning the country to the Viet Cong and a major intensification of their effort in South Vietnam;

(e) the military situation is unlikely to show much improvement during the next twelve months although the successful conclusion of the strategic hamlet programme would have a long-term effect. The struggle is therefore likely to continue on much the same lines as in the past few months.

-11-

SECRET - GUARD

Document Eighteen continued

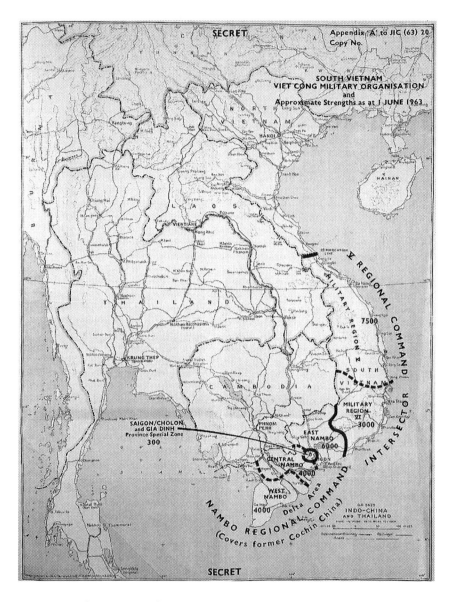

Document Eighteen continued

necessary basis for achieving a greater understanding of British perspectives in the region.[10]

Special National Intelligence Estimate (SNIE)[11] 53–2–63 came into the public domain as part of the so-called 'Pentagon Papers'. This is a short-hand term for *United States-Vietnam Relations, 1945–1967: A Study Prepared by the Department of Defense*, a 47-volume history of the US involvement in the Vietnam War. The study was commissioned in 1967 when Secretary of Defense Robert McNamara appointed the Pentagon's Director of Policy Planning and Arms Control for International Security Affairs, Leslie H. Gelb, to oversee a comprehensive review of US involvement with Vietnam since 1945. Gelb, working with a staff of 36 military officers, policy experts and historians, produced a body of work containing some 4,000 pages of documents (from the 1945–67 period) with 3,000 pages of analysis. The majority of these were leaked to the *New York Times* by Daniel Ellsberg, a former State Department official, and the newspaper used them as the basis for a series of articles beginning on 13 June 1971.[12] On 29 June 1971, Senator Mike Gravel (D-AK) entered 4,100 pages of the Papers into the Congressional Record and this portion of the Papers was subsequently published.[13] Despite this, the whole of the documentation has never been released and resides in the LBJ Presidential Library – closed to the public.[14]

Any analysis of the two reports must focus upon the differing national priorities of London and Washington in 1963. The direct nature of US involvement in Vietnam meant that South-East Asia was accorded a far higher priority than was the case with Britain. Yet, it is significant that the British government felt the situation in South-East Asia of sufficient importance to ask the JIC to produce this document at all, given that the JIC is primarily tasked with the production of definitive top-level all-source assessments for British ministers, the armed forces and senior civil servants.[15] But it is as well to recall that a former Chairman of the JIC comments that Britain focussed its Cold War intelligence efforts primarily on the USSR, with Vietnam very much a secondary consideration.[16]

In assessing British policy on US involvement in Vietnam we might usefully refer to Arnold Wolfers's concept of 'possession' and 'milieu' goals. Possession goals are direct and concrete; milieu goals are indirect and more abstract. Wolfers identifies the nature of 'possession' goals as meaning that they are praised by some for being in the national interest and condemned by others as 'indicating a reprehensible spirit of national selfishness or acquisitiveness'. 'Milieu' goals, by contrast, are characterised by nations seeking not to defend or increase possessions they hold to the exclusion of others, but instead to 'shape conditions beyond their national boundaries'.[17] In Wolfers's model, Soviet penetration of South-East Asia – by means of a Viet Cong victory – did not represent a mortal threat to British interests. For the United States, conversely, the loss of South-East Asia was increasingly viewed as a potential disaster. For the USA, the preservation of South Vietnamese independence was a 'possession goal'. For the British, it was a 'milieu goal'.

On 21 July 1954, the Geneva Accords – reached under the co-Chairmanship of Britain and the USSR – granted Indochina independence from France. Vietnam was divided and Ho Chi Minh's Viet Minh retreated north of the 17th Parallel to await elections for a unified Vietnam – scheduled for July 1956.[18] But Diem, with the tacit backing of the United States, managed to block these elections (which Ho Chi Minh would probably have won).[19] For their part, the British, despite their role as Geneva co-Chair, effectively turned a blind eye to Diem's obstructionism, evading periodic Soviet attempts to enforce the Geneva Accords more rigorously.[20] Naturally, the British were acutely aware of US sensitivity to their stance on Vietnam. The British thus behaved primarily as an ally of Washington rather than a co-Chair of the Geneva Conference. In return, the British expected American backing for their interests in Malaya and Rab Butler (Foreign Secretary, 1963–4), told the Cabinet that British support for the US position in Vietnam since 1954 had seen a straight swap 'for the support of the US government in seeking to maintain our position in South-East Asia'.[21] In 1955 the then Foreign Secretary, Harold Macmillan, had recorded his assurance to the Americans that 'although we were only indirectly interested in Vietnam . . . it was a very real interest a) because of the Geneva Treaty [and] b) because of the effect on Malaya etc'.[22] But this was as far as London wanted to go. As a co-Chair of the Geneva Conference, the British did not want to close the door on dialogue with the USSR in the Far East.[23] Furthermore, when the Malayan Emergency ended in 1960, British interest in South-East Asia diminished. Against this background, when the Americans became involved on the ground in Vietnam, not even right-wing Conservative MPs had any real desire for renewed direct military engagement in South-East Asia.

When Kennedy became president in 1961 he had no intention of committing US troops to a ground war in Vietnam. This feeling was reinforced by the strong opposition to direct intervention in South-East Asia in Congress, and even General Douglas MacArthur 'expressed his old view [to Kennedy in July 1961] that anyone wanting to commit American ground forces to the mainland [of Asia] should have his head examined'.[24] Yet much was to change in the two years of Kennedy's presidency, for, although ground troops were not deployed, the path to the large-scale intervention of the Johnson years was laid. For the historian, SNIE 53–2–63 is nothing less than a sign-post along that road.

Analyses of intelligence assessments revolve around a number of questions. First, was the intelligence accurate in its reading of the situation at certain junctures? Second, if the intelligence was correct and ignored, why was its advice discarded? Third, if the intelligence community was incorrect, but its advice heeded, what damage was done? Fourth, did the intelligence community itself fall prey to the phenomenon known as the 'politicisation of intelligence' and seek to tailor their targets and conclusions accordingly?[25] As Harold P. Ford notes in his study of the CIA and Vietnam:

> DCIs and senior intelligence professionals face [a dilemma] in cases when they know that unvarnished intelligence judgments will not be welcomed by the President, his policy managers, and his political advisers. At such times intelligence officers must decide just what balance to make between the ever-present contradictory forces of whether to tell it like it is (and so risk losing

their place at the President's advisory table), or to go with the flow of existing policy by accenting the positive (thus preserving their access and potential influence).[26]

We might usefully refer here to the precursor of SNIE 53–2–63, NIE 53–63, 'Prospects in South Vietnam' (17 April 1963) and the manner in which we see a blatant distortion of its conclusions as a prime example of the 'politicisation of intelligence'. The draft version of NIE 53–63, submitted by the Intelligence Community's representatives to the US Intelligence Board on 25 February 1963 stated that:

> The struggle in South Vietnam at best will be protracted and costly [because] very great weaknesses remain and will be difficult to surmount. Among these are lack of aggressive and firm leadership at all levels of command, poor morale among the troops, lack of trust between peasant and soldier, poor tactical use of available forces, a very inadequate intelligence system, and obvious Communist penetration of the South Vietnamese military organization.

Yet, the final version of the NIE 53–63 painted a wholly different, and far more optimistic, picture:

> We believe that Communist progress has been blunted and that the situation is improving . . . Improvements which have occurred during the past year now indicate that the Viet Cong can be contained militarily and that further progress can be made in expanding the area of government control and in creating greater security in the countryside.[27]

JIC 63(20) (Document Eighteen) is far more similar in tone to the original US draft: 'Of South Vietnamese military weaknesses, the most important are indifferent leadership at many levels and a heavy reliance on sophisticated support, which . . . slow down infantry operations'. Indeed, it was concluded that 'these two factors endanger the satisfactory conduct of a basically anti-guerrilla war.'[28] Thus, while JIC 63(20) lacks the source base enjoyed by the final version of NIE 53–63, the 'politicisation' of the American final version makes the British report rather more accurate in assessing the weaknesses of the South Vietnamese government (and, thus, the mounting troubles of the Americans). We therefore find ourselves in the curious position that the archival record of JIC 63(20) might seem more accurate – or at least more prescient – than NIE 53–63. This example demonstrates nothing so much as the necessity that, in this case, the scholar be aware of both the phenomenon of 'intelligence politicisation' and the political, institutional and bureaucratic background of intelligence production and policy-making in the United States in 1963.

JIC 63(20), by contrast, must be set against the background of British scepticism, at the very highest levels, of the rationale behind, and the future intentions of, US policy in Vietnam. Macmillan recalled that he had warned Kennedy at Key West in March 1961 'of the danger of being sucked into these inhospitable areas without a base, without any clear political or strategic aims and without any effective system of deploying armed forces or controlling local administration'.[29] Concern over US policy in Vietnam had deep roots in British policy circles. This went back to the Attlee government (1945–51) and its view of American support of the French attempts to re-assert control over Indochina after the Second World War.[30] In 1961, the British (and the French) had warned President Kennedy of the 'danger and foolishness' of any US-led ground war in Vietnam. Such views resonated strongly with the US president, who having seen what had happened to the French in Indochina, was determined to avoid any repetition.[31] But, while British warnings to the Americans were tempered by a desire to avoid offending Washington unnecessarily, Charles de Gaulle was less inhibited and had warned Kennedy that Vietnam would trap the United States in 'a bottomless military and political swamp'.[32]

When advising Kennedy, de Gaulle no doubt recalled the disastrous French war in Indochina (1946–54) and British perspectives on Vietnam were, naturally, similarly informed by their own recent history. British interest in Vietnam therefore arose chiefly from the experience of the Malayan Emergency (1948–60), where British forces had faced their own prolonged Communist insurgency. And, even after 1960, it was Malaya that had top priority in British policy formulation towards South-East Asia. The relationship between the British experience in Malaya and their perspectives on American involvement in South Vietnam came to be personified by Sir Robert Thompson, a major figure in the defeat of the Communist insurgency in Malaya, who came to serve both London and Washington in Vietnam.[33] Thompson's stock in Washington was raised by virtue of the fact that US Vice-President Lyndon Johnson returned from Saigon in 1961 convinced that British experiences in fighting Communism in Malaya could be of great utility in Vietnam.[34] Always keen to exert influence in Washington, the British government was naturally keen to encourage the notion that the Americans could learn from their experience in Malaya.

In September 1961, Macmillan appointed Thompson chief of the newly established BRIAM (British Advisory Mission) to South Vietnam to assist the United States in its fight against Communism. In his final report of February 1962, Thompson suggested that South Vietnam adopt a single body (provisionally termed the Security Intelligence Bureau or SIB) to co-ordinate efforts against all internal threats, as the British had done in Malaya.[35] Thompson urged the creation of something like the British JIC in order to generate accurate intelligence assessments in the political, economic and military fields so as to ensure that intelligence would serve stated policy goals. But, as Aldrich comments, Thompson was right and wrong in equal measure here because South Vietnam, unlike Malaya, lacked a viable civil infrastructure in which the people could have confidence.[36] JIC 63(20) concurs on this point and much is made of the weaknesses of the South Vietnamese government – especially at the top. JIC 63(20) also incorrectly asserts that Thompson and BRIAM were directly responsible for the genesis of the 'Strategic Hamlets' programme. In actual fact, the JIC could well have been misled by

Thompson himself as, following the rejection of his Delta Plan, Thompson had sought to ensure his continued influence by a rapid conversion in his thinking. In fact, after initial opposition, Thompson had only resigned himself to the idea of 'Strategic Hamlets' with some reluctance. Yet, with all the zeal of the convert, by early 1963 Thompson was telling President Kennedy that 'Strategic Hamlets' were making a significant contribution to what he foresaw as imminent victory.[37] The lesson here, again, was clear: if you want influence over policy and doctrine then you had better ensure that you are in step with official thinking.

Thus, Thompson found that his proposed remedies to the failings of the Diem had to take account of US policy imperatives. While the weaknesses of the Diem regime are also evident in JIC 63(20) and in Foreign Office traffic, there is a subtle difference in language between British and American assessments.[38] In contrast with British reports, SNIE 53–2–63 discusses the Diem regime in a manner that is rather sanguine with regard to the notion of American culpability for the situation in mid-1963. The question remains as to the extent that the British were aware of the American slide into a large-scale commitment in Vietnam. But clues as to the confidential deliberations of the British government on US involvement in Vietnam could be gleaned by the use of secondary sources long before official (non-JIC and JIC) British records become publicly available. In 1965, Brian Crozier, a writer and anti-Communist with extensive contacts within SIS, wrote a book, based in part on sources in MI6, condemning the United States for relying on regional 'strong men', commended only by their anti-Communism, to lead key allies.[39] Writing in 1973, Harold Macmillan noted that American policies in Vietnam 'produced the very situation against which' he had warned Kennedy of from 1961 onwards.[40] JIC 63(20) certainly differs in tone in its criticism of Diem from Macmillan's memoirs in that it is far more willing to highlight US deficiencies in their handling of the South Vietnamese president. British misgivings were publicly evident in 1963, and Diem, for all his shortcomings, certainly recognised the tensions between London and Washington, seeking to play the British off against the Americans whenever possible.[41] The United States also faced the problem that in calling Diem to heel, they only strengthened Communist charges that Diem was a 'tool' of American policy.[42] Indeed, such were the effectiveness of these charges, JIC 63(20) noted that, despite Saigon's military deficiencies, 'A token reduction in United States servicemen ... would be welcome to the South Vietnamese'.[43] SNIE 53–2–63 concurs with this but additionally speculates on Diem's desire to safeguard his position against being deposed by the Americans themselves:

> The [Government of South Vietnam] has always shown some concern over the implications of US involvement in South Vietnamese affairs and from time to time has felt moved to restrict US activities and presence in South Vietnam. This attitude springs partly from legitimate, if hypersensitive, concern for the appearance as well as the fact of Vietnam's recently acquired sovereignty. To a considerable degree, however, it springs from the Diem government's suspicion of US intentions toward it, and from its belief that the extensive US

presence is setting in motion political forces which could eventually threaten Diem's political primacy.[44]

This leads us to one of the more controversial events in the long history of US involvement in South-East Asia – the coup that deposed, and then killed, Diem on 1 and 2 November 1963.[45] What is certain is that American patience with Diem was wearing very thin by mid-1963. The US ambassador in Saigon, Henry Cabot Lodge, cabled Washington in unambiguous terms on 29 August:

> We are launched on a course from which there is no respectable turning back: the overthrow of the Diem government. There is no turning back in part because U.S. prestige is already publicly committed to this end in large measure and will become more so as the facts leak out. In a more fundamental sense, there is no turning back because there is no possibility, in my view, that the war can be won under a Diem administration[46]

The US belief that Diem had been *the* central obstacle to the stabilisation of South Vietnam had provided a useful excuse for failures thus far and his removal therefore stimulated a handy bout of American optimism. In a briefing for the new president, Lyndon Johnson, on 23 November 1963, the State Department reported that 'The outlook is [now] hopeful. There is better assurance than under Diem that the war can be won.'[47] To what extent had the US brought this situation about by deliberately engineering Diem's demise? While the CIA's director, John McCone, had twice vetoed plans to assassinate Diem, President Kennedy and Assistant Secretary of State for Far Eastern Affairs Roger Hilsman[48] had encouraged plots to remove him.[49] This causes one to question the manner in which SNIE 53–2–63 portrays domestic opposition to Diem as being independent of, and largely unaffected by, US policy. In particular, SNIE 53–2–63 particularly stresses the Buddhist opposition to Diem (which had precipitated an extended crisis in 1963):

> The Buddhist crisis in South Vietnam has highlighted and intensified a widespread and longstanding dissatisfaction with the Diem regime and its style of government. If – as is likely – Diem fails to carry out truly and promptly the commitments he has made to the Buddhists, disorders will probably flare again and the chances of a coup or assassination attempts against him will become better than even.[50]

JIC 63(20) concurs with this view, albeit in less melodramatic fashion:

> In May and early June of this year [1963], inept handling of Buddhist demonstrations provoked by discontent over discrimination in favour of Vietnamese Catholics led to a crisis . . . [and although an] agreement on outstanding issues was reached in mid-June . . . but only after the Government, or rather the Ngo family, had gone dangerously far towards alienating unnecessarily a large and normally loyal part of the population. There is now likely to be further trouble.[51]

Yet, JIC 63(20) also notes that despite Senator Mike Mansfield's report to Kennedy of December 1962 containing 'well-considered misgivings' about the ineffective nature of the massive US aid given to Diem since 1955, the administration was not at all 'discouraged'. Ominously, however, JIC 63(20) warned that Congress and the American press will soon begin to seriously question the wisdom of further funding of the Diem regime.[52] Thus, while JIC 63(20) acknowledges the Buddhist dimension in South Vietnam, the manner in which the US government itself is responsible for, and enmeshed in, the situation in South Vietnam is also made clear in the document. Accepting the British notion of American responsibility for events in Vietnam raises certain issues. For instance, the fact that Diem was assassinated in November 1963 poses questions as to US foreknowledge and culpability. Did the US government seek to nullify Congressional criticism by seeking to topple Diem? Certainly, regardless of whether or not Diem had continued in office, the British were certain that the United States was being drawn deeper into Vietnam. JIC 63(20) is very straightforward on this:

> [T]he United States is deeply committed in South Vietnam and, although President Kennedy has indicated that the United States is unlikely to feel able to get itself further committed, it would be hard for them not to do so if faced with a choice between abandoning the country to the Viet Cong and a major intensification of their effort in South Vietnam.[53]

Once Diem was gone, British suspicions that the underlying problems in South Vietnam would not be solved by the installation of the new military government were quickly confirmed.[54] On the last day of 1963, a Foreign Office official concluded that the war in Vietnam was now an 'all-American show' and that Britain could only watch from the sidelines.[55] And so it was to prove.

Significantly, JIC 63(20) and SNIE 53–2–63 emerged at a point between British failure at Suez in 1956, and the increasing isolation of the United States from its allies in the second half of the 1960s. Paradoxically, while the United States compelled the British to cease their Suez adventure in 1956, Washington was increasingly desperate to secure British backing over Vietnam some ten years later.[56] Even 'one regiment [of the] Black Watch' in Secretary of State Dean Rusk's famous phrase, would have been invaluable.[57] Denis Healey, British Defence Secretary between 1964 and 1970, later recalled that: 'The United States, after trying for thirty years to get Britain out of Asia . . . was now trying desperately to keep us in.'[58] As it was, once the war in Vietnam escalated after 1964, the Labour government of Harold Wilson opted instead to attempt to mediate between the warring parties.[59] (Although Wilson did authorise MI6 co-operation with the CIA over Vietnam, as Johnson had demanded).[60] Predictably, Wilson's decision to effectively revert (publicly) to the role of Geneva co-Chair only enraged the United States and Johnson later remarked bitterly:

> I have no doubt . . . that the British government's general approach to the war and to finding a peaceful solution would have been considerably different if

a brigade of Her Majesty's forces been stationed just south of the demilitarized zone in Vietnam.[61]

The mounting criticism of American policy in Vietnam only increased the defensiveness of the successive Johnson and Nixon administrations. In 1971, the doubts of the American public grew massively as a result of Ellsberg's revelations as to the ineptitude and – more importantly – the deliberate deceit of both the American public and Congress by policy-makers. Furthermore, the fact that whatever the details of the November 1963 coup against Diem, the US had certainly been pessimistic about his prospects and had conspired against him. Because of the subsequent course of events in Vietnam, the debates about the removal of Diem has inevitably become increasingly enmeshed with the fallacious (or at least unfounded) notion that Kennedy would have withdrawn from Vietnam – most likely after the 1964 presidential election.[62] In support of the idea that Kennedy would never have gotten so deep into Vietnam, his televised interview of 2 September 1963 is often invoked:

> In the final analysis, it is their war. They are the ones who have to win it or lose it. We can help them, we can give them equipment, we can send our men out there as advisers, but they have to win it – the people of Vietnam.[63]

Yet, does this prove that Kennedy would not have sent in ground forces if he had come to believe that they were required to help the 'people of Vietnam' attain victory? Does this prove that Johnson was unaware of the need for popular support in South Vietnam to ensure the long-term defeat of Communism? Nixon certainly recognised the logic in Kennedy's statement when he enunciated the 'Nixon Doctrine' – and its South-East Asian variant, 'Vietnamization' – in 1969.[64] Yet, by the end of the 1960s, the United States was deeply mired in Vietnam and deeply divided at home. With domestic opposition to the war mounting, the disclosures made in the Pentagon Papers were to strike a near-mortal blow to the credibility of American policy in South-East Asia.

The leaking of the Pentagon Papers in 1971 had an impact on American society that was quite startling. The disclosure of such a large amount of classified information massively increased the (already gaping) credibility gap in the Nixon administration's Vietnam policy. Further, the fact that SNIE 53–2–63 was leaked in 1971, two years *before* direct US involvement in Vietnam ended, made it a part of US involvement in Vietnam *per se*. Consequently, in addition to SNIE 53–2–63's original role as a confidential intelligence document, its afterlife as a leaked document gives it a significance way beyond either its content or its British JIC counterpart. In 1971, the 'damage' to the US cause in Vietnam caused by the leak of such information was further exaggerated by enraged policy-makers (perhaps understandably so given the exploitation of such revelations by political opponents).[65] White House Chief of Staff H.R. Haldeman told President Richard M. Nixon that:

But out of [all of this] . . . comes a very clear thing: . . . you can't trust the government; you can't believe what they say; and you can't rely on their judgment; and the – the implicit infallibility of presidents, which has been an accepted thing in America, is badly hurt by this, because it shows that people do things the President wants to do even though it's wrong, and the President can be wrong.[66]

On 30 June 1971, the US Supreme Court voted 6–3 to allow the *New York Times* and the *Washington Post* to continue publication of the 'Pentagon Papers'.[67] This ruling caused Nixon to comment that that Ellsberg's behaviour could set a precedent to 'every disgruntled bureaucrat' who disagreed with the conduct of his or her government.[68] Henry Kissinger, Nixon's National Security Advisor, later identified a recurring theme in the endless balancing act between the 'national interest' and the right of access in democratic societies. Kissinger professed to believe that while the Pentagon Papers appeared to be most damaging to the Kennedy and Johnson administrations,

Our foreign policy could never achieve the continuity on which other nations must depend, and our system of government would surely lose all trust if each president used his control of the process of declassification to smear his predecessors or if his discretion in defending the classification system became a partisan matter.[69]

But, in reality, the 'Pentagon Papers' had performed two great services. First, they had demonstrated that American policy in Indochina had been fallacious almost from the outset and, second, they illustrated that the American people and the Congress had been consistently misled as to the true picture in South-East Asia.

SNIE 53–2–63 appeared in the wake of President John F. Kennedy's assurance, in his State of the Union address of January 1963, that 'the spearpoint of [Communist] aggression has been blunted in South Vietnam'.[70] Such unfounded public declarations of imminent victory are inimical to the conduct of military and intelligence activities, inviting humiliation should success not be achieved.[71] In the short term, such rhetoric encourages intelligence agencies to simply identify the best method of achieving a pre-ordained goal when, in fact, the goals themselves should only be set after comprehensive assessments have been made. Long after Kennedy had departed the scene, General William Westmoreland, US commander in Vietnam between 1964 and 1968, claimed that victory was in sight in Vietnam in a speech he gave to the National Press Club on 21 November 1967. This came back to haunt him with a vengeance when the Communists launched the Tet Offensive in January 1968.[72] While Tet was eventually a military victory for the United States, it also represented the decisive political defeat of the war by virtue of its effect on the faith of the American people in the possibility of victory. The rhetoric of Westmoreland and others, which had sought to bridge the gap between American military means and the unattainable political ends in Vietnam, had been a contributory factor in this. The inability of military power to overcome the shortcomings of US policy in South-East Asia had been evident to more perceptive observers for some years. In 1965, Hans J. Morgenthau railed against the underlying weakness in US Vietnam policy:

> [T]he indiscriminate crusade against Communism [has led to the adoption of] counterinsurgency as a technically self-sufficient new branch of warfare [and] the conception of foreign and military policy as a branch of public relations . . . [These] misconceptions . . . conjure up terrible dangers for those who base their policies on them. . . . Beyond the present crisis . . . one must hope that the confrontation between these misconceptions and reality will teach us a long overdue lesson – to rid ourselves of these misconceptions altogether.[73]

US intelligence naturally sought to facilitate the goals of policy-makers in the conduct of policy in South-East Asia. Unfortunately, in order to be taken seriously, the US intelligence community was forced to accept a series of erroneous notions that policy-makers insisted upon as an essential starting point. Of the years 1962–63, Harold P. Ford has rightly noted that the 'Distortions of reality, some wishful, some more deliberate, persisted until the expulsion of the American presence in Vietnam 12 years later – and definitely contributed to that outcome.'[74] Yet, with policy based on such false premises, the CIA could only ever mitigate the disaster and, for the United States, the 'lesson' of Vietnam would be learned the hard way.

Notes

Overview: The US and Vietnam in 1963

Andrew Priest

1   Peter Busch, *All the Way with JFK? Britain, the US, and the Vietnam War* (Oxford: Oxford University Press, 2003), p. 9.
2   Ibid., pp. 126–9.
3   Foreign Relations of the United States (FRUS), 1961–63, Vol. 2, Vietnam 1962 (Washington, DC: United States Government Printing Office, 1990), Hilsman to Harriman, 19 December 1962, pp. 789–92.
4   Foreign Relations of the United States (hereafter FRUS), 1961–63, Vol. 3, Vietnam January-August 1963 (Washington, DC: United States Government Printing Office, 1991), Memorandum for the Record by Hilsman, 2 January 1963, pp. 12–13.
5   For an overview, see David Kaiser, *American Tragedy: Kennedy, Johnson and the Origins of the Vietnam War* (Cambridge and London: Belknap, 2000), pp. 213–47.
6   FRUS, 1961–63, Vol. 3, Central Intelligence Agency Report, 8 July 1963, pp. 473–8.
7   FRUS, 1961–63, Vol. 4, Vietnam August–December 1963 (Washington, DC: United States Government Printing Office, 1991), Bundy to Lodge, 5 October 1963, p. 379.
8   FRUS, 1961–63, Vol. 4, NSAM 263, 11 October 1963, pp. 395–6.
9   John Newman, *JFK and Vietnam: Deception, Intrigue, and the Struggle for Power* (New York: Warner Books, 1992); *JFK* (directed by Oliver Stone, 1991).
10 Although McNamara acknowledges that Kennedy would have had to deal with the consequences of Diem's assassination. Robert S. McNamara, *In Retrospect: The Tragedy and Lessons of Vietnam* (New York: Times Books, 1995), pp. 95–6; William

E. Colby, *Lost Victory: A Firsthand Account of America's Sixteen-Year Involvement in Vietnam* (Chicago: Contemporary Books, 1989).

11   Howard Jones, *Death of a Generation: How the Assassinations of Diem and JFK Prolonged the Vietnam War* (Oxford: Oxford University Press, 2002). See also William J. Rust, *Kennedy in Vietnam* (New York: Scribner, 1985), pp. 179–82.

12   Frederik Logevall, for example, suggests that Kennedy would have most likely continued with his 'middle course'. Frederik Logevall, *Choosing War: The Lost Chance for Peace and the Escalation of War in Vietnam* (Berkeley, CA: University of California Press, 2001), pp. 34–8. See also Noam Chomsky, *Rethinking Camelot: JFK, the Vietnam War, and US Political Culture* (London: Verso, 1993); Frederik Logevall, 'Vietnam and the Question of What Might Have Been', in Mark J. White, *Kennedy: The New Frontier Revisted* (New York: New York University Press, 1998), pp. 19–62.

13   Logevall, *Choosing War*, pp. 70–1.

14   While Johnson told Congress on 27 November 1963, 'We will keep our commitments from South Vietnam to West Berlin', privately he was more circumspect. On 24 November 1963, of a meeting with a number of high-level advisors including DCI John McCone in Washington, Johnson recalls that he told them, 'I thought we had been mistaken in our failure to support Diem.' Lyndon B. Johnson, *The Vantage Point: Perspectives on the Presidency 1963–1969* (New York: Popular Library, 1971), pp. 43, 44.

Commentary: *'In the final analysis, it is their war': Britain, the United States and South Vietnam in 1963*

R. Gerald Hughes

1   Shockley, memorandum given to the House Select Committee on Intelligence, 1975, attachment to George Carver, Memorandum for the Director, 'Lt. Col. Shockley's Critique of Intelligence on the ARVN', 29 November 1975. Quoted in Harold P. Ford, *CIA and Vietnam Policymakers: Three Episodes, 1962–1968* (Langley, VA: CIA Center for the Study of Intelligence, 1998), p. 8.

2   Arthur M. Schlesinger, Jr., *Robert Kennedy and His Times* (New York: Mariner Books, 2002 edn. [1978]), p. 712.

3   For an interesting perspective on the situation reversed, see Richard J. Aldrich, 'American Intelligence and the British Raj: The OSS, the SSU and India, 1942–1947', in Martin S. Alexander (ed.), *Knowing Your Friends: Intelligence inside Alliances and Coalitions from 1914 to the Cold War* (London: Frank Cass, 1998), pp. 132–64.

4   On the wider aspects of British policy, see Matthew Jones, *Conflict and Confrontation in South-East Asia, 1961–1965: Britain, the United States and the Creation of Malaysia* (Cambridge: Cambridge University Press, 2002).

5   On the phenomenon of spying on allies, see Martin S. Alexander, 'Introduction: Knowing your friends, assessing your allies – perspectives on intra-alliance intelligence' in 'Knowing Your Friends Intelligence inside Alliances and Coalitions from 1914 to the Cold War', Special Issue of *Intelligence & National Security*, 13/1 (1998), pp. 1–17.

6   Our knowledge of the 'special' Anglo-American intelligence relationship throughout the Cold War naturally leads us to speculate as to the degree of information exchange when examining these documents. On intelligence and the 'Special Relationship', see Richard J. Aldrich, 'British Intelligence and the Anglo-American "Special Relationship"', *Review of International Studies*, 24/1 (March 1998): 331–51.

7   Stephen Dorril, *MI6: Fifty Years of Special Operations* (London: Fourth Estate, 2004), pp. 719–20; Payne Harrison, *Black Cipher* (Carmarthen: Crown, 1994), p. 33; Jonathan

Bloch and Patrick Fitzgerald, *British Intelligence and Covert Action: Africa, Middle East, and Europe Since 1945* (Dingle, Republic of Ireland: Brandon, 1983), p. 64.

8   Richard J. Aldrich, *The Hidden Hand: Britain, America and Cold War Secret Intelligence* (London: John Murray, 2001), p. 644.

9   (Public Records Office, National Archives, Kew) PRO: 371/ 160107 [1011], Hohler to Home, 21 January 1961. Other instances including, 'Armed Forces in South Vietnam: Military Operations against Viet Cong Forces' are dealt with in British diplomatic correspondence for 1963 in eight separate files (FO 371/ 170131–FO 371/ 170137). Class FO 1095, 'Foreign Office: Embassy, Vietnam: Various Records [1960–1966]', contains files such as the 1960 file 'Vietnamese Army' (FO 1095/ 1). In the Prime Ministerial class see, for instance, PREM 11/ 4759, 'Situation in Vietnam: Part 2' (1963) and PREM 11/ 4760, 'Situation in Vietnam: Part 3' (1964).

10 See, for instance, the 1963 documents on the 'Threat of Communist Subversion in SEATO Area' (FO 371/ 170055 and FO 371/ 170056).

11 The NIE/SNIE was a crucial component in intelligence dissemination. Following the outbreak of the Korean War in 1950, the Director of Central Intelligence (DCI), Lt. Gen. Walter Bedell Smith, used the recommendations of the Dulles Report of January 1949 to form the Board of National Estimates to coordinate and produce National Intelligence Estimates. Michael Warner and J. Kenneth McDonald, *US Intelligence Community Reform Since 1947* (Washington, DC: Central Intelligence Agency: Center for the Study of Intelligence, 2005), p. iii. Traditionally, the DCI has had a dual role within the US government as both head of the CIA and with responsibility for coordinating the entire intelligence effort among the plethora of American agencies. Smith (DCI, 1950–53) was particularly notable for promoting this 'two hats' approach of the DCI's role within the US intelligence community. Douglas F. Garthoff, *Directors of Central Intelligence as Leaders of the US Intelligence Community* (Washington, DC: Central Intelligence Agency: Center for the Study of Intelligence, 2005), pp. 22, 27–8.

12 For Ellsberg's account of his career, his involvement with Vietnam, the leaking of the papers and his subsequent trial, see Daniel Ellsberg, *Secrets: A Memoir of Vietnam and the Pentagon Papers* (New York: Viking, 2002).

13 *The Pentagon Papers: The Defense Department History of United States Decision-making on Vietnam*, 5 volumes (Boston, MA: Beacon Press, 1971–72).

14 The LBJ Library has released portions of the remaining classified sections of the Pentagon Papers periodically. On 6 June 2002, for instance, 115 more pages were released into the public domain. On this, see http://www.lbjlib.utexas.edu/johnson/ Press.hom/tonkinpentagonpapers.shtm

15 Crucially, as Percy Cradock notes, 'I should perhaps stress that we are dealing here not with intelligence collection . . . but with . . . [the] second stage in the process, analysis and evaluation, their interface between intelligence and policy.' Percy Cradock, *Know Your Enemy: How the Joint Intelligence Committee Saw the World* (London: John Murray, 2002), p. 1.

16 Ibid., pp. 4, 294.

17 Arnold Wolfers, *Discord and Collaboration: Essays on International Politics* (Baltimore, MD: Johns Hopkins University Press, 1962), p. 74.

18 A.J. Stockwell, 'Southeast Asia in War and Peace: The End of European Colonial Empires 1941–1957', in Nicholas Tarling (ed.), *The Cambridge History of Southeast Asia*, vols Two, part Two, *From World War II to the Present* (Cambridge: Cambridge University Press, 1992), p. 45.

19 On 'The Non-election of 1956', see Kathryn C. Statler, *Replacing France: The Origins of American Intervention in Vietnam* (Lexington, KY: University Press of Kentucky, 2007), pp. 155–82.

20 In New York on 28 September 1955, Soviet Foreign Minister Molotov asked Macmillan why Diem had not implemented Geneva. Macmillan recorded that he 'said

we must have patience, but we were doing our best'. Harold Macmillan, diary entry for 28 September 1955. Peter Catterall (ed.), *The Macmillan Diaries: The Cabinet Years 1950–1957* (London: Pan, 2004), p. 484.

21   Quoted in Dorril, *MI6*, p. 716.

22   Harold Macmillan, diary entry for 7 May 1955. Catterall (ed.), *The Macmillan Diaries*, p. 423.

23   Antonio Varsori, 'Britain and US Involvement in the Vietnam War during the Kennedy Administration, 1961–63', *Cold War History*, 3/2 (January 2003), pp. 89, 93.

24   Arthur M. Schlesinger, Jr., *A Thousand Days* (Boston, MA: Houghton Mifflin, 1965), p. 339. See also, Theodore C. Sorenson, *Kennedy* (New York: Bantam, 1966), p. 723.

25   On the 'politicisation of intelligence' in Vietnam, see Thomas L. Cubbage, 'Westmoreland vs. CBS: Was Intelligence Corrupted by Policy Demands?' *Intelligence and National Security*, 3/3 (July 1988), pp. 118–80.

26   Ford, *CIA and Vietnam Policymakers*, p. 151.

27   Ibid, p. 1.

28   PRO: CAB 158/ 48, JIC 63(20), 'The Outlook', para. 28, p. 10.

29   Harold Macmillan, *At the End of the Day, 1961–1963* (London: Macmillan, 1973) pp. 238–9. By the time Macmillan left office in October 1963 he was distinctly pessimistic about Vietnam. Alastair Horne, *Macmillan 1957–1986*, volume II of the official biography (London: Macmillan, 1989), p. 418.

30   On this see, for instance, Mark Atwood Lawrence, *Assuming the Burden: Europe and the American Commitment to Vietnam* (Berkeley, CA: University of California Press, 2005), pp. 104–15, 210–15.

31   Orrin Schwab, *Defending the Free World: John F. Kennedy, Lyndon Johnson, and the Vietnam War, 1961–1965* (Westport, CT: Praeger, 1998), p. 24. On Kennedy and Indochina in 1961, see Geoffrey Warner, 'President Kennedy and Indochina: The 1961 Decisions', *International Affairs*, 70/4 (1994), pp. 685–700.

32   Stanley Karnow, *Vietnam: A History* (London: Pimlico, 1991), p. 265.

33   For Thompson's personal recollections, see Robert Thompson, *Defeating Communist Insurgency: Experiences from Malaya and Vietnam* (London: Chatto & Windus, 1966). In London, Thompson's role in Vietnam was lauded as it seemed the British, for a relatively low cost, were exerting a degree of influence over US policy: Varsori, 'Britain and US Involvement in the Vietnam War', p. 96.

34   Varsori, 'Britain and US Involvement in the Vietnam War', p. 86; *Foreign Relations of the United States* (FRUS), *1961–1963*, vol. 1, *Vietnam, 1961* (Washington, DC: United States Government Printing Office, 1988), pp. 149–51.

35   Aldrich, *The Hidden Hand*, pp. 593–4.

36   Ibid., p. 596. On British intelligence success in Malaya, see Brian Stewart, 'Winning in Malaya: An Intelligence Success Story', in *The Clandestine War in Asia: Western Intelligence, Propaganda and Special Operations* (London: Frank Cass, 2000), pp. 267–83.

37   On Thompson, BRIAM and 'Strategic Hamlets', see Peter Busch, 'Killing the "Vietcong": The British Advisory Mission and the Strategic Hamlet Programme', *Journal of Strategic Studies*, 25/1 (March 2002), pp. 135–62.

38   On Hohler's criticisms of Diem in 1963, see, for example, FO 371/ 170100, FO 371/ 170118, FO 371/ 170131.

39   Dorril, *MI6*, pp. 716–7. Quote, p. 717; Brian Crozier, *South-East Asia in Turmoil* (London: Penguin, 1965); Brian Rossiter Crozier (b. 4 August 1918, Australia) was an anti-Communist writer who founded the Institute for the Study of Conflict, a London-based group that studied insurgency. At various junctures, Crozier advised SIS, the Information Research Department (IRD) and the CIA on the Communist threat. He was also on good terms with Sir Robert Thompson. For his autobiography, see Brian Crozier, *Free Agent: The Unseen War 1941–1991: The Autobiography of an International Activist* (London: HarperCollins, 1993).

40   Macmillan, *At the End of the Day*, p. 246.
41   On this, see Busch, *All the Way with JFK? Britain, the US, and the Vietnam War* (Oxford: Oxford University Press, 2003), p. 100.
42   James E. King, Jr., 'Collective Defense: the Military Commitment' in Arnold Wolfers (ed.), *Alliance Policy in the Cold War* (Baltimore, MD: Johns Hopkins University Press, 1959), p. 133.
43   PRO: 158/ 48, JIC 63(20), 'The Outlook', paragraph 26, p. 9.
44   SNIE 53–2–63, 'III: The Effect of Recent Developments on US-GVN Relations', paragraph ten.
45   On US deliberations over whether or not to depose Diem in a coup, see Lawrence Freedman, *Kennedy's Wars: Berlin, Cuba, Laos and Vietnam* (Oxford: Oxford University Press, 2002), pp. 365–82, 384–9.
46   Ambassador Lodge to Secretary Rusk, 29 August 1963: *The Pentagon Papers*, vol. 2, p. 738. Macmillan noted that when he left office, in October 1963, the prospects for South Vietnam 'looked gloomy'. Macmillan, *At the End of the Day*, p. 245.
47   Christopher Andrew, *For the President's Eyes Only: Secret Intelligence and the American Presidency from Washington to Bush* (New York: HarperCollins, 1996), p. 314.
48   In 1962, Hilsman, the then Director of the State Department's Bureau of Intelligence and Research (INR), reported:

> Ineffectiveness in administration at the national level, in carrying out the control functions of the government, and in extending services to the country-large measure, is due to the limited authority [of] President Diem . . . [who] continues to represent the Vietnamese Government's main weakness . . . Diem continues to make virtually all major decisions and even many minor ones, to rely largely on his inner circle of official and unofficial advisors rather than on his cabinet officers and the formal channels of military and civil command in formulating and executing policy, and to interfere personally in purely and often minor operational matters. Discontent within the government bureaucracy and the military establishment with these tactics by Diem and his lieutenants does not appear to have decreased substantially during the past year. The prospects that Diem may change his method of operation are not favorable. (Roger Hilsman, Department of State, Bureau of Intelligence and Research, Research Memorandum, RFE-27, 18 June 1962, 'Progress Report on South Vietnam', *The Pentagon Papers*, vol. 2, pp. 680–1).

49   Rhodri Jeffreys-Jones, *The CIA and American Democracy*, 3rd edn (New Haven, CT: Yale University Press, 2003), p. 138.
50   SNIE 53–2–63, 'Conclusions: A', 10 July 1963. (See also, 'The Buddhist Affair', paras 2–9.)
51   PRO: CAB 158/ 48, JIC 63(20), 'Consequences of United States [and] South Vietnamese Counter-measures: Internal', para. 24, pp. 8–9. The Buddhist problem had also been drawn to the British government's attention through Foreign Office reports in 1963. See the 1963 files, 'Buddhism in South Vietnam: Conflict with the Diem Government', FO 371/170142, FO 371/170143, FO 371/170144, FO 371/170145, FO 371/170146.
52   PRO: CAB 158/ 48, JIC 63(20), 'Consequences of United States [and] South Vietnamese Counter-measures: External', para. 25, p. 9. On Mansfield and Vietnam, see Gregory Allen Olson, *Mansfield and Vietnam: A Study in Rhetorical Adaptation* (East Lansing, MI: Michigan State University Press, 1995).
53   PRO: CAB 158/ 48, JIC 63(20), para. (d) of the 'Summary of Report and Conclusions', p. 2.
54   Varsori, 'Britain and US Involvement in the Vietnam War', pp. 103–5.
55   PRO: FO 371/ 170097 [DV 1015/ 145], 'South Vietnam', FO minute by J.E. Cable, 31 December 1963: cited in ibid., p. 103. The language used by the British official

here immediately puts one in mind of Kennedy's statement of 2 September 1963 ('In the final analysis, it is their war').

56   Richard Nixon, Vice-President in 1956, later regretted this:

> In retrospect I believe that our actions were a serious mistake . . . Britain . . . [was] so humiliated and discouraged by the Suez Crisis that [it] lost the will to play a major role on the world scene. From this time forward the United States had to 'go it alone' in the foreign policy leadership of the free world.
>
> (Richard M. Nixon, *RN: The Memoirs of Richard Nixon* (New York: Grosset & Dunlap, 1978), p. 179)

57   Louis Heren, *No Hail, No Farewell: The Johnson Years* (London: Weidenfeld & Nicolson, 1970), p. 231. See also Geoffrey Wheatcroft, 'Downing Street Secrets', *Boston Globe*, 19 June 2005.

58   Karl Peiragostini, *Britain, Aden and South Arabia: Abandoning Empire* (London: Macmillan, 1991), p. 13.

59   Most notably in the Wilson-Kosygin talks of 1967. On this, see Harold Wilson, *The Labour Government 1964–70: A Personal Record* (London: Weidenfeld & Nicolson/Michael Joseph, 1971), pp. 345–51, 353, 355–66; Yoshihiko Mizumoto, 'Harold Wilson's Efforts at a Negotiated Settlement of the Vietnam War, 1965–67', *Electronic Journal of International History*, March 2005, http://www.history.ac.uk/ejournal/Mizumoto.pdf

60   Dorril, *MI6*, p. 717.

61   Lyndon Baines Johnson, *The Vantage Point: Perspectives on the Presidency 1963–1969* (London: Weidenfeld & Nicolson, 1972), p. 255.

62   As suggested by Robert S. McNamara's *In Retrospect: The Tragedy and Lessons of Vietnam* (New York: Vintage, 1995) and, more dubiously, in Oliver Stone's far-fetched film, *JFK* (1991). Such ideas are demolished in Diane Kunz, 'Camelot Continued', in Niall Ferguson (ed.), *Virtual History: Alternatives and Counterfactuals* (London/Basingstoke: Papermac, 1998), pp. 368–91. Against this, however, Harold Macmillan was also of the opinion that Kennedy would have never have allowed the US to get bogged down in Vietnam. Horne, *Macmillan 1957–1986*, p. 575.

63   Schlesinger, Jr., *Robert Kennedy and His Times*, p. 712.

64   'Vietnamization' was designed to gradually shift the burden of the war onto the South Vietnamese. For an interesting discussion of the concept and its possibilities in modern Iraq, see Melvin R. Laird, 'Iraq: Learning the Lessons of Vietnam', *Foreign Affairs*, November/December 2005, http://www.foreignaffairs.org/20051101faessay84604/melvin-r-laird/iraq-learning-the-lessons-of-vietnam.html. Laird was Nixon's Secretary of Defense between 1969 and 1973.

65   Nixon saw how opponents of his conduct of the war would be fortified, despite the fact that 'under Kennedy and Johnson [many of these critics] had led us into the Vietnam morass in the first place'. Richard M. Nixon, *The Memoirs of Richard Nixon*, vol. 1 (New York: Warner, 1979), p. 630.

66   Haldeman to Nixon, Monday, 14 June 1971 (3:09 p.m. meeting). 'The Pentagon Papers: Secrets, Lies and Audiotapes (The Nixon Tapes and the Supreme Court Tape)', National Security Archive Electronic Briefing Book, 48, http://www.gwu.edu/~nsarchiv/NSAEBB/NSAEBB48

67   Cornell Law School: Supreme Court Collection: http://supct.law.cornell.edu/supct/cases/403us713.htm. On this, see David Rudenstine. *The Day the Presses Stopped: A History of the Pentagon Papers Case* (Berkeley, CA: University of California Press, 1998).

68   Nixon, *Memoirs*, I, p. 630.

69   Henry A. Kissinger, *The White House Years* (London: Weidenfeld & Nicolson & Michael Joseph, 1979), pp. 729–30.

70   Quoted in Ford, *CIA and Vietnam Policymakers*, p. 4.

71 A notable example here being British Prime Minister Lloyd George's claim about the British campaign against the IRA ('we have murder by the throat') in his London Guildhall Speech of 9 November 1920. Quote: Kenneth O. Morgan, *Consensus and Disunity: The Lloyd George Coalition Government, 1918–1922* (Oxford: Oxford University Press, 1979), p. 130. Lloyd George's rhetoric was soon exposed when, on Sunday 21 November 1920, fourteen key British intelligence agents were assassinated by the IRA in Dublin.

72 On Westmoreland's speech, see James J. Wirtz, *The Tet Offensive: Intelligence Failure in War* (Ithaca, NY: Cornell University Press, 1991), p. 168.

73 Hans Morgenthau, 'We Are Deluding Ourselves in Vietnam', *New York Times Magazine*, 18 April 1965.

74 Ford, *CIA and Vietnam Policymakers*, p. 23.

9   British intelligence on the Arab–Israeli military balance, 1965

James R. Vaughan and Yigal Sheffy

OVERVIEW: BETWEEN SUEZ AND THE SIX DAY WAR: WESTERN INTELLIGENCE ASSESSMENTS AND THE ARAB–ISRAEL CONFLICT, 1957–67

James R. Vaughan

No one really expected a major war between Israel and its Arab neighbours to break out in 1967. In many respects, this is somewhat surprising, given the fact that Arab–Israeli relations in the decade between the 1956 Suez-Sinai War and the outbreak of the 'Six Day' War in June 1967 were predictably marked by persistent tension and escalating violence on Israel's frontiers. Under pressure from the United States, Israel was forced to withdraw from the territory it had conquered during the 1956 war, but nevertheless succeeded in extracting two important security guarantees, namely, the stationing of a United Nations Emergency Force (UNEF) in Sinai, and a guarantee of freedom of passage for Israeli shipping through the Straits of Tiran. It was President Nasser's unexpected bid, in May 1967, to reverse these gains by demanding the removal of the UNEF peacekeepers in Sinai and closing the Straits of Tiran, that provoked Israel into its pre-emptive strike against Egypt on the morning of 5 June.[1]

Nasser's gamble cannot be understood in isolation from the background of the growing regional tensions caused by a combination of Palestinian guerrilla raids into Israel from bases in Lebanon, Syria and Jordan, and Israel's often disproportionate retaliation against the areas believed to be harbouring and supporting the *fedayeen*. The March 1965 Joint Intelligence Committee (JIC) report under consideration here was produced within three months of the first raid into Israel undertaken by Arafat's al-Fatah organisation. Indeed, during the two years before the June War, there was an increase in border violence that, on more than one occasion (as at the West Bank village of Samu in November 1966, and over the skies of Damascus in April 1967), brought a very real possibility of escalation to full-scale conflict between Israel and one or more of its Arab neighbours. Among Western observers, however, the consensus opinion was that such escalation remained unlikely. In March 1966, Foreign Secretary, Michael Stewart, wrote to the British Ambassador to Israel, Michael Hadow, to inform him:

The danger of serious hostilities between Israel and the Arabs lies almost entirely in the accidental escalation of frontier incidents. (The other dangers are a second pre-emptive attack by Israel, or one by Egypt, perhaps caused by the belief that Israel is about to acquire nuclear weapons. Neither is likely.)[2]

Such analyses failed to consider the possibility that the Soviet Union might choose to provoke a Middle Eastern crisis and draw Nasser into the border conflict between Israel and Syria. This was precisely what the Soviet Union proceeded to do when, on 13 May 1967, it fed misleading intelligence reports about an imminent Israeli attack on Syria to the Egyptians. Historians now dismiss the Soviet move as a major blunder but, as Britain's Ambassador in Moscow later pointed out, the benefit of hindsight serves to obscure the logic of Soviet tactics at the time:

> The miscalculations are obvious now. They were not so obvious then. The moment could have seemed ideal; Arab unity was at an apparent optimum; there seemed well-founded grounds for believing that the rest of the world would not unite to prevent Nasser scoring a fait accompli off the Israelis & the staggering wealth of Soviet armaments in Arab hands could surely be expected to deter Israel from preventing this herself. . . . If the US & UK intervened on Israel's side, they would severely damage their position in the Middle East to the advantage of the Soviet Union. If they did nothing, the Arabs would be left with a significant gain & Soviet prestige would rise. The short-sightedness of this calculation . . . was demonstrated tragically on the 5th of June.[3]

If the Soviets were guilty of a major miscalculation, British intelligence assessments were better but still flawed in several important respects. Perhaps the biggest failure was a tendency towards complacency and wishful thinking in relation to the likelihood of war in the Middle East. British policy towards the Arab-Israel dispute was, in the decade after the Suez Crisis, governed by a desire to reduce regional commitments and thus to minimise the chances of being caught up in any Arab–Israeli conflagration. In May 1966, the head of the Foreign Office's Eastern Department, Willie Morris, stated that the British objective was 'to try gradually to withdraw from involvement in this dispute by avoiding intervention as far as possible'.[4] A key policy document, 'British Policy Towards the Arab/Israel Dispute', circulated in March 1966, outlined Britain's desire to avoid entanglement in Arab–Israeli affairs. 'Since the American role in preserving the peace is already so predominant,' it was argued, 'the general Western interest, and our own national interests, would be served by a further reduction of our involvement in the Arab/Israel dispute.' It was recognised that 'Such an evolution can only be gradual and incomplete, and we must be careful not to cause trouble with the Americans by trying to rush it',[5] but the general thrust of British policy was to put as much distance as possible between Britain and the quicksand of Arab–Israeli conflict.

In February 1966, Michael Stewart reported that his Israeli counterpart, Abba Eban, was 'happy to say that Israel was not now in a "crisis area" and that the situation of the Arab/Israel dispute was one of relative tranquillity.'[6] Michael Hadow notoriously reported to the Foreign Office on 4 June 1967 that 'the day of the firebrand in the Israel Defence Forces is over. . . . [Moshe Dayan] will be in favour of a longish pause and a "détente".'[7] Given Hadow's subsequent acknowledgement that 'Next day [the Israelis] embarked upon one of the most ruthlessly efficient military campaigns in modern history', it is hardly surprising that he would later characterise the weeks immediately preceding the outbreak of war as a period of 'Overtaken Intelligence Appreciations'.[8]

If British diplomats and intelligence analysts got it wrong in their assessment of the likelihood of a major war between Israel and the Arab states, they (together with their American counterparts) were much nearer the mark in their appreciation of what might happen if a war were indeed to break out. In the United States, the Central Intelligence Agency predicted on 26 May 1967:

> Israel could almost certainly attain air superiority over the Sinai Peninsula in 24 hours after taking the initiative . . . We estimate that armored striking forces could breach the UAR's double defense line in the Sinai within several days . . . Israel could contain any attacks by Syria or Jordan during this period.[9]

British analysts were rather more circumspect about the extent of Israeli military superiority, but remained in general agreement with the American interpretation. On 17 April 1967, the JIC reported:

> Despite some numerical and material inferiority Israel would have the best of any conflict with the UAR, owing to the greater fighting efficiency and higher morale of the Israel forces, who are maintained at a high state of readiness and backed by an efficient intelligence organisation . . . Any military support for the UAR from other Arab countries is unlikely appreciably to reduce the extent of Israel's military superiority . . . An improvement in the efficiency and morale of the UAR and other Arab forces sufficient to offset the present Israeli superior capabilities is inconceivable.[10]

While elements within the British foreign policy and defence elites, such as Rear-Admiral Josef Bartosik (Assistant Chief of the Naval Staff (Operations)) argued that 'The State Department's estimate of Israeli strength was that they were much more powerful than we, in this country, believed',[11] most British observers were content that Israel would have the better of any conflict with Egypt and its Arab allies. Patrick Dean, Britain's Ambassador in Washington and a former Chairman of the JIC, effectively summarised the consensus view in Britain when, after discussions with Dean Rusk and Robert MacNamara, he reported:

> The Israelis certainly believed that for up to about another ten days they could take the military initiative and win a decisive victory. The US appreciation agreed with this though apparently some experts thought that the Israelis could retain the military advantage for another three weeks depending on their

capability to destroy the Egyptian Air Force in the first day or two and follow up with an armoured thrust across Sinai. We on our side said we were rather less optimistic about Israeli prospects but did not fundamentally disagree with the US assessment. There was a general agreement that the conflict would be a bloody one.[12]

COMMENTARY: ASSESSING THE ASSESSORS:
JIC ASSESSMENT AND THE TEST OF TIME

Yigal Sheffy

The British Joint Intelligence Committee's (JIC) (Document Nineteen) report on the military balance between Israel and the Arab World up to the end of 1966 comes under what the intelligence terminology calls 'analysis of capabilities', to distinguish it from 'analysis of intentions' (or decisions). Such a report is the end product of a long process in which the intelligence service is required to examine potential scenarios, without necessarily assessing the probability of their actual occurrence.[1] In our case, the analysis compared the military capability of Israel, on the one hand, with several Arab states, on the other hand, while the JIC was anxious to point out that 'we do not attempt to assess the likelihood of war between them'.[2] Yet, implicitly, it left the impression that such a war was not imminent; as the report laid emphasis on the fact that a significant portion of the Egyptian army – the prime mover of any armed confrontation with Israel – was tied up by the war in Yemen, while some of the Iraqi forces were confined to mountainous Kurdistan.

The JIC was not alone in such an assessment. The Israeli intelligence and defence community also did not expect an Arab-initiated major war to be launched before 1970. Moreover, it predicted that even Israeli military action aimed at disrupting the Arab project of diverting the Jordan River tributaries originating in Lebanon and Syria (and perceived by the Israelis as a much greater national threat than Palestinian terror and sabotage activity at the time) would not provoke Egyptian president Gamal Abd al-Nasser to become prematurely entangled in war.[3]

Analysis of the 'capability' element in any intelligence assessment entails examination of both the various resources available to the protagonists (including human, material, organisational, spiritual, morale, etc.) and the means by which they might exploit these resources against each other. Comparison of 'capabilities' is in fact a judgement about which side might make better use of its resources, on the one hand, while more effectively neutralising its foe's resources on the other. In this sense, the JIC report presented a cautious assessment, perhaps over-cautious. Thus, the report stated: 'if the U.[nited]A.[rab] R.[epublic] withdrew significant numbers of troops from the Yemen, a reassessment would be required'.[4] However, from a 'capability' perspective, not only could the JIC hypothetically take the segment of the Egyptian army in Yemen into account as if it had already returned to Egypt, but, judging by its own criteria according to which efficiency and quality, not numerical strength, were given priority among the factors determining combat

The circulation of this paper has been strictly limited.
It is issued for the personal use of _e/L ._

TOP SECRET

Copy No. 93

J.I.C.(65)20(Final)

18th March, 1965

CABINET

JOINT INTELLIGENCE COMMITTEE

THE MILITARY BALANCE BETWEEN ISRAEL
AND THE ARAB WORLD UP TO THE END OF 1966

Report by the Joint Intelligence Committee

SUMMARY AND CONCLUSIONS

In the report at Annex we assess the military balance between Israel and the Arab World up to the end of 1966. We do not attempt to assess the likelihood of war between them.

2. We have allowed for the build up of Arab forces under the United Arab Command (U.A.C.) and have taken into account all known agreements to supply arms to both sides.

3. We have for the purposes of this report interpreted the "Arab World" as those states whose forces might be placed under the U.A.C. in the event of war with Israel, and whose deployment in the early stages of such a war are considered logistically feasible. These forces are those of the U.A.R., Lebanon, Syria, Jordan, Iraq and Saudi Arabia. Although Algeria, Libya, the Sudan and other states are represented in the U.A.C. staff in Cairo we do not consider that significant elements of their forces are likely to be employed in a war with Israel during the period under review. Effectively the forces to be considered are those of the U.A.R. and Jordan, and to a lesser extent Iraq and Syria.

4. The capability credited to the U.A.R. takes into account their present commitments in the Yemen. If the U.A.R. withdrew significant numbers of troops from the Yemen, a reassessment would be required.

5. We conclude that –

    (a) It is probable that Israel would at present have the best of any conflict with the Arab World, but this superiority is due solely to greater efficiency and higher morale, and to the inefficiency of the United Arab Command and Arab armies and air forces;

–1–

TOP SECRET

Document Nineteen: JIC (65)20 'The Military Balance between Israel and the Arab World up to the end of 1966', National Archives, Kew: CAB 158/ 57. Produced with permission of the National Archives.

TOP SECRET

(b)　the balance of power will depend on the extent to which the U.A.R. can at any given moment rely on effective military support from other members of the U.A.C. The advantage is unlikely to pass to the Arabs if the Israelis maintain roughly the ratios of equipment forecast for the end of the period. But this situation could change if the U.A.C. were to succeed in improving its will to fight and efficiency, particularly in the air; and if the Yemen, Kurdish and other military distractions were removed;

(c)　in total holdings of sea, land and air major equipments, the U.A.C. is much superior to Israel;

(d)　the present re-equipment programme for Israel's armour will substantially improve her present position during the period. Nevertheless at the end of 1966, the U.A.C. will have a three to one advantage in both modern and obsolescent tanks. In armoured cars and APCs, the imbalance will have reached nearly six to one against the Israelis, while in field artillery the figure will be nearly four to one. However, the U.A.C. would be unable to deploy against Israel much of the heavy equipment available to them;

(e)　if comparison is made with the U.A.R. alone, the equipment balance is markedly less unfavourable to Israel. By the end of 1966 the ratios U.A.R./Israel will be 6:5 in modern tanks; 1:2 in light tanks; 2:1 in armoured cars and APCs; about 2:1 in artillery, 3:2 in jet fighters; and 7:1 in jet bombers;

(f)　in terms of operational formations, Israel has the capability to mobilise her full force of twenty-six brigades (including four armoured) within forty-eight hours, against a maximum of twenty-four U.A.C. brigades (including five armoured) in the same period. However, the mobilisation plan might be disrupted by air attack;

(g)　at the end of a week the U.A.C. could deploy against the Israelis a total of thirty-one brigades (including eight armoured). However, this U.A.C. numerical superiority would be offset by the superior training and fighting efficiency of the Israelis;

(h)　the battle for air supremacy would be between the Israeli Air Force and the U.A.R. Air Force, with the air forces of Syria, Iraq and Jordan playing a comparatively minor role. The U.A.R. Air Force is numerically superior to that of the Israelis, in particular in bomber aircraft, but this advantage is offset by shortage of sound leadership and suspect operational capability;

--2--

TOP SECRET

Document Nineteen continued

(j) the Israeli Air Force, although highly efficient,
has to contend with the problem of operating
from a small number of airfields in a confined
area, exposed to attack by up to ninety
bomber aircraft from the U.A.R., Iraq and
Syria;

(k) it is most unlikely that any Arab navy other than
that of the U.A.R. could play a significant part
in a conflict with Israel. The U.A.R. Navy has
a considerable numerical superiority but is not
efficient. Although the training and morale
of the Israeli Navy are high, they do not fully
counter-balance its inferiority in numbers,
and the Israelis have no effective naval counter
to the U.A.R. missile-firing FPBs. However,
we do not consider that naval action would
necessarily play a significant part in military
operations. A sea blockade against Israel,
although it is unlikely to have much effect in
the short term, would become increasingly
important after the first fortnight of
hostilities.

(Signed) BERNARD BURROWS

Chairman, on behalf of the
Joint Intelligence Committee

Cabinet Office, S.W.1.

18th March, 1965.

-3-

Document Nineteen continued

TOP SECRET

Annex to J.I.C.(65)20(Final)

THE MILITARY BALANCE BETWEEN ISRAEL
AND THE ARAB WORLD UP TO THE END OF 1966

In this report we assess the military balance between
Israel and the Arab World up to the end of 1966. We do not
attempt to assess the likelihood of war between them.

2.   We have allowed for the build up of Arab forces under the
auspices of the United Arab Command (U.A.C) in our detailed
assessment of available equipment and operational capabilities
which are set out at the Appendices to this paper. We have also
taken into account recent military aid agreements with Russia,
signed in the latter half of 1964, by the U.A.R., Syria and Iraq
for delivery in 1965/66· and the Western military aid which
certain Arab States, notably Jordan and Iraq, are likely to
receive during the same period. Approved Western military aid to
date for Israel is also covered in this paper.

3.   We cannot exclude the possibility that during the period
under review Western Powers e.g. France and West Germany, might
supply additional military equipment to Israel: nor, for that
matter, that the Soviet Union might supply more equipment to the
U.A.R. than at present envisaged.

4.   The capability credited to the U.A.R. takes into account
their present commitments in the Yemen. If the U.A.R. withdrew
significant numbers of troops from the Yemen, a reassessment
would be required.

MILITARY UNITY OF THE ARAB WORLD

5.   We interpret the term "Arab World" in the military sense as
consisting of those Arab States whose forces might be placed under
the United Arab Command in the event of war with Israel and whose
deployment in the early stages of such a war are considered to be
logistically feasible. This definition has reduced our study
of Arab forces to those of the U.A.R., Lebanon, Syria, Jordan,
Iraq and Saudi Arabia. A map is attached.

6.   Many other states, notably Algeria, Libya and the Sudan, are
represented in the United Arab Command staff structure based in
Cairo, but in the period under review we consider that no significant elements of these forces are likely to be employed directly
against Israel. We have also discounted in the period under review
the military capability of the Palestine Army which is being
recruited among Palestinian refugees in Jordan.

7.   The United Arab Command is still in the early stages of
development and it is arguable whether it will ever be capable of
exercising co-ordinated combat command of Arab land and air forces
in battle. However, this does not preclude the possibility of
simultaneous military action by a combination of Arab countries.

GROUND FORCES

Military Capability

8.   The Israeli Army. Since Suez no major Israeli unit has
engaged in battle. Battle experience among junior ranks up to
company commander level is therefore limited to patrol actions
and border clashes. Commanders and staff, however, are
very experienced. This fact, combined with realistic
and thorough Israeli training methods which include large

-4-

TOP SECRET

Document Nineteen continued

scale formation exercises every year, ensures that the army
is capable of operating efficiently at every level. Morale
remains high. The increasing intake of non-European Jews in
the armed forces may result in a slight deterioration in
the combat efficiency of junior ranks. Israel maintains
nine strong brigade groups in peace (one armoured, one
mechanised, six infantry and one parachute) and in war would
have twenty-six brigade groups (four armoured, four
mechanised, sixteen infantry and two parachute). Reserve
brigades contain a strong regular cadre in peace.
Reservists carry out three to four weeks training annually
and these formations can be regarded as at least as
effective as any opposing Arab force.

9. U.A.C. Armies. The U.A.R. and Iraqi Armies have had
recent experience in dealing with guerillas in the Yemen
and against the Kurds, but no true battle experience against
a fully equipped enemy. The Jordan Arab Army retains some
measure of its former efficiency. On the whole however
Arab armies are not well trained above unit level, although
assistance from the Soviet Bloc in the provision of training
teams and courses in the U.S.S.R. is resulting in an
improvement. Commanders and staffs have very little
experience of the operational and logistical problems of
controlling formations of troops in battle because of the
continued failure to hold realistic exercises. The holding
of such exercises under U.A.C. auspices can be expected
in due course, but until they take place regularly the Arab
armies will have only a very limited offensive capability.
The concept of Israel as a common enemy coupled with the
arrival of much first class new military equipment has
contributed to an improvement in morale.

10. The United Arab Command can commit quickly, i.e. within
one week, only those forces which are stationed close to the
Israeli border and for which supporting logistic facilities
exist. The capability and strength of these forces is
assessed as follows –

Brigades

Country	Armoured	Mechanised	Infantry	Remarks
Lebanon	–	–	2	With some armour. Units are under-strength with a limited defensive capability only.
Syria	2	2	4	Well equipped with Soviet arms, poorly trained, capable of defensive operations and with a limited offensive capability.

–5–

Document Nineteen continued

TOP SECRET

Country	Armoured	Mechanised	Infantry	Remarks
Jordan	2 (weak)	–	6	Equipment is a mixture of modern and obsolete Western types, very comparable with that of Israel. Command capability, training and morale are all inferior to the Israeli but better than the Arab average. We have included three of the five new infantry brigades which are planned, in the expectation that they will have been formed by the end of 1966.
Iraq	1	–	–	Well equipped but morale, training and leadership are all, at best, fair.
Saudi Arabia	–	–	1	One lightly equipped brigade with U.S. equipment. Morale is probably high but otherwise operational capability is very limited.
U.A.R.	3	1	6	The best equipped of the Arab armies, it sho should be capable of sustained and effective defensive operations. Offensive capability is limited by lack of training.

Syria, Iraq, Jordan and the U.A.R. all have some parachute troops. The total parachute forces which might be committed, probably in a good role only, amount to the equivalent of one brigade, up to strength in men, but probably weak in equipment.

Mobilisation Capability

11. A table giving the comparative rate of build up of the U.A.C. and Israeli Armies during the first week is at Appendix A.

12. Israel. Israel's mobilisation plan is to increase her forces within forty-eight hours from the peace-time strength of 60,000 (nine active brigades) to a total of 250,000, including twenty-six brigades plus supporting arms and strong static defensive units. The mobilisation scheme is efficient and well practiced, but it is liable to disruption by U.A.R. bombing, or possibly missile attack, particularly in the narrow belt of land between the westernmost Jordan frontier and the sea.

-6-

TOP SECRET

Document Nineteen continued

TOP SECRET

furthermore, complete mobilisation. which was not even fully carried out at the time of Suez, would probably take up to four days, although all key fighting formations would be available after forty-eight hours.

13. <u>United Arab Command</u>. The U.A.C. does not rely on the mobilisation of reserve formations. It is prepared to fight with its peacetime forces although these, which are under strength in peace-time, require individual reinforcements for which man-power is available. In peace, the U.A.C. has a total of sixty-four active brigades (350,000), but only sixteen of these are stationed close to the Israeli border. After forty-eight hours (when the Israeli mobilisation should be complete) a further eight brigades could reach the battle area, followed by another six after a further five days. Within one week the U.A.C. could muster thirty-one brigades (including the mixed parachute force).

14. <u>Comparative rate of build up</u>. Although the Israelis are outnumbered by the U.A.C. in peace-time by sixteen brigades to nine, their mobilisation system enables them to make up this deficit and keep pace with a U.A.C. build up, although after one week the U.A.C. would again have a slight advantage (thirty-one brigades against twenty-six brigades). U.A.C. slowness in providing individual reinforcements to bring their units up to war-time strength will probably nullify this advantage. After the first week a slow U.A.C. build-up of seven infantry brigades is possible, with by the end of 1966 an additional capability of three armoured and one mechanised brigades. In a prolonged contest the balance of forces would move progressively in favour of the U.A.C.

<u>Equipment</u>

15. At Appendix B is a comparative table of U.A.C. and Israeli present and forecast holdings of major army equipment, allowing for all known military aid agreements. A programme for the re-equipment of Israel's armies will improve her position during the period under review. Nevertheless at the end of 1966 the U.A.C. will have a three to one advantage in both modern and obsolescent tanks. In armoured cars and APCs the imbalance will have reached nearly six to one against the Israelis, while in field artillery the figure will be nearly four to one. Ratios between Israel and the U.A.R. alone are of course significantly less unfavourable to Israel, e.g. five to six in modern tanks by the end of 1966. All these ratios are of total holdings, which will not be reflected on the battlefield because Arab countries must retain a proportion of their forces at home for security reasons and have difficulty in training sufficient men to handle the more complex weapons. Excellent maintenance standards in peace-time and field repair and recovery capability in war give the Israelis marked advantage over Arab armies, whose maintenance in peace is probably satisfactory but who have no recovery and repair organisation which could stand the test of operational conditions. As regards artillery, the U.A.R. and Syria have received numbers of more modern Soviet guns which considerably outrange their Western counterparts with which the Israelis are equipped.

-7-

TOP SECRET

Document Nineteen continued

TOP SECRET

AIR FORCES

16. Details of relative air strengths are at Appendix C.

Israel

17. Because of her geographical position and the
small size of her territory, Israel has to contend from
the start with a difficult air situation. The main threat
at present is from the U.A.R. light and medium bomber force,
particularly if used at low level or alternatively at night.
In a bid to counter this threat Israel has already acquired
from the U.S.A. 144 Hawk surface-to-air missiles. The
Matra 530, a French air-to-air missile, is fitted in
limited numbers to the Mirage 3C fighters. This weapon
system, directed by FPS6 and FPS20 radars, which should
arrive this year, will raise the effectiveness of the air
defence system. Even so the kill rate is unlikely to be
sufficiently high to protect major Israeli military and
civil installations from appreciable damage, which could
possibly impair their mobilisation arrangements. The air
defence of Israel will depend more on the ability of the
Israelis to destroy or immobilise the U.A.R. bombers
at their bases.

18. The efficiency, flexibility and morale of the Israeli
air force is high. It has recently demonstrated that it can
carry out ground attack operations in Arab territory and
should be well able to maintain local air superiority.
Although Israeli tactics do not call for a large bomber
force, their existing Vautour bombers are obsolescent and the
Israelis have shown interest in the Mirage 4 or Buccaneer
as replacements. Their transport force is experienced and
has a lift capability of 1,500 paratroops. Reconnaissance
and anti-shipping capability is satisfactory. The total aircraft holdings of the Israeli Defence Force Air Force
(I.D.F.A.F.) are shown at Appendix C. Of these holdings it
is estimated that the following would be available for
operations in the event of a clash –

	1965	1966
Jet Bombers	6	10
Jet Fighters	230	230
Transports	39	50
Helicopters	30	40

The U.A.C. Air Forces

19. There is no evidence at present that the U.A.C. has
engaged in the planning of any joint air strike operations
against Israel although there has been some co-operation
over air defence. The development of airfields in Syria and
Iraq might by the end of the period under review permit a
deployment which would constitute a greater threat to Israel.

20. U.A.R.

(a) Strength. The total U.A.R.A.F. aircraft holdings are
shown at Appendix C. Of these holdings it is
estimated that the following would be available for
operations in the event of a clash –

	1965	1966
Jet Bombers	60	60
Jet Fighters	165	182
Transports	67	60
Helicopters	36	48

–8–

TOP SECRET

Document Nineteen continued

TOP SECRET

(b) Capability. The U.A.R. Air Force is now almost wholly dependent on the Soviet bloc for equipment and military supplies, and continues to receive guidance from Russian technical staff. An improvement in capability has been achieved over the last three years and is likely to continue: the rotation of air and ground crews through the Yemen since 1963 has provided operational experience in the field to the tactical element of the U.A.R.A.F. The light and medium bomber force provide a night bombing threat of some weight. Ten SAM sites, of a total of twenty-one seen under construction since 1962, have now been completed and these, all in the Cairo, Alexandria and Suez areas, could probably be manned towards the end of this year in emergency. It is likely that all twenty-one sites will be completed in 1966 and that these could also be manned by that time. Training schemes in the U.A.R. and Russia are now maturing and the man-power is becoming available slowly to utilise more efficiently the sophisticated air defence equipment possessed and to build up a modern fighter force. But Egypt still possesses far more operational air-craft than she has pilots and crews to fly them. The U.A.R. is well aware of its inability to prevent determined low level strikes by the Israeli Air Force, and also of Israel's utter reliance upon maintaining air superiority at all times if she is to survive in attack or defence. Thus the future development of the U.A.R.A.F. is likely to be guided by these factors. However, their ability to press home and sustain attacks with vigour and tenacity remains suspect.

21. Syria. Air support could be given by up to seventy aircraft by the end of 1966, and would be limited to ground attack and air defence by day. The day intercept capability is at present low.

22. Jordan. The Royal Jordanian Air Force (R.J.A.F.) is a small but reasonably effective force. Morale is good, but there is lack of experience in the higher ranks. Some air support in the ground attack role could be given by about fifteen Hunter aircraft in addition to very limited air defence. The R.J.A.F. is anxious to acquire supersonic jet fighters but is unlikely to receive any during the period under review. Jordan's potential major contribution to U.A.C. plans lies in her geographical position which allows her radars, if integrated into the U.A.R. network, to provide an element of early warning of Israeli attacks, even at low level.

23. Iraq. Air support might come from fifty-two ground attack/fighter aircraft, although the need to retain some aircraft for operations against the Kurds could well reduce this number. Towards the end of the period under review some twenty-two light and medium bombers may be operational. Shortage of aircrew does not at present allow the Iraqis to operate their medium bombers. Aircraft utilisation is low, as are leadership and technical training. Political loyalty amongst all ranks is expected to preclude any major improve-ment in the next twelve months. Air defence of Iraq is generally poor, although the defence of Baghdad is of a slightly higher standard.

–9–

TOP SECRET

Document Nineteen continued

TOP SECRET

24. <u>Lebanon</u>. It is unlikely that the Lebanese air force would play any significant role in an Arab/Israeli conflict.

25. <u>Saudi Arabia</u>. It is unlikely that Saudi Arabian aircraft would take part in any conflict.

NAVAL FORCES

26. Both sides are likely to avoid a naval engagement unless the clash of land forces developes into a full scale war. There are no signs of naval plan ing between the Arab countries, nor does the U.A.R. Navy use Syrian, Lebanese or Jordanian ports. The U.A.R. Navy is the only one which has an offensive capability at present, and it is unlikely that the other Arab Navies will be capable of serious offensive operations during the period under review. Details of Israeli and U.A.C. naval strengths are given at Appendix D.

The Israeli Navy

27. The Israeli Navy, although relatively efficient and well trained, is the Cinderella of the forces, and is at present ill-equipped to meet the considerable potential threat posed by the U.A.R. Navy. Its two available submarines are likely to be used for offensive reconnaissance and anti-submarine patrols, while the small surface force (comprising three Destroyer types and six FPBs) will be retained to defend the approaches to the main Mediterranean ports. There is also a Naval Commando unit, about 150 strong, which is well trained in sabotage and clandestine operations, while the FPBs can be specially fitted for landing assault parties. The Israeli force available at Eilat would be unable to counter a blockade of the Gulf of Aqaba by the U.A.R.

28. The Naval Command is acutely aware of its deficiencies and is making every effort to acquire a force of large fast gunboats, armed with a powerful weapon (preferable a ship to ship missile); this it considers the only effective answer, in the absence of adequate air support, to the U.A.R. missile firing FPBs. The re-organisation is however unlikely to take place during the period covered by this paper.

U.A.R. Navy

29. The U.A.R. Navy continues to suffer from poor leadership and ship maintenance, although there has been some improvement in the last twelve months. Although it has considerable offensive capability it is probable that the U.A.R. Navy would not be used effectively against the Israelis. Its main role would probably be to stop shipping bound for the port of Eilat from entering the Gulf of Aqaba, and to attempt a blockade of Israeli Mediterranean ports with its surface ships and submarines. In this latter it would generally be careful to remain out of range of Israeli counter-measures, but might mount hit and run raids against coastal shipping, possibly using its eight missile firing patrol boats.

–10–

TOP SECRET

Document Nineteen continued

TOP SECRET

24. Lebanon. It is unlikely that the Lebanese air force would play any significant role in an Arab/Israeli conflict.

25. Saudi Arabia. It is unlikely that Saudi Arabian air-craft would take part in any conflict.

NAVAL FORCES

26. Both sides are likely to avoid a naval engagement unless the clash of land forces developes into a full scale war. There are no signs of naval plan ing between the Arab countries, nor does the U.A.R. Navy use Syrian, Lebanese or Jordanian ports. The U.A.R. Navy is the only one which has an offensive capability at present, and it is unlikely that the other Arab Navies will be capable of serious offensive operations during the period under review. Details of Israeli and U.A.C. naval strengths are given at Appendix D.

The Israeli Navy

27. The Israeli Navy, although relatively efficient and well trained, is the Cinderella of the forces, and is at present ill-equipped to meet the considerable potential threat posed by the U.A.R. Navy. Its two available submarines are likely to be used for offensive reconnaissance and anti-submarine patrols, while the small surface force (comprising three Destroyer types and six FPBs) will be retained to defend the approaches to the main Mediterranean ports. There is also a Naval Commando unit, about 150 strong, which is well trained in sabotage and clandestine operations, while the FPBs can be specially fitted for landing assault parties. The Israeli force available at Eilat would be unable to counter a blockade of the Gulf of Aqaba by the U.A.R.

28. The Naval Command is acutely aware of its deficiencies and is making every effort to acquire a force of large fast gunboats, armed with a powerful weapon (preferable a ship to ship missile); this it considers the only effective answer, in the absence of adequate air support, to the U.A.R. missile firing FPBs. The re-organisation is however unlikely to take place during the period covered by this paper.

U.A.R. Navy

29. The U.A.R. Navy continues to suffer from poor leadership and ship maintenance, although there has been some improvement in the last twelve months. Although it has considerable offensive capability it is probable that the U.A.R. Navy would not be used effectively against the Israelis. Its main role would probably be to stop shipping bound for the port of Eilat from entering the Gulf of Aqaba, and to attempt a blockade of Israeli Mediterranean ports with its surface ships and submarines. In this latter it would generally be careful to remain out of range of Israeli counter-measures, but might mount hit and run raids against coastal shipping, possibly using its eight missile firing patrol boats.

–10–

TOP SECRET

Document Nineteen continued

TOP SECRET

<u>SURFACE-TO-SURFACE GUIDED MISSILES AND WARHEADS</u>

<u>Nuclear weapons</u>

30.   It is highly unlikely that either Israel or any
of the Arab countries could develop a nuclear weapon
during the period under review;   though it is just
conceivable that Israel could carry out a test in late
1966, if the decision to develop nuclear weapons had been
taken some time ago. We do not know whether such a
decision has been taken.

<u>Missiles</u>

31. <u>Israel</u>. To counter the missile threat from the
U.A.R. (see paragraph 33 below) Israel has con-
tracted for short range (300 nm) surface-to-surface
missiles from France.   However, it is most
unlikely that any of them would be available within the
period under review.

32. <u>U.A.R.</u>

(a) The two types of rocket which were first demonstrated
in Egypt in 1962 have since probably been developed with
the help of West German technicians, but are not yet
operational.   The bigger of these could probably reach
any part of Israel from the Delta area. There is
evidence that guidance problems have still to be overcome, and it is probable therefore that the accuracy
of these rockets is poor. It is possible that a few
missiles of acceptable accuracy could be produced by the
end of the period, but it is doubtful if these would be
available for deployment.

(b) These missiles could be fitted with either HE or
CW warheads. The U.A.R. is believed to have a limited
potential to produce CW agents, but it is unlikely
this would include nerve gas. Unless available in
quantity, which we do not expect during the period under
review, these missiles would have very limited effect
except possibly on morale.

<u>CONCLUSIONS</u>

33. We conclude that –

(a) It is probable that Israel would at present
have the best of any conflict with the
Arab World, but this superiority is
due solely to greater efficiency and
higher morale, and to the inefficiency
of the United Arab Command and Arab armies
and air forces;

–11–

TOP SECRET

Document Nineteen continued

(b) the balance of power will depend on the extent to
     which the U.A.R. can at any given moment rely on
     effective military support from other members
     of the U.A.C. The advantage is unlikely to pass
     to the Arabs if the Israelis maintain roughly the
     ratios of equipment forecast for the end of the
     period. But this situation could change if the
     U.A.C. were to succeed in improving its will
     to fight and efficiency, particularly in the air;
     and if the Yemen, Kurdish and other military
     distractions were removed;

(c) in total holdings of sea, land and air major
     equipments, the U.A.C. is much superior to
     Israel;

(d) the present re-equipment programme for Israel's
     armour will substantially improve her present
     position during the period. Nevertheless at the
     end of 1966, the U.A.C. will have a three to one
     advantage in both modern and obsolescent tanks.
     In armoured cars and APCs, the imbalance will
     have reached nearly six to one against the
     Israelis, while in field artillery the figure
     will be nearly four to one. However, the U.A.C.
     would be unable to deploy against Israel much
     of the heavy equipment available to them;

(e) if comparison is made with the U.A.R. alone,
     the equipment balance is markedly less unfavour-
     able to Israel. By the end of 1966 the ratios
     U.A.R./Israel will be 6:5 in modern tanks;
     1:2 in light tanks;   2:1 in armoured cars and
     APCs;   about 2:1 in artillery, 3:2 in jet
     fighters;   and 7:1 in jet bombers;

(f) in terms of operational formations, Israel has the
     capability to mobilise her full force of twenty-
     six brigades (including four armoured) within
     forty-eight hours, against a maximum of twenty-
     four U.A.C. brigades (including five armoured)
     in the same period. However, the mobilisation
     plan might be disrupted by air attack;

(g) at the end of a week the U.A.C. could deploy
     against the Israelis a total of thirty-one
     brigades (including eight armoured). However,
     this U.A.C. numerical superiority would be offset
     by the superior training and fighting efficiency
     of the Israelis;

(h) the battle for air supremacy would be between
     the Israeli Air Force and the U.A.R. Air Force,
     with the air forces of Syria, Iraq and Jordan
     playing a comparatively minor role. The U.A.R.
     Air Force is numerically superior to that of
     the Israelis, in particular in bomber aircraft,
     but this advantage is offset by shortage of sound
     leadership and suspect operational capability;

-12-

Document Nineteen continued

(j)   the Israeli Air Force, although highly efficient,
      has to contend with the problem of operating
      from a small number of airfields in a confined
      area, exposed to attack by up to ninety
      bomber aircraft from the U.A.R., Iraq and
      Syria;

(k)   it is most unlikely that any Arab navy other than
      that of the U.A.R. could play a significant part
      in a conflict with Israel. The U.A.R. Navy has
      a considerable numerical superiority but is not
      efficient.   Although the training and morale
      of the Israeli Navy are high, they do not fully
      counter-balance its inferiority in numbers,
      and the Israelis have no effective naval counter
      to the U.A.R. missile-firing FPBs. However,
      we do not consider that naval action would
      necessarily play a significant part in military
      operations. A sea blockade against Israel,
      although it is unlikely to have much effect in
      the short term, would become increasingly
      important after the first fortnight of
      hostilities.

-13-

Document Nineteen continued

TOP SECRET

Appendix A to J.I.C.(65)20(Final)

COMPARATIVE BUILD UP OF U.A.C. AND ISRAELI LAND FORCES

MOBILISATION DAY (M DAY)

	BRIGADES				
	Armoured	Mechanised	Infantry	Parachute	Total
Lebanon	–	–	1	–	1
Syria	1	1	3	–	5
Jordan	1	–	3	–	4
Iraq	–	–	–	–	–
Saudi Arabia	–	–	–	–	–
U.A.R.	–	–	6	–	6
Total U.A.C.	2	1	13	–	16
Total Israel	1	1	6	1	9

M + 48 hours

Lebanon	–	–	1	–	1
Syria	1	2	3	–	6
Jordan	2	–	6	–	8
Iraq	–	–	–	–	–
Saudi Arabia	–	–	–	–	–
U.A.R.	2	1	6	–	9
Total U.A.C.	5	3	16	–	24
Total Israel	4	4	16	2	26

M + 1 week

Lebanon	–	–	2	–	2
Syria	2	2	4	–	8
Jordan	2	–	6	–	8
Iraq	1	–	–	–	1
Saudi Arabia	–	–	1	–	1
U.A.R.	3	1	6	–	10
Plus the equivalent of one parachute brigade					4
Total U.A.C.	8	3	19	–	31
Total Israel	4	4	16	2	26

Note. Both the U.A.R. and Iraq could in due course move
additional brigades towards Israel. Iraq might find
up to three more infantry brigades and the U.A.R. an
additional four. By the end of 1966, the U.A.R.
could also find a further three armoured and one
mechanised brigades.

-14-

TOP SECRET

Document Nineteen continued

TOP SECRET

Appendix B to J.I.C.(65) 20 (Final)

U.A.C. AND ISRAEL GROUND FORCES HOLDINGS

NOTE: Figures given are present holdings with forecasts for 1966 in brackets

Serial	Type	U.A.R.	SYRIA	LEBANON	IRAQ	JORDAN	SAUDI ARABIA	TOTAL U.A.C.	ISRAEL	REMARKS
(a)	(b)	(c)	(d)	(e)	(f)	(g)	(h)	(j)	(k)	(l)
1	Medium & heavy tanks									
	modern	350(600)	130(180)	—	446(446)	192(250)	67(137)	1,155(1,533)	240(530)	
	obsolescent	410(360)	300(300)	58(53)	76(76)	97(97)	58(58)	999(949)	310(310)	
2	Light tanks	75(100)	—	22(22)	36(36)	—	—	133(158)	150(200)	
3	Armoured cars and APCs	675(1,000)	445(500)	86(86)	590(670)	343(450)	104(154)	2,243(2,860)	400(500)	
4	Field, medium and heavy artillery including Rocket launchers and heavy mortars	864(1,056)	530(530)	72(72)	725(800)	146(200)	101(101)	2,438(2,759)	655(655)	Over 60 per cent of Israeli artillery is obsolete or obsolescent

–15–

TOP SECRET

Document Nineteen continued

Appendix C to J.I.C.(65) 20 (Final)

U.A.C. AND ISRAEL AIR FORCES

STRENGTHS 1965

	U.A.R.	SYRIA	LEBANON	IRAQ	JORDAN	SAUDI ARABIA	TOTAL U.A.C.	ISRAEL
Operational Aircraft on Squadrons								
Jet Fighters	184	60	8	50	28	19	349	198
Jet Bombers	64	4	–	22	–	–	90	9
Transports	67	11	–	17	6	10	111	39
Helicopters	40	10	8	31	4	1	94	30
Operational aircraft in use unassigned to squadrons	–	–	–	42	–	–	42	60
Operational aircraft in stored reserve	208	34	–	–	–	–	242	9
Total inventory	563	119	16	162	38	30	928	345

FORECAST STRENGTHS – 1966

	U.A.R.	SYRIA	LEBANON	IRAQ	JORDAN	SAUDI ARABIA	TOTAL U.A.C.	ISRAEL
Aircraft on squadrons unassigned or in Stored Reserve								
Jet Fighters	357	96	10	123	30	19	635	252
Jet Bombers	91	10	–	22	–	–	123	13
Transports	62	15	–	19	6	10	112	50
Helicopters	52	15	10	36	5	1	119	40
Total Inventory	562	136	20	200	44	30	989	355

–16–

Document Nineteen continued

TOP SECRET

Appendix D to J.I.C.(65) 20 (Final)

U.A.C. AND ISRAEL NAVAL FORCES

Note: Figures given are present holdings with forecasts for 1966 in brackets

Serial	Type	U.A.R.	SYRIA	LEBANON	IRAQ	JORDAN	SAUDI ARABIA	TOTAL U.A.C.	ISRAEL	REMARKS
(a)	(b)	(c)	(d)	(e)	(f)	(g)	(h)	(j)	(k)	(l)
1	Destroyers	6(7)	-(-)	-(-)	-(-)	-(-)	-(-)	6(7)	2(2)	
2	Frigates	3(2)	-(-)	-(-)	-(-)	-(-)	-(-)	3(2)	1(1)	
3	Submarines	9(10)	-(-)	-(-)	-(-)	-(-)	-(-)	9(10)	2(3)	
4	FPBs	40(40)(a)(b)	16(18)(c)(d)	-(2)	12(12)	-(2)(e)	-(-)	68(74) 9 (9)		
5	Minesweepers & Coastal escorts	12(14)	5(5)	-(-)	3(3)	-(-)	-(-)	20(22)	-(-)	

NOTES: (a) Including eight KOMAR missile firing boats

(b) Including twelve KOMARs

(c) Including four KOMARs

(d) Including six KOMARs

(e) Acquired from U.A.R.

-17-

TOP SECRET

Document Nineteen continued

strength, it could easily reach the conclusion that the homecoming of the Egyptian formations at that point of time would not substantially alter the picture.

The main points of the JIC report were as follows:

1   It is probable that the Israel Defence Forces (IDF) would gain the upper hand in case of armed conflict with the major Arab armies under the United Arab Command.
2   The main reason for such an assessment is that although in terms of force ratio – namely, the number of operational formations and main weapon systems, Israel is at a disadvantage, in terms of total combat power, which is the decisive factor in any military engagement – the balance is tilted towards the IDF.
3   This supremacy derived from the IDF's better morale and efficiency as well as superior command and combat effectiveness, which grant it greater offensive superiority.
4   Israeli superiority is best expressed by the IDF's capability for rapid mobilisation and deployment of its entire combat force within only 48 hours. This grants the Israelis a week of temporary force superiority and, subject to its effectual utilization, blunts the significance of the growing Arab numerical strength after the first week of fighting.
5   The major threat to Israeli mobilisation is air attacks and bombardments. However, the Egyptian air force's numerical superiority, primarily in bombers, is offset by what the JIC described as 'shortage of sound leadership and suspect operational capability'.

Until this very moment Arab authorities have released no official figures and facts about order of battle and numerical strength of their armies for the period under discussion (or, for that matter, for almost any other period). Consequently, our only touchstone is a comparison between the JIC's figures and those reached at by the Israeli Directorate of Military Intelligence (DMI) after the 1967 War, based on its findings, captured documents and interrogation of POWs. This comparison reveals that the JIC's estimates of available weapon systems both for 1965 and 1966 were basically on the mark, revealing an efficient surveillance of Arab arms deals.[5] The JIC was also correct when mentioning overall figures of Israeli main weapon systems such as the total number of tanks, guns, aircraft or warships, although overestimating by about 20 per cent the number of modern weapons that the IDF would possess in 1966 and underestimating by no less than 50 per cent the number of its armoured personal carries (estimated at 400 to 500 as compared to the correct number of 1130).[6] The JIC systematically underestimated the number of combat formations – infantry for the most part – available to the Arab armies in the first week of a potential war. It ignored the existence of divisional structure in Egypt and Syria, failed to mention the existence of reserve infantry brigades in both armies (proved, in the Egyptian case, to be combat-worthy during the 1967 War) and underestimated by 50 per cent the number of Egyptian regular infantry brigades and by 25 per cent the number of Egyptian armoured brigades (see Table 9.1). It also misjudged the Egyptian capability of a rapid build-up on the Israeli border, already demonstrated five years earlier, in February 1960, in what had been called by Israel 'The Rotem Affair', when one armoured and two infantry divisions (11 brigades) had massed in eastern Sinai, geared for combat in much less than a week.[7]

The report was less accurate in its portrayal of the IDF's points of strength and weakness, demonstrating that British intelligence had not completely grasped the operational rationale behind the Israeli organisation and force design. First and foremost, the report made no distinction between the striking force (designed for rapid decision in offence and as the centre of gravity in defence) and the territorial force (for securing the state's territory and creating a firm base for offence). This is perhaps the reason why the JIC's estimate tripled the actual number of field formations available to the IDF in peacetime. While the report mentioned nine strong standing brigade groups (1 armoured, 1 mechanised, 1 parachute and 6 infantry), Israel in fact possessed only three undermanned regular field brigades (one each of armoured, parachute and infantry) and five territorial brigades (each responsible for a specific sector along the border). In peacetime, the latter were only skeleton formations of very small regular army staff and logistic elements, while the battalions and support units were all comprised of reservists, mobilised only in emergencies. For their day-to-day activity the territorial brigades employed temporarily assigned troops from the three standing brigades or periodically called up reservists, usually in the ratio of no more than an infantry company per brigade. Putting both types of formations together, the JIC, in fact echoed a deceptive component of Israel's pre-1967 deterrence doctrine – portraying the peacetime (regular) army as much stronger than it actually was. In this matter, even London's Institute for Strategic Studies had done better, counting in its *Military Balance* only three (in 1964) or four (in 1965) Israeli regular brigades (it erred, though, in most other figures).[8]

The JIC erred by underestimation as well, as it was not apparently fully aware of the IDF's contemporary expansion of its manoeuvring arm, in particular armoured and mechanised elements, at the expense of the traditional infantry. Thus, the report exaggerated the total number of Israeli brigades (26 instead of 22), doubled, on the one hand, the number of infantry brigades (16 instead of 9) and overrated the instant combat efficiency of the reserve brigades (most reached a good level of efficiency in the 1967 War mainly due to the three weeks of intensive training forced upon the IDF during the 'waiting period' before 5 June). However, on the other hand, it cut down the actual number of the mobile brigades (10 instead of 13), underestimated the manoeuvrability of the infantry brigades, and ignored the existence of four functional divisional HQs, each capable of assuming ad hoc command of several brigades, which significantly enhanced the operational and tactical flexibility and manoeuvrability of the IDF (see Table 9.2).

British intelligence was absolutely correct in placing emphasis on the rapid mobilisation of the protagonists. The IDF, having learned the lesson of the fast deployment of the Egyptian army in Sinai during the Rotem Affair, made every effort to minimise the timeframe from a decision to call up reserve formations to final ready-for-battle deployment. Ironically, when an unpredicted war actually

Table 9.1 Arab order of battle, 1965–67 (forces able to reach the border within a week/participated in 1967 War)

Country + Type of brigade	JIC estimate (March 1965)	DMI estimate (September 1965)[1]	Actual strength (June 1967)[2]
Lebanon – infantry	1	1 (equivalent)	irrelevant
Syria – total	8	10–11	11
Armoured	2	2	2
Mechanised	2	2	1
Infantry	4	6–7[3]	8[4]
Jordan – total	8	11	11
Armoured	2	2	2
Infantry	6	9	9
Egypt – total (excluded those in Yemen)	10	18	27
Armoured	3	4	7[5]
Mechanised	1	1	1
Infantry	6	14[6]	18[7]
Parachute		1	1
Iraq – infantry		2	irrelevant[8]
Armoured	1		
Saudi Arabia – infantry	1	–	irrelevant
Total	31	40	49
Armoured	8	8	11
Mechanised	3	3	4
Infantry	18	28	33
Parachute	1 (equivalent)	1	1

Notes:
1 IDF, DMI, 'The Arab Armies', special edition prepared for the National Defence College, September 1964, revised September 1965. In author's possession.
2 IDF Intelligence Branch, 'The Egyptian Army in Light of the Six Days War', September 1968, Basic Research Report 1/68, pp. 26–8, IDF Archive, 2595/535/2004; Matitiahu Mayzel, *Ha-ma'arahcah 'al ha-golan, juni 1967* [The Golan Heights Campaign, June 1967] (Tel Aviv, Ma'arachot 2001), pp. 127–30; Efraim Kam (ed.), *Husayn poteach be-milhama: milhemet sheshet ha-yamim be-einyi ha-yardenim* [Hussein Goes to War: The Six Day War in the Eyes of the Jordanians] (Tel Aviv: Ma'arachot, 1974), pp. 311–12 (all in Hebrew).
3 Including 2–3 reserve brigades.
4 Including 3 reserve brigades.
5 Including a brigade returned from Yemen and another organised ad-hoc on the eve of the war.
6 Including 3 reserve brigades.
7 including 4 reserve brigades and brigades returned from Yemen.
8 An expeditionary force of 1 armoured, 1 mechanised and 2 infantry brigades, despatched to the front on 6 June, reached the area only after the war after being attack by the IAF.

Table 9.2 Israeli order of battle, 1966–67

Type of brigade/ weapon system regular + (reserve)	JIC estimate for 1966 regular + (reserve)[1]	Actual strength, 1966	Actual strength (June 1967)[2]
Brigades – total	9 + (17) = 26	3 + (19) = 22	22
Armour	1 + (3) = 4	1 + (5) = 6 (including 3 indep. batts.)	6
Mechenized	1 + (3) = 4	(4) = 4	4
Parachute	1 + (1) = 2	1 + (2) = 3	3
Infantry		1 + (3) = 4 (field) (5) = 5 (territorial)	
	6 + (10) = 16	1 + (8) = 9	9
Tanks – total	1,040	974	1,093
Medium modern	530	425	
Medium obsolescent	310	365	
Light	200	184	
Artillery	655		681
APCs	500	1,150	About 1,100
Aircraft – total	355 (without trainers)	291 (+ 58 jet trainers)	296 (+ 47 jet trainers employed in a war for ground support missions)
Fighters	252	192 (+ 58 jet trainers)	181 (+ 47 jet trainers)
Bombers	13	23	19
Transport and helicopters	90	76	96
Warships – total	15	14	14
Destroyers	3	3	3
Submarines	3	2	2
FPB/MTBs	9	9	9

Notes:
1 Wallach and Lissak, *Atlas carta le-toldot medinat yisrael, a'asor sheni*, p. 52.
2 IDF, Operation Branch, 'Organisation of the IDF, Volume I: Order of Battle', December 1966, pp. 4–6, IDF Archive, 94/160/1968; IAF, Air Branch 2, 'Three Years Plan 1966/67–1968/69', 16 May 1965, IDF Archive, 49/777/2005; Israeli Navy HQ, Naval Branch 1, 'Naval Order of Battle as of 1 April 1965', 1 April 1965, IDF Archive, 160/68/1994.

broke out in 1967, it emerged out of a scenario in which the confronting armies had already been facing each other and fully deployed long before the first shot was actually fired.

An interesting point is the JIC's treatment of the aerial dimension of the expected confrontation. Looking at the military balance in the air, the committee concluded that the gravest threat to the IDF lay in the Egyptian bomber force, which, if successful in destroying or damaging even one of the only three air bases available to the Israelis, might impair mobilisation (especially along the narrow Sharon Plain between the Jordanian border on the east and the Mediterranean on the west) and reduce Israeli air activity. The conclusion was clear-cut: 'The air defence of Israel will depend more on the ability of the Israelis to destroy or immobilise the U.A.R. bombers at their bases'.[9] Confining this issue to air strength balance alone, the JIC went only half-way, not realising that according to the Israeli perception, not air defence alone depended on neutralisation of the Arab air forces, but ground operations as well, that is, the outcome of the entire war. But the British, probably unconsciously, put their finger on the most guarded secret of the Israeli war plans, as they implicitly pointed to an opening move by a strike from the air as the most plausible course of action.

The 'Moked' operational plan, which met with unprecedented success in the 1967 War, was the ace Israel kept up its sleeve as a force multiplier to achieve strategic surprise. Its objective was to open an initiated war by a surprise air attack on all surrounding Arab airfields (including several in Iraq) in order to destroy as many aircraft as possible, gaining air superiority and battlefield dominance in the first hours of the war not in Sinai alone (as predicted by later British and American assessments, referred to in Dr Vaughan's introduction), but throughout the entire region.[10]

Among the measures taken to keep the plan secret was a long-term strategic deception, in which a reliable double agent passed false information to Egyptian intelligence, according to which the mission of the Israeli Air Force (IAF) was primarily defensive – to keep the Israeli skies clear of Arab bombers. The secondary mission was defined as ground support. The IAF's real offensive mission was purposely obscured. Pre-1967 Egyptian intelligence assessment corresponded indeed with the Israeli story, but whether this mindset should be attributed, completely or partially, to the Israeli deception is still a matter of speculation.[11] The editors of the JIC report apparently did not realise the complete significance of these findings, otherwise they would, most probably, have included it in their summary – the only part by and large that was read by the constantly busy decision-makers. But even this mere pointing to the air-attack option bears witness to the fact that in order correctly to assess the probable (although not always the chosen) course of action by the assessment's subject, one is not compelled to first penetrate decision-making circles, nor to employ elite spies, nor to develop extraordinary means of collection (which, as far as it is known, were not used by British intelligence to cover Israel). It is apparently sufficient for intelligence services to be properly familiar with the strength and security perception of their subject and to intelligently analyse parameters of time, space and geography. Nothing prevented

Arab intelligence from reaching the identical conclusion on their own and Arab armies, or from introducing appropriate preventive counter-measures, such as multiplying the number of their air bases, enhancing air defence or dispersing their aircraft. Luckily for Israel, they did not. Notwithstanding all the JIC's errors, at the end of the day, it correctly assessed the military balance between Israel and its Arab neighbours, envisaging the two factors that indeed dictated the June 1967 War's outcome: an opening air strike against Arab airfields and overall battlefield superiority by the IDF during the first – in fact, the only – week of the war, that ended with a decisive Israeli military victory.

Notes

Overview: Between Suez and the Six Day War: Western intelligence assessments and the Arab–Israel conflict, 1957–67

James R. Vaughan

1   Recent historical analysis of the Arab-Israel dispute in the period up to and including the 1967 war includes: Uri Bar-Joseph. 'Rotem: The Forgotten Crisis on the Road to the 1967 War', *Journal of Contemporary History*, 31/3 (July 1996), pp. 547–66; Jeremy Bowen, *Six Days: How the 1967 War Shaped the Middle East* (London Simon & Schuster, 2003); Tom Segev, *1967: Israel, the War, and the Year that Transformed the Middle East* (London: Metropolitan Books, 2007); Frank Brenchley, *Britain, the Six Day War and its Aftermath* (London: I.B. Tauris, 2005); Fawaz A. Gerges, 'The 1967 Arab–Israeli War: U.S. Actions and Arab Perceptions', in David Lesch (ed.), *The Middle East and the United States* (Boulder, CO: Westview Press, 1996), pp. 185–203; Isabella Ginor, 'The Cold War's Longest Cover-up: How and Why the USSR Instigated the 1967 War', *Middle East Review of International Affairs*, 7/3 (September 2003), pp. 34–59; Isabella Ginor and Gideon Remez, 'The Spymaster, the Communist, and Foxbats over Dimona: the USSR's Motive for Instigating the Six-Day War', *Israel Studies*, 11/2 (2006), pp. 88–130; Isabella Ginor and Gideon Remez, 'Un-Finnished Business, Archival Evidence Exposes the Diplomatic Aspect of the USSR's Pre-planning for the Six Day War', *Cold War History*, 6/3 (2006), pp. 377–95; Isabella Ginor and Gideon Remez, *Foxbats over Dimona: The Soviets' Nuclear Gamble in the Six-Day War* (New Haven, CT: Yale University Press, 2007); Galia Golan, 'The Soviet Union and the Outbreak of the June 1967 Six-Day War', *Journal of Cold War Studies*, 8/1 (2006), pp. 3–19; Haim Gordon (ed.) *Looking Back at the June 1967 War* (Westport, CT: Praeger, 1999); Laura M. James, *Nasser at War* (Basingstoke: Palgrave Macmillan, 2006); Robert McNamara, 'Britain, Nasser and the Outbreak of the Six Day War', *Journal of Contemporary History*, 35/4 (October 2000), pp. 619–39; Michael Oren, *Six Days of War: June 1967 and the Making of the Modern Middle East* (New York: Oxford University Press, 2002); Richard B. Parker (ed.), *The Six-Day War: A Retrospective* (Gainesville, FL: University Press of Florida, 1996); Moshe Shemesh, 'The IDF Raid on Samu: The Turning Point in Jordan's Relations With Israel and the West Bank Palestinians', *Israel Studies*, 7/1 (2002), pp. 139–67.
2   The National Archives, Kew, (henceforward TNA), PREM 13/1617, Stewart to Hadow, No. 53, 29 March 1966.
3   TNA, PREM 13/1622, Sir Geoffrey Harrison to George Brown, 20 July 1967.
4   TNA, FO 371/186443/E1891/1, Memorandum by W. Morris, 12 May 1966, 'Middle East Heads of Missions Conference, 16–20 May'.

5   TNA, PREM 13/1617, Stewart to Hadow, 29 March 1966, 'British Policy Towards the Arab/Israel Dispute'.
6   TNA, PREM 13/1582, Foreign Office to No. 10, 18 February 1966, Enclosing 'Record of Meeting of the Foreign Secretary with Mr. Eban on 14 February, 1966'.
7   TNA, PREM 13/1619, Michael Hadow to Foreign Office, No. 469, 4 June 1967.
8   TNA, PREM 13/1622, Michael Hadow to George Brown, 6 July 1967.
9   *Foreign Relations of the United States, 1964–1968*, vol. XIX, *Arab–Israeli Crisis and War, 1967* (Washington, DC: United States Government Printing Office, 2004), pp. 138–9, No. 76, Intelligence Memorandum Prepared in the Central Intelligence Agency, 'Military Capabilities of Israel and the Arab States', 26 May 1967.
10   TNA, CAB 158/66, JIC(67)26(Final), Report by the Joint Intelligence Committee, 'A Comparison of the Armed Forces of Israel and those of Certain Arab States up to the End of 1967', 17 April 1967.
11   TNA, DEFE 4/218, COS 41st Meeting/67, Minutes of a Meeting held in Room 5301, Ministry of Defence, 26 May 1967.
12   TNA, PREM 13/1618, Patrick Dean to Foreign Office, No. 1897, 3 June 1967.

Commentary: *Assessing the assessors: JIC assessment and the test of time*

Yigal Sheffy

1   A further discussion of analysis of 'capabilities' versus analysis based on 'intentions': Cynthia M. Grabo, *Anticipating Surprise: Analysis for Strategic Warning* (Lanham, MD: University Press of America, 2004), pp. 17–24.
2   TNA, CAB: 158/57, JIC 65(20), 'The Military Balance between Israel and the Arab World', p. 1, para. 1.
3   On the Israeli intelligence assessment in 1964–66, see Ami Gluska, *The Israeli Military and the Origins of the 1967 War* (Oxon: Routledge, 2007), pp. 48–58.
4   TNA, CAB: 158/57, JIC 65(20), 'The Military Balance between Israel and the Arab World', p. 1, para. 4.
5   Jehuda Wallach and Moshe Lissak (eds), *Atlas carta le-toldot medinat yisrael, a'asor sheni* [Carta's Atlas of Israel: the Second Decade, 1961–1971] (Jerusalem: Carta, 1980) (in Hebrew), pp. 52–7.
6   IDF, Operation Branch, Department of Staff Duties, 'The IDF Order of Battle 1965/66 – Competence for War', 31 January 1965, IDF Archive, 35/69/1992.
7   Yigal Sheffy, *Parashat 'Rotem' ve-tfisat ha-hatra'ah shel yisrael 1957–1960* [The 'Rotem' Affair and the Emergence of Israeli Early Warning Perception, 1957–1960] (Tel Aviv: IDF, Department of Military History, 2006) (in Hebrew). 'Rotem: The Forgotten Crisis on the Road to the 1967 War', *Journal of Contemporary History*, 31/3 (July 1996), pp. 547–66.
8   The Institute for Strategic Studies, *The Military Balance 1964–65* (London: The Institute for Strategic Studies, November 1964), pp. 32–3; Institute for Strategic Studies, *The Military Balance 1965–66* (London: Institute for Strategic Studies, November 1965), p. 35.
9   TNA, CAB: 158/57, JIC 65(20), 'The Military Balance between Israel and the Arab World', p. 8, para. 17.
10   Ezer Weizman, *On Eagle's Wings: The Personal Story of the Leading Commander of the Israeli Air Force* (London: Weidenfeld and Nicolson, 1975), pp. 221–7; Ehud Yonay, *No Margin for Error: The Making of the Israeli Air Force* (New York: Pantheon Books, 1993), pp. 309–17; Kenneth M. Pollack, 'Air Power in the Six Day war', *Journal of Strategic Studies*, 28/3 (2005), pp. 471–503; Danny Shalon, *Ke-raa'm be-yom bahir: mivtza moked be-milhemet sheshet ha-yamim* [Like a Bolt Out of the

Blue: Moked Operation in the Six Day War] (Rishon le-Zion: Bavir, 2002) (in Hebrew).

11   Yossi Melman and Eitan Haber, *Ha-meraglim: parshot rigul be-medinat yisrael* [The Spies: Israel Counter-espionage Wars] (Tel Aviv: Yedioth Aharonoth and Chemed Books, 2002) (in Hebrew), pp. 67–83.

10   A KGB view of CIA and other Western espionage against the Soviet Bloc, 1983

Paul Maddrell and Matthias Uhl

OVERVIEW: WESTERN SPYING ON THE SOVIET UNION'S MILITARY-INDUSTRIAL COMPLEX DURING THE SECOND COLD WAR

Paul Maddrell

Introduction

Document Twenty is a minute of the address of the principal KGB delegate to a meeting of representatives of the directorates of the Soviet Bloc security services responsible for the security of the economy. The KGB officer in question was Lieutenant-General Fyodor Shcherbak, who led the delegation sent by the responsible KGB department, the Sixth Directorate (it was charged with 'Economic Counter-intelligence and Industrial Security'). Shcherbak had previously been deputy head of the Second Chief Directorate, the directorate principally responsible for internal security within the USSR. The Sixth Directorate was its little brother. Ironically, given his strong condemnation of the Central Intelligence Agency (CIA) in this minute, when *glasnost* reached the KGB in 1989, he was one of the officers sent by the Chairman, Vladimir Kryuchkov, to discuss counter-terrorist operations with former CIA officers.[1] The minute was made by the Sixth Directorate's East German counterpart, Main Department 18 (*Hauptabteilung XVIII*) of the German Democratic Republic's (GDR) Ministry of State Security (*Ministerium für Staatssicherheit*, or MfS), and is held in the MfS archive. It is written in a rather clumsy secret police form of German and is partly in note form.

Shcherbak surveys the operations of the Western secret services against the Soviet Bloc, focusing on their spying and 'sabotage' in the economic field (this field included science and, most importantly, scientific research and development for military purposes). Given the light it sheds on Western spying, the most surprising thing about the document is the source from which I have obtained it. This is the Birthler Authority, the German government agency which controls the MfS archive.[2] The Authority was established to enable research to be undertaken into the history of the MfS.[3] In 1996 its governing law, the *Stasi-Unterlagen-Gesetz* (StUG), was amended to allow the Authority to make records available to researchers to study Nazism, on which the MfS had collected much information. However, the Authority is not meant to make available to researchers records relating to secret services other than the MfS. Indeed, it is specifically instructed to hold information on their officers, 'methods and practices' separately; this information the Federal Minister of the Interior may order to be withheld from researchers in the public interest.[4] This strict legal regime was meant to protect the interests of secret services like the CIA. Nevertheless, this document has slipped through the net. Once this has happened, it can be published. The civil rights movement which helped to overthrow the Communist dictatorship and so destroy the GDR was appalled at the MfS's secret coercion; it demanded that its murky, brutal role in maintaining Communist power be revealed and that (subject to controls) its records be used to do this. Consequently, Section 3(2) of the *Stasi-Unterlagen-Gesetz* provides that, 'Every individual has the right to use the information and records which he receives from the Federal Commissioner consistently with the general law.' In accordance with the StUG, towards the end, the names of West German companies which, according to Shcherbak, had engaged in activities which disrupted the USSR's economy, have been blacked out. I have also put in quotation marks abbreviations which I have left in their original German form.

The East–West intelligence competition in the 1980s

Document Twenty contains much of interest about the activities of the CIA and other Western secret services in the early 1980s, when the Reagan Administration was taking a highly confrontational course in foreign and defence policy which provoked furious hostility from the Kremlin. The document shows that policy towards intelligence collection followed suit. Indeed, what Shcherbak says breaks some new ground in academic study of US intelligence and its partners. According to him, the 'imperialist' (Western) secret services were in the early 1980s operating 'enormous networks of agents' in the Soviet Bloc, including the USSR (of course, the word 'agents' is broad enough to include dissidents under Western influence as well as spies). He depicts the American services as particularly aggressive and unscrupulous in their efforts to recruit agents, targeting above all emigrants from the USSR, people who wanted to migrate from it and Soviet officials sent abroad. Indeed, the CIA is presented as positively reckless, approaching people in such places as pedestrian tunnels without having investigated their character beforehand. Shcherbak's allegations of Western aggression include ones of deliberate economic disruption. He even maintains that a British secret service – presumably either the Secret Intelligence Service or the Security Service – tried to recruit Soviet scientists by threatening to murder them if they refused to cooperate (this probably reflects more an ideological tendency to damn the class enemy than reality).

The issue the minute raises is how reasonable was the view which Communist security officials had of their enemy. Their mentality was subject to two competing influences. On the one hand, to fight the 'imperialists' effectively, they had to be able to uncover their operations; for this, they had to be able to analyse evidence of Western activities sensibly and well. On the other hand, the Communist regimes needed virulent hostility towards the West in order to survive; the Leninist tenet that the capitalist world could only be their enemy and needed to overthrow them encouraged security officials to exaggerate the West's bad faith. Hatred of the West was deliberately inculcated in them. The minute reflects both tendencies. There is plenty of evidence to support some of the claims made in it; there is not enough to accept allegations of deliberate delivery of defective industrial equipment or that scientists were threatened with murder.

That William Casey, as Director of Central Intelligence, intensified American espionage in the Bloc is well established.[5] It is highly likely that in so doing the CIA tried to exploit emigrants who had already left it, using them to recruit former colleagues and relatives and friends of theirs who continued to live in the Bloc states. That was a standard method of recruiting spies behind the Iron Curtain. It is also likely that the Agency and other Western secret services tried to recruit people who wanted to emigrate from the USSR. This is one way in which both US intelligence agencies and West Germany's *Bundesnachrichtendienst* (BND) tried to recruit spies in the GDR, as ample evidence in the MfS's records shows.[6] One celebrated group of would-be emigrants were Soviet Jews, who wanted to make their home in Israel. One bar to emigration from the USSR was the applicant's knowledge of secrets; this consideration applied particularly strongly in the defence sector. Many Jewish scientists – among them some of the greatest names in Soviet science – worked in secret scientific institutions. Targeting such would-be emigrants for recruitment promised to yield intelligence directly relevant to American defence at a time when the Reagan Administration was conducting a furious arms race with the USSR. Certainly the KGB feared such recruitments. Even though he seems to have had no evidence to this effect, Yuri Andropov, when its Chairman in the 1970s, steadfastly maintained to the East German foreign intelligence chief Markus Wolf that the 'refusenik' Anatoly Shcharansky – a computer scientist in a research institute – was a CIA spy. It was owing to his work for this institute that he was denied permission to emigrate to Israel in 1973.[7] The CIA succeeded in this period in penetrating at least one Soviet defence research laboratory: among the spies betrayed by the traitors Aldrich Ames and Edward Lee Howard was Adolf Tolkachev, an avionics engineer at the Moscow Aviation Institute.[8] Former MfS officers have confirmed that in the 1980s Western secret services made strenuous efforts to recruit Communist officials who had been sent abroad.[9] As far as the use of economic disruption is concerned, adequate evidence for this is lacking, though it should be noted that MfS officers believed this claim: in his memoirs the former MfS general Josef Schwarz has also made it.[10]

Indeed, perhaps the most interesting point about the minute is what it does not say: namely, that the Soviet Bloc's repression was both the Western secret services' main problem and their chief opportunity. In many respects, secret police methods were effective in deterring, preventing and uncovering spying; this is the main reason why the Western services devoted so much effort to trying to recruit Communist officials sent abroad. However, the Bloc's very repression caused many who lived there to try to leave it for countries which would take them – West

Germany, in the case of East Germans, and Israel, in the case of Soviet Jews. The desire to emigrate enabled the Western secret services to recruit spies by promising to exfiltrate them. The Communist regimes' repression also prompted dissidents to make common cause with the West. Emigration and dissidence were key resources exploited by the West in its espionage and subversion against the Communist Bloc. The document does not mention the importance to the 'imperialist' secret services of Communism's repressiveness because, even if the officers who attended the conference had allowed themselves to realize it, they would not have dared to express this view.

DOCUMENT TWENTY:

Multilateral conference of the organs responsible for the security of the economy [illegible word or number], Sept. 1983, BStU, ZA, MfS-HA XVIII/2524.

[Translated by Paul Maddrell]

Main points in the content of the remarks made by the leader of the delegation of the Sixth Directorate of the KGB of the USSR, Comrade Lieutenant-General Shcherbak

Greetings to the conference from the Chairman of the Committee for State Security of the USSR and his deputy;

Agreement to the assessment of the situation and the conclusions drawn from it [contained] in the address of the leader of the Eleventh Directorate of the 'KfNS'[1] of the CSSR;[2]

Since Sofia 1979[3] significant change had taken place in the political-operational situation; the securing of the people's economies of the Socialist countries had increased in significance as a material basis for politics and security; economic warfare occupies a particular place in the 'anti-Communist crusade' of the imperialists against Socialism; complex of spying, sabotage, diversion and PID;[4]

Strategy of the USA and its allies: to destabilize and smash Socialism; Regan [sic] Administration has created appropriate 'preconditions' for that; e.g. Regan [sic] directive on work of USA secret services;[5] USA secret service doctrine: right to intervention in other countries, particularly the organization and activation of underground and counter-revolutionary movements in the Socialist countries;

Secret services have constructed <u>enormous networks of agents</u>, which are principally meant to work against the USSR and other Socialist countries;

Targets in the USSR are <u>the defence industry</u> and related sectors; in its large-scale <u>operations to recruit citizens of the USSR</u> (on its territory as also beyond its borders) the USA secret service shows particular aggression and unscrupulousness;

Secret service operations form part of economic warfare; meant to create particular requirements for stepping up disruptions of the foreign economic relations of the USSR, obstruction of scientific-technical exchange, undermining of export-import relations; considerable attacks are concentrated on <u>disrupting</u> 'SÖI'[6] as well as on undertaking <u>sabotage/diversion in developing countries</u>;

The imperialist secret services are particularly stepping up agent work in the USSR. In this connection the <u>secret service residencies[7] in the USA embassy</u> play a particular role. Recently intensified efforts to use homes of USSR citizens for spying purposes.

CIA makes contacts with USSR citizens without having made a thorough study of them (e.g. speaking to them in pedestrian tunnels, railway, telephone etc.);

At the same time the secret services are stepping up their targeted approaches to would-be emigrants and emigrants from the SU with the aim of recruiting them;

Intensified recruitment operations of the USA secret service, particularly with regard to citizens of the USSR who are staying on business in the capitalist world; approximately 500,000 citizens of the USSR a year in states of the capitalist world; important target groups for secret service activities e.g. of the CIA are above all scientists, 'RK',[8] 'AK';[9] February 1983 example of attempts to recruit several USSR specialists[10] using brutal methods, CIA spoke to all USSR scientists who were staying in USA and invited them to emigrate; similar approach also on the part of the British secret service, in event of refusal to cooperate threat of physical extermination;

Imperialist secret services increasingly abuse tourism for espionage purposes; USA-England-Japan und FRG number of tourists has consistently increased; travellers tasked with gathering intelligence information;

In connection with the development of the foreign economic relations of the USSR with the states of the non-Socialist world, the visits of representatives of the economic, finance and banking sectors have further increased; 1983 up to now approx. 100,000 foreign trade representatives of companies and other enterprises have travelled to the USSR; of these 100 people were expelled, among them 40 suspected of spying;

Imperialist secret services, particularly 'BND',[11] continually interested in information on 'SÖI' and COMECON with the aim of searching for opportunities for targeted undermining;

Important element in economic warfare is the economic disruptive activity organized by the imperialists; displays itself particularly in delivery of out-of-date equipment; delaying installation, sabotage and other forms of influence;

Securing the people's economy is in the new operational conditions a complicated process. It is not only a matter for domestic security but also for foreign intelligence.

The creation of the Sixth Directorate of the KGB was a response to the new security requirements; Sixth Directorate of the KGB has an experienced staff.

Main task: on the basis of the resolutions of the 26th Party Congress and other Party resolutions to organize long-term security work, focusing on the main tasks, whereby unity of prevention and of directly fighting the enemy are the highest principle.

Important in this connection the complex treatment of all issues of giving security to the people's economy, because enemy operates along various lines:3

- 'IM'[12]-network defence industry, keeping secrets;
- Undertaking operational games – getting rid of opposing organizations and people being used by secret service;
- Bringing together operational capabilities, continually adding to the picture of the enemy and making it more precise; better prepare informers among 'RK'/'AK' for service in non-Socialist world;
- Necessity of investigating incidents and accidents in the people's economy because this makes a significant contribution to making the picture of the enemy more precise and to improving security work; objective, comprehensive <u>investigation of causes in cases of incidents</u> essential; e.g. imported factory for plastic production in USSR 1982 guarantee expired, <u>only now are deficiencies becoming visible</u> ([name blacked out] Company FRG)[13]

    Change in silicon production technology of [name blacked out] Company, FRG, caused explosion and poisoning of workers;
- Necessary to evaluate knowledge of disruptive activity of capitalist companies, firms and enterprises more effectively in public, compromise such companies in the press and other mass media;
- A special operational group created within Sixth Directorate of the KGB to investigate causes of/conditions favouring incidents/accidents and other disturbances;

    In the bi- and multilateral <u>cooperation</u> of the brother services to give security to the people's economy <u>the following main issues should take precedence</u>:
- More operational structuring of information exchange about fundamental questions of security work;
- Securing of processes and common institutions of 'SÖI'/COMECON especially defence and supply industries;
- Improvement in quality in preparing and using scientist-informers;
- Objective and current assessment of the situation in the individual security sectors to establish development tendencies and main points of coordinated cooperation;
- Perfecting the leadership, planning and organization of the political-operational working process with the aim of realizing new ideas/methods of improving quality and effectiveness in securing multilaterally the people's economy/'SÖI';

- Extending the coordination of operational measures in securing the people's economy with and between the various Lines.

1 'Komitee für Nationale Sicherheit', meaning 'Committee for National Security' and thus referring to the Security Service ('Statni Bezpec[v]nost', StB).
2 Czechoslovakia.
3 Referring to a previous conference.
4 PID stood for 'politisch-ideologische Diversion': political-ideological diversion, best translated as subversion.
5 This is probably a reference to Executive Order 12333, which President Reagan signed on 4 December 1981.
6 'Sozialistische Ökonomische Integration', meaning 'Socialist Economic Integration'.
7 Stations, in American terminology.
8 'Reisekader' (travelling cadres): officials allowed to travel abroad.
9 'Auslandskader' (cadres abroad): officials resident abroad.
10 Meaning scientists, engineers or people with technical knowledge.
11 *Bundesnachrichtendienst* (Federal Intelligence Service). This was West Germany's foreign intelligence service and is now that of the reunited Germany.
12 'Inoffizielle Mitarbeiter', meaning informer.
13 Federal Republic of Germany.

COMMENTARY: INSIDE THE SOVIET BLOC IN 1983

Matthias Uhl

Since Paul Maddrell in his Overview has chiefly analysed the activities of the Western secret services against the Soviet Union and the Eastern Bloc in the period of the Second Cold War, in my commentary I would like to focus on the internal conditions within the Socialist camp which led to this document being written and outline its effects.

In 1983, the Cold War was approaching one of its high points. The Soviet invasion of Afghanistan at the end of 1979, the Polish Crisis of 1980–81, and the imminent deployment of intermediate-range nuclear missiles in Western Europe pursuant to NATO's twin-track decision markedly increased the political, military and economic tensions between the Blocs.[1]

The new arms race which was caused by the intensification of the confrontation above all put great strain on the Socialist economies. More strain was added by the failed foreign trade-oriented growth strategy and the failed attempts at integration within Comecon, which further increased the economic misery of the

individual Warsaw Pact states. At the beginning of the 1980s, the Socialist economies were close to collapse.

However, the Eastern secret services saw the cause of these economic difficulties
less in failings of the centrally-planned economy than in the meddling of Western
intelligence services. Leading Eastern secret service officers even believed
themselves faced with Western economic warfare (see Document Twenty, p. 247).
In accordance with these assumptions, for instance, in March 1982, the Stasi's chief,
Erich Mielke, issued Service Instruction 1/82 on 'the political-operational securing
of the economy'. The Instruction was meant above all to ensure internal stability
and prevent economic crises which were supposed to be caused from outside:[2]

> The aim of securing the GDR economy involves the prevention, timely
> uncovering, consistent fighting and foiling of all subversive attacks, the
> preventive foiling of disruptions and harm to the productive process, as well
> as supporting state and economic management organs in guaranteeing
> considerable internal stability in all economic branches, economic units and
> processes.[3]

The securing of the economy by the secret police was to concentrate on carrying
out five tasks:

1   Collecting intelligence on enemy plans.
2   Uncovering 'hostile-negative' activities.
3   Maintaining internal stability.
4   Preventative, harm-averting work and active support for measures enhancing
    the performance of the economy.
5   Guaranteeing the constant up-to-date analysis of the political-operational
    situation.[4]

It was not only in the GDR that supposed Western 'economic warfare' led to an
intensification of secret police security operations. In the USSR, on 25 October
1982, by Order No. 00210, 'Concerning measures to strengthen counter-espionage
in the defence of the economy of the country against underground activity of the
enemy', the Sixth Directorate, for the 'Protection of the Economy', was formed
out of Administration 'P' of the Second Chief Directorate of the Committee for
State Security of the USSR (KGB), which was responsible for counter-espionage.
Fyodor Shcherbak, who had previously been First Deputy Chairman of the Second
Chief Directorate, was appointed its head; at the same time, the secret service
leadership made him a member of the KGB Collegium, the innermost leadership
circle of the Soviet secret police.[5]

After this reorganization of KGB structures, the international cooperation of
the Eastern secret services in the field of economic counter-espionage was stepped
up. After, first, bilateral consultations had taken place in early 1983, leading secret
service officers of the economic counter-espionage units of the Comecon states met

in September 1983 to discuss how jointly to take action against the Western 'attacks' on the Socialist economies.

However, first, Shcherbak analysed the situation. He spoke of 'enormous networks of agents' of the Western intelligence services, which were operating against the Socialist alliance. The KGB appeared above all to be shocked that the CIA, in building its agent networks in the Soviet Union, blatantly dispensed with all previous precautions and even 'made contact with USSR citizens without having made a thorough study of them' (see Document Twenty, p. 247). The Soviet secret service also saw a direct threat in the persistent increase in so-called *Reisekader* (officials authorized to travel abroad). Soviet security officials likewise viewed growing Western tourism with disquiet; after all, the KGB assumed that the travellers from the West had instructions to collect intelligence.

It is indisputable that this was in fact the case. For example, the *Bundes-nachrichtendienst* (Federal Intelligence Service, or BND) questioned GDR visitors to the West extensively to gather intelligence on the situation in the East German state. In doing so, it realized – approvingly – that nine out of ten GDR sources were 'playing for both sides' – that is to say, were double agents of the Ministry of State Security (MfS). After all, the knowledge 'obtained so without risk' could flow to the BND and be used to inform political decision-makers in Bonn. Moreover, each piece of information 'sooner or later could be checked against further information obtained, among other sources, from travellers to the West who were not actively controlled by the MfS, including foreigners'.[6] This is also an indication that Western travellers were deliberately used to collect intelligence in the Socialist camp. Nonetheless, it is doubtful whether in reality – as the KGB thought – use was made of entire legions of agents. If, in 1983, out of 100,000 people a mere 40 were expelled from the Soviet Union on suspicion of espionage, this represented just 0.04 per cent of all visitors. The number of agents among the Eastern *Reisekader* was probably considerably higher.

All in all, the Eastern secret services were faced with the dilemma that the persistent increase in contacts with the West led to a consistently growing communication, which could barely be kept under surveillance any more. As a result, the effort devoted to assessment and reporting got out of hand, just as did the surveillance of *Auslandskader* (officials posted abroad) and *Reisekader*. The Main Directorate XVIII of the MfS alone, which was responsible for 'Economic Security', wrote 6,934 information reports in 1982–83. In accordance with Service Instruction 1/82, in 1983–84, the Main Directorate XVIII carried out more than 20,100 investigations of *Reisekader* (and that with a staff which was not increased).[7]

All in all, the secret police efforts of the Eastern intelligence services to secure their economies against 'attacks from the West' were doomed to fail. For the cause of the economic difficulties of the Socialist camp hardly lay in the 'delivery of out-of-date equipment' from the West or 'economic disruptive activity organized by the imperialists' (Document Twenty, p. 248). Nor did it lie in the mismanagement or embezzlement on the part of some economic officials of the Eastern Bloc which the secret services uncovered.[8] Among other factors, these economic problems resulted chiefly from the wholly excessive armaments policy, which tied up and absorbed all the resources of the Socialist economies. Therefore, there was no capital for investment which was urgently needed to renew their aged and worn-out production facilities. So it is also not surprising that, despite intensifying 'security operations', the number of serious accidents, for instance, in the GDR continually increased from 1983.[9] However, the decisive factor was that, in addition to the secret services, the political leaderships of the Eastern Bloc also obstructed the change in the economic system which was necessary for successful reforms. The economic decline of the Soviet Union and its satellites could not be held in check by even the most extensive and sophisticated secret service measures. The collapse of the Socialist world system in 1989 was hardly caused by the activities against the Eastern Bloc of the Western secret services. The lack of political and economic prospects and solutions made the people of Eastern Europe rebel against dictatorships which deprived them of any opportunity of free development. Like their economies, the apparently all-powerful secret services collapsed like houses of cards.

Notes

Overview: Western spying on the Soviet Union's military-industrial complex during the Second Cold War

Paul Maddrell

1   C. M. Andrew and O. Gordievsky, *KGB: The Inside Story of its Foreign Operations from Lenin to Gorbachev* (London: Hodder & Stoughton, 1990), p. 534 and Appendix C1.
2   The proper name for this institution is the *Bundesbeauftragte für die Unterlagen des Staatssicherheitsdienstes der ehemaligen Deutschen Demokratischen Republik* (BStU for short). In English, the name means 'Federal Commissioner for the Records of the State Security Service of the Former German Democratic Republic'.
3   Section 1, *Gesetz über die Unterlagen des Staatssicherheitsdienstes der ehemaligen Deutschen Demokratischen Republik*. For short, this law is known as the *Stasi-Unterlagen-Gesetz* (StUG).
4   Section 37(1)(3d), StUG. For an explanation of how the law works, see P. Maddrell, 'The Revolution Made Law: The Work since 2001 of the Federal Commissioner for the Records of the State Security Service of the Former German Democratic Republic', *Cold War History*, 4/3 (2004): 153–62.
5   K. Eichner and A. Dobbert, *Headquarters Germany: Die USA-Geheimdienste in Deutschland* (Berlin: edition ost, 1997), p. 181; see also J. Persico, *Casey: From the OSS to the CIA* (Harmondsworth: Penguin Books, 1991), pp. 283, 360.
6   P. Maddrell, *Spying on Science: Western Intelligence in Divided Germany, 1945–1961* (Oxford: Oxford University Press, 2006), pp. 56–8, 119–20, and 251–3; P. Maddrell, 'The Scientist Who Came in from the Cold: Heinz Barwich's Flight from the GDR', *Intelligence and National Security*, 20/4 (2005): 608–30.
7   M. Wolf, *Man Without a Face* (London: Jonathan Cape, 1997), pp. 218–19; C. Whitney, *Spy Trader* (New York: Times Books, 1993), pp. 188–9.
8   J. Richelson, *The US Intelligence Community* (Boulder, CO: Westview Press, 1999), p. 262.

9   W. Großmann, *Bonn im Blick* (Berlin: Das Neue Berlin, 2001), p. 286; Eichner and Dobbert, *Headquarters Germany*, pp. 259–61.
10 See J. Schwarz, *Bis zum bitteren Ende* (Schkeuditz: GNN-Verlag, 1995), pp. 73–4.

Commentary: Inside the Soviet Bloc in 1983

Matthias Uhl

1   In this connection, see, for example, brochures distributed both by the Soviet Union and USA: *Whence the Threat to Peace* (Moscow: Military Publishing House, 1982); *Soviet Military Power* (Washington, DC: US Government Printing Office, 1982); *Die sowjetische Rüstung. Pentagon-Papier zur sowjetischen Rüstung* (Bonn: Bernard & Graefe Verlag, 1981).
2   See Siegfried Suckut, Clemens Vollnhals, Walter Süß and Roger Engelmann (eds), *Anatomie der Staatssicherheit: Geschichte, Struktur, Methoden – MfS-Handbuch: Die Hauptabteilung XVIII: Volkswirtschaft* (Berlin: Der Bundesbeauftragte für die Unterlagen des Staatssicherheitsdienstes der ehemaligen Deutschen Demokratischen Republik, 1995), pp. 74–9; Jens Gieseke, *Die DDR-Staatssicherheit. Schild und Schwert der Partei* (Bonn: Bundeszentrale für Politische Bildung, 2001), p. 62 et seq..
3   Dienstanweisung 1/82 'zur politischen-operativen Sicherung der Volkswirtschaft', 10/3/1982, p. 5; BStU, ZA, DSt 102836.
4   Ibid., pp. 13–15.
5   See A.I. Kokurin and N.V. Petrov (eds), *Lubjanka: Organy VCK-OGPU-NKVD-NKGB-MGB-MVD-KGB 1917–1991. Spravocnik* (Moscow: Mezhdunarodnyj fond 'Demokratija', 2003), p. 173.
6   See Ullrich Wössner, 'Angriffe des MfS auf den Bundesnachrichtendienst', in Georg Herbstritt and Helmut Müller-Enbergs (eds), *Das Gesicht dem Westen zu ... DDR-Spionage gegen die Bundesrepublik Deutschland* (Bremen: Edition Temmen, 2003), p. 401.
7   See Siegfried Suckut, Clemens Vollnhals, Walter Süß and Roger Engelmann (eds), *Anatomie der Staatssicherheit: Geschichte, Struktur, Methoden – MfS-Handbuch: Die Hauptabteilung XVIII: Volkswirtschaft* (Berlin: Der Bundesbeauftragte für die Unterlagen des Staatssicherheitsdienstes der ehemaligen Deutschen Demokratischen Republik, 1995), p. 94. All in all, in 1983, the HA XVIII had a staff of 478; in 1984, 475. Only in 1985 did it increase to 491; thereafter, it fell again to less than 460.
8   In 1983, at the order of Yuri Andropov, who was both the Soviet Communist Party's General Secretary and the President of the USSR, a whole series of economic trials took place under the direction of the KGB. The one which made the biggest impact on public opinion – the trial of the directors of several Moscow trading organizations – was followed by the execution of several people. See R.G. Pichoja, *Sovetskij sojuz: Istorija vlasti 1945–1991* (Moscow: Izdatel'stvo RAGS, 1998), p. 421 *et seq.*
9   See Suckut, Clemens Vollnhals, Walter Süß & Roger Engelmann (eds.), *Anatomie der Staatssicherheit: Geschichte, Struktur, Methoden – MfS-Handbuch: Die Hauptabteilung XVIII: Volkswirtschaft* (Berlin: Der Bundesbeauftragte für die Unterlagen des Staatssicherheitsdienstes der ehemaligen Deutschen Demokratischen Republik, 1995), pp. 96–8.

11 A conversation with former DCI William E. Colby

Spymaster during the 'Year of the Intelligence Wars'

Loch K. Johnson

In 1975, the Church Committee carried out its sweeping inquiry into charges that the Central Intelligence Agency (CIA) had violated its charter by spying on citizens within the United States. This year is remembered by historians as the most extensive probe into the CIA since its founding in 1947. Many intelligence professionals inside the Agency recall the investigation as a period of great trauma – the 'Year of the Intelligence Wars' between the CIA and the Congress.[1] At the helm of U.S. intelligence at the time was William Egan Colby, the Director of Central Intelligence (DCI). In that capacity, he was the titular leader of the entire intelligence community and directly in charge of the CIA, where the Office of the DCI was located at the time (and until 2005) on the seventh floor of the Agency's headquarters building.

As DCI, Colby had conceded to *New York Times* reporter Seymour M. Hersh that a laundry list of wrongdoing by CIA officers, dubbed the 'family jewels' (and released in full in 2007)[2] by Agency insiders, had been compiled by his predecessor, James R. Schlesinger, who during his few months as DCI in 1973 had decided to clean house. It was, to say the least, a turbulent time for Colby – 'one of the worst times in Agency history to become DCI,' notes an Agency historian.[3] Colby found himself torn between a White House (under President Gerald R. Ford), which wanted him to be less forthcoming with lawmakers, and the Church Committee, which hounded him each day of the inquiry for more documents, more witnesses, and more candor. He attempted to strike a balance between the two demands, feeling that he had to be reasonably forthright with the Committee or else its members might react angrily by emasculating his beloved Agency. Convinced that lawmakers might even abolish the CIA if Colby failed to cooperate with the investigation, the DCI decided to court the Church Committee and demonstrate to its members that intelligence could be made accountable to Congress. His mantra became another form of the CIA acronym: 'Constitutional Intelligence for America', a slogan that seemed to many Ford administration officials as far too conciliatory to the Church panel. Another of Colby's predecessors, Richard Helms – highly regarded among members of the Operations Directorate, where both Helms and Colby had pursued their intelligence careers – scorned Colby's deferential approach, arguing privately among colleagues that the best response to Congress was to hunker down until the storm subsided.

Perilous circumstances were nothing new to Colby, and nor was controversy. As a young intelligence officer in the Second World War, he had joined forces with Norwegian insurgents in parachuting expeditions behind German lines to conduct sabotage operations against the Nazis in Scandinavia. During the Vietnam War, he had headed up Operation Phoenix from 1968–71, a program designed to 'neutralize' – read apprehend or kill – the Viet Cong infrastructure in South Vietnam. The Phoenix program led to the death of some 20,000 (Colby's estimate) to 60,000 suspected Viet Cong fighters or sympathizers. Colby maintained after the war that these deaths were a necessary part of the conflict, a byproduct of warfare. His critics, though, viewed the program as a massive assassination operation, anathema to American values.[4]

The critics had long memories. In 1979, when I was a staffer member of the House Permanent Select Committee on Intelligence and responsible for organizing a series of hearing for Rep. Les Aspin (D-WI) on CIA relations with the media, then-retired Colby came to testify on this subject. Waiting for him in the back row of the hearing room were two young men with buckets of red paint that they intended to throw over him in a protest against Operation Phoenix. The two were apprehended by Capitol Hill police before Colby arrived.

Just as Colby had performed well under fire in Norway and had responded calmly to the criticism rising from Operation Phoenix, so did he take on the task of steering the CIA and the other intelligence agencies through the Charybdis of the Ford White House and the Scylla of the Church Committee in 1975. Certainly there are legions of intelligence officers who viewed him as too soft during that *annus horribilis* – even a turncoat – but many others inside and outside the intelligence profession admired his skillful navigation through this tight strait in rough seas. As Frank Church's assistant during this time, I found him charming, bright, more or less cooperative in meeting document requests and call for witnesses, and clearly correct about the need to work with the Congress – or face the prospects of an infuriated investigative committee at a time when there was unambiguous evidence that the CIA and other agencies had improperly spied against innocent Americans exercising their First Amendment rights to protest against the war in Vietnam and in favor of the civil rights movement.

From the point of view of the Church Committee, Colby – however charming – was no pushover. For example, he strongly and successfully resisted the Committee's plan to hold public hearings on several covert actions that at the time were (and still remain) classified. He negotiated with Senator Church over every step of the inquiry, and often persuaded the Committee to back away from some subjects that had nothing to do with illegal domestic espionage. On the subject of domestic improprieties, however, he was fully forthcoming and personally unhappy that they had occurred.

Colby was born on January 4, 1920, in St. Paul, Minnesota, the son of a U.S. Army officer who traveled with his family in tow to a number of assignments during Colby's youth, including a stint in China.[5] A fine student, Colby went to Princeton and graduated in 1940, then followed his father's footsteps into the Army, volunteering for active duty as a 2nd Lieutenant in August 1941. In 1943, he shifted over to the Office of Strategic Services (OSS), operating behind enemy lines in France as well as in Norway. He earned a law degree at Columbia University after the war, practiced his profession briefly in New York (1947–49) and then with the National Labor Relations Board in Washington, D.C. (1949–50). He joined the CIA in 1950. He rose through the ranks of the CIA's Operations Directorate, serving as Chief, Far East Division, from 1962–67, before becoming Director of Civil Operations and Rural Development Support in Saigon and head of the Phoenix program, under the cover of the Agency for International Development, from 1968–71.

Upon returning to Agency Headquarters in Langley, Virginia, he became the Executive Director-Comptroller from 1972–73 and – the plumb position for an operations officer, Deputy Director for Operations – for six months in 1973. At the end of this brief period of service at the pinnacle of his home Directorate, Colby was selected as the nation's top spymaster, serving as DCI from September 4, 1973, to January 30, 1976, in the midst of the Watergate and domestic spying scandals.

After retirement, Colby authored two well-received books, his memoir entitled *Honorable Men*, and a book on his experiences in Vietnam entitled *Lost Victory*.[6] In the French language edition of the memoir, the CIA accused him of revealing classified information about an intelligence collection operation that employed a deep-sea mining vessel, the *Glomar Explorer*, to salvage a Soviet submarine that had exploded and sunk in the Pacific Ocean near Hawaii during his tenure as DCI. Colby agreed to pay $10,000 in an out-of-court settlement. For some, it seemed a petty retaliation by certain elements in the Agency against Colby for his 'coziness' with the Church Committee. More conspiratorial still, some Colby supporters wondered if his death on a canoeing trip in 1996 might have sinister causes. Police accounts, though, concluded that he had suffered a stroke or heart attack while canoeing near his home at Rock Point, Maryland, with no evidence of foul play.

On January 22, 1991, as U.S. troops were involved in the first Persian Gulf War against Iraq, I sat down with him in his Washington, D.C., law office to discuss his career and observations about the evolution of intelligence in the United States. Tanned and relaxed, he leaned back in his chair and smiled as I began the recorded conversation (published here for the first time) with questions about the Church Committee and the system of intelligence oversight it had established in the aftermath of the 1975 investigation.

Intelligence oversight

JOHNSON: Let me begin by asking you about this 'grand experiment' we have been having in intelligence oversight. Do you think it has worked out all right?

COLBY: I think it's worked out very well. Of course, there are glitches here and there, and some arguments. I think that Iran-*contra* was a direct violation of the deal, in both the respects of the refusal to send the finding over [to the congressional Intelligence Committees] on the Iranian part, and then coming up with the thesis that the Boland Amendment did not apply to the NSC, which was pure sophistry. I'm surprised [then DCI William J.] Casey didn't pick that up, because the Amendment very clearly says: '. . . *any* agency engaged in intelligence activities'. So if you engage, you're automatically included; it doesn't give you it by name. You will have that kind of thing forever: little things that happen here and there.

JOHNSON: The quality of intelligence oversight often seems uneven.

COLBY: It's the same throughout the government. Sometimes people on the Agriculture Committees worry about what is happening in the Agriculture Department, and sometimes they don't. I think that's typical.

JOHNSON: Do you think that legislators tend to focus in when something goes wrong?

COLBY: Oh, sure. That's the way the Hill works, which is fair enough; but they also look at things in the annual budget, which is down to a line-item thing. I remember one incident. Some people came to me with the idea of putting a bug out in one of the trust territories in the Pacific. I sent it up to the lawyers. I said, 'Look, this is a trust territory. Is it outside the United States, or is it inside the United States?' And a lawyer came back and said, 'It's outside.' And I said, 'Well, I don't think this will be worth a helluva lot, but okay, let's try it for three months and see what happens.' Well, it leaked and Congress complained. I told them the operation had been there all along in the line-item budget. 'It was there for you to ask about,' I reminded them.

   As I say, I never thought it was going to do a helluva lot of good, but I didn't want to put out the word throughout the Agency: 'We're going to stop everything because of fear.' So let's do the things: if they work, fine; if they don't, the hell with it.

JOHNSON: How do you develop comity between the branches?

COLBY: I don't think you get comity. It's a deliberate separation of powers. I explained our government to a foreigner one time. I said, 'Look, you're familiar with establishing a coalition government in your country. You establish a coalition, you agree on a program, and then everything more or less goes through because you have party discipline. You have to realize that in this country we have to establish a new coalition on each issue. There's no party discipline, so each issue has to have its own coalition.' So it's consensus that you need, rather than comity.

   There was a case here, I noticed in the paper, though it's a little fuzzy, that apparently before the attack in Panama somebody came up with the idea of running a coup against Noriega. The possibility was mentioned in the *PDB* [*President's Daily Brief*]. This idea apparently got all the way to one of the [congressional oversight] committees, as was proper. The committee's members were being briefed on it, as they should have been. And it got into a discussion. If he's killed in the middle of the coup, is that an assassination? And it went back and forth, they mulled it over, and they finally decided not to do it. Instead [of a covert action], they [the first Bush administration] sent 24,000 troops and killed several hundred Panamanians; but I suspect that was the correct decision, because you'd still be hearing about the assassination of Noriega for the next hundred years – and you will not be hearing about the attack on Panama for the next hundred years.

JOHNSON: I think I've heard you say before that you would not even have ordered an assassination against Hitler before we declared war in 1941.

COLBY: Before, no. After, it's an act of war; generals are just as subject to being killed as privates.

JOHNSON: What about assassinating Saddam Hussein instead of going to war against Iraq and inflicting perhaps thousands of casualties?

COLBY: I basically think, no. You have to say, that's what happened in Panama. It's a tough moral issue. It's a very close call; but I think from the country's point-of-view, it's better to have a flat prohibition – except in war. And I don't mean to be fancy about war; I mean when our young men are dying, and the other country's young men are dying, then you can go after the top man.

JOHNSON: Are we likely to have another DCI in the future like Casey who does not appreciate oversight?

COLBY: Yeah, sure.

JOHNSON: There is no way to get around that?

COLBY: No, you just count on the tension in the Constitutional system to work; and if it doesn't work and gets caught, then there's a back-up that's supposed to work for a while when someone goes off the reservation. It's like the laws against murder: murders take place even though we have laws, and we punish them when it happens.

JOHNSON: What about the question of access to information by Congress? Is the 'sources and methods' argument a bit phony when it's brought up by the Agency in this context, as means for avoiding the sharing of information with legislators?

COLBY: I think it's pretty sincere, though they undoubtedly stretch it. Particularly on agent names, we did convince both Church and Pike to leave out the names [in their committee reports].[7] We pretty well got through that whole thing without names. It was critical. And the return on it was to be reasonably responsible. There's your comity; even when you're antagonists, you can have comity.

JOHNSON: Unless you're dealing with Otis Pike and some of his people?[8]

COLBY: Oh, they were impossible!

JOHNSON: A lot of this depends upon personality.

COLBY: Yes, of course it does: the character of the person and so forth. Back to sources and methods, the technological people – especially the cryptography people – are hyper about revealing anything, because it's just indoctrinated in them since the Year One that if the other side learns you're reading their stuff, then they change their codes and there you are: you're lost. They just learn that from childhood. So that's why they get so upset. And when they have some new whizmo up in the sky that does something new and different, they want to keep a monopoly on the information. But, you know, you can buy satellite photography now that is probably better than what we were guarding when I was DCI.

Humint

JOHNSON: If Congress were to examine the quality of humint [human intelligence, collected by agents, as opposed to technical intelligence – 'techint' – gathered by satellites and other machines], wouldn't it have to get into some aspects of sources?

COLBY: Yes, but you don't have to get into details. You see, you have undoubtedly seen some of the DDO [Deputy Directorate for Operations] reports and there's a source part: it's descriptive of the source, but it's also fuzzed enough so that you couldn't put it right smack on point. Now if you take the text and it says, 'He [the agent] and I were in the garden and we had the following conversation . . .' and you get that back to the originator, he knows damn well who was in the garden and you've got trouble.

JOHNSON: No Member of Congress would want to know a name anyway, would he or she?

COLBY: I don't think so. Once in a while there was a demand for a name of who was receiving subventions [money and other forms of remuneration from the CIA]. There were a few of those, where there were prominent people around the world who were getting help from us. They might also want to know who the intermediary was: 'Are you sure these guys don't just pocket the money and run away with it?' This is a legitimate question, and you explain what you do to cross-check with some reasonable control; but, quite honestly, you say, 'I can't guarantee there isn't any waste here.' Yes, it can happen; but still and all, we see the results and the activity that we're paying for, and therefore they seem reasonably happy about it.

Congressional access to information

JOHNSON: What about the timing of Congress's access to information?

COLBY: I think Stan Turner [Admiral Stansfield Turner, DCI from 1977–81] said it about as well as anyone. He said at one point, when they were talking about this 48-hour stuff,[9] 'Look, before Desert One, I had sent people over there [to Iran] in little planes to check out the desert to see whether it would hold the weight of a C-15. I am not able to look a young man like that in the face and tell him that I'm not going to tell ten congressmen [about the mission]; at the same time, I'm not going to lie to him. So, I need that kind of flexibility.' I don't think you can write a law to cover it, but I think what you can say is [that] after the event, then the Congress would have the right to review whether it was reasonable to withhold the information. In that case, they would have said yes.

But if it had been a jackass operation from the word go, then it might be that it would be reasonable to withhold that individual's involvement and the particular thing he did; but, in the same way, the Congress should have been informed that there was an overall program – as it probably was on the hostage rescue thing. I imagine there was some kind of briefing: that we are going to run some kind of operation some day, without any particular specifics. I would be surprised if [President Jimmy] Carter hadn't arranged for a few of the leadership [in Congress] at least to be brought into the fact that we're going to do something to try to get these people out.

JOHNSON: And if Congress doesn't like the rationale . . .?

COLBY: Then it can raise a fuss.

A Grand Charter for intelligence

JOHNSON: What do you think about the idea of a 'Grand Charter' for intelligence?[10] Has that gone the way of the dinosaurs?

COLBY: That's gone. I was for it, I was for it. You could diddle with the details, but I've always been interested in getting intelligence a charter – a solid, statutory base – for its functions within the American government. The history of our intelligence is that we use it when we need it, and we throw it away when we don't. We throw away the organization. After World War I, after World War II – Truman tried to throw it away. It's sufficiently institutionalized now that I don't think you can throw it away, but that's part of what the charter proposal was about.

JOHNSON: I guess we're getting little pieces of the charter.

COLBY: You've got little bits of it. I mean, this Agent Identity legislation, the 'graymail' thing, the special court [for wiretaps] – that's a fabulous idea.[11] Star Chamber! [Laughter.] It's so fascinating that the American citizen carries his constitutional protections with him even when he goes abroad.

Funding for intelligence

JOHNSON: Does the CIA have access to money outside the appropriations process?

COLBY: No.

JOHNSON: One example might be proprietaries. . . .

COLBY: We ran into that when we sold Air America when I was there. I've forgotten how much money we made off that – several millions of dollars, I guess. And I said, 'Why don't we save the taxpayers some money? We've got this money; why don't we subtract it from next year's appropriation and use this?' I said, 'Go up and talk to the Hill about it.' They were interested, and then they ran into this general provision of law that says, 'No agency of the government will spend non-appropriated funds.' It was determined that the only thing one could do with that money was turn it in to the Treasury as miscellaneous receipts, and you had to get your full appropriation out of the Congress, which is basically a good idea, because various intelligence services around the world have gotten into trouble by self-financing and going into their own deals, totally out of control, as the French did at one time.

JOHNSON: How do we know DCIs have indeed turned such profit over to the Treasury?

COLBY: It's set into the rules. Now a proprietary will turn its own money over while it's still alive; in other words, you set up an air-transport proprietary, you tell it to go out and do a certain amount of legitimate business so that you have cover for its other business. It'll turn over that basic capital.

JOHNSON: What if it makes huge profits?

COLBY: Huge profits just build up; you can't take it anywhere. Now you may bet a bigger airline, which is a little bit what happened to Air America. It got too big, in my mind.

JOHNSON: In the Iran-*contra* case, private American and foreign governments were willing to give money to pay for our intelligence operations . . .

COLBY: Well, with respect to foreign governments, I don't know if they did or not; I can't answer that question.[12] There is an attempt in Congress now to write law that says, 'Thou shall not urge a third country to do what you have not had authority from our Congress to do.' President [George H.W.] Bush pocket-vetoed this, because he said it would stop you even from having diplomatic conversation with another country.

JOHNSON: That seems stretching it to me.

COLBY: If you make the distinction that, 'Why don't you help those guys,' and it's a direct relationship between those two; but 'Why don't you give me money to help those guys,' – no, that's wrong. But I don't object to our government suggesting to the French government that it help the opposition against [Col. Muammar] Qaddafi [the leader of Libya].

JOHNSON: But should that be reported to the congressional oversight committees?

COLBY: You don't have to report everything from a diplomatic exchange. It becomes a matter of whether it's an operation, or whether it's just chit-chat. Again, how are you going to define that? If it's cooperation, then clearly you have to report it; but if it's just suggesting that somebody else do something useful, that's not quite the same.

White House detailees

JOHNSON: What about this question of detailees?[13] The argument that they run operations against the White House . . .

COLBY: You wouldn't have a Director [DCI] very long.

JOHNSON: Where is the loyalty of these individuals?

COLBY: It's like military officers. In my experience with military officers, you tell them what their chain-of-command is, and they salute. The same is true with the CIA. Whether there's a little back-channel chatter on what's going on, I'm sure that occurs in the military and everywhere else; but in terms of someone using the position to spy for the Agency, I can't believe that. I would say that if you have a CIA career officer and you send him on TDY [temporary leave to serve as a designee] that you don't put him in the Peace Corps.

JOHNSON: And you don't make them Fulbright Scholars.

COLBY: Right. Obviously we put people undercover all the time. Some of the political sections in the embassies are upset about this.

JOHNSON: You've spoken about the problem of 'vanishing cover'.[14]

COLBY: Oh, it drives me up the wall. It's a serious problem. . . . So, obviously we've put people undercover, but in those situations they normally have a dual commitment; but what you're referring to is ostensibly, but not actually, a single commitment. I would have doubts that that would be at all feasible. There might be some informal chatter. And old friend calls up and says, 'What the hell are you guys doing?' That's part of Washington.

More on humint

JOHNSON: Is humint valuable?

COLBY: It's one of those things, you can't afford to say no – because sometimes it can be. It's a very difficult subject. If in times of crisis, you have an agent in Baghdad, you would have a helluva time communicating to him right now. On the other hand, if he were reasonably close to the Revolutionary Command in the week before the crisis, he might have been able to give us a tip – that 'He [Saddam Hussein] really is going [to invade Kuwait in 1990]. This is no bluff.' I gather that was the analytical conclusion anyway. And, of course, you go through years with nothing much happening, and then you cut off the relationship. We were in the process of closing the stations in El Salvador and Portugal just before [these countries] blew up; nothing had happened there for ten years! [Laughter.] And I was under a lot of pressure to squeeze down in personnel. So it's a tough subject. But I think that . . . well, when the Soviet Union was a monolith, then a little window into this section was quite valuable, because you had a reasonable case that what you saw there was probably typical of what was going on in the rest of the monolith.

Nowadays, with the Soviet Union spilling all over hell's half-acre and all sorts of voices coming from all sides, using a human agent doesn't have the same value. A human agent in the United States would be absolutely worthless [for a foreign intelligence agency], unless you want some highly technical subject. So, it's a tough subject; but I think you'll always have some, and they'll pay off. And remember that the human agent is also available to somehow manipulate [a foreign government].[15]

The dissemination of intelligence

JOHNSON: What can be done about the dissemination side of intelligence?[16]

COLBY: Not very much. You do now pretty well disseminate it – you know, the estimates and that sort of thing to the Congress. When Webster had to say that he thought the situation in Eastern Europe was irreversible, and [Secretary of Defense Dick] Cheney was trying to get a budget for Defense, Cheney was sore as hell. But it had its effect. It didn't have an effect on the administration's budget, but undoubtedly it's going to have an effect on the Congressional budget.

JOHNSON: Where do you come down on the Sherman Kent argument versus those who think intelligence officers ought to be closer to policy-makers?[17]

COLBY: I think it ought to be closer – not supportive, but it has to be close enough to be related to what the hell is going on. When intelligence was sort of way over here in the early Nixon years . . . that was when Henry [Kissenger] was saying, 'Oh, what is all this crap?' – it was true.

JOHNSON: Did [DCI] Casey carry this closeness too far?

COLBY: I don't know that any allegation has been made that even Casey was warping the conclusions to fit the policy. I haven't heard that, one way or the other. Some guy [analyst] is always going to say that, if the DCI doesn't agree with him. That's one of the protections you have. The Agency is not a disciplined monolith. If you get something that does upset somebody, it'll come out sooner or later; then, you either defend it or admit that you shouldn't have done it. But that's a pressure point.

Intelligence collection and analysis

JOHNSON: Are there any breakthroughs in methodologies for analyzing intelligence?

COLBY: I know we were experimenting with some quantitative stuff. As you know, I did break up the Board of National Estimates, because I thought it was so generalist it was lacking in expertise. Then you need some protection against the Agency being the only source of opinion, and I think you get that through the [Intelligence] Community – having the arguments with the Navy, the Army, or whatever.

JOHNSON: Do we try to gather too much intelligence?

COLBY: Not for a big nation. If I were Israel, I'd spend my time on the neighboring Arab armies and I wouldn't give a damn about what happened in China. We are a big power, and we've got to worry about all of the world.

Covert action

JOHNSON: Is covert action really all that useful?

COLBY: I think it would be a mistake to get rid of it. Did we overuse it? Probably in some cases. But I think some of the major covert actions were very effective: the Laos case, Western Europe.

JOHNSON: What about Afghanistan? Was covert action effective there [in the 1980s]?

COLBY: Afghanistan, certainly. Even you might say Cambodia. I don't know about Angola. All that was part of the Cold War, the containment policy. The Bay of Pigs was a disaster, of course. But what if it had worked?

DCI/White House relations

JOHNSON: What about DCI access to the White House? Can you mandate it?

COLBY: I don't think you can mandate it. I think Casey had too much. I think [Richard] Helms had about the right amount with [President Lyndon B.] Johnson

– the Tuesday 'lunch group,' you know. He was in the circuit. He was quite meticulous about not taking a policy position. But he was still in the President's agonizing, so he knew how to manipulate the machinery, too. You either support the President, or offer advice that he was on the wrong track. I think the Pentagon Papers are quite a tribute to Helms; you know, Johnson was not the most patient guy in the world.

JOHNSON: What about your own access?

COLBY: I had very little. I had all I wanted to [national security adviser] Brent [Scowcroft]. I was on the phone to him every day or so. [Secretary of State] Henry [Kissinger] I'd see fairly frequently. President [Richard M.] Nixon was such a retired fellow that you didn't see him very much – though [on those occasions when he did talk to Colby] he would listen and often disagree, which was fair enough. [President Gerald R.] Ford was more regularized. He'd have the meetings in the NSC on the various issues, so you'd prepare for those. He wasn't very informal on that sort of thing.

JOHNSON: So Nixon wasn't very interested in meeting with DCIs?

COLBY: No, I think one time he called me up and asked me what was happening in China – just out of the blue.

JOHNSON: Ford didn't seem to treat you well.

COLBY: I understood what his problem was. He was taking such a pasting on [intelligence] issues that by stepping in and putting his own man in [in other words, Colby as a replacement for DCI James R. Schlesinger] – and, remember, one of the motives of this thing was to conceal the dumping of a vice-president [Spiro Agnew]; that was behind the scenario – and, of course, Ford never understood Schlesinger, so he just threw me in as an also-ran.

Counterintelligence

JOHNSON: What about the Nosenko case?[18] Did [CIA Chief of Counter-intelligence James J.] Angleton order that confinement?

COLBY: No, apparently he did not. Apparently there is even some doubt that he had anything to do with the actual confinement. I don't know. This was before my time. Obviously, he was in the loop of the whole thing, but what he knew about the confinement, I don't know. And I can't name you who did. It's the thing that scared me the most: the assassination of a foreign leader may be dumb, but to take someone and put him in jail in the United States . . . what the hell happened to habeas corpus? This is pretty fundamental. For an intelligence agency to do that in this country – Jesus! Though I gather Nosenko accepted it as 'So what's new?' [Laughter.]

JOHNSON: What are the chances that the CIA is currently penetrated at the top? Especially by the Soviets?[19]

COLBY: It would be my guess, no. I can't say no absolutely. If it is, you don't know. We did have Alger Hiss, and those punks at various levels; then that Chinese fellow at FBIS, which was a surprise to me.[20] I don't say it's impossible. I just don't think so. Frankly, I think we would have heard about it by now. The big thing we have, which the British did not have, was the security clearances and the polygraph. Now I don't believe in the polygraph either, but it sure as hell helped us. My security people told me that, faced with the polygraph, people told us things that caused us not to hire them. As far as I'm concerned, it paid for itself right there.

JOHNSON: But the polygraph is no fool-proof system?

COLBY: No, and the real weakness was, once you get in there wasn't enough periodic checking.

CIA oversight

JOHNSON: How well has the IG [Inspector General] system worked inside the CIA?

COLBY: Well, it's like the IG in the military. They do periodic inspections, and they're a useful investigating team for the Director if something is strange. He just tells the IG to look into it. It's a bureaucratic mechanism to get something done; but as a great safety valve, I'm not so sure – any more than the IOB [Intelligence Oversight Board, a panel for intelligence accountability established in the White House in 1976]. I mean, it's there, but I don't think . . . Congress is the real safety check.

JOHNSON: And the press?

COLBY: And the press certainly; and the feeling that if something is wrong, people will make it known. I have no idea how many sources someone like Seymour Hersh has, but it must be dozens; they must be all over the place. And so if anything serious is wrong, it'll come out.

JOHNSON: Some say the FOIA [Freedom of Information Act] is the most important source of oversight . . .

COLBY: Well, in a way, but now they've exempted the operations files from that – for good reason; it was just a useless exercise. I think it's the press and the Congress, and the sort of the traditional feeling that if something is bad you should do something about it. The normal, good, loyal American citizen will think.

The role of the DCI

JOHNSON: Is the DCI biased towards the CIA?

COLBY: If anything, the DCI is inclined to take kind of a position showing that he is not biased. He obviously knows [the CIA] better; his contact with the rest of the services is episodic.

JOHNSON: Do we need a more powerful DCI?

COLBY: I think you've got to have a very close, coordinating mechanism. We use to have weekly meetings of the U.S. Intelligence Board, at which you get the senior representatives of each of the agencies there. This was very useful, because you could argue things out, you know, discuss them. And it was helpful not only in the substantive discussion of what's happening in Argentina (if you're making an estimate or something), but also in the practical sense – you know, how many of these goddamn satellites do we really need? Do we need fifty, or do we only need ten? And you work through those things. You do a lot of staff work beforehand – each agency does.

JOHNSON: As DCI, does one feel in control of the Agency?

COLBY: I think you have to work at it, and that means you have to use your chain-of-command. You also have to have some independent reporting as to what's going on. You get out of your chair and go out and look . . . talk to people. It's like running General Motors. You're not going to run everything in General Motors; but you can have the auditors and you have the other people to keep it under some semblance of control. I think that business of being in control also has something to do with the attitude of people. When George [H.W.] Bush came into the office [as DCI, following Colby in 1976], there was this wonderful story about him. Three days after he got there, they were having this meeting and somebody said, 'Well, there's a story in the press that says we did this or that.' And Bush said, 'What are they trying to do to us?' *Us* after three days. [After that], he had the place in the palm of his hand.

Turner was at the opposite end. He was afraid of them.

I use to say that one should have an outsider [as DCI], with an insider deputy, because the inside deputy will give the local knowledge and the outsider will give you a little of the independence. You take somebody who comes up through the career [ranks of the CIA]; your ideas are shaped by what you did during the career. I always thought the best Director I ever knew, including myself or anyone else, was John McCone [DCI, 1961–65], and he was an outsider. His first deputy was an outsider, too, General [Charles Pearre] Cabell; but, there were other professionals who ran the different Directorates.

JOHNSON: Why was McCone so good?

COLBY: He was just such a consummate manager. He would say, 'I want this done by tomorrow morning. I want this. I want this. Where is it?' No softness. 'Goddamn it, let's get it done!' He had the place totally excited. He'd go down to the White House, and write up six questions on a piece of paper on his way back in the car. He turned this over to [the dean of the CIA's intelligence analysts] Sherman Kent or whoever and say, 'I want these answered by 8:00 o'clock tomorrow morning': 'If we do this, what will China do? If we do that, what will the Soviets do?' 'Answer those questions.' And, of course, they [the analysts] loved it. Absolutely loved it. They worked like hell, and he would then go in and make no bones about what he thought about it [the analytic products].

JOHNSON: We've drifted away from the notion that we ought to have a military person as DDCIA [Deputy Director of the CIA, the second-in-command at the time after the DCI]. . . .

COLBY: Yeah, we used to feel we had to, but I don't think you do now. I think the reason you don't need to now is that the DIA [Defense Intelligence Agency] fulfills that function – giving senior status to the military. It used to be we thought that to keep some semblance of comity with the military that we had to have a military deputy [at the CIA, as deputy to the DCI]. This is not so important now.

Colby's self-appraisal

JOHNSON: What were your most important contributions as DCI?

COLBY: Well, I think the thing that will last longest is this constitutional thing – just getting through it [the Church Committee inquiry and related investigations] alive. I think that is the longest-term effect that I had. Oh, I fooled around with some of the internal machinery. The other thing I think I started, and Casey finished, was the NIO [National Intelligence Officer] system, which led to the reorganization of the analytical side. Sherman Kent points out in his book, *Strategic Intelligence*, published in 1947,[21] that you organize intelligence either by subject or by area. He said there are arguments for and against both ways. He said that, on balance, 'I think it ought to be area,' but he wasn't very strong about. So, we organized it by discipline: political, economic, scientific, military, all those.

And I got in and I remember one time asking to see some people talk about China, and, Jesus, fifteen people came in! And I realized I was the only central figure of all of those fifteen. I said, 'I can't do this for China, for the Soviet Union, and for everything else – this is crazy.' We had this Board, which I had doubts about anyway; so I set up the NIO system. I considered whether we should go ahead and try to re-organize the analysts; and I said, 'Christ, we have enough turmoil around here: no, not now.'

Casey did, and he did it very quickly after he went into office; he just reorganized. And, of course, I often wondered why the hell we did it this way, until somebody pointed out, 'That's the way you organize universities' – which have a different function than intelligence. Intelligence is supposed to react to problems and opportunities, and they come largely in geographic terms – not in economic terms or political terms. They come by geographic area.

JOHNSON: Say, 'What are we going to do in China?'

COLBY: Sure. This was one of the reasons – that inadequate organization in the early stage – that analysts didn't play a bigger role during those twenty-odd years, because they were all divided up. I remember there was a time, when I was Chief of the Far East Division, I was the one going to talk to State or the military about the Far East – not the analysts. I never read NSA [National Security Agency] traffic, yet here I would be representing intelligence in a meeting on policy, and I was the worst one to do it; it should have been an analyst. Now that is very much the case: the Chief of China, he's the guy who goes to the White House meetings for the Director.

JOHNSON: Can you recall any mistakes you made as DCI?

COLBY: Obviously, the Yom Kippur War[22] we didn't distinguish ourselves on.

JOHNSON: I guess there will always be surprises.

COLBY: There is that thesis. But my contention – in a way, a mental game – is that if intelligence does its work well and anticipates some problem arising and communicates this that to policy-makers, and policy-makers act so that the thing does not happen in a bad way but happens in a good way, intelligence turns out to be wrong – but wrong for the right reasons. So I think your record is: How many things do you get policy to move on, and how few bad surprises? I use to say, 'I don't mind good surprises, but I don't want any bad surprises.' And I think that is a legitimate demand. But you should be braced for the bad. On that Yom Kippur one, we just had convinced ourselves that it didn't make sense. And it didn't! But. . . .

Looking back on the 'Year of Intelligence'

JOHNSON: Would the CIA have been in big trouble if you hadn't cooperated with the Church and Pike Committees?

COLBY: I thought so. I was walking along by the Library of Congress one time – five, maybe eight, years ago-and this fellow who was Counsel for the House [Appropriations] Committee crossed the street to me, and he said, 'I just want to tell you something. I heard that you thought that, if you weren't cooperative with Congress, they would have gone out to destroy the Agency. I just want to tell you, you're absolutely right. We would have.' They were out for blood, so I was throwing things at them, trying to be *reasonably* responsive and trying to protect the Agency. And I considered, really, the greatest victory in that was the Church Committee report, which is not a bad report, it really is not an unbalanced report. It's a little more sanctimonious than I'd like to have had; but when they came down to that part about covert action, I thought we'd come home free – you know, we shouldn't use it very often, but we shouldn't dismiss it. I was really a little surprised, because I thought we'd have a little more antagonistic [report]. The Pike Committee report was useless; but the Church Committee report, if you read it through, hangs together pretty well.[23]

Economic espionage

JOHNSON: Should the CIA be more involved in economic intelligence and assisting American industry?

COLBY: My answer to that is it certainly ought to be more active in the economic analytical area, because economics is going to be a big subject for the next decade or so. It's a major subject and CIA has excellent capabilities in this area. Collection? Overt collection, fine, no problem; covert collection, very rarely and only when there is some strategic reason for it. If you're engaged in illegal espionage in another country, you're entitled to do it for your security; but you really don't [if your objective is simply] to save a few bucks. You don't need to use satellites to count Toyotas.

And what do you do with it [the intelligence]? Suppose you have the information that Toyota is going to come out with a new model, and you got it through a secret penetration – what do you do with it? Both I and Stan Turner experimented with putting out some [public] economic reports, and it was hopeless. It would be met with: 'Oh, this is spying!' And it had nothing to do with spies at all. Either they over-believed it, or just laughed about it – giggled. We did work up a set of relations with the other departments, comparable to the one we have with the Defense Department, where we funneled the information over to Commerce, to Treasury, to Agriculture, I guess, wherever else. Then they absorb it into their business, and they put it out. And they don't just put it out to Ford; they can't. They put it out evenly; and that means it has to go to the foreigners, too, who are by now smart enough to know how much information there is in this city.

But I think the risk factor is such that I would be sort of dubious about this. I won't say never – you know, never say never. But it would have to be something very vital. And, of course, controlling the illegal diversion of military-related equipment, that sort of thing, proliferation of weapons, all that sort of thing, that's fine sure.

The future of intelligence

JOHNSON: Will the future mission of U.S. intelligence change much?
COLBY: Not a helluva lot. [Colby referred me to a piece he had written recently on intelligence].[24]
JOHNSON: Thank you for spending this time with me.
COLBY: Thank you.

COMMENTARY: LOCH JOHNSON'S ORAL HISTORY INTERVIEW WITH WILLIAM COLBY, AND JOHNSON'S INTRODUCTION TO THAT INTERVIEW

Rhodri Jeffreys-Jones

William Colby's story is one of darkness and redemption. But he did not necessarily see that split. A proclivity to invest his life with uniform virtue comes across in his retrospective writings, and shows up also in the rather special oral history interview published in this volume. Of interest here are the background of the interviewer as well as the interviewee, and the problem of oral history as evidential genre as well as the issues that Colby addresses in the interview itself.

Loch Johnson notes that his interview with Colby took place in January 1991, at the time of the first American war against Iraq. Johnson is flagging up the important point that interviews are affected by the times in which they are conducted. Equally, it is appropriate to consider another influence on the interview: the interviewer.

Loch Johnson took his Ph.D. in Political Science from the University of California, and is currently Regents Professor at the University of Georgia. On the road to that senior academic post, he distinguished himself in public service. *Inter alia*, he was Staff Director for the Subcommittee on Intelligence Oversight, Permanent Select Committee on Intelligence, U.S. House of Representatives (1977–79), and Special Assistant to the Chairman of the 1990s Aspin-Brown Commission on intelligence reform. Of particular relevance to the Colby interview, Johnson was Special Assistant to the Chairman of the Select Committee on Intelligence, U.S. Senate (commonly known as the Church Committee). He was one of a number of gifted scholars retained by the famous inquiry. John Elliff and Athan Theoharis, for example, helped it to probe the affairs of the FBI. But it was Johnson who became pre-eminent among these scholars for his erudition on the CIA.

Johnson's public service took place in Democratic administrations, and his extensive publication record marks him as a thoughtful advocate of an intelligence establishment that is both effective and democratically accountable. But although his mission has yielded a variety of crops, one of them is only partially harvested. For Johnson has interviewed every CIA director from Richard Helms to George Tenet, covering, in this way, the direction of central intelligence from 1966 to 2004. The Helms interview appeared in the journal *Intelligence and National Security*, and Johnson hopes one day to collect all of the interviews within a single volume. Thus far, however, the Colby text that appears here is only the second to see the light of day.[1]

As an evidential genre, oral interviews with governmental figures fall roughly into the category of official memoir. Like other memoirists, the interviewee can be expected to put the best possible spin in his period of office, and to withhold information that might embarrass him, or discredit his motives. In the case of secret intelligence there are, of course, further considerations that militate against candour.

In the case of the Johnson series of interviews, there are further potential complications. One of these has to do with the possibly inverse relationship between immediacy and objectivity. Some of Johnson's interviewees were still in office as CIA chiefs, while others had retired. According to Johnson, directors 'were likely to be more candid when out of office'. However, he believes that those interviewed in post, like James Woolsey and William Webster, still 'seemed to be forthcoming'.

Another complication is that Johnson had an agenda. The transcripts of his interviews depart from the memoir genre pure and simple, for Johnson exercised the interviewer's prerogative to steer. He wanted 'to capture the sentiments of a collection of intelligence chiefs during the period after the Cold War (1991–98) – as it turned out, an interlude before the spate of new wars America would enter against terrorism and suspected WMDs in Iraq; a time of horrendous intelligence failures'. He is thus asking Colby not just to comment on his time in office at the CIA, but also to act as an expert witness on events in later years. Since Johnson's questions, as well as the answers to them, were frozen in time (the transcripts are based on 'verbatim recordings'), they were clearly not influenced by events subsequent to 1991. But Johnson's, and others', subsequent take on the interview can hardly fail to have been influenced by the harsh winds of partisanship that blew in the 1990s and subsequently.[2]

With regard to the troubled 1970s, Johnson's comment that Colby pursued a policy of propitiation carries authority, as Johnson was at the receiving end of the propitiation initiative, and in a position to judge its sincerity at first hand. The interview confirms that Colby was in favour of a legislative charter for the CIA, and that he was never highly regarded by President Ford, a point on which the former director is refreshingly candid and unresentful. He is also remarkably gracious about George H.W. Bush, the official Ford appointed in his stead after

Colby was fired from the CIA directorship in 1976. His opinion of Stansfield Turner is, however, less generous. Turner found it difficult to match Bush's in-house popularity when he took over in 1977, came under fire for being a 'political' appointee, and incurred the wrath of neoconservatives of the Reagan stripe by preferring technical to human intelligence. Turner provoked deep hatreds when he pruned Colby's old domain, the operations directorate.

Though hated by conservatives on account of his cooperation with the Church inquiry, Colby adopts a conservative anti-Turner stance, for a reason that hints at his bias. For William Colby was a covert operator by trade. It is perhaps because of this background that he enlists with the conventionally-minded snipers who aim not just at Turner, but also at the House intelligence inquiry chaired by Otis Pike, an investigation that commented adversely on the Agency's policy on Kurds and Iraq (with devastating prescience, as later events have confirmed), and focussed on what Richard Aldrich terms the cost benefit approach to intelligence (again, with the wisdom of hindsight, not a bad thing). It makes one wonder how qualified Colby was to absorb the theoretical approach of Sherman Kent, to which he alludes, and to shake-up the estimating process.[3]

According to your point of view, Colby on the post-1970s years comes across as a voice of reason, or as someone with a subjective dislike for the Reaganites and all they stand for. Not for him, he claims, the Iran-Contra show. Nor does he approve of the cross-contamination of politics and intelligence. This timeless stricture seems to have been lost on those who govern(ed) in Johnson's 'time of horrendous intelligence failures'. Colby comes across as slightly dated on some issues, such as the sale of proprietaries. The modern problem seems to be the selling on of proprietaries' equipment such as worn-out operations choppers with wound-back odometers. Sadly, his concern about cavalier attitudes to habeas corpus rights seems to be even more out of date.

Turning to Colby's remarks about the pre-1970s, he seems to sanction practices of the type that he condemned in Iran-Contra. Even allowing for the nature of his career, his emphatic approval of 1950s/1960s covert operations is striking. It does not occur to Colby that the problem with the Bay of Pigs operation was its initiation, rather than its failure. As the journalist Thomas B. Morgan found in a persuasive study in 1967, the CIA's covert operations were the main reason why the world's most charismatic democracy was losing hearts and minds, even when competing with the vilest of enemies.[4]

This is the dark side of Colby, and it could not be much darker. He was ruthless to the point of committing crimes against humanity. In the course of his OSS operation in Norway, he persuaded a German patrol to surrender, but, according to his biographer John Prados, one of the surrendering soldiers shouted out, and Colby's trigger-happy men wiped out the entire German unit.[5] When Colby took over the CIA's East Asian division, he had a hand in the execution of more than a million suspected communists in Indonesia. And then, as Johnson indicates, there was the higher-profile Phoenix operation in Vietnam, with at least 20,000 people killed. The 1970s tears that Colby shed over the CIA's assassination policy seem, at first sight, to have been of the crocodile variety.

However, this brings us to the redemption of William Colby, and to a question that every civilized interviewer would shudder to ask. Colby's daughter Catherine suffered from depression, and was upset by Phoenix. She died from complications of anxiety in 1973. Is it possible that the father went from grief to remorse, and played the good boy in American public affairs for at least a couple of years? Loch Johnson refrained from asking this indelicate question, just as Prados did not entertain the theory in his book. It must remain a matter for speculation whether Colby's mid-1970s support for democratic oversight was a form of atonement.

Notes

A conversation with former DCI William E. Colby: Spymaster during the 'Year of the Intelligence Wars'

Loch K. Johnson

1   For an account of this period, see Loch K. Johnson, *A Season of Inquiry: The Senate Intelligence Investigation* (Lexington, KY: University Press of Kentucky, 1985).
2   The 'jewels' included details on CIA assassination plots against foreign leaders, drug testing on unwitting subjects, opening the mail of selected American citizens without a warrant, and spying on Vietnam War protesters. On their emergence into the public domain, see National Security Archive, 'The CIA's Family Jewels: Agency Violated Charter for 25 Years, Wiretapped Journalists and Dissidents', 21 June 2007, http://www.gwu.edu/~nsarchiv/NSAEBB/NSAEBB222/index.htm The entirety of the 'family jewels' were released – and posted on-line – on 26 June 2007 and are available at: http://www.gwu.edu/~nsarchiv/NSAEBB/NSAEBB222/family_jewels_full.pdf
3   David S. Robarge, Book Review: 'Lost Crusader: The Secret Wars of CIA Director William Colby by John Prados', *Studies in Intelligence*, 47/ 4 (2003): https://www.cia.gov/library/center-for-the-study-of-intelligence/kent-csi/docs/v47i4a07p.htm
4   See Dale Andradé, *Ashes to Ashes: The Phoenix Program and the Vietnam War* (Lexington, MA: D.C. Heath, 1990).
5   For a biography, see John Prados, *Lost Crusader: The Secret Wars of CIA Director William Colby* (New York: Oxford University Press, 2003).
6   William E. Colby with Peter Forbath, *Honorable Men: My Life in the CIA* (New York: Simon & Schuster, 1978); William E. Colby and James McCargar, *Lost Victory: A Firsthand Account of America's Sixteen-Year Involvement in Vietnam* (Chicago, IL: Contemporary Books, 1989).
7   Rep. Otis Pike (D-NY) headed up a panel of inquiry in the House of Representatives during 1975. By mutual agreement, the Church Committee focused on questions of intelligence improprieties at home and abroad, while the Pike Committee examined questions related to the quality of intelligence collection and analysis.
8   The Pike Committee engaged in a running battle with Colby and the Ford administration during its investigation, whereas the Church Committee attempted to have a more cordial relationship, based on the notion that more flies could be attracted by honey. The vitriol between the Pike panel and the administration led to the failure of that committee to win the trust of House members and the investigation faltered in a whirlwind of dissension inside the panel and with the administration. See Frank J. Smist, Jr., *Congress Oversees the United States Intelligence Community, 1947–1989* (Knoxville, TN: University of Tennessee Press, 1990).
9   According to the Hughes-Ryan Act of 1974, covert actions were to be reported to Congress 'in a timely fashion', which the floor colloquia preceding passage of this law seemed to define as within two days.

10   In 1976–78, the Senate Select Committee on Intelligence attempted to draft an omnibus charter for intelligence to replace the sketchy details of the National Security Act of 1947. This proposed law became long and convoluted and eventually collapsed under its own weight, with the help of lobbying against it by the intelligence bureaucracy. See Loch K. Johnson, 'Legislative Reform of Intelligence Policy,' *Polity* 17 (Spring 1985), pp. 549–73.

11   In 1982, Congress passed the Intelligence Identities Act to protect intelligence officers and their agents against the disclosure of their names by outsiders, whether newspaper reporters or enemies of the United States seeking to destroy the CIA and the other intelligence services. Four years earlier, in 1978, Congress passed the Foreign Intelligence Surveillance Act (FISA) – a major Church Committee recommendation – that required judicial warrants for intelligence wiretaps and other forms of surveillance, instead of just an order from a president or some other executive branch official.

12   For evidence that money was raised from foreign nations, see Senate Select Committee on Secret Military Assistance to Iran and the Nicaraguan Opposition and House Select Committee to Investigate Covert Arms Transactions with Iran, *Hearings and Final Report* (Washington, DC: Government Printing Office, 1987).

13   Detailees are individuals loaned to the Executive Office of the Presidency from various government agencies around Washington, DC, for employment by the president without cost to the White House.

14   See William E. Colby, testimony, 'The CIA and the Media,' *Hearings*, Permanent Select Committee on Intelligence, U.S. House of Representatives (Washington, DC: Government Printing Office, 1979).

15   That is, human agents don't just gather intelligence, they can also engage in covert actions as well as counter-intelligence deceptions and penetrations.

16   This refers to the connection between intelligence professionals and policy-makers. Transferring intelligence from the former to the latter is rife with difficulties, perhaps the most important being the distortion of intelligence by policy-makers to suit their own political needs.

17   Yale University history professor Sherman Kent served in the CIA as a high-level analyst and argued consistently for a strong barrier between analysts and policy officials, as a means of preserving the neutrality and integrity of analysts.

18   Yuri Ivanovich Nosenko was a Soviet defector banished to the CIA's training facility at Camp Perry ('The Farm') in Virginia, where he was confined and interrogated at length to test his bona fides. For one account, see Edward Jay Epstein, *Legend: The Secret World of Lee Harvey Oswald* (New York: Reader's Digest Press, 1978).

19   We now know that Aldrich H. Ames was a Soviet/Russian mole at the time of this interview, as was FBI agent Robert P. Hanssen.

20   Larry Wu-tai Chin became a translator for the United States on Okinawa and later gained employment at the CIA as a translator for its Foreign Broadcast Information Service. See Ronald Kessler, *Inside the CIA* (New York: Pocket Books, 1992), p. 155.

21   Sherman Kent, *Strategic Intelligence for American World Policy* (Princeton, NJ: Princeton University Press, 1949).

22   The unpredicted war between Egypt and Israel in 1973.

23   For the Church Committee Report, see Select Committee to Study Governmental Operations with Respect to Intelligence Activities, *Final Report*, Sen. Rept. No. 94–755, 6 vols., 94th Cong., 2nd. Sess. (Washington, DC: Government Printing Office, November 20, 1975). The Pike Report was leaked to a New York City magazine: 'The CIA Report the President Doesn't Want You to Read: The Pike Papers', *Village Voice*, February 16 and 23, 1976. A third investigation in 1975, this one by the White House under the leadership of Vice President Nelson Rockefeller, was expected to whitewash the intelligence abuses, but instead produced a hard-hitting report focused

on illegal CIA domestic operations; see Commission on CIA Activities within the United States, *Report to the President* (Washington, DC: Government Printing Office, 1975).

24   William E. Colby, 'Intelligence in a New World', *Mediterranean Quarterly* 1 (Fall 1990), pp. 46–59.

Commentary: Loch Johnson's oral history interview with William Colby, and Johnson's introduction to that interview

Rhodri Jeffreys-Jones

1   Loch Johnson, 'Spymaster Richard Helms: an interview with the former US Director of Central Intelligence', *Intelligence and National Security*, 18/3 (Autumn 2003), pp. 24–44; Johnson, email to author, 10 August 2006.
2   All quotations from Johnson, email to author, 10 August 2006.
3   Richard J. Aldrich, *Espionage, Security and Intelligence in Britain, 1945–1970* (Manchester: Manchester University Press, 1998), p. 5.
4   Thomas B. Morgan, *The Anti-Americans* (London: Michael Joseph, 1967), pp. 9–10.
5   John Prados, *Lost Crusader: The Secret Wars of CIA Director William Colby* (New York: Oxford University Press, 2003), p. 33.

12   The Butler Report, 2004

*Peter Jackson, Robert Jervis and
Loch K. Johnson*

OVERVIEW: THE BUTLER REPORT AS AN HISTORICAL DOCUMENT

Peter Jackson

The Butler Report, which is the result of an investigation conducted in 2004 by a high-profile Committee of Privy Counsellors chaired by Lord Butler of Brockwell, marked the culmination of a 'season of inquiry' into British intelligence reporting on Iraq prior to the invasion of that country in March 2003.[1] The report is the fourth of a series of official inquiries conducted in 2003–4.[2] It was drafted within a context of intense public criticism in the United Kingdom over the government's policy toward Iraq in general and its use of intelligence to justify this policy in particular. This criticism paralleled similar charges levelled against the Bush Administration in the United States, which also commissioned a series of official investigations into American intelligence reporting on Iraq.[3] The published reports resulting from these various inquiries provide a wealth of information concerning the manner in which secret intelligence on Iraq was collected, collated and analysed by British and American intelligence services. They therefore constitute an important source for the study of foreign and security policy-making at the opening of the twenty-first century.

The Butler Report will be of particular interest to scholars of British intelligence. It provides extensive excerpts from the assessments of the Joint Intelligence Committee (JIC). This material is supplemented by numerous references to, and quotations from, key policy documents (several of which have since been leaked to the press) that serves to set the collection and assessment of intelligence information within its wider policy context. In addition to bringing this material into the public domain, the report also discusses in detail the nature of the human intelligence reports provided by the Secret Intelligence Service (SIS) as well as the role these reports played in the assessment process. All of this is without precedent in the history of British intelligence. The excerpt of the report printed below is the Butler Committee's 'Conclusions on Iraq'. While these conclusions are fascinating in their own right, they can only be understood properly when they are read within the wider context of the rest of the report. This introductory essay is therefore a discussion of the report as a whole with specific reference to the findings and recommendations of the committee concerning the case of Iraq.

The character of the document

The five-person 'Committee of Privy Counsellors' appointed to conduct the inquiry was chaired by Lord Butler of Brockwell. Before his retirement, Robin Butler was a distinguished civil servant whose career had included service as private secretary to Prime Ministers Edward Heath, Harold Wilson and Margaret Thatcher and then as Cabinet Secretary and Head of the Home Civil Service during the premierships of Margaret Thatcher, John Major and Tony Blair. After his retirement in 1998, Butler was appointed Master of University College Oxford and had also served as a member on the Royal Commission for the Reform of the House of Lords. Butler was joined on the committee by Sir John Chilton, another retired civil servant who had occupied a range of important posts within the Home Office; Field Marshal the Lord Inge, a former Chief of the General Staff and Chief of Defence Staff; Ann Taylor, a Member of Parliament, former Labour Party Chief Whip and Chair of the Parliamentary Intelligence and Security Committee; and Michael Mates, a Conservative Member of Parliament, also on the Intelligence and Security Committee and a former Chair of the House of Commons Select Committee on Defence.[4] All five authors of the Butler Report had extensive experience in dealing with intelligence and security-related issues. All, moreover, had spent much or all of their careers immersed in the committee culture of the British government machinery. There were no genuine 'outsiders' on the Butler Committee. This explains, at least in part, the report's reluctance to address the operating assumptions and fundamental structures of the British system for the collection, analysis and use of intelligence.

The terms of reference set for the Butler Committee by the government were an issue of considerable controversy. On 3 February 2004, Foreign Secretary Jack Straw outlined the committee's remit to the House of Commons as follows:

> [T]o investigate the intelligence coverage available in respect of WMD programmes in countries of concern and on the global trade in WMD, taking into account what is now known about these programmes; as part of this work, to investigate the accuracy of intelligence on Iraqi WMD up to March 2003, and to examine any discrepancies between the intelligence gathered, evaluated and used by the Government before the conflict, and between that intelligence and what has been discovered by the Iraq survey group since the end of the conflict; and to make recommendations to the Prime Minister for the future on the gathering, evaluation and use of intelligence on WMD, in the light of the difficulties of operating in countries of concern.[5]

The committee was thus instructed to consider the performance of the intelligence services in supporting counter-proliferation policy, to evaluate the accuracy of intelligence on Iraqi non-conventional weapons programmes and to make recommendations for improving the collection and assessment of intelligence on weapons of mass destruction (WMD). The Butler Committee took oral evidence in camera from an impressive range of ministers that included Prime Minister Tony Blair, Foreign Secretary Jack Straw, and Attorney-General Lord Goldsmith. It also interviewed key policy advisers from both the Prime Minister's staff and the Cabinet Office, including John Scarlett, the chair of the Joint Intelligence Committee.

The Butler Committee interpreted these terms of reference as a mandate to concentrate 'principally on structures, systems and processes rather than on the actions of individuals'. The widespread expectation that the report would attribute individual blame and pass judgement on government policy was therefore bound to be disappointed. The Butler Report does neither. At the same time, the committee's investigations were rigorous and its final report ranged well beyond the accuracy of intelligence reporting to consider the decision-making procedures of the Blair government. Although it is expressed in the cautious and understated language of the Whitehall officialdom, the report contains detailed criticisms not only of the manner in which some intelligence assessments were drafted but also of what it judged to be a subversion of the time-honoured procedures of Cabinet government in the formulation of policy toward Iraq.

In addition to its interesting findings, the Butler Report provides a wealth of raw material that will be invaluable to scholars researching questions ranging from the role of intelligence in British counter-proliferation policy to the importance of international intelligence cooperation to the effectiveness of the British system of 'joint intelligence' and 'government assessment' during the crucial period leading up to the invasion of Iraq. Of particular interest are the appendices – which contain lengthy excerpts from JIC assessments of 12 March 2002, 21 August 2002, 9 September 2002 and 24 September 2002. There are, finally, interesting quotations from earlier JIC assessments dating back to the early 1990s. This material would normally be closed to researchers for at least thirty years. There are also illuminating analyses of the British intelligence effort against the proliferation of biological, chemical and especially nuclear weapons from Libya to Malaysia. These sections of the report suffered relative neglect in media reporting as a result of the national and international fixation on Iraq.

The political context of the report

British participation in the invasion and 'pacification' of Iraq cast a long shadow over the final two terms of the Labour government under Prime Minister Tony Blair. The failure of the invading coalition to turn up substantial evidence of non-conventional Iraqi weapons programmes gave rise to widespread charges that the British public was deceived into believing that such programmes existed and posed a threat to the United Kingdom. These charges had particular resonance because the Blair government had made public use of British intelligence assessments of Iraqi weapons programmes in an effort to garner public support for its increasingly hard-line policy towards the regime of Saddam Hussein.

At the centre of the controversy were a series of confident assertions about Iraq's ongoing production of chemical and biological weapons made in an official dossier published by the government on 24 September 2002. The dossier was drafted by the chair of the JIC, John Scarlett. In a foreword to this document, Prime Minister Blair asserted that, although the government 'cannot publish everything we know', intelligence assessments had 'established beyond doubt' that 'Saddam has continued to produce chemical and biological weapons' and 'continues in his efforts to develop nuclear weapons'. Blair further claimed that these weapons were 'vital to [Saddam's] strategic interests, and in particular his goal of regional domination'. Most sensationally, the Prime Minister also stressed that Iraqi 'military planning allows for some of the WMD to be ready within 45 minutes of an order to use them'. He concluded that '[t]he threat is serious and current'. All of these claims were supported in the text of the dossier, which was expressed in the language of JIC 'judgements'.[6] Significantly, the contrast between the term 'we judge' deployed in the text of the dossier and the Prime Minister's assertion that the JIC had 'established' the existence of Iraqi non-conventional weapons programmes 'beyond doubt' was not picked up by observers during the period leading up to the invasion the following March.

It is worth emphasising that the decision to publish current JIC assessments in an official dossier was entirely without precedent. As one distinguished historian of British intelligence has observed: 'No government had ever previously published a JIC assessment, and no JIC assessment had ever been prepared with public consumption in mind.'[7] The assertions made in this dossier would become the focal point of four public inquiries into the role of intelligence in British policy towards Iraq.

Despite its efforts to shape opinion through the public disclosure of intelligence, the Blair government took the decision to make war in the face of widespread opposition to its policy. The government had been trying to build public support for a more hard-line posture towards Iraq since early 2002. But the credibility of the government's case was undermined seriously in February 2003 when it circulated a 'briefing document' entitled 'Iraq: its infrastructure of concealment, deception and intimidation' – much of which was exposed as having been plagiarised from the research of a doctoral student.[8] An ICM poll conducted on the eve of the invasion found that 52 per cent of Britons opposed war with only 29 per cent expressing approval for government policy.[9] The high level of popular opposition to the war was central to the government's decision to publish its two dossiers on the Iraqi threat. As the Prime Minister recalled in testimony to the Butler Committee, it was this opposition that prompted publication of the government's dossier:

> the purpose of the dossier was simply to say 'here is the intelligence . . . there is a real issue here' . . . there was a tremendous clamour coming for it and I think a clamour to the extent that, had we resisted, it would have become completely impossible.[10]

The opposition to which Blair referred did not abate even after significant military successes were achieved during the initial phases of the conflict. Indeed, it was further stimulated in late May 2003 by press allegations that the intelligence information in the September 2002 Dossier had been 'sexed up' by government officials in order to make a stronger case for war. Particular controversy surrounded the '45 minute claim' in both the Dossier and the Prime Minister's foreword.[11] These charges led to an inquiry by the House of Commons Select Committee on Foreign Affairs (FAC) in June 2003, which concluded that there had been no improper government influence in the drafting of the Dossier. This inquiry was not granted access to either raw intelligence reports or JIC assessments but was forced to rely on private briefings by intelligence officials.[12]

Public interest in the role of intelligence assessments of the Iraqi threat in the decision for war surged again with the suicide of Dr David Kelly in July 2003. Dr Kelly had been an expert on chemical and biological weapons within the Proliferation and Arms Control Secretariat at the Ministry of Defence (MOD). In this capacity he had been charged with providing advice to both the MOD's Defence Intelligence Staff (DIS: the largest assessment organ within the British intelligence community) as well as the Secret Intelligence Service. Most importantly, Kelly had been the central source for media reporting on political interference in the drafting of the September dossier.[13] It was in the immediate aftermath of his suicide that the Parliamentary Intelligence and Security Committee (ISC) conducted a second inquiry, this time into the assessment of intelligence on Iraqi 'weapons of mass destruction'. The ISC inquiry was able to consult ninety-three JIC assessments as well as various drafts of the September dossier. It too found that there had been no improper government interference in the intelligence material contained in this Dossier. But it did offer the notable criticism that the 'uncertainty' inherent in the process of assessing Iraqi weapons programmes should have been made 'clearer' in the published Dossier.[14] Yet the ISC was not well placed to conduct a thorough analysis of the assessment process because it did not have access to the raw intelligence upon which the JIC assessments were based. As Richard Aldrich has observed, 'The ISC is only just inside the ring of secrecy and to an extent has to believe what it is told'.[15]

The events of May-July 2003 prompted a third government inquiry into the intelligence-related issues, when Lord Hutton was appointed to conduct an investigation into 'the circumstances surrounding the death of Dr David Kelly'. The focus of this inquiry, however, remained fixed overwhelmingly on the question of inappropriate political interference in the drafting the September Dossier. Lord Hutton's investigations turned up a host of official emails and memoranda pertaining to the compilation of the government's Dossier. This evidence provides fascinating insights into the way key Downing Street officials understood intelligence reporting and assessment and sought to present intelligence material to the British public. It also details dissent expressed by the Nuclear, Biological and Chemical Technical Intelligence section within the Defence Intelligence Staff. This dissent was focused on the level of certainty conveyed in the Dossier in general and on the '45 minute claim' in particular.[16]

The evidence gathered by the Hutton Inquiry is published on its official website. In addition to minutes and memoranda drafted by DIS officials, it includes interviews with senior intelligence officials and sensitive email exchanges between Jonathan Powell, the Prime Minister's Chief of Staff, Alastair Campbell, the Blair government's Director of Communications, and JIC Chair, John Scarlett. Official disclosure of this kind was unprecedented and anticipated the implementation of the UK Freedom of Information Act in January 2005. Under the existing regime of weeding and filtering, some of the evidence on the Inquiry website would almost certainly never have made it into the National Archives and much of that which did would have been held back for fifty years. And yet, despite the fascinating material made available by Lord Hutton's investigations, there is a danger that the new legislation may not be an unalloyed benefit for scholars. Disturbing rumours that the Freedom of Information Act has given rise to a 'new culture of destruction' within the machinery of government have prompted one veteran researcher to observe that its implementation may be 'a good thing for journalists who want an easy way of chasing issues such as the expense accounts of ministers' but it is also likely to prove 'a bad thing for political historians who hope that even sensitive records will eventually be available [to researchers]'.[17]

Lord Hutton endorsed the conclusion of the House of Commons Foreign Affairs and the Intelligence and Security Committees that the September dossier did not contain deliberate distortions of available intelligence. At the same time his inquiry uncovered clear evidence that key members of the Prime Minister's staff had played a role in shaping the language in which intelligence judgements were expressed in the document. Hutton judged that:

> I do not consider that it was improper for Mr Scarlett and the JIC to take into account suggestions as to drafting made by 10 Downing Street and to adopt those suggestions if they were consistent with the intelligence available to the JIC. However, I consider that the possibility cannot be completely ruled out that the desire of the Prime Minister to have a dossier which, whilst consistent with the available intelligence, was as strong as possible in relation to the threat posed by Saddam Hussein's WMD, may have subconsciously influenced Mr Scarlett and the other members of the JIC to make the wording of the Dossier somewhat stronger than it would have been if it had been contained in a normal JIC assessment.[18]

Hutton's conclusions led to further controversy. The Blair government, and in particular its former director of communications Alastair Campbell, claimed vindication. But in the British public sphere the report was widely branded a 'whitewash'.[19] Pressure on the government to revisit the question of intelligence assessments intensified as it became clear that the Iraq Survey Group, established in June 2003 to investigate Iraqi weapon's programmes, was unlikely to turn up evidence of non-conventional weapons. Before the US Congress, the Director of the Iraq Survey Group, Dr David Kay, judged that 'It turns out we were all wrong probably, in my judgement, and that is most disturbing.'[20] Once it became clear that the Bush administration intended to establish a commission to investigate the shortcomings of the US intelligence effort, calls to set up a similar inquiry in Great Britain could not be resisted. Foreign Secretary Straw cited Kay's judgement when he announced the appointment and remit of the Butler inquiry to the House of Commons on 3 February.[21]

To sum up, the decision to appoint a committee to investigate the quality of intelligence on Iraqi weapons programmes, like the decision to publish a dossier on this subject in 2002, was taken in response to widespread public disquiet over the government's policy towards Iraq.

Diagnoses

Informed observers have underlined the 'understated language' of the Butler Report and its emphasis on collective responsibility – an almost inevitable consequence of the committee's decision to focus on 'structures and processes'. Yet the report does not refrain from making a range of robust criticisms of the quality of intelligence collected on Iraqi weapons systems, the way this intelligence was assessed and the way it was integrated into the policy-making process. In its consideration of the decision-making process, in particular, it goes further than the much longer report prepared by the WMD Commission in the United States.[22]

The international context and inspection regimes

One aspect of the report that is often missed in commentary is the fact that, following the terms of reference set down by the government, it places the intelligence effort against Iraqi chemical, biological and nuclear weapons programmes within the larger context of British counter-proliferation policy. One of the government's aims in setting the terms of reference in this way was almost certainly to underline the fact that British policy towards Iraq should be understood within the wider context of multiple but inter-connected proliferation threats from a various regions. In addition to the two substantial chapters devoted to Iraq, there is a chapter entitled 'Countries of concern other than Iraq and global trade', another that focuses on terrorism and another that examines the role of intelligence in British counter-proliferation machinery. The first of these examines British intelligence and policy efforts against Libya, Iran and North Korea as well as against a clandestine network established to promote the trade of nuclear technology established by renegade Pakistani scientist Abdul Qadeer (AQ) Khan. The Butler Report judged all four of these cases to have been 'to a greater or lesser extent success stories' characterised by 'an impressive performance by the intelligence community and policy-makers in each case, and overall'. This point is emphasised again in the concluding sections of the report – which make clear that the case of Iraq should be understood as one failure within a wider context of considerable success against the proliferation of non-conventional weapons systems.[23]

Among the interesting points made in the sections on Iraq in the report are a series of observations concerning the role of the international inspection regime established in the aftermath of the 1991 Gulf War. The Butler Committee concluded:

> The most authoritative information on the status of Iraq's nuclear, biological, chemical and ballistic missile programmes in this period came from reports produced by the United Nations Special Commission [UNSCOM] and by the International Atomic Energy Agency [IAEA] derived from their inspection activities on the ground.

It is clear that, when the inspection activities of these agencies were disbanded in 1998, the flow of intelligence on Iraqi programmes to the British government fell off dramatically. This judgement, significantly, rests largely on JIC assessments during this period. One such assessment from May 2001, for example, admitted, 'Our knowledge of developments in Iraq's WMD and ballistic missile programmes since Desert Fox air operations in December 1998 is patchy.' Another prepared on 15 March 2002 described the state of intelligence reporting as 'sporadic and patchy'.[24] One of the chief criticisms made in the Butler Report is that these caveats were not carried through to the judgements expressed in the Dossier published by the government the following September.

The secret intelligence service and human intelligence

Of the many conclusions reached by the Butler Committee, the best-known is almost certainly the judgement that the British intelligence lacked well-placed human sources reporting on Iraqi chemical and biological weapons programmes during the period leading up to the invasion of 2003. The report indicates that, in the period leading up to the publication of the September Dossier, SIS possessed five 'main' sources of intelligence on Iraqi capabilities. A sixth 'new source on trial' came on stream only in September 2002. Of the five, the two 'dominant' sources are judged to have been reliable when reporting on questions upon which they possessed first-hand knowledge. Crucially, however, neither had direct knowledge of Iraqi chemical or biological weapons programmes. Over the course of 2002 both were asked for information on this issue as a result of the British government's increased desire for intelligence on Iraqi violations of UN Security Council Resolution 687. The reports they provided on this question were based on 'hearsay' in the case of the first dominant source and 'sub-sources' in the case of the second. The Report observes that attempts to validate this reporting in the aftermath of the invasion had raised 'serious doubts' about its reliability. Similarly, the validity of the third main SIS source, which appears to have provided the information upon which the '45 minute claim' was based, has also 'come into question'.[25]

The sixth SIS source began reporting on 10 September 2002 – just as the September Dossier was being drafted. The information received from this 'new source on trial' (recruited from within the Iraqi military) complemented existing intelligence on Iraqi production of chemical and biological agents. The timely arrival of this intelligence played an important role in the decision to overrule the dissent expressed from within the DIS concerning the level of certainty conveyed in the government's dossier.[26] Further reporting received since April 2000 from 'a liaison service' suggested that Iraq was developing mobile biological agent production facilities. This source was the notorious agent 'Curveball' run by the German *Bundesnachrichtendienst* (BND) since 1999.[27] While SIS has yet to dismiss all of the information provided from this source, the Butler Report nonetheless concludes that 'Reports received from the liaison service on Iraqi production of biological agent were seriously flawed.'[28] The precise role played by 'Curveball' information in the construction of British intelligence assessments on Iraqi capabilities remains mysterious.

Not all SIS sources provided corroborating information on Iraqi chemical and biological weapons programmes however. In fact, two of the five 'main sources' forwarded intelligence that the Butler Report describes (with frustrating vagueness) as 'less worrying'. This intelligence, significantly, is now regarded as having been reliable.[29] In assessing the overall quality of intelligence collection on Iraqi chemical and biological weapons capabilities, the committee observed that the most serious problems emerged when 'agents who were known to be reliable were asked to report on issues beyond their normal territory'. This led to hearsay and sub-source information that was unreliable. '[B]ecause of the scarcity of sources and the urgent requirement for intelligence', the report concluded, 'more credence was given to untried agents than would normally be the case.'[30] In sum, SIS had difficulty meeting ever-more urgent demands for intelligence on a difficult subject (chemical and biological weapons programmes) from a 'hard' target (Iraq). In his testimony before the committee, the Chief of SIS, Sir Richard Dearlove, alluded to 'pressure on the service to produce good intelligence'.[31]

The Joint Intelligence Committee

The Butler Report provides important insights into the way intelligence was interpreted by the assessment machinery of the British government. The Report's judgements focus primarily on three assessments prepared on 15 March, 21 August and 9 September 2002 and on their relationship to the government's September Dossier. The Butler Committee made three chief criticisms of the JIC's role. The first concerned the quality of JIC assessments under consideration. The Report judges that the incomplete and inferential character of received intelligence was not always reflected sufficiently in the language used in the JIC judgements concerning Iraqi capabilities. The second criticism is that the JIC, which assumed the responsibility for drafting the government Dossier, failed to convey to the public the inferential character of its reasoning and assessments. It thus left the impression of a greater level of certainty concerning the nature of the threat posed by Iraq. Third, the report pointed to a breakdown in the process of all-source analysis and 'government assessment' resulting from a failure to share vital information across relevant agencies within the UK intelligence community.

All three of the JIC assessments cited at length in the report contain repeated references to the 'sporadic and patchy' nature of available intelligence on Iraqi non-conventional weapons programmes. The Butler Report notes that the conclusion that Iraq possessed chemical and biological weapons and was likely to use them - expressed with growing certainty in the assessment of 21 August and especially that of 9 September – was based in part on a single human intelligence report from one source but 'mainly on the JIC's own judgements'.[32]

The Butler Committee made four important criticisms of the quality of JIC assessments during this period. First, it stressed, 'we were struck by the relative thinness of the intelligence base supporting the greater firmness of the JIC's judgements on Iraqi production and possession of chemical and biological weapons, especially the inferential nature of much of it'. Second, the report judged that the intelligence which was represented by the JIC as 'confirming' the information received from 'Curveball' should instead have been described as 'complementary'. Third, the Committee admonished the JIC for failing to mention that material in one of the human intelligence reports suggested that most members of the Iraqi leadership were not confident that it would be possible to make use of chemical and biological weapons. The report judges that this information should have been included in the 9 September Assessment, even if only to be discounted by the JIC.[33] Fourth, alluding to the tendency toward worst-case analyses, the Butler Committee pointed to the iniquitous effects of 'layering': a process in which estimates are based on previous judgements without carrying forward qualifications and uncertainties. 'As a result' the report concludes, 'there was a risk of over-cautious or worst-case estimates, shorn of their caveats, becoming the "prevailing wisdom".'[34] This syndrome was also highlighted by American investigators as having undermined US intelligence estimates of the Iraqi threat.[35] All four of these criticisms are substantial. And yet, after detailing these errors in assessment, which, it is important to remember, were made within the context of a decided hardening of British policy toward Iraq, the Butler Committee nonetheless concluded that it found 'no evidence of JIC assessments and the judgements inside them being pulled in any particular direction to meet the policy concerns of senior officials on the JIC'.[36]

The report also makes trenchant criticisms of the manner in which intelligence assessments were presented to the public in the September Dossier. The report undertakes a detailed comparison of the language used in the three key JIC assessments, on the one hand, and that deployed in the Dossier, on the other. The result is compelling evidence that the qualifications and cautions contained in all three assessments were either edited out or systematically played down in the published Dossier.[37] This was despite warnings expressed by Dr Brian Jones, head of the Nuclear, Biological and Chemical Weapons section of the DIS, that 'We have not seen intelligence which we believe "shows" that Iraq has continued to produce C[hemical] W[eapons] agent in 1998–2002, although our judgement is that it has probably done so.'[38] This passage is of particular interest to scholars of intelligence. It highlights the importance attributed to precision and nuance by those responsible for interpreting intelligence and drafting assessments to inform policy.

In his warning, Jones was emphasising the difference between judgements taken on the balance of evidence, on the one hand, and the existence of compelling evidence, on the other. It is precisely this distinction that was lost when the JIC assessments of March, August and September 2002 were transformed into a document intended to support the government's hard-line policy. This problem was underlined by the Butler Committee: 'We conclude that it was a serious weakness that the JIC's warnings on the limitations of the intelligence underlying its judgements were not made sufficiently clear in the dossier.'[39] This is the strongest language deployed by the Committee in any of its criticisms of the intelligence process.

Butler also identified a significant breakdown in the British system of 'government assessment' and 'all-source analysis'. The dissent expressed by Brian Jones and his colleagues within the DIS lay at the centre of this breakdown. Jones challenged not only the certainty of the language employed in the dossier but also its lack of precision concerning the types of weapons to which the '45 minute claim' applied. This dissent was overruled by Jones's superiors within the DIS (both of whom also sat on the JIC) on the basis of a single report received by SIS from its 'new source on trial' on 10 September 2002. Crucially, the report was withheld, however, from the Nuclear, Biological and Chemical Intelligence experts within the DIS. In the event, this source proved unreliable and the intelligence it provided was withdrawn by SIS in July 2003. The Butler Report is highly critical of the fact that it was not scrutinised by the relevant experts on Jones's staff. It judges that this breakdown in the system of all-source analysis resulted in 'a stronger assessment in the dossier in relation to Iraqi chemical weapons production than was justified by the available intelligence'.[40]

The handling of intelligence from the new SIS source illuminates the importance attached by the British government to any information that confirmed existing convictions that Iraq possessed chemical and biological weapons. In the first instance, the new intelligence was sent directly to the Prime Minister's office. Two days later the Chief of SIS briefed Tony Blair personally on the potential importance of the new source.[41] The result was that the JIC assessment machinery was circumvented and unvalidated intelligence reached the very highest levels of the British government. The provision of raw intelligence to the Prime Minister is by no means unprecedented. Winston Churchill, for example, insisted on receiving a daily selection of the most interesting intercepts from Bletchley Park during the Second World War.[42] This episode nonetheless underlines the dangers inherent in using secret intelligence to build a case for a pre-determined policy. Given the urgency attached to acquiring intelligence on clandestine Iraqi weapons pro-grammes, it is hardly surprising that unjustifiable significance was attached to intelligence from this untried source at a crucial juncture in the preparation of the government's dossier. And yet, in circumstances such as these, it is arguably even more important that incoming information is scrutinised by all available expertise and that a sceptical perspective is brought to bear on intelligence reporting that reinforces prevailing assumptions. Paradoxically, it is under precisely such circumstances that ambient pressures are most likely to act to prevent such scrutiny. The case of the breakdown in the machinery of assessment in September 2002 is a good illustration of this frustrating paradox.

The role of government

The most forceful criticisms made by the Butler Committee were directed at the Blair government. The Committee used its stated focus on structures and procedures as justification for a critical examination of the decision-making practices of the Blair government regarding Iraq. Indeed, the Committee went well beyond a strict interpretation of its remit to focus on three aspects of the government's use of intelligence: (1) the decision to involve the JIC in the public Dossier; (2) the role of the Chair of the JIC in this process; and (3) the functioning of Cabinet government leading up to the invasion of March 2003.

Some of the most critical passages in the entire report pertain to the way the JIC was used to provide credibility for the government's insistence that Iraq posed a 'serious and current threat to the UK national interest'.[43] The report judges that using the JIC in this way 'put a strain' on efforts to 'maintain . . . normal standards of neutral and objective assessment' for those members of its Assessments Staff who were charged with drafting the Dossier.[44] Another unfortunate result of the decision to publish the Dossier was to 'put the JIC and its Chairman into an area of public controversy'. The Committee concluded that use of the JIC in this way was a 'mistaken judgement', the result of which was that 'more weight was placed on the intelligence than it could bear'.[45] The implicit but unmistakable message in all of this is that chief responsibility for the problems arising from the public Dossier lies with the government's decision to draw on the JIC's authority to support its policy'.[46]

The Butler Committee was just as explicit in its criticisms of the decision-making processes which intelligence assessments were meant to inform. The report deploys understated but nonetheless unequivocal language to censure the Blair government for subverting long-established Cabinet procedures. The Prime Minister's practice of using small groups and informal meetings (without minutes) to hammer out policy is singled out for criticism. The effect, the report underlines, was to concentrate deliberation and policy-formulation in 'fewer minds' around the Prime Minister at the expense of the rest of the Cabinet.[47] The Butler Committee's view of this practice merits citing at length:

> Without papers circulated in advance, it remains possible but is obviously much more difficult for members of the Cabinet outside the small circle directly involved to bring their political judgement and experience to bear on the major decisions for which the Cabinet as a whole must carry responsibility. The absence of papers on the Cabinet agenda so that Ministers could obtain briefings in advance from the Cabinet Office, their own departments or from the intelligence agencies plainly reduced their ability to prepare properly for such discussions, while the changes to key posts at the head of the Cabinet

Secretariat lessened the support of the machinery of government for the collective responsibility of the Cabinet in the vital matter of war and peace.[48]

The Cabinet had been sidelined. The result, the Committee observed in a final broadside of the practice, was to restrict unnecessarily 'the scope for informed collective political judgement' on an issue where 'hard facts are inherently difficult to come by and the quality of judgement is accordingly all the more important'.[49] The Blair government's approach to policy-making is the target of the most powerful criticisms made in the Butler Report.

This fact has not been always been acknowledged in media coverage of the Butler Report – which continues to focus on the question of purposeful distortion of intelligence rather than the larger issue of the subversion of Cabinet government. Lord Butler therefore reprised his committee's criticisms in an interview with *The Spectator* in December 2004 in which he asserted that the practices of the Blair government were driven by 'too much emphasis on selling . . . too much central control and . . . too little of what I would describe as reasoned deliberation which brings in all the arguments'. He then called on the government to 'restore open debate . . . at all levels up to the Cabinet. The Cabinet now – and I don't think there is any secret about this – doesn't make decisions.'[50] Butler went further in the House of Lords on 22 February 2007 when he charged that the Prime Minister had been 'disingenuous' in asserting that intelligence on Iraqi weapons programmes was 'extensive, detailed and authoritative'.[51] The tone of these criticisms illustrates the extent of both Butler's disapproval and his frustration at the fact that the critiques advanced in the report have not been taken up in a sustained way by either the press or the opposition.

Lacunae and final observations

The Butler Report is the most wide-ranging and penetrating public inquiry into the role of intelligence ever undertaken in Great Britain. It offers unprecedented insight into the quality of human intelligence reporting, the process of assessment and the interplay between intelligence and policy-making. Its recommendations have resulted in a number of important measures aimed at improving the quality of both collection and assessment. It is therefore a document of extraordinary interest for scholars of intelligence.

And yet there are interesting lacunae in this document. There is little, for example, about communications intelligence. The agency responsible for collecting this type of information, Government Communications Headquarters (GCHQ), is Britain's largest and most expensive foreign intelligence service. Yet it is mentioned only once in the text of the report.[52] This is a glaring omission which raises important questions about the comprehensiveness of the Butler Inquiry and possibly even the scope and the character of the British intelligence effort against Iraq between 1990 and 2003. Without a clear idea of both the scale and nature of communications intelligence on Iraqi capabilities, our understanding of the role of intelligence remains incomplete.[53] Another frustrating aspect of the Butler Report is that, despite its avowed focus on 'structures and processes', its pays only cursory attention to the question of relations between different agencies responsible for collection and assessment within the British intelligence community.

A final notable omission is any explicit discussion of the extent to which the JIC's classified and public assessments of the Iraqi threat were politicised. There are indirect references to this issue: the allusions to the 'strain' placed on intelligence officials by the government's request for a public dossier, for example, or to the need for the JIC chair to be a senior official 'demonstrably beyond influence'. There are also long passages detailing the way what remained basically the same intelligence picture was presented in a progressively more alarming light in the JIC assessments of March, August and September 2002, a process that culminated in the publication of the government dossier on 24 September of that year. The Committee's reluctance to go further and to consider the origins and nature of this politicisation is to be regretted.

The Committee's judgement that JIC assessments were not 'pulled in any particular direction to meet the policy concerns of senior officials on the JIC' may well reflect a desire not to see the JIC blamed for the decision to invade Iraq. As the report makes clear, this decision was made elsewhere and intelligence assessments played at best a secondary role in policy calculations. But the result is that an important dimension to the role of intelligence in policy-making has been obscured. The British system of assessment is particularly vulnerable to political distortion because the assessment machinery of the JIC is so firmly embedded within the government's decision-making apparatus. The JIC is, if anything, even more 'customer driven' than its US counterpart. Indeed, policy-makers from the Foreign and Commonwealth Office, the Ministry of Defence and other departments sit on the JIC alongside the heads of intelligence agencies. In this function they perform a peculiar dual role. In their role as policy-makers, they play a central role in commissioning intelligence assessments that are intended to inform policy. And in their role as members of the JIC, they are responsible for approving these assessments once they have been forwarded upwards from the Assessments Staff.[54]

The potential for the 'pull' architecture of the British system to produce politicised assessments has received little attention in the existing literature.[55] Yet this is precisely what may have happened in the case of assessments of the threat from Iraq. The Report *is* critical of the fact that no re-assessment of both received intelligence and the judgements concerning Iraqi capabilities were undertaken after the team of UN inspectors led by Dr Hans Blix failed to turn up evidence of illegal weapons programmes in early 2003.[56] But it does not go further to consider the possibility that this failure may well have been because no such assessments were commissioned by the policy-makers sitting on the JIC itself. Commitment to a policy of force had by this time almost certainly made any such assessments redundant and even undesirable.

Similarly, there is little evidence in the three JIC assessments reproduced in Annex B of the Butler Report that the Assessments Staff was tasked with assessing the threat Iraqi clandestine weapons programmes posed to British interests in contexts other than a military confrontation. This despite that fact that the 21 August JIC assessment was entitled 'Iraq: Saddam's Diplomatic and Military Options' and that of 9 September 'Iraqi Use of Chemical and Biological Weapons: Possible Scenarios'. Significantly, the political and strategic ramifications of Iraq's presumed non-conventional capabilities *in peacetime* are scarcely considered at all in these two documents. Both assessments instead focus tellingly on the way these capabilities would be deployed *in the context of a war between Iraq and over-whelming coalition forces.*[57] It is, of course, important not to jump to conclusions on the basis of limited evidence. We do not know whether the Assessments Staff produced other assessments of the wider ramifications of the Iraqi threat in the run-up to the war that have not been reproduced. Based on the evidence of the Butler Report, however, it appears that the government's decision to pursue a hard-line policy toward Iraq precluded searching assessments of the strategic significance of Iraqi weapons programmes in contexts other than a military confrontation with a US-British-led coalition. The fact that the Butler Committee did not remark upon this fact is surprising and may illustrate the extent to which the terms of reference set by the government were successful after all in limiting the conceptual horizons of this public inquiry.

DOCUMENT TWENTY-ONE:

Excerpt from the Butler Report, 'Conclusions on Iraq' (pp. 104–17, paras. 424–74).

5.10 CONCLUSIONS ON IRAQ

THE POLICY CONTEXT

424. We have deliberately started our description of the policy context in 1998. It was clear to us, especially from the evidence we heard from the Prime Minister, that the challenge posed by the Iraqi regime in 1998 to the United Nations inspections regime and the Government's response to it had a significant influence on policy towards Iraq in later years. Thus, the Prime Minister's statement in the House of Commons in February 1998 contained themes that would be equally applicable four years later – the need to preserve the authority and standing of the United Nations; the need in particular to prevent the Iraqi government thwarting the United Nations inspection regime; and

in that context the need to back United Nations' demands that
Iraq meet its obligations with the threat of force.

425. A review of Government policy towards Iraq in 1999 noted that
the policy of containment had '*kept the lid on*' Saddam Hussein.
In the absence of internationally acceptable alternative options,
it recommended continuation of the policy of containment,
despite its disadvantages. In parallel, however, key policy-
makers were receiving increasing intelligence on the developing
nuclear, chemical and biological programmes of other states of
concern and the proliferation activities of the AQ Khan network,
described more fully at Chapter 2. They also had intelligence,
described at Chapter 3, of efforts by Usama bin Laden to seek
unconventional weapons. The Prime Minister described to us his
perception of the longer-term risks to international security and
stability posed by such programmes and activities. Other
witnesses spoke of a sense of a '*creeping tide*' of proliferation
and growth in the nuclear, biological, chemical and ballistic
missile capabilities of states of concern.

426. The Prime Minister told us that, even before the attacks of
11 September 2001, his concern in this area was increasingly
causing him to examine more proactive policy options. He also
described to us the way in which the events of 11 September
2001 led him to conclude that policy had to change. He and
other witnesses told us of the impact on policy-making of the
changed calculus of threat that emerged from those attacks – of
the risk of unconventional weapons in due course becoming
available to terrorists and extremists seeking to cause mass
casualties unconstrained by the fear of alienating their
supporters or the public, or by considerations of personal safety.
The Prime Minister's view was that a stand had to be taken, and
a more active policy put in place to prevent the continuing
development and proliferation of nuclear, biological and
chemical weapons and technology in breach of the will of the
international community. We describe at Chapter 4 the new
counter-proliferation machinery put in place in summer 2002 to
implement that policy.

427. The developing policy context of the previous four years, and especially the impact of the events of 11 September 2001, formed the backdrop for changes in policy towards Iraq in early 2002. The Government's conclusion in the spring of 2002 that stronger action (although not necessarily military action) needed to be taken to enforce Iraqi disarmament was not based on any new development in the current intelligence picture on Iraq. In his evidence to us, the Prime Minister endorsed the view expressed at the time that what had changed was not the pace of Iraq's prohibited weapons programmes, which had not been dramatically stepped up, but tolerance of them following the attacks of 11 September 2001. When the Government concluded that action going beyond the previous policy of containment needed to be taken, there were many grounds for concern arising from Iraq's past record and behaviour. There was a clear view that, to be successful, any new action to enforce Iraqi compliance with its disarmament obligations would need to be backed with the credible threat of force. But there was no recent intelligence that would itself have given rise to a conclusion that Iraq was of more immediate concern than the activities of some other countries.

428. Other factors clearly influenced the decision to focus on Iraq. The Prime Minister told us that, whilst on some perspectives the activities of other states might be seen as posing more direct challenges to British interests, the Government, as well as being influenced by the concerns of the US Government, saw a need for immediate action on Iraq because of the wider historical and international context, especially Iraq's perceived continuing challenge to the authority of the United Nations. The Government also saw in the United Nations and a decade of Security Council Resolutions a basis for action through the United Nations to enforce Iraqi compliance with its disarmament obligations.

429. The Government considered in March 2002 two options for achieving the goal of Iraqi disarmament – a toughening of the existing containment policy; and regime change by military means. Ministers were advised that, if regime change was the chosen policy, only the use of overriding force in a ground campaign would achieve the removal of Saddam Hussein and

Iraq's re-integration with the international community. Officials noted that regime change of itself had no basis in international law; and that any offensive military action against Iraq could only be justified if Iraq were held to be in breach of its disarmament obligations under United Nations Security Council Resolution 687 or some new resolution. Officials also noted that for the five Permanent Members of the Security Council and the majority of the 15 members of the Council to take the view that Iraq was in breach of its obligations under Resolution 687, they would need to be convinced that Iraq was in breach of its obligations; that such proof would need to be incontrovertible and of large-scale activity; but that the intelligence then available was insufficiently robust to meet that criterion.

430.   This advice, and a parallel JIC assessment, formed part of the background for the Prime Minister's meeting with President Bush at Crawford on 6–7 April 2002. The themes of the British Government's policy framework established as a result of that meeting and work in subsequent months echoed those of 1998 – the importance of the United Nations; the need to get United Nations inspectors back into Iraq; and the value of increasing pressure on the Iraqi regime, including through military action.

431.   Intelligence on Iraqi nuclear, biological, chemical and ballistic missile programmes was used in support of the execution of this policy, for three main purposes:

a.   To inform planning for a military campaign if that should be necessary, in particular, in relation to unconventional weapons, for providing the necessary safeguards for coalition troops, diplomatic personnel and others; and for targeting.

b.   To inform domestic and international opinion of the UK's assessment of Iraq's holdings, programmes and intentions, in support of the Government's advocacy of its changing policy towards Iraq.

c.   To obtain and provide information to United Nations inspectors about the likely locations of weapons and programmes which contravened the terms of United Nations Security Council resolutions.

432. We draw our Conclusions on the sources, assessment and use of intelligence in the following paragraphs against that policy background. In doing so, we are conscious that Iraq was not the only issue on which the intelligence agencies, the JIC and the departments concerned were working during this period. It is a common temptation for reviews of this nature to comment as if those concerned were doing nothing else and should have had their attention concentrated full-time on the subject under review. In this case, for much of the period up to mid-2002, many other issues were more demanding of the intelligence community's and policy-makers' time and attention. Iraq loomed large from mid-2002 onwards. But even then other matters, including terrorism and the activities of other countries of concern, were requiring intensive day-to-day observation and action, including continuing operations in Afghanistan and the crisis between India and Pakistan.

THE SOURCES OF INTELLIGENCE

433. Iraq was a very difficult intelligence target. Between 1991 and 1998, the bulk of information used in assessing the status of Iraq's biological, chemical and ballistic missile programmes was derived from UNSCOM reports. In 1995, knowledge was significantly boosted by the defection of Hussein Kamil. But, after the departure of United Nations inspectors in December 1998, information sources were sparse, particularly on Iraq's chemical and biological weapons programmes.

434. In Spring 2000, intelligence was obtained from a significant new source via a liaison service on mobile biological agent production facilities. During 2002, additional human intelligence reporting was obtained by the UK. Nevertheless the number of primary human intelligence sources remained few (although they drew on a wider number of sub-sources and sub-sub-sources). As Section 5.9 explains, SIS had five main sources. Two of those were dominant, in terms of both the number of reports and influence on JIC assessments.

435. Furthermore, SIS did not generally have agents with first-hand, inside knowledge of Iraq's nuclear, chemical, biological or ballistic missile programmes. As a result, intelligence reports were mainly inferential. Other intelligence sources provided valuable information on other activity, including overseas procurement activity. They did not generally provide confirmation of the intelligence received from human sources, but did contribute to the picture of the continuing intention of the Iraqi regime to pursue its prohibited weapons programmes.

436. Validation of human intelligence sources after the war has thrown doubt on a high proportion of those sources and of their reports, and hence on the quality of the intelligence assessments received by Ministers and officials in the period from summer 2002 to the outbreak of hostilities. Of the main human intelligence sources described above:

   a.   One SIS main source reported authoritatively on some issues, but on others was passing on what he had heard within his circle.

   b.   Reporting from a sub-source to a second SIS main source that was important to JIC assessments on Iraqi possession of chemical and biological weapons must be open to doubt.

   c.   Reports from a third SIS main source have been withdrawn as unreliable.

   d.   Reports from two further SIS main sources continue to be regarded as reliable, although it is notable that their reports were less worrying than the rest about Iraqi chemical and biological weapons capabilities.

   e.   Reports received from a liaison service on Iraqi production of biological agent were seriously flawed, so that the grounds for JIC assessments drawing on those reports that Iraq had recently-produced stocks of biological agent no longer exist.

437. We have considered why such a high proportion of human intelligence reports should have been withdrawn or subsequently be subject to doubt.

438. One reason which is frequently suggested is that, in the case of Iraq, there was over-reliance on émigré' and dissident sources,

who had their own motives for exaggerating the dangers presented by the Iraq regime. But, after examination, we do not believe that over-reliance on dissident and émigré sources was a major cause of subsequent weaknesses in the human intelligence relied on by the UK. The important source on Iraqi biological agent production capabilities was a refugee. But his reporting was treated with some caution by the JIC until it appeared to be confirmed by other human intelligence. The subsequent need to withdraw a key part of the reporting received through the liaison service arose as a result of misunderstandings, not because of the source's status.

439. A new sub-source to another main source, who provided a significant proportion of influential human intelligence reporting, turned out to have links to opposition groups of which SIS only later became aware. But SIS, once they knew of those links, warned readers in their reports of the risk of embellishment. And the serious doubts that have subsequently arisen on the quality of his reporting do not arise from issues connected with his dissident status.

440. One reason for the number of agents whose reports turned out to be unreliable or questionable may be the length of the reporting chains. Even when there were sources who were shown to be reliable in some areas of reporting, they had in other areas of intelligence concern where they did not have direct knowledge to draw on sub-sources or sub-sub-sources. This was the case with the first of the two dominant sources.

441. Another reason may be that agents who were known to be reliable were asked to report on issues going well beyond their usual territory, leading to intelligence reports which were more speculative than they would have provided on their own specialisms. We believe this to have been the case with some aspects of the reporting of the second of the two dominant sources.

442. A third reason may be that, because of the scarcity of sources and the urgent requirement for intelligence, more credence was

given to untried agents than would normally be the case. This was the case with the report received between the JIC assessment of 9 September 2002 and the publication of the Government's dossier in September 2002.

443. We believe that a major underlying reason for the problems that have arisen as the difficulty of achieving reliable human intelligence on Iraq. Part of the difficulty faced by SIS in recruiting and running reliable agents came from the nature and brutality of the Iraqi regime. The nature of Iraq after the war might also have had its own effect, with the risk that some of the informants may have reported reliably but had reasons after the war to deny having provided information.

444. However, even taking into account the difficulty of recruiting and running reliable agents on Iraqi issues, we conclude that part of the reason for the serious doubt being cast over a high proportion of human intelligence reports on Iraq arises from weaknesses in the effective application by SIS of its validation procedures and in their proper resourcing. We received evidence from two witnesses about the impact of organisational changes in parts of SIS relevant to our Review. Following reductions in SIS's budget in the mid-1990s, these were made with the goal of making overall staff savings and freeing experienced case officers for operational work. This weakened SIS's internal processes for the quality assurance of agents. One of those witnesses also noted that the level of staff effort applied to geographical and functional tasks relevant to our Review was too thin to support SIS's responsibilities. We believe that the validation of some sources on Iraq suffered as a consequence of both problems.

445. The Chief of SIS acknowledged to us that a problem had arisen. He attributed it primarily to the shortage of experienced case officers following the rundown of the size of SIS in the 1990s. Our Review has shown the vital importance of effective scrutiny and validation of human intelligence sources and of their reporting to the preparation of accurate JIC assessments and high-quality advice to Ministers. We urge the Chief of SIS to ensure that this task is properly resourced and organised to

achieve that result, and we think that it would be appropriate if the Intelligence and Security Committee were to monitor this.

ASSESSMENT

446. We have examined the way in which raw intelligence was analysed and assessed over the period and then incorporated into JIC assessments for Ministers and other senior readers. In particular, we have looked at whether:

   a. The material in intelligence reports was correctly treated as it passed along the chain from agent reports through analysis into JIC assessments, and that it did not suffer as a result of compression or incorrect translation from one stage to the next.

   b. Analysis or assessment appears to have been coloured by departmental policy or other agendas.

   c. Assessment had access to and made full use of available technical expertise.

447. Drawing on our conclusions on these issues, we have then examined and drawn conclusions on the quality of the JIC assessments we read on Iraq's nuclear, biological, chemical and ballistic missile programmes. We have looked in particular at the degree of analytical rigour applied across the range of assessments we have read, especially to see whether there developed within the intelligence community over a decade of analysis and assessment 'Group Think' or a 'prevailing wisdom'. That has led us to look at whether sufficient challenge was applied to analysis and assessment, and whether readers of JIC assessments and the JIC itself were sufficiently alerted to the existence of dissenting or alternative views.

448. In doing so, we decided to study JIC assessments and the intelligence reports that underlay them as far back as 1990, to seek to establish in particular:

   a. Whether there were any issues surrounding the operation of the intelligence assessment process over more than a decade which might have affected JIC assessments in the period prior to the second Gulf war.

b.   Whether assessments made about the scale of Iraq's nuclear, biological, chemical and ballistic missile programmes at the time of the first Gulf war and during the early- and mid-1990s had an impact which was still reflected in JIC assessments made in 2002 and 2003.

The treatment of intelligence material

449. In general, we found that the original intelligence material was correctly reported in JIC assessments. An exception was the '45 minute' report.

But this sort of example was rare in the several hundred JIC assessments we read on Iraq. In general, we also found that the reliability of the original intelligence reports was fairly represented by the use of accompanying qualifications. We should record in particular that we have found no evidence of deliberate distortion or of culpable negligence.

The effect of departmental policy agendas

450. We examined JIC assessments to see whether there was evidence that the judgements inside them were systematically distorted by non-intelligence factors, in particular the influence of the policy positions of departments. We found no evidence of JIC assessments and the judgements inside them being pulled in any particular direction to meet the policy concerns of senior officials on the JIC.

Access to technical and other expertise

451. We conclude in general that the intelligence community made good use of the technical expertise available to the Government, for example in the DIS or from the Atomic Weapons Establishment at Aldermaston and the Defence Science and Technology Laboratory: Porton Down, both through consultation and secondments. An example of the strength of this network of expertise came in the assurances we were given that technical experts both in the DIS and elsewhere were consulted on the

question of whether the aluminium tubes were likely to have been intended for a centrifuge facility for nuclear enrichment.

452. We accept the need for careful handling of human intelligence reports to sustain the security of sources. We have, however, seen evidence of difficulties that arose from the unduly strict 'compartmentalisation' of intelligence which meant that experts in DIS did not have access to an intelligence report which became available in September 2002 and played a major role for the JIC in confirming previous intelligence reports that Iraq was producing chemical and biological weapons. The report was later withdrawn in July 2003. We accept that this report was from a new source who was thought to be of great potential value and was therefore of extreme sensitivity. Nevertheless, it was wrong that a report which was of significance in the drafting of a document of the importance of the dossier was not shown to key experts in the DIS who could have commented on the validity and credibility of the report. We conclude that arrangements should always be sought to ensure that the need for protection of sources should not prevent the exposure of reports on technical matters to the most expert available analysis.

The quality of JIC assessments

453. We were impressed by the quality of intelligence assessments on Iraq's nuclear capabilities. They were in our view thorough, balanced and measured; brought together effectively human and technical intelligence information; included information on the perceived quality of the underlying intelligence sources to help readers in interpreting the material; identified explicitly those areas where previous assessments were wrong, and the reasons why; and at each significant stage included consideration of alternative hypotheses and scenarios, and provided an explanation of the consequences were any one to arise, to aid readers' understanding.

454. Partly because of inherent difficulties in assessing chemical and biological programmes, JIC assessments on Iraq's chemical and biological weapons programmes were less assured. In our view,

assessments in those areas tended to be over-cautious and in some areas worst case. Where there was a balance of inference to be drawn, it tended to go in the direction of inferring the existence of banned weapons programmes. Assessments were as a consequence less complete, especially in their considerations of alternative hypotheses, and used a different burden of proof.

455. There are some general factors which will always complicate assessments of chemical and biological weapons programmes. In our review of intelligence on the nuclear, biological and chemical programmes of other states, we saw an equivalent complexity in making judgements on their status. The most significant is the 'dual use' issue – because chemical and biological weapons programmes can draw heavily on 'dual use' materials, it is easier for a proliferating state to keep its programmes covert.

456. There were also Iraq-specific factors. The intelligence community will have had in mind that Iraq had not only owned but used its chemical weapons in the past. It will inevitably have been influenced by the way in which the Iraqi regime was engaged in a sustained programme to try to deceive United Nations inspectors and to conceal from them evidence of its prohibited programmes. Furthermore, because SIS did not have agents with first-hand knowledge of Iraq's nuclear, chemical, biological or ballistic missile programmes, most of the intelligence reports on which assessments were being made were inferential. The Assessments Staff and JIC were not fully aware of the access and background of key informants, and could not therefore read their material against the background of an understanding of their motivations for passing on information.

457. We have also noted in the papers we have read that the broad conclusions of the UK intelligence community (although not some particular details) were widely-shared by other countries, especially the assessment that it was likely that Iraq had, or could produce, chemical and biological weapons which it might use in circumstances of extremity. We note that Dr Blix, Executive Chairman of UNMOVIC, has said[1] that:

My gut feelings, which I kept to myself, suggested to me
that Iraq still engaged in prohibited activities and retained
prohibited items, and that it had the documents to prove it.

Where doubts existed, they were about the extent to which the
intelligence amounted to proof, as opposed to balance of
probability.

458. However, we detected a tendency for assessments to be
coloured by overreaction to previous errors. Past under-
estimates had a more lasting impact on the assessment
process than past over-estimates, when both should have
been as deserving of attention. We have also noted that
where for good reasons[2] the JIC chose to adopt a worst
case estimate (which in most cases it described as such) there
was a tendency for that basis of calculation not to be made clear
in later assessments. As a result, there was a risk of over-
cautious or worst case estimates, shorn of their caveats,
becoming the 'prevailing wisdom'. Subsequent Iraqi declarations
being tested against such estimates for truthfulness would have
been seen as falling short – a view that will have been reinforced
by proven shortfalls in Iraqi declarations during the early- and
mid-1990s and by Iraqi prevarication, concealment and
deception.

459. The JIC may, in some assessments, also have misread the nature
of Iraqi governmental and social structures. The absence of
intelligence in this area may also have hampered planning for the
post-war phase on which departments did a great deal of work.
We note that the collection of intelligence on Iraq's prohibited
weapons programmes was designated as being a JIC First
Order of Priority whereas intelligence on Iraqi political issues
was designated as being Third Order. The membership of the
JIC is broad enough to allow such wider evidence to be brought
to bear. We emphasise the importance of the Assessments
Staff and the JIC having access to a wide range of information,
especially in circumstances (e.g. where the UK is likely to become
involved in national reconstruction and institution-building) where
information on political and social issues will be vital.

THE USE OF INTELLIGENCE

The Government's dossiers

460. The main vehicle for the Government's use of intelligence in the public presentation of policy was the dossier of September 2002 and accompanying Ministerial statements. (The dossier of February 2003 has been fully dealt with in the ISC Report and we make no further comment on it here, except to endorse the conclusion accepted by the Government that the procedures followed in producing it were unsatisfactory and should not be repeated.)

461. The dossier broke new ground in three ways: the JIC had never previously produced a public document; no Government case for any international action had previously been made to the British public through explicitly drawing on a JIC publication; and the authority of the British intelligence community, and the JIC in particular, had never been used in such a public way.

462. The dossier was not intended to make the case for a particular course of action in relation to Iraq. It *was* intended by the Government to inform domestic and international understanding of the need for stronger action (though not necessarily military action) – the general direction in which Government policy had been moving since the early months of 2002, away from containment to a more proactive approach to enforcing Iraqi disarmament. The Government's wish to give its case greater objectivity and credibility led to the Government's decision to commission the JIC to produce the dossier and to make public the JIC's authorship of it. The Chairman of the JIC accepted responsibility for its production with the intention of ensuring that it did not go beyond the judgements which the JIC had reached. He and the JIC therefore took on the ownership of it.

463. The Government wanted an unclassified document on which it could draw in its *advocacy* of its policy. The JIC sought to offer a dispassionate *assessment* of intelligence and other material on Iraqi nuclear, biological, chemical and ballistic missile

programmes. The JIC, with commendable motives, took responsibility for the dossier, in order that its content should properly reflect the judgements of the intelligence community. They did their utmost to ensure this standard was met. But this will have put a strain on them in seeking to maintain their normal standards of neutral and objective assessment.

464. Strenuous efforts were made to ensure that no individual statements were made in the dossier which went beyond the judgements of the JIC. But, in translating material from JIC assessments into the dossier, warnings were lost about the limited intelligence base on which some aspects of these assessments were being made. The Government would have seen these warnings in the original JIC assessments and taken them into account in reading them. But the public, through reading the dossier, would not have known of them. The dossier did contain a chapter on the role of intelligence. But the language in the dossier may have left with readers the impression that there was fuller and firmer intelligence behind the judgements than was the case: our view, having reviewed all of the material, is that judgements in the dossier went to (although not beyond) the outer limits of the intelligence available. The Prime Minister's description, in his statement to the House of Commons on the day of publication of the dossier, of the picture painted by the intelligence services in the dossier as '*extensive, detailed and authoritative*' may have reinforced this impression.

465. We conclude that it was a serious weakness that the JIC's warnings on the limitations of the intelligence underlying its judgements were not made sufficiently clear in the dossier.

466. We understand why the Government felt it had to meet the mounting public and Parliamentary demand for information. We also recognise that there is a real dilemma between giving the public an authoritative account of the intelligence picture and protecting the objectivity of the JIC from the pressures imposed by providing information for public debate. It is difficult to resolve these requirements. We conclude, with the benefit of hindsight, that making public that the JIC had authorship of the dossier was

a mistaken judgement, though we do not criticise the JIC for taking responsibility for clearance of the intelligence content of the document. However, in the particular circumstances, the publication of such a document in the name and with the authority of the JIC had the result that more weight was placed on the intelligence than it could bear. The consequence also was to put the JIC and its Chairman into an area of public controversy and arrangements must be made for the future which avoid putting the JIC and its Chairman in a similar position.

467. We recognise that there will be a dilemma if intelligence-derived material is in future to be put into the public domain. If future documents are published solely in the name of the Government, it is inevitable that Ministers will be asked if the JIC has endorsed the intelligence assessments inside them. But we believe that there are other options that should be examined for the ownership of drafting, for gaining the JIC's endorsement of the intelligence material and assessments that are quoted and for subsequent 'branding'. One is for the government of the day to draft a document, to gain the JIC's endorsement of the intelligence material inside it and then to publish it acknowledging that it draws on intelligence but without ascribing it to the JIC. Or the Government, if it wishes to seek the JIC's credibility and authority, could publish a document with intelligence material and the JIC's endorsement of it shown separately. Or the JIC could prepare and publish itself a selfstanding assessment, incorporating all of its normal caveats and warnings, leaving it to others to place that document within a broader policy context. This may make such documents less persuasive in making a policy case; but that is the price of using a JIC assessment. Our conclusion is that, between these options, the first is greatly preferable. Whichever route is chosen, JIC clearance of the intelligence content of any similar document will be essential.

468. Furthermore, we conclude that, if intelligence is to be used more widely by governments in public debate in future, those doing so must be careful to explain its uses and limitations. It will be essential, too, that clearer and more effective dividing lines

between assessment and advocacy are established when doing so.

469. In reaching these conclusions, we realise that our conclusions may provoke calls for the current Chairman of the JIC, Mr Scarlett, to withdraw from his appointment as the next Chief of SIS. We greatly hope that he will not do so. We have a high regard for his abilities and his record. Once the Government had decided to produce a dossier based on intelligence, he and the JIC took on ownership of it with the excellent motive of ensuring that everything it said was consistent with JIC judgements. We have said above that it was a mistaken judgement for the dossier to be so closely associated with the JIC but it was a collective one for which the Chairman of the JIC should not bear personal responsibility.

Intelligence and the legality of the use of military force

470. As described in Section 5.7, the part played by intelligence in determining the legality of the use of force was limited. The criterion which the Attorney General advised the Government to apply was the degree of Iraq's compliance and co-operation with United Nations Security Council Resolution 1441.

471. The Government received on 18 December the JIC's initial assessment on the quality of Iraq's declaration of 7 December, called for under Resolution 1441, on the status of its prohibited programmes. The Government also received in the period between September 2002 and March 2003 a significant stream of intelligence reports about attempts by the Iraqi regime at concealment, as well as information about the results of UNMOVIC and IAEA inspections inside Iraq, captured in the reports provided to the United Nations Security Council.

472. Even so we have noted that, despite its importance to the determination of whether Iraq was in further material breach of its obligations under Resolution 1441, the JIC made no further assessment of the Iraqi declaration beyond its *Initial Assessment*'. We have also recorded our surprise that policy-

makers and the intelligence community did not, as the generally negative results of UNMOVIC inspections became increasingly apparent, re-evaluate in early-2003 the quality of the intelligence.

VALIDATION OF THE INTELLIGENCE

473.   As we set out at the start of this Chapter, we sought in our Review to assess the intelligence on Iraqi capabilities to enable us to answer three broad questions:
   a.   What was the quality of the intelligence and other evidence, and the assessments made of it, about the strategic intent of the Iraqi regime to pursue nuclear, biological, chemical or ballistic missile programmes in contravention of its obligations under United Nations Security Council Resolution 687?
   b.   What was the quality of the intelligence or other evidence, and the assessments made of it, about Iraq seeking to sustain and develop its indigenous knowledge, skills and materiel base which would provide it with a 'break-out' capability in each of those fields? Was there in particular good intelligence or other evidence of Iraq pursuing activities to extend and enhance those capabilities in contravention of its obligations under United Nations Security Council Resolutions?
   c.   What was the quality of the intelligence or other evidence, and the assessments made of it, about Iraqi production or possession of prohibited chemical and biological agents and weapons, nuclear materials and ballistic missiles?

474.   Even now it would be premature to reach conclusions about Iraq's prohibited weapons. Much potential evidence may have been destroyed in the looting and disorder that followed the cessation of hostilities. Other material may be hidden in the sand, including stocks of agent or weapons. We believe that it would be a rash person who asserted at this stage that evidence of Iraqi possession of stocks of biological or chemical agents, or even of banned missiles, does not exist or will never be found. But as a result of our Review, and taking into account the evidence which has been found by the ISG and de-briefing of

---

Iraqi personnel, we have reached the conclusion that prior to the war the Iraqi regime:

a. Had the strategic intention of resuming the pursuit of prohibited weapons programmes, including if possible its nuclear weapons programme, when United Nations inspection regimes were relaxed and sanctions were eroded or lifted.

b. In support of that goal, was carrying out illicit research and development, and procurement, activities, to seek to sustain its indigenous capabilities.

c. Was developing ballistic missiles with a range longer than permitted under relevant United Nations Security Council resolutions; but did not have significant – if any – stocks of chemical or biological weapons in a state fit for deployment, or developed plans for using them.

1 Dr Hans Blix, *Disarming Iraq* (London: Bloomsbury, 2004), p. 112. (In the original this is marked footnote 19).
2 In particular, in relation to chemical and biological weapons it would have been irresponsible in the highest degree to send armed forces into battle on the assumption that Iraq did not have chemical or biological weapons and would not use them. (In the original this is marked footnote 20).

COMMENTARY: THE BUTLER REPORT

Robert Jervis

To American eyes, the Butler Report reads like a very British document – or at least not an American one. Of course, it can only be fully appreciated in its entirety, but the section printed above gives its flavor. The Report runs only a bit over 150 pages. While this may be more than enough for some readers, the American counterparts[1] (and the American government being quite pluralistic, there are several of them) are many times longer. This may reflect a combination of the size of the staffs available and national style, as American National Intelligence Estimates (NIEs) tend to be longer than reports by the Joint Intelligence Committee (JIC). The Butler Report then provides less detail than the parallel American documents, but also avoids distractions.

The Report also is more analytically sophisticated than the American documents, which tend to equate incorrect conclusions with faulty reasoning and deficient processes. The Report's opening chapter, 'The Nature and Use of Intelligence' can stand on its own as a fine introduction to the subject, making important conceptual distinctions and drawing on historical cases. Although its reaching back to World War II may not impress British readers, this is a long memory in the American context. This is more than background; it helps explain what can and cannot be expected from intelligence and why glib statements like 'intelligence has to connect the dots' or 'policy should never be based on intelligence derived from a single source' are misleading.

The most significant contrast, however, involves politics, both the politics that the reports describe and the politics they embody. The Butler Report spends much more time on what it calls 'the political context' than do the American documents. This is partly because in America intelligence and policy are kept much more separate than they are in the UK, or at least are supposed to be. The physical remove of Langley from Washington and the informal rule that intelligence should avoid commenting on American policy are symptomatic, and may stem from the American traditional fear of centralized power and the association of strong intelligence with the Nazi regime, which was particularly important because US intelligence came of age during and after World War II. In Britain, the intelligence establishment grew more slowly and with less impetus for a sharp separation from policy. Indeed, the JIC, the peak intelligence body, is lodged in the Cabinet Office and produces a 'government assessment' rather than an 'intelligence assessment.'[2] Of course this does not mean in Britain intelligence should be twisted to support policy. Indeed, the Butler Report and other investigations sought to see whether the integrity of intelligence had been subverted, and one of the Report's recommendations was that the unprecedented preparation of a public JIC dossier not be repeated. But the report also understands that the political context in which intelligence is prepared will inevitably influence its content, that, especially in the smaller British world, intelligence and policy officials breathe the same air, and that one cannot expect the two to exist in sealed compartments. Relatedly, the report implies (e.g., pp. 105, 150–1, 154), although it does not clearly state, that the intelligence errors played only a secondary role in the government's decision to go to war.

The stress on the political context in combination with the sophisticated understanding of the limits on intelligence gives the Butler Report a somewhat exculpatory tone in comparison to the American counterparts. It is striking that while the two communities had more or less the same information and came to more or less the same conclusions, the American reports, especially that by the Senate Select Committee on Intelligence (SSCI), are excoriating while the Butler Report is chiding. In part, we may be seeing the American tendency towards bombast and British understatement, but I think it is more than that. In the US, intelligence has few powerful defenders. It is almost always a handy whipping-boy, and this was nowhere more true than in the case of Iraq. Republicans had an obvious incentive to blame war intelligence, and while Democrats also wanted to point a finger at White House misuse of information and pressure on CIA, those who had voted for the war also had reason to fault the assessments. Furthermore, to have recognized the limitations on what intelligence can do would have been much more threatening in the American case because its role as the sole superpower meant that it would have to take strong actions on the basis of limited and contestable information, something that would be true even in the absence of Bush's doctrine of 'pre-emptive' (really preventive) war.

The Butler Committee, by contrast, not only dwells less on the failure of intelligence, going so far as to say that 'we were impressed by the quality of intelligence assessments on Iraq's nuclear capabilities' (p. 111 – a judgment repeated in the summary on p. 153), but by stressing the political context takes much of the weight off the shoulders of intelligence. Indeed, when a colleague in CIA read the Butler Report, he said to me: 'Bob, now I know how we can avoid these criticisms. All we have to do is move to London.' Indeed, the Report urges that the chairman of the JIC not lose his planned promotion to Chief of SIS, a vindication that would have been inconceivable in the US. Although the Report does not find explicit government pressure on intelligence, it does conclude that there is a 'a strong case for the post of Chairman of the JIC being held by someone with experience of dealing with Ministers in a very senior role, and who is demonstrably beyond influence, and thus probably in his last post' (p. 144). The Butler Report then simultaneously limits its criticisms of British intelligence and attributes some of the blame to the political leadership. It documents in great detail the ways in which the public dossier on Iraq's WMD programs removed many of the qualifications and uncertainties in the secret intelligence. While blaming the JIC as well as the government for the misleading claim that Saddam Hussein could use chemical and biological weapons within 45 minutes of a decision to do so (it later became clear that this report also was incorrect), the Butler Report had the effect, and probably the intent, of shielding intelligence from the strongest possible criticisms.

One reason for this may be that, unlike American intelligence, British intelligence stands by its original claim that Saddam Hussein was seeking uranium from Africa. The infamous forged documents played no role in its initial assessment, and so their debunking did not lead to a change of heart. But it remains unclear why the British and Americans reached different conclusions after the war, as well as how the British position can be sustained in light of the fact that the rest of the Iraqi nuclear program was in suspension and post-war interrogations failed to supply evidence of attempted procurement. One should not think that the British were generally more alarmist than the Americans, however. The Butler Report makes clear that British analysts differed from their CIA counterparts in concluding that the aluminium tubes alluded to in intelligence reports on Iraqi weapons programmes were almost surely destined for use in rockets, not uranium enrichment, a judgment that was later confirmed.

The British report blames intelligence less than do the American reports and public opinion in part because it understands that intelligence is almost always fragmentary and so requires extensive interpretation. Here the political context is crucial, not only and even not so much in the sense of what government policy is, but what images have formed in the minds of intelligence officials at all levels, images that are developed in the context of recent world affairs. No less than the policy-makers, intelligence officials knew that Saddam Hussein had developed extensive WMD programs before the Gulf War, tried to conceal them afterwards, refused to cooperate with international inspectors, and used gas against the Iranians and the Kurds. Given his situation and revealed ruthlessness, it made perfect sense for him to continue his illicit programs. What the Prime Minister said in 1998 was undoubtedly the view of intelligence as well: 'The Saddam Hussein we face today is the same Saddam Hussein we faced yesterday. He has not changed. He remains an evil, brutal dictator' (p. 54). Furthermore, the discovery of the A.Q. Khan network and the growing danger of proliferation, of course multiplied by the fear generated by the attacks of September 11, meant that few threats could be dismissed.[3] Within this context, even intelligence reports of questionable reliability fit nicely together to show that forbidden programs almost surely continued, albeit in a form and at a pace that were devilishly hard to discern (pp. 105, 112, 153, 157).

Although some of the information used to reach this conclusion rested on technical intelligence (little discussed in the Butler Report), most came from human sources (HUMINT). The Report shows that the British, like the Americans, relied heavily upon information from international inspectors and that, when they were forced to withdraw, few sources were recruited to continue the information flow. The Report does a great service by its detail, moving source by source and noting that in many cases important information came from sub-sources (that is, people who were recruited by the sources) or sub-sub-sources. Assessing the validity of the reports and the reliability of the sources (and those they relied on) is extraordinarily difficult, and the Report indicates that SIS did not do as good a job as it should have in part because of weakness in its validation procedures (pp. 109, 152).[4] The pressures for more information may also have contributed to accepting sources and reports without proper scrutiny, but, contrary to popular impression, few of the errors were attributable to information supplied by the organized Iraqi opposition which of course sought to exaggerate the threat posed by Saddam. Another obstacle to validating sources arose when they were recruited not by SIS, but by a counterpart service. The Report then hints at the general importance of liaison relationships. Even more than most other aspects of intelligence, the extent of cooperation between services is kept secret. But it is clear that, on the one hand, even close allies do not fully share their sources with one another, and that, on the other hand, countries with tense relations may engage in significant information sharing.

Also interesting are the points not made and the questions not raised. There is little in here about why the Americans and British reached different conclusions on some aspects of the Iraqi weapons programs or the extent of Anglo-American conversations on these issues. The Report, like the intelligence itself, also misses the significance of 'negative evidence', i.e., the frequent cases in which sources who were in a position to have observed or at least heard of WMD activities, in fact, made no reports. The problem is that silence is both easy to miss and can be very important, as it was here. Also important and difficult to detect are the subtle but pervasive pressures on intelligence stemming from the knowledge of what will please the policy-makers. This is difficult to investigate and rarely will definitive conclusions be possible, but the Report's recommendation that the

Chairman of JIC be someone 'in his last post' may speak to this. Finally, the Report mentions but does not dwell on the fact that the JIC did not prepare a new assessment based on the information received after the inspectors were allowed back in (p. 87). Although the inspectors had time to follow up on only 'a little over half of the leads provided by the British Government' (p. 91), it is still striking that the absence of evidence of WMD did not lead to a reassessment. (The same was true in the US.) One does not have to be obsessed with political pressure to think that the most likely explanation was that everyone knew that war was coming and that the government would hardly welcome news that it might not be necessary. One also does not have to expect retrospective reports to be perfect to believe that the lack of coverage of this topic reveals a desire not to explore a topic that would embarrass both intelligence and the government.

Sometimes the most important discoveries are re-discoveries. The Butler Committee begins its report by quoting Clausewitz: 'Much of the intelligence that we receive in war is contradictory, even more of it is plain wrong, and most of it is fairly dubious.' This is a sad lesson that we still need to learn, and unfortunately will re-learn after the next intelligence failure.

COMMENTARY: THE BUTLER REPORT: A US PERSPECTIVE

Loch K. Johnson

This brief commentary offers some comparisons between the British panel of inquiry into intelligence failures surrounding the mistaken prediction of unconventional weapons in Iraq and similar investigations carried out in the United States. The focus here is on three features of the inquiries: the approaches used by the British and the Americans; their findings; and their recommendations for reform.

Investigative approaches

In both the United Kingdom and the United States, the question of intelligence failure regarding suspected – but, as it turned out, absent – Iraqi weapons on mass destruction (WMDs) stirred exhaustive probes, once the scale of the error became evident when British and American troops invaded the Persian Gulf nation in March of 2003. The British undertook four separate inquiries into the mistaken intelligence: one by Parliament's Foreign Affairs Committee; a second by Parliament's intelligence oversight group, the Intelligence and Security Committee; a third by the former Lord Chief Justice of Northern Ireland, Lord Hutton, at the request of the Prime Minister; and the Butler panel.[1] The Americans engaged in a Senate probe (the Roberts Report, after the chairman of the chamber's intelligence oversight committee, Pat Roberts, R-Kansas) and a presidential commission (the Robb-Silberman Commission, after former Senator Chuck Robb, D, Virginia, and the former judge Laurence Silberman).[2] Although all of these investigations had their shortcomings, their very existence stood as an impressive testament to the health of democracy in both nations, displaying a laudable capacity for self-criticism and reform.

The two nations approached self-criticism with some similarities and a major difference. Limiting the focus in this commentary to the Butler Report and its American counterparts, one is impressed by the thoroughness of these inquiries as they explored the flaws of their respective intelligence agencies. Both fell short, however, in coming to grips with the second half of the equation: the role of policy officials in mishandling ('politicizing') the intelligence reports provided to them – although the Butler Report is somewhat more successful in addressing this aspect than either the Roberts or Robb-Silberman Reports. In looking at their intelligence agencies, each of the three panels held extensive hearings, marshaled an enormous amount of data, and questioned key witnesses in a serious manner. These were not whitewashes, in the manner of so many American probes into national problems over the years. The Americans spent much more time and money on their probes, enjoyed the benefits of larger staffs and subpoena powers, and interrogated a larger number of witnesses; but, even with its more limited investment of resources, the Butler Inquiry establishes in a convincing manner the sequence of British intelligence errors and provides a thorough evaluation of the dynamics involved.

All three investigations faced what the Americans call 'stonewalling' or 'slow rolling' by their respective executive authorities, with document requests coming in more slowly than the panels wanted (and sometimes not at all) and witnesses sometimes being less than fulsome. Indeed, on both sides of the Atlantic, the President and the Prime Minister opposed any inquiries, only giving in to public pressure for investigations when they had to. The failure of executive officials to cooperate with lawmakers with respect to the sharing of information about intelligence activities, even in times of properly authorized official investigations, remains an unfortunate commonality for both nations.

The primary difference between the British and American inquiries was the marked partisanship that plagued the U.S. effort. While the members of the Butler panel no doubt had political perspectives that colored their judgements to one degree or another (no investigative committee is free of human foibles), the American panels – and especially the Roberts Committee – became something of a political battleground over who should be blamed for the WMD mistakes: the 'blame game'. Regrettably, since the early 1990s intelligence has become as much a partisan football in the United States as health care or welfare reform. This partisan dimension has prevented the Roberts Committee from fulfilling its original promise to examine the misuses of intelligence by Bush administration officials in the lead-up to war in 2003, with Republican Roberts himself stonewalling and slow-rolling his own committee (supported by fellow GOP members) and with the Democrats crying out for completion of the WMD investigation.

Findings

The Roberts Committee placed blame for the fault WMD analysis squarely on the shoulders of the intelligence agencies, rejecting the notion that the Bush administration had selectively incorporated ('cherry-picked') only those snippets of intelligence that supported the case for war against Saddam Hussein's regime in Iraq, or otherwise 'politicized' intelligence to suit its preordained hawkish intentions. The Robb-Silberman panel also came down hard on intelligence professionals but, in ambiguously worded passages in its report, left the door open to the possibility that the Bush White House may have unduly pressured the intelligence agencies to provide 'intelligence to please'. At any rate, the panel concluded, 'it is hard to deny the conclusion that intelligence analysts worked in an environment that did not encourage scepticism about the conventional wisdom'.[3] A few members of these U.S. committees expressed the view as individuals that Bush administration officials had flatly distorted intelligence to suit policy, but they were in the minority; most skirted the political side of the equation and limited their criticism to the weaknesses of intelligence collection and analysis.

The Butler Inquiry, too, focused chiefly on the shortcomings of intelligence agencies, especially (as in the American case) the poor quality of human-source intelligence in Iraq prior to the war and the inadequate vetting of the few dubious sources that did exist. The British panel, though, pointed somewhat more forcefully – though still more guardedly than the facts warrant – to the possible political contamination of the intelligence process, with distortion of intelligence reporting by the Prime Minister's media chief and too many politicians weighing in during the final shaping of intelligence conclusions on the top U.K. analysis group, the Joint Intelligence Committee (JIC).

Recommendations

The panels of inquiry in both the United Kingdom and the United States came to similar conclusions about the need for improvements in the operations of their intelligence agencies. Among the litany of reforms common to both nations: the requirements for better human sources, shorter reporting chains in the intelligence hierarchy, better vetting of sources, clearer presentations in intelligence reports about the limitations of any data that may be included in the findings, and more extensive sharing of information among intelligence services and their analysts. In both nations, though, the investigative panels fell short of fulfilling their obligations for full reporting to the citizenry; they never emphasized sufficiently (or, in the case of the Roberts Report, at all) the most serious failures in the WMD disaster.

The first pre-eminent failure had less to do with political pressures from No. 10 Downing Street or from the White House on those involved in intelligence analysis ('assessment', in the British phrase), than with the unwillingness of intelligence professionals to object – publicly if necessary – to the subsequent twisting ('cooking') of intelligence by policy officials. Here is the vital step from professional intelligence assessments to government dossiers of a political nature, where distortions can creep in because policy officials may be inexperienced in understanding the nuances of intelligence or may simply choose to ignore nuances that may run counter to their political predilections. The Butler panel did not go far enough in scolding intelligence professionals for their quiescence when policy officials in Great Britain turned assessment into advocacy by publicly evoking the good name of the JIC in support of the war.

The second failure was the unwillingness or inability of policy officials to aggressively question the pro-WMD assessments they were receiving from the intelligence agencies. The lack of scepticism at high policy levels may have been a result, of course, of not wanting to have additional information, since the intelligence they were getting fit perfectly well into their pro-war policy designs. Nonetheless, all three panels of inquiries should have had – at the heart of their recommendations – commentary about the importance of policy officials examining carefully and understanding the nuances of intelligence, and taking more seriously dissenting opinions within their intelligence agencies.

When the policy officials are unwilling to probe for softness in intelligence data, intelligence managers themselves must insist that they pay attention to the nuances, caveats, uncertainties, speculations, and incomplete data in the reports. Instead, the American intelligence chief, George Tenet – evidently swept up into the vortex of White House politics and the drumbeat for war – did not emphasize for the President the nuances in U.S. intelligence reporting on Iraqi WMDs and famously told him that the existence of the weapons was a 'slam dunk'.[4] In Britain, the senior intelligence official, JIC Chairman John Scarlett, also crumbled in the face of political pressure favoring war, allowing intelligence concerns about Iraqi tactical WMDs to become inflated in the rhetoric of the Prime Minister's media spokesman into strategic threats to the United Kingdom itself.

A close reading of the intelligence reports on Iraq in both nations in 2002 reveals that the analysts who wrote them hardly claimed perfect knowledge about the state of Saddam Hussein's unconventional weapons program. In the United States, in fact, the Intelligence and Research Bureau in the Department of State, the intelligence unit in the Energy Department, and Air Force Intelligence all raised serious doubts about the existence of WMDs in Iraq. Their views were outflanked, however, not so much by the President or by Vice President Dick Cheney, but by majority opinions among analysts generally favoring the WMD hypothesis in the Central Intelligence Agency (CIA) and other larger organizations within the U.S. intelligence community.

In was incumbent upon the U.S. intelligence chief, though, to warn the President about the divergence of opinion, the softness of the data (much of it based on extrapolations from the last time the CIA had people in Iraq, earlier in the 1990s), and the dubious quality of sources like the German intelligence asset 'Curveball', the Iraqi defector Ibn al-Shaykh al-Libi, and the politically motivated Iraqi exile Ahmed Chalabi.[5] A briefing to the President or the Prime Minister along these lines would have highlighted the need for a delay in the invasion plans until UN weapons inspectors had cleared up the intelligence ambiguities. Instead, both the White House and No. 10 Downing Street appear to have been all too ready to accept the convenient findings of some intelligence analysts that happened to run parallel to their own policy ambitions, namely, regime change in Iraq. Intelligence became the linchpin in support of a political and foreign policy agenda for the President and the Prime Minister. The politicians cherry-picked and smiled happily at the abundance of supportive intelligence, while the intelligence professionals stood by, looking at their shoes instead of demanding greater appreciation of the limitations in the Iraq reporting.

So the WMD problem reduced to a question of speaking truth to power, never an easy task for intelligence professionals who enjoy their special status in government, not to mention having mortgages to pay and families to feed. The Turks have an old adage, 'He who brings bad news should keep one foot in the saddle.' In one of its few veiled criticisms of the top British intelligence chief, the Butler Inquiry noted – in what may be its paramount recommendation, applicable to all governments and all intelligence services: the Chair of the JIC should be someone 'demonstrably beyond influence and thus probably in his [sic] last post'.[6]

Notes

Overview: The Butler Report as an historical document

Peter Jackson

1   This phrase is inspired by the title of Loch Johnson's path-breaking account of the Church Committee hearings into US intelligence operations of 1975: *A Season of Inquiry: The Senate intelligence investigation* (Lexington, KY: University of Kentucky Press, 1985).

2   For excellent preliminary assessments of the impact of these four investigations, see Richard Aldrich, 'Whitehall and the Iraq War: The UK's Four Intelligence Enquiries', and Eunan O'Halpin, 'British Intelligence and the Case for Confronting Iraq: Evidence from the Butler and Hutton Reports', both in *Irish Studies in International Affairs*, 16 (2005), pp. 73–88 and 89–102 respectively. On the third of these enquiries, chaired by Lord Hutton, see Anthony Glees and Philip H.J. Davies, *Spinning the Spies: Intelligence, Open Government and the Hutton Enquiry* (London: Social Affairs Unit, 2004). Alex Danchev's rather impressionistic 'The Reckoning: Official Inquiries and the Iraq War', *Intelligence and National Security*, 19/3 (2004), pp. 436–66 can also be consulted.

3   For insightful discussions of the conduct and conclusions of the British and American investigations see Robert Jervis, 'Reports, Politics and Intelligence Failures: The Case of Iraq', *Journal of Strategic Studies*, 29/1 (2006), pp. 3–52 and Anthony Glees and Philip H.J. Davies, 'Intelligence, Iraq and the Limits of Legislative Accountability during Political Crisis', in a special issue of *Intelligence and National Security* entitled 'Intelligence, Crises and Security', edited by Len Scott and R. Gerald Hughes, 21/5 (2006), pp. 848–83.

4   This information is drawn from the biographical information provided on members of the Butler Committee by the committee's official website at: http://www.butler review.org.uk/biography/lordbutler.asp.

5   *House of Commons Debates [Hansard]*, volume 417, 3 February 2004, column 625.

6   *Iraq's Weapons of Mass Destruction: The Assessment of the British Government* (London: HMSO, 2002), pp. 3–4. This document can also be consulted on the Downing Street website at http://www.pm.gov.uk/output/Page271.asp and downloaded at: http://www.pm.gov.uk/files/pdf/iraqdossier.pdf.

7   O'Halpin, 'Case for Confronting Iraq', p. 90.

8   The briefing document is still available on the Downing Street website: http://www.
      number-10.gov.uk/files/pdf/Iraq.pdf. This document was drawn principally from the
      work of Ibrahim al-Marashi (at the time a research fellow at the United States Naval
      Postgraduate School at Monterrey and doctoral student at St Antony's College, Oxford)
      on the Iraqi secret services. Some material was also drawn from Jane's Intelligence
      Review. See the evidence submitted by Dr Glen Rangwala (who originally exposed
      the plagiarism on 5 February 2003) to the Parliamentary Select Committee on Foreign
      Affairs on 16 June 2003, available at: http://www.middleeastreference.org.uk/fac
      030616.html. The largest portion of the plagiarised dossier was drawn from an article
      by al-Marashi entitled, 'Iraq's Security and Intelligence Network: A Guide and
      Analysis', *Middle East Review of International Affairs*, 6/3 (2002), pp. 1–13.
9   The question put to those polled was 'Would you approve or disapprove of a military
      attack on Iraq to remove Saddam Hussein?'. See: http://www.icmresearch.co.uk/
      reviews/2003/guardian-february-2003.htm.
10   Cf. *Butler*, p. 72 and again p. 77.
11   The initial charge was broadcast by Andrew Gilligan on the BBC Radio Four *Today
      Programme* that morning. For the full text of the story, see http://news.bbc.co.uk/
      1/hi/uk_politics/3090681.stm.
12   House of Commons Select Committee on Foreign Affairs, 'The Decision to Go to War
      with Iraq', session 2002–2003, HC 813–1, vol. 1, 3 July 2003. This document is
      available online at: http://www.publications.parliament.uk/pa/cm200203/cmselect/
      cmfaff/813/813.pdf. See also the analysis in Aldrich, 'Whitehall and the Iraq War',
      pp. 76–8.
13   The most comprehensive discussion of Dr Kelly's role is in the published report
      compiled by Lord Hutton, *Report of the Inquiry into the Circumstances Surrounding
      the Death of Dr David Kelly C.M.G* [cited hereafter as *Hutton Report*], (London,
      HMSO, 2004), especially pp. 4–5 for his career. The 'Hutton Report' is also available
      at www.the-hutton-inquiry.org.uk/content/report/index.htm.
14   Intelligence and Security Committee, *Iraqi Weapons of Mass Destruction: Intelligence
      and Assessments*, Cm. 5972, 9 September 2003, pp. 31 and 43. This report is also
      available at: http://www.cabinetoffice.gov.uk/publications/reports/isc/iwmdia.pdf. The
      Intelligence and Security Committee is a committee of parliamentarians responsible
      for oversight of the intelligence services that reports to the Prime Minister.
15   Cf. Aldrich, 'Whitehall and the Iraq War', p. 82.
16   See, for example, CAB/33/0116, 'Iraqi WMD Dossier: Comments on Revised draft
      (15 Sept. 203)', 17 September 2002 and especially CAB/33/0114, 'Iraq Dossier', 20
      September 2002, both available online in the 'Evidence' section of the Hutton Enquiry
      website: http://www.the-hutton-inquiry.org.uk/content/evidence.htm.
17   Cf. Aldrich, 'Whitehall and the Iraq War', p. 83.
18   *Hutton Report*, p. 320.
19   See, for example, 'Hutton a Whitewash Say 56 Per Cent', *Daily Telegraph*, 30 January
      2004. This article refers to a 'YouGov' poll in which 56 per cent of those surveyed
      responded that Lord Hutton was 'too sympathetic with the government' while only
      34 per cent felt that the report was 'impartial'. See also, 'UK Press Mauls Hutton
      "Whitewash"', CNN.com, 29 January 2004: http://www.cnn.com/2004/WORLD/
      europe/01/29/hutton.press/index.html; 'Widespread Scepticism to Hutton "White-
      wash"', *The Guardian*, 29 January 2004 and 'Hutton Breaks Silence to Deny Claims
      of "Whitewash"', *The Independent*, 2 November 2004.
20   The Iraq Survey Group was a 1,400 strong team of investigators established by the
      invading coalition in spring 2003 to identify WMD and programmes for research and
      development of WMD in Iraq. Its final report was submitted on 30 September 2004
      and is entitled 'Comprehensive Report of the Special Advisor to the DCI on Iraq's
      WMD' (although it is also known as the 'Duelfer Report' after Special Advisor Charles

Duelfer). The report, which runs to more than 1,000 pages, can be consulted at: https://www.cia.gov/library/reports/general-reports-1/iraq_wmd_2004/index.html.

21 *House of Commons Debates [Hansard]*, vol. 417, 3 February 2004, column 625. President Bush announced the formation of 'The Commission on the Intelligence Capabilities of the United States Regarding Weapons of Mass Destruction' on 6 February 2006. See http://www.wmd.gov/20040206.pdf.

22 See *Commission on the Intelligence Capabilities of the United States Regarding Weapons of Mass Destruction: Report to the President* [cited hereafter as *WMD Commission Report*] (Washington, DC: US Government Printing Office, 2005).

23 Cf. *Butler*, p. 26; see also pp. 142 and 149. The report was written more than two years before the nuclear test carried out by North Korea on 9 October 2006. But recent developments in the nuclear standoff do not undermine the conclusions reached by the Butler Committee concerning the North Korean case.

24 Cited in *Butler*, pp. 56 and 67 respectively.

25 *Butler*, p. 127.

26 *Butler*, pp. 100 and 138–9.

27 The American WMD Commission provides by far the most detailed and comprehensive discussion of the Curveball saga. See *WMD Commission Report*, especially pp. 84–111 and 91–2.

28 Cf. *Butler*, p. 102; see also ibid., pp. 101, 108 and 152.

29 *Butler*, pp. 100, 102, 108 and 152.

30 *Butler*, p. 108.

31 *Butler*, p. 103.

32 Cf. *Butler*, p. 73.

33 *Butler*, p. 75.

34 *Butler*, p. 112.

35 Jervis, 'Reports, Politics and Intelligence Failures', pp. 22–3, and the *WMD Commission Report*, pp. 124, 172–3, 425, 562.

36 *Butler*, pp. 110, 152.

37 See especially *Butler*, pp. 81–6.

38 Cf. *Butler*, p. 138.

39 *Butler*, p. 154.

> [I]n translating material from JIC assessments into the dossier, warnings were lost about the limited intelligence base on which some aspects of these assessments were being made. Language in the dossier may have left with readers the impression that there was fuller and firmer intelligence behind the judgements than was the case.
>
> In the process of translating JIC assessments into the public Dossier, 'precautionary JIC judgements . . . were subsequently taken up into the dossier, and were taken up in an abbreviated form in which points were run together and caveats on the intelligence were dropped'.

40 *Butler*, p. 139.

41 *Butler*, p. 139. Sir Richard Dearlove recalled that, when briefing the Prime Minister, he indicated that the new source remained 'unproven'.

42 Christopher Andrew, 'Churchill and Intelligence', *Intelligence and National Security*, 3/3 (1988), pp. 181–93; see also the observations of O'Halpin in 'Case for Confronting Iraq', pp. 93–4.

43 Cf. the Prime Minister's Foreword to *Iraq's Weapons of Mass Destruction* [September Dossier], p. 3.

44 Cf. *Butler*, p. 113.

45 Cf. *Butler*, p. 114.

46 *Butler*, p. 113. Scarlett became Chief of SIS in August 2004.

47   *Butler*, p. 147.
48   *Butler*, pp. 147–8.
49   Cf. *Butler*, p. 148.
50   Lord Butler interviewed by Boris Johnson in *The Spectator*, 11 December 2004.
51   Cf. *Hansard*, House of Lords Debates, vol. 689, column 1231.
52   In a general discussion of the various agencies responsible for intelligence collection, *Butler*, p. 8.
53   A point also made by Aldrich in 'Whitehall and the Iraq War', pp. 84, 86.
54   Assessments are also forwarded for scrutiny to Current Intelligence Groups as part of the JIC process; see especially Michael Herman, *Intelligence Power in Peace and War* (Cambridge: Cambridge University Press, 1996), pp. 295–7, 310–14; M. Herman, 'Intelligence and the Iraqi Threat: British Joint Intelligence after Butler', *Journal of the Royal United Services Institute*, 194/4 (2004), pp. 21–2 and Philip H.J. Davies, *MI6 and the Machinery of Spying* (London: Frank Cass, 2004) pp. 13–16, 340–7.
55   See, for example, Herman, *Intelligence Power*, pp. 295–14 and Davies, *MI6 and the Machinery of Spying*, pp. 340–7.
56   '[W]e are surprised that neither policy-makers nor the intelligence community, as the generally negative results of UNMOVIC inspections became increasingly apparent, conducted a formal re-evaluation of the quality of the intelligence and hence of the assessments made on it'. Cf. *Butler*, p. 92.
57   My italics. The three assessments are in Appendix B of the *Butler Report*, pp. 163–76.

Commentary: The Butler Report

Robert Jervis

1   The two most important are *Report on the U.S. Intelligence Community's Prewar Intelligence Assessments on Iraq*, Senate Select Committee on Intelligence, July 7, 2004; and *Report to the President of the United States*, The Commission on the Intelligence Capabilities of the United States Regarding Weapons of Mass Destruction, March 31, 2005.
2   Michael Herman, *Intelligence Power in Peace and War* (Cambridge: Cambridge University Press, 1996), p. 275.
3   On this network, see Jackson, 'The Butler Report', this volume, pp. 283–4.
4   For more on this, see Philip H.J. Davies, 'Collection and Analysis on Iraq: A Critical Look at Britain's Spy Machinery', *Studies in Intelligence*, 49/4 (2005), pp. 41–54.

Commentary: The Butler Report: a US perspective

Loch K. Johnson

1   Foreign Affairs Committee, *The Decision to Go to War in Iraq*, HC 813–1 (London: HMSO, 2003); Intelligence and Security Committee, *Iraqi Weapons of Mass Destruction: Intelligence and Assessments*, Cm 5972 (September 2003); Brian Hutton, *Report of the Inquiry into the Circumstances Surrounding the Death of Dr. David Kelly CMG*, HC 247 (London: HMSO, 2004).
2   Senate Select Committee on Intelligence, *Report on the U.S. Intelligence Community's Prewar Intelligence Assessments on Iraq* (Washington, DC: U.S. Government Printing Office, June 2004); and Commission on the Intelligence Capabilities of the United States Regarding Weapons of Mass Destruction, *Report, 2005* (henceforth 'Robb-Silberman Report').

3   Robb-Silberman Report, p. 11.
4   Bob Woodward, *Plan of Attack* (New York: Simon & Schuster, 2004), p. 249.
5   See Loch K. Johnson, 'A Framework for Strengthening U.S. Intelligence', *Yale Journal of International Affairs* 1 (Winter/Spring 2006), pp. 116–32.
6   Butler Report, p. 144.

Index